This book is dedicated to the two people
who made the Edelbrock name emblematic of the American Family.
They were pioneers in the rudiments of high-performance and loving parents
to the continuing future of the name Edelbrock.

TO **KATIE HIGGINS EDELBROCK** AND **OTIS VICTOR EDELBROCK SR.**

Dedicated by Vic Jr., Nancy, Camee, Christi, and Carey Edelbrock

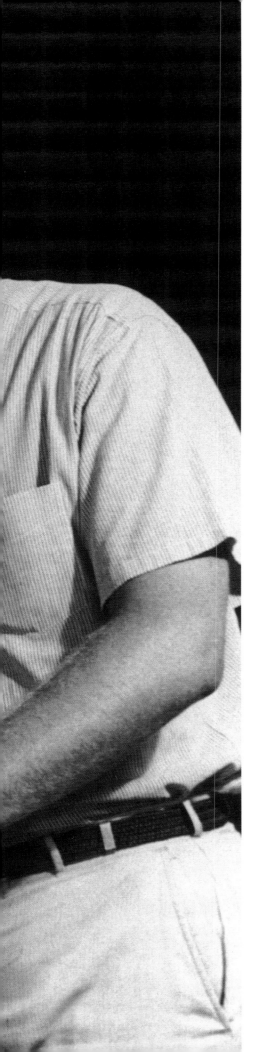

MADE IN USA

TOM MADIGAN
FOREWORD BY BENNY PARSONS

MOTORBOOKS
INTERNATIONAL

A TEHABI BOOK

I would like to express a special word of gratitude to my wife, Darlene,
for her unwavering support during this project.
Without her help this piece of history would not have been recorded.
—Tom Madigan

Tehabi Books designed and produced *Edelbrock: Made in USA* and has conceived and produced many award-winning books that are recognized for their strong literary and visual content. Tehabi works with national and international publishers, corporations, institutions, and nonprofit groups to identify, develop, and implement comprehensive publishing programs. Tehabi Books is located in San Diego, California. www.tehabi.com

President and Publisher: Chris Capen
Senior Vice President: Sam Lewis
Vice President and Creative Director: Karla Olson
Director, Corporate Publishing: Chris Brimble

Senior Art Directors: John Baxter, Charles McStravick
Art Director: Curt Boyer
Production Artists: Mark Santos, Helga Benz

Editor: Terry Spohn
Editorial Assistant: Emily Henning
Developmental Editor: Louise Noeth
Copy Editor: Marco Pavia
Proofreader: Dawn Mayeda

This edition published in 2005 by Motorbooks International, an imprint of MBI Publishing Company, Galtier Plaza, Suite 200, 380 Jackson Street, St. Paul, MN 55101-3885 USA

Motorbooks International titles are also available at discounts in bulk quantity for industrial or sales-promotional use. For details write to Special Sales Manager at Motorbooks International Wholesalers & Distributors, Galtier Plaza, Suite 200, 380 Jackson Street, St. Paul, MN 55101-3885 USA.

ISBN 0-7603-2202-3
Library of Congress Cataloging-in-Publication Data

Madigan, Tom, 1938-
  Edelbrock : made in USA / by Tom Madigan ; foreword by Benny Parsons.
    p. cm.
  ISBN 0-7603-2202-3 (hardcover : alk. paper)
  1. Edelbrock, Victor, 1913-1962. 2. Edelbrock Corporation--History. 3. Automobiles, Racing--Parts.
4. Automobile supplies industry--United States--Biography. 5. Automobile mechanics--United States--Biography. I. Title.
  TL140.E33M33 2005
  629.28'78'092--dc22

                    2004030365

Printed in China by Toppan

10 9 8 7 6 5 4 3 2 1

By Vic Edelbrock Jr. People often ask, if you had your life to do over, what would you change? In my case, although it may sound old-fashioned, the truth of the matter is I would not change a moment. As I see things, the good in my life has rewarded me generously. The bad experiences have made me stronger and more appreciative of my blessings. The Edelbrock family of the past and the Edelbrock family in the present are bound together by tradition, a strong faith in our values, and the love of family.

From the very first days of my memory, two recollections linger: the warm feelings of being with my mom and dad and the sights and smells of the automobile. Later those early sensations turned to fascination. As years passed, the bond between my feelings and the automobile heightened. By the time I reached school age, my dad's shop became ground zero for my dreams; its many secrets kept me craving more. Listening to my dad and his crew tell stories in the hours after work

Never suffering from the spoiled child syndrome often found with an only child, Vic Jr., above, at Marine Stadium in Long Beach, had a wonderful childhood, loved his parents, and worked for his dad. Beginning at the bottom, he swept floors and cleaned restrooms before he moved on to running the dyno, above right, and building engines.

entertained me like no toy or game. As I got older, my dad offered me the opportunity to experiment and learn about the world of the automobile. A simple task like washing the clay from a racecar after its night of battle never seemed like work to me; it was a privilege. As time passed I learned to love what my father did for a living: As long as I met my responsibilities at school, I could then rush to his shop to be a part of the excitement. If I did not stray from my chores, on weekend nights I could accompany my dad to the colorful, noisy world of racing. I would watch in total fascination, unable to control the rush of sensations as my dad's car would race. I could taste the competitive energy as dirt flew and smoke filled the air. After the race I would return to being a child and laugh at being teased by the drivers and become anxious for my dad to supply me with a hot dog and a soda pop.

I learned the rules of being an honorable person and a racer not only from my parents, but also from the racing family that was part of our lives. Friends like Bobby Meeks, Don Towle, Fran Hernandez, Mary Faulkner, Perry Grimm, Rodger Ward, and Murray Jensen all watched over me and gave me a poke if I strayed from the path.

My father was a rugged, honest, and fair man who raised his only son with a firm hand, and his rules were simple and highly principled. He never forced his will on anyone, and as a father, he allowed me to make my own choices. As this story will show, my father was a competitor, an innovator, and a pioneer. He was one of a very select few who created the high-performance industry. He built a business based on his skill, his word, and results. He made products for racers and gave them an honest chance to become a winner.

As the Edelbrock name grew, my father protected his reputation with great resolve, impressing upon me many times in my life that a stain on the family name was not to be tolerated. I kept this in mind as I matured and experienced the lessons of college and sports. I met and married my wife,

Nancy. We have three wonderful daughters. Through it all, my love for the business and the automobile remained an integral part of everything I tried to accomplish.

When I lost my dad, a perfect world suddenly became a painful place, and for a moment, I was unsure of my ability to meet the challenges I faced. My wife, my mother, and those who had stood with my dad gave me the courage to continue his vision. Over the years, the performance industry has grown into a global market and the products created at Edelbrock Corporation are part of that expansion.

My dad believed that your products and your reputation were only as good as the people who stood behind them. Throughout the years, Edelbrock Corporation has had the good fortune of an exceptional work force. Today every employee, from the youngest novice to the most experienced executive, remains part of the family, just as it was when the company began. It would be thoughtless and foolish to believe that the growth of Edelbrock Corporation came about without help. The performance industry has reached its position through the efforts of many. Over the years, I have been privileged to work with or be a part of many of these efforts. I would like to thank the following organizations for their efforts in making our industry a major component of our nation's economy, providing products for millions plus jobs and security for our families. Thanks to the NHRA, NASCAR, SEMA, to the many other organizations too numerous to list, and to the enthusiast.

The story you are about to read is not just the story of a single American family making good. It is the story of an industry that grew from backyard garages, the arid dry lakes of California, the rough-and-tumble dirt tracks of the Midwest, the moonshiners in the South, and the young inventors of the East. Hot rodding is truly an all-American institution and will remain rooted in our country's culture for all time. The name Vic Edelbrock Sr. will also remain as an honored pioneer of this American legacy.

Vic Edelbrock Jr., 2005

When Vic Sr. passed away in 1962, many in the performance industry scoffed at the idea of the "kid" taking over the business. Many of the hardliners said they would give him a couple years, and then he would be gone. They were all wrong; Vic Jr. took the business to the top of the performance mountain.

By Benny Parsons As a young man growing up in rural Wilkes County, North Carolina, my initiation into the world of the automobile came mainly from the tales told by men who knew what going fast was all about. My hometown had a history that was both exciting and controversial. It may have been the 1950s, but since 1920 and the beginning of Prohibition, Wilkes County was, in a manner of speaking, ground zero to those who manufactured and transported moonshine whiskey. The old boys who ran the back country blacktop were heroes to those who loved fast cars, and young men like me just couldn't resist listening to the stories told at the local garage or service station. If you kept your mouth shut and your ears open you could overhear the owners of the fastest booze-runners talk about their drivers' skill and daring. You could hear accounts of running hard and making horsepower from hopped-up flathead engines. Whenever the stories flew through the air, the name Edelbrock was always part of the conversation. The boys would say, "Edelbrock this and Edelbrock that." The fast guys used the best parts, and Edelbrock was the choice of many. I never had the chance to meet Vic Sr.—he was gone before I really got started racing. The locals said he came down South once to see first-hand how his products were used. He went to the shops to meet the boys and talk racing. In those days, moonshining and racing went hand in hand. The only thing I knew for sure back then was if you wanted to go fast and run hard, Edelbrock was a name to remember.

Years later, in the 1970s, I had been working on and driving racecars for a number of years, and I got pretty good at the driving part. I had won the ARCA championship in 1968 and 1969, and joined NASCAR in 1970. The winning continued with my first Winston Cup race in 1971 and the Winston Cup Championship in 1973. In 1975 the dream of every NASCAR driver came true: I won the Daytona 500. You can't win in NASCAR racing without a hard-working crew and help from people in the racing business. During the 1970s, I became a driver/team manager. It was during this period we had to switch race engines, from the monster big-blocks like the 427 Chevy and Chrysler Hemi, to small-blocks. I don't know what we would have done without the Edelbrock Corporation and Vic's crew. People like Murray Jensen, Bobby Meeks, Jim McFarland, and young Curt Hooker were running the Edelbrock dyno facility and they spent many long days helping us put things together.

I remember we came out to California for the Riverside race—my crew chief was Travis Carter and my engine builder was Waddell Wilson. We spent what seemed like months in the Edelbrock dyno room running engine tests. It was more fun than you can imagine. One of my sponsors was an apple grower, and when we shipped the engines to Edelbrock, a couple of crates of apples came along. We would run tests all day, eating apples and telling jokes non-stop. At the end of the day the engines ran strong and we were all sick from laughing and eating too many apples. Vic Jr. would always stick his head in to find out what was going on. He was always good for lunch or dinner or a few cocktails at the end of the day. He didn't just sell parts, he was a racer, and he wanted his products to do some good. He didn't want any stains on his dad's name.

We ran an Edelbrock manifold on our Daytona-winning Chevy in 1975, and if I recall, I was a poster guy for a couple of Edelbrock ads. On a personal level, I would like to thank Vic Edelbrock Jr. for getting behind stock car racing for all these many years and for his friendship both in business and in life. Our type of racing needs people like Edelbrock to continue a tradition of excellence and a spirit of competition. Although I'm no longer in the driver's seat for NASCAR events, I have been lucky enough to continue being part of the action as a commentator for ESPN-NBC and TNT. Every time I witness the spectacle that is NASCAR racing I marvel at the excitement it generates. It is truly a family sport and a genuine product of the United States. I am thankful that I have been a part of the phenomenon. I hope the readers of this story will feel some of the history of a sport we all love.

Benny Parsons, 2004

I n 1904, the John Edelbrock family moved from Coffey County, Kansas, to a 160-acre farm just northeast of the town of Eudora. The farm lay in slightly undulating terrain surrounded by thickets of trees. A small creek ran through the center of the property, providing the water that was carried by hand for the house and to the livestock. The house was a large wood frame, with two bedrooms, kitchen, parlor, dining room, living room, and storeroom downstairs. More bedrooms and a bath were upstairs. The house was flanked by two main barns and one smaller barn used as a smokehouse and storage for animal feed. Aligning the road leading to the house were rows of cherry and peach trees and an apple orchard. At some point the farm was home to a herd of dairy cows and beef cattle. At harvest time, gypsies would camp under the shade trees near the house, after a hard day's work in the fields and orchards, and they would build fires and sing and dance, with the Edelbrock children joining in the fun.

The children of John Edelbrock grew up knowing the value of hard work, a love of nature, and the meaning of taking fruits of the fields to feed the soul. The remaining chronicle of the John Edelbrock family is shrouded in uncertainty. One popular scenario has John Edelbrock Sr. and family moving to a second farm in the Eudora area that was eventually taken over by his son Peter. As for the children, Cleva died in 1916 at age 23. John Edelbrock Jr. fought in France during World War I, suffered from shell shock, and remained in poor health for many years. He returned to Eudora with his wife, Mildred, and built a house close to his father. There was an unconfirmed story that Elmer Edelbrock left his wife and five children and was never heard from.

William Edelbrock became a truck driver and continued to live in Kansas. John's daughter Mary lost her first husband at a very young age, remarried, was again widowed, and died in a home for the aged in Eudora. Grant, born in 1891, married but had no children. Edith Effie, the

Many years before he would see the dry lake beds of California, Otis Victor Edelbrock was just a boy on his tricycle, above. The Edelbrock family settled in Kansas in the mid-1880s and when Kate Hoover married John Edelbrock in 1881, they had nine children, one of whom was also named John. John Jr. had three sons, above center, Ross (left), Otis Victor (center), and Carl (right). Far right, Victor (left) came West with his brother Carl (right) and Carl's wife Esther in the early 1930s.

youngest girl, raised six children. She passed away at age 94. Nelson, the oldest son, married a woman named Margaret, who may have been part Shawnee Indian, a member of the Fish Tribe that help settle Eudora.

Nelson and Margaret had three sons, Ross, Carl, and Otis Victor Edelbrock, the youngest, who was born August 16, 1913. Nelson and his family moved from Eudora to Furley, then to Augusta, Kansas. Otis Victor Edelbrock came into a world on the brink of great change, although at the time of his birth the family was only concerned with farming their crops, unaware of the fact that they were poor, accepting what the land provided and being thankful. However, shortly after his birth, an event that would be most significant in the life of Victor Edelbrock took place on October 7, 1913: Henry Ford created the world's first automotive assembly line to turn out the Model T at Ford's Highland Park plant. Ford's automobiles and Otis Victor Edelbrock were fated to meet on a road both would travel into the pages of automotive history.

Other monumental events were about to change the world forever. In August 1914, a year after Victor Edelbrock was born, President Woodrow Wilson was busy with the opening of the Panama Canal, linking the Pacific and Atlantic Oceans. In Europe, the First World War had begun. The United States was now a huge nation, explored and mapped basically by horse. The automobile would change exploration from a mandatory reconnaissance to a fun-filled adventure. As the 1920s began, there were over eight million automobiles in the United States with

Ford Motor Company pumping Model Ts off its assembly line as fast as customers would buy them—that number grew to ten million by 1924. The automobile had attained mass appeal, and there were so many automobile manufacturers it was hard to keep track. Among the many autos available were the Ajax 6 and Auburn, Buick, Chalmers, Chevrolet, Chrysler, Cleveland, Essex, Ford, Gray Haynes, Jordan, Lincoln, Moon, Overland, Packard, Pierce-Arrow, REO, Stearns, Studebaker, Stutz, Wills St. Claire, and Winton.

Most of the automobiles manufactured in the early 1920s used parts built by vendors who created components for all manufacturers, so many of the finished products were similar. In spite of this similarity, there was a marked lack of stability in pricing and resale value. For example, a new 1920 Franklin Brougham sold for about $3500, yet six years later it was valued at $125.00. A Model T sold new in 1922 for $364, but you could get a used one in 1926 for about $60.00. Despite its depreciation, the car allowed people a great independence and mobility. It set them free, and the movement would never be stopped. If owning an automobile set a body free, then racing an automobile set the spirit free, and racing automobiles became an obsession for some. Young men raced cars all over the continent, from Pike's Peak in Colorado to racetracks in Indianapolis, and on fairgrounds throughout the heartland. They raced on board tracks in Beverly Hills, California and on the sands of Daytona Beach, Florida. There was even talk of places in the deserts of California called dry lakes, where you could drive an automobile without restrictions. Automobile racing began to build its own heroes. Men like Howard Wilcox, Tommy Milton, Peter DePaolo, Jimmy Murphy, and

Above, Vic Sr. was a dapper young man. Above right, sitting on a hay wagon with his brother Carl.

Joe Boyer not only became legendary at the Indianapolis 500, but they raced on high-banked tracks made of wood that were terrifying to drive and mind-boggling to watch. Racing and the Roaring Twenties were a perfect match.

But the fun and excess of the early 1920s did not filter down to the Nelson and Margaret Edelbrock family. Times were hard, and raising three growing boys required working a farm and other sources of income as well. Nelson took jobs working the oil fields around Augusta. As the older boys, Carl and Ross, grew, so did their duty to contribute to the family. In the mid-1920s, Nelson and Margaret opened a small grocery store and conditions improved slightly. Any plan for building a future was dashed in 1927 when the tiny store burned to the ground. At this point just surviving became a daily effort. Caught up in the crisis, young Victor, only 14, had to quit school and find work. With no desire to farm the fields, Victor found work at a local automobile repair shop. He took to the work like he had been preordained to master the art of mechanics. To supplement his income he began delivering Model T Fords to local farmers for a dealer in town. He quickly learned to be an expert driver, and running the lonely, rutted farm roads out of town he had to make on-the-spot repairs when the unyielding trails caused parts and pieces to unhinge from mountings.

Vic's widow, Katie, remembers something else about this time. "Vic told me when he was sixteen he used to run some moonshine for local bootleggers. He would pick up a couple dollars spending money. Of course he never told his parents, his dad would have been disgraced having

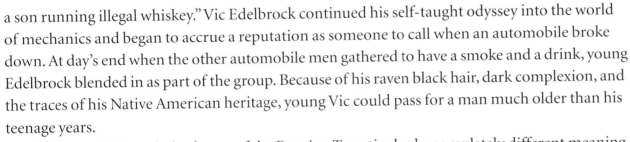

Victor Edelbrock Sr., above and left, (front row) came to California in 1931, finding work in a filling station. He met his wife Katie and married her in 1933 and opened his first shop the same year. He welcomed his son into the world in 1936. During those early years, Vic Sr. never imagined that someday his name would be known around the world.

a son running illegal whiskey." Vic Edelbrock continued his self-taught odyssey into the world of mechanics and began to accrue a reputation as someone to call when an automobile broke down. At day's end when the other automobile men gathered to have a smoke and a drink, young Edelbrock blended in as part of the group. Because of his raven black hair, dark complexion, and the traces of his Native American heritage, young Vic could pass for a man much older than his teenage years.

For Victor Edelbrock the frenzy of the Roaring Twenties had a completely different meaning. The automobile had captured his interest. There were more cars than buggies, and paved highways began to appear. Traffic signals and service stations appeared in cities, and places called motels popped up along roadsides. Victor Edelbrock found he had a mechanical gift. He also formed a philosophy that would remain with him for the rest of his life: When you do a job, do it right, and do it better than anyone else, because then people will ask you to do more.

In 1930, Ross Edelbrock, the oldest son of Nelson, decided to join the thousands of pilgrims heading west to California to find a better life. Within months, Carl followed his brother. For a time young Victor remained with his mother and father. But the lure of adventure and the chance for a fresh start proved too tempting and Victor soon followed his brothers. According to his widow Katie, "He packed every possession he owned, and he headed for California with Carl and Carl's wife, Esther, in an aluminum-bodied 1920's Studebaker. It was Carl's second trip." The year was 1931.

PHOTOGRAPHY CREDITS

His ideas destined one day to become legend,
Otis Victor Edelbrock Sr. strides toward his future.

1 Palm Trees and Movie Stars

I n 1931, the population of Los Angeles was near 1.3 million—not crowded, given the size of the landscape. There was a creative energy and hopefulness to the place that was hard to express but, once experienced, seemed to enter the soul. Los Angeles was the place of unlimited potential where an entrepreneur could experiment without bounds. Vic Edelbrock had reached the Promised Land. His wife Katie, when asked about coming to California as a young girl said, "It was Utopia after the hardships we faced in Texas. You didn't have to face harsh winters, there was more work than in the rest of the country, and you could pick oranges off of the trees."

With a youthful idealism, and motivated to pull his family out from the hardships, eighteen-year-old Edelbrock focused on the problem at hand—he accepted the blessings of Los Angeles and gravitated toward cars. In California, automobile racing was a serious interest to many by 1931. Although racing was popular all over the country, the mild weather and free spirit of California allowed a longer growing season for invention. Racing had actually played a part in the development of California in general and Southern California in particular. Since the early 1900s, in places like Santa Monica and San Diego, automobiles raced on the same roads and trails they shared with horse and buggies.

Historic events were not limited to Southern California. Events like the Vanderbilt Cup garnered national media coverage in publications such as the Los Angeles Times. One of the more captivating events was created in the tiny farming community of Visalia located in the central valley of California. Inaugurated on July 4, 1912, the Visalia Road Races attracted nearly ten thousand spectators. A 444-mile road race ran a year later—from Los Angeles to Sacramento—with Visalia as the focal point and the halfway stop. In 1917, the Visalia Road Races ended with America's entrance into World War I, but not before young Dale Drake, half of the Meyer-Drake partnership that would one day rule the Indy 500, won the final event.

Auto racing flourished in California for two basic reasons, good weather and free-spirited young men who loved speed. For those who craved the ultimate in daring, Los Angeles offered the board tracks—huge, high-banked ovals constructed of wooden planks. Speeds over the boards were unheard of in the 1920s. California boosted board tracks in Beverly Hills, Oakland, Playa Del Rey and Culver City. Playa Del Rey was the first and Culver City was the fastest. High speeds, death and flying splinters held the allure of the boards.

15c   15c

Official Program

AMERICAN LEGION
SPEEDWAY

AUTO RACES

AUSPICES GLENDALE POST NO. 127

AMERICAN AUTOMOBILE ASSOCIATION
SANCTION NO. 2127

2:30 P. M.   Sunday, March 10, 1929

Back in Los Angeles, road racing in the early 1900s gave way to track racing, which would dominate by the 1920s. On the West Coast—Los Angeles being the nucleus— racetracks grew like orange groves. There were dirt tracks, cinder tracks, long and short tracks as well as spectacular wooden tracks. Born in Playa del Rey, California in 1910, board tracks quickly spread across the country. They ranged in size from a half-mile to monsters like the high bank 1½ mile track in Beverly Hills, California. Consisting of millions of board feet of two-by-fours laid on their sides, this super smooth-track allowed speeds of over 140 mph. But for the average working class enthusiast, the local quarter-and half-mile dirt tracks called bullrings were the most popular. Los Angeles had plenty in places like Legion Ascot Park and Culver City. There were tracks up and down the coast, from Oakland to San Diego. One of the most significant was Gilmore Stadium. Opened in 1934 by oil magnet Earl Gilmore, this track played a vital role in the history of Southern California racing and in the history of Vic Edelbrock.

Another influential development in the local car culture was the evolution of gas stations, which had become private businesses owned by individual entrepreneurs rather than the original bulk centers owned by gasoline manufacturers. Oil companies wanted to sell their products in large quantities and experiment with the fundamentals of a credit card or charge system for payment. As early as the 1930s the dealer/owner lease service station came into vogue. This was an innovation for the Depression-starved worker; a service station could support an owner as well as several workers. Money could be made not only from selling gas and oil, but from mechanical services as well. Soon gas stations took on personalities, evolving from a wooden box office and free-standing fuel pumps to covered islands with larger buildings and service garages. In Los Angeles, many stations adopted the Spanish adobe style, while others blended with the neighborhood

> *"If you were neat and presentable you got a job. But people looked down on maids as second-class citizens. I didn't care, because by living in, everything I earned, I kept."* —**Katie Edelbrock**

landscape. Companies like Richfield, Standard Oil, Union 76, Flying A, Sunset, Texaco, Sinclair, Associated, and Gilmore competed against each other by trying to provide better service. Los Angeles was a rich environment for Vic Edelbrock.

Vic Sr. opened his own shop in 1934 at the corner of Venice and Courtland in West Los Angeles. It wasn't much, a four stall repair shop and a three pump Gilmore Service Station, below.

Vic, his brothers and Katie

When Vic first came to California, he shared an apartment with his brother Carl, and Carl's wife, Esther. Older brother Ross, who had come to Los Angeles several years earlier, was in the banking business, but the poor health of their son Robert forced them to move to the clearer air of Fresno, California. Things were tough for Carl and Esther. Carl spent time bouncing from job to job, working at everything from selling bars of soap on the street corner to odd jobs at the movie studios. Then the couple opened a small coffee shop called Karl's Koffee Kup on the corner of Gower and Vine, near movie studios. Young, struggling actors like John Wayne and Ward Bond would often run tabs for coffee and donuts until they could pay at the end of the week.

Although loyal and hard working, the three brothers were never close as a family, and they would each make their own way. Each respected what belonged to the other and never asked for help unless it was life and death. Vic took this family ideology very seriously and would demand complete loyalty from his friends and those who would work for him. He had a gift for mechanics and he soon found work at a service station doing general repair, which meant fixing anything that was broken. As his reputation quickly grew, so, too did his knowledge and insight into the automobile. Even at age nineteen, Vic Edelbrock knew that the way to survive the Depression and make something of yourself was to own the business, not work for someone who could take advantage of your skills.

By the spring of 1933 Vic Edelbrock had established himself as an efficient, skillful mechanic. He began to buy his own tools, but lacked the funds to break away from the chains of being an employee. To

Route 66

Victor's journey to California had been arduous. In the 1930s, the highway system was only beginning to emerge from dirt trails and rutted country roads. Crossing the country meant that at some point you would have to find the "Mother Road"—Route 66. Its point of departure was Chicago, Illinois, and its termination was Santa Monica, California. Between the two cities lay the heart of our developing nation. Although a major artery of travel, Route 66 was not exactly the Yellow Brick Road. On the contrary, the Mother Road was 2,448 miles long, with only 800 miles paved in 1926, It would be nearly 11 years—1937—before it was completed. It bumped and twisted through eight states, and three time zones. Today we drive the highways at speeds unheard of in 1931. We cruise in air-conditioned comfort with our favorite music filling our ears. A swipe of a plastic card and we get gas, food is mass-produced and placed in throwaway containers. We stop for rest at a sanitized, comfortable establishment complete with a swimming pool and free continental breakfast. In 1931, you were basically on your own. Gas stations were few and far between, with most dispensing fuel from hand-operated pumps. Rest at the end of the day meant either sleeping in your vehicle, on the ground under the vehicle or, if you were very fortunate, there were what were called tourist courts—usually providing a one-room box with beds and a place to park a vehicle. Restrooms were communal and showers may or may not have been available. Each day on the road had to be carefully planned to ensure a fuel supply and food. Most often, meals were taken at the side of the road, and when you could find a cafe, the chances of getting a good meal were less than 50-50. Water bags and hand tools were a necessity, and a breakdown was always a serious matter. All things considered, driving cross-country was a challenge in the best of times.

earn extra money, he spent his evening hours parking cars at a large apartment complex near downtown Los Angeles. The job paid tips and offered a chance to perform some on-the-spot repairs for tenants who didn't have time to bring the car to a garage. Soon the tips paid for the first month's rent on a very small one-room apartment.

Vic and Katie

At the parking complex, Edelbrock met an attractive, auburn-haired woman named Katherine (Katie) Collins, a nineteen-year-old Irish lass tempered by the harshness of the Depression but still filled with a lust for life. She had worked since her early teens and was trying to make a living like the rest of the population. She was engaged to a young aviator named Jimmy Barton, but the relationship was rocky at best. Working as a day maid, Katie met Vic by accident as he ran from parking lot to building, driving tenants' automobiles.

Tall and handsome with dark features, young Mr. Edelbrock was a noticeable figure to a young girl. When Vic asked Katie out on a date she told him she was engaged. Vic was insistent and she relented, and it quickly got serious. "It was like a soap opera," Katie said. "All my friends were wondering who was going to win. Vic was so competitive and once he got his mind set there was no stopping him. Poor Jimmy didn't have a chance in hell." Eight weeks after meeting, Vic Edelbrock and Katie Collins were married in Santa Ana, California, by a justice of the peace for two dollars.

Life was not easy for the newlyweds. Although Los Angeles was better off than other areas of the country in 1933, earning a living was still a day-to-day struggle. Katie changed jobs and took work in Beverly Hills as a domestic housekeeper and live-in maid. The only time together would be during Katie's free time.

In typical Hollywood fashion, like an actor trying to break into the movies, Vic bounced from garage to service station all over the west Los Angeles area, always short of money and always missing his young bride. Within several months of their wedding, the stress of their constant separation began to wear on the couple. Both were young and hot-tempered, and as arguments became common, Vic became introverted, spending more time working and less time with Katie.

Unable to cope with his feelings and depressed about the lack of money, Vic put together an old Ford sedan and decided he would return to Kansas to see if going back to familiar surroundings would ease the pain. He missed Katie so much that he began to write love letters every day from the moment he arrived in Kansas. In only a few weeks, heartbroken and overwhelmed by his mistake, Vic packed up his old car and headed back to Los Angeles. The couple reunited and began working twice as hard to make enough money to get Katie out of the live-in maid business and make Vic his own boss.

In spite of his family taboo against working with a relative, Vic joined forces with Katie's brother, Wes, and her brother-in-law, Buck Bryce, in a gas station and garage on Wilshire Boulevard and Small Drive in West Los Angeles. The trio worked hard and things improved. Meanwhile, Katie took a new job as a companion to the child of songwriters Grace and Gus Kahn. The Kahns wrote show songs for Hollywood films and Broadway plays. They wanted someone Katie's age to look after their daughter, who was diabetic. Katie worked days and evenings in their lavish Beverly Hills home, complete with swimming pool and chauffeur-driven car. The Kahns loved Katie and they remained friends for years after Katie moved on.

The early days were a great time for Vic and Katie Edelbrock. Katie worked for the great song writers Gus and Grace Kahn, below and Vic worked at becoming a great mechanic and dry-lakes racer. Vic, (bottom), spent a great deal of time with Katie's brother Wes Collins both working and racing.

Vic Sr.'s 1932 Roadster, left, was not only a family car and daily driver, but a dry lakes racer and test vehicle. Wes Collins, Katie's brother, is riding shotgun in this mid-1930s photograph. Below, a young Vic Edelbrock Sr. stands on the steps of an ivy covered home in Los Angeles. It was unusual to see Vic Sr. without a '32 Roadster or a dry lake bed close by.

Vic's Garage

The outlook at the gas station didn't stay bright for long. Vic decided that he wanted to find a place of his own. While chasing down some parts for a customer, he caught sight of a "for rent" sign at a three-pump Gilmore Service Station one block from Hoover and Venice at Cortland Street. Inquiring, Vic was told that the vacancy was behind the wood frame office of the station, in a four-stall repair shop, adjacent to single-car rented garages. The garage area needed some serious cleaning and restoring. Without much haggling, Vic and the owner came to a handshake agreement; Vic would run the garage and the owner would pump the gas and handle the garage rents. Since Vic had come to California, he had experienced tough times and hard work. He had gotten married and had lived through the Long Beach earthquake of March 10, 1933, so the challenge of a new business was not going to intimidate the young man from Kansas.

He began moving his equipment into the shop and cleaning up the place after its years of neglect. While building workbenches and a storage bin, Vic noticed a young boy standing just outside the doors of the stall that he was working in, staring at the mess. He had come from an apartment across the street and his name was Robert E. Meeks. Young Bobby, as he was called, had come to California with his father after the elder Meeks had divorced in St. Louis, Missouri. Bobby seemed drawn to the mystery of what was going on in the indistinct confines of the garage and had come over to investigate. He wondered who this man was with the complexion of an Indian. Suddenly, the man moved in the boy's direction and asked, "You lookin' for work?" Meeks replied, "Yeah, I guess so." "Well, come over here and grab a broom and I'll show you what to clean up."

Katie & Vic Sr. in the Early Years

Vic and Katie were married in June of 1933, at the height of the Depression years. Still, they enjoyed life, (above) spending all their free time together. They even took trips to places like Las Vegas (Katie, right, poses by a truck on the way). *Opposite:* These photos offer some idea as to the life Katie and Vic shared in these early years. Vic Sr., top left, liked getting dressed up on Sunday and taking in a movie or dinner at a local eatery. Katie center, loved the outdoors, and liked to venture to places like the Redwood and Sequoia National Parks. Katie moved to California from Waxahachie, Texas, when she was just a teenager. She came to California with a strong tie to the automobile, as shown, bottom, in a photo of her sitting in front of a gathering of cars bought by her older brother for $10 to $15 each. Individual portraits of Vic and Katie, far right, show them in later years, but their love of doing things together remained strong.

So Little Time for Fun

The story of the Edelbrock family reflects a life of hard work and struggle. Consider that both Katie and Vic Sr. were of the generation that faced the two most devastating events of the Twentieth Century; the Great Depression and World War II. They learned that if you wanted to get ahead during this period, you had to work as hard as you could and save every penny. Despite the bleak outlook, Katie and Vic loved to have a cocktail or two, dance to a big band, and spend time enjoying family affairs. In these rare family photos, the social sides of Vic Sr. and Katie are revealed. Top left, Vic Sr. and Katie pose with her niece Rose Marie. A candid shot of Katie and Vic Sr., top right, on a trip to the California Redwoods. Vic and Katie enjoy the Christmas season, below, not knowing that the following December would bring World War II, and the saddest Christmas they would experience. *Opposite:* This candid photo of Katie and Vic at Katie's sister's home circa 1960 shows a very typical Los Angeles neighborhood during that era. Note the 1960 Ford Falcon behind the couple. Vic Sr. was not showing any signs of the cancer that would take his life on November 11, 1962, only two short years after this photo.

At the conclusion of World War II, midget racing in California went over the top. Up and down the state, racers ran seven nights a week, often sleeping in their tow vehicles and washing up in gas station restrooms. Drivers and owners could make up to $1,500 a week in prize money. Vic Sr., shown relaxing in his number 27 at Gilmore, collected his share of the winnings. Bobby Meeks (left) and Bob Bradford (center) check out the scene.

Meeks was fascinated that his new acquaintance worked on cars and appeared to be capable of handling any situation. Over the next few weeks, Bobby would sprint the three blocks home from school and show up at Vic's garage for work. Vic would demand that all schoolwork was completed before any job could be started. Bobby's tasks grew from sweeping floors to cleaning tools and returning them to their proper position on wooden racks hung on the walls of the shop.

Once the simple jobs were perfected, Meeks moved on to cleaning carbon from piston tops and washing engine parts in solvent. While performing these mundane tasks, the youngster studied his teacher up close. Every evening, Vic would sit his young charge down and they would discuss the happenings of the day. Sometimes Vic would have a little shot of whiskey and Bobby would have a cold Coke. It was the start of a tradition as important as doing good work. As the two grew in friendship, Vic assigned Bobby more responsibilities. He was soon fixing tires, installing batteries, and washing cars before they were delivered to the customers. The relationship between Vic and Bobby was like an older and younger brother, with Vic in his early twenties. Although work was serious, the two often teased and joked out of the earshot of customers. For Meeks, it was a kind of family closeness he had missed in his early childhood.

Vic would take in any job, no repair was too small or too big. A good mechanic had to be prepared to work on cars, trucks, tractors, bicycles, and even horse-drawn wagons. The Depression was always lurking. Most of Vic's customers had little money and tried to keep the worst looking wrecks running long past their time. The variety of automobiles roaming the streets of Los Angeles in the 1930s was astonishing. There were the most popular models like Model T Fords, Hudsons, Chryslers, Buicks, Chevrolets, Lincolns, Packards, Studebakers, and Willys. But there were also the rare birds like the Elcar, Franklin, Maxwell, Peerless, Durant, Diana 8, Premier, and a few Marmon-built Roosevelt straight eights.

Bobby had only been working for Vic a short time when an honest-to-goodness gold prospector came flying into the shop honking his horn and cussing up a storm. It seems the old guy had punched a rod out the side of the block on his 1931 Cadillac Fleetwood Touring car. Considered an automobile for the upper class, the 140-inch wheelbase Caddy cost over $4,000, but the old miner could not have cared less. Top down, the seven-passenger machine was filled with picks and shovels, water bags, camping gear, a sluice box, and a 12-gauge shotgun. Vic looked under the car and sure enough, a rod had poked its way through the block, blowing oil everywhere.

As the old-timer headed for a local hotel, Vic began repairs on the V-12. He made a steel patch to cover the hole, then drilled and tapped holes in the block to mount the patch, complete with a handmade gasket. Then he dropped the oil pan, pulled the rod and piston out, ordered new parts, polished the crankshaft journal, replaced the rod, bearings, and piston, added new oil, and fired up the engine. It ran fine. The old prospector paid in cash, jumped in his car, and headed off to the Mojave Desert.

Several weeks later, with horn blowing and dust flying, the old guy returned, charging into the shop to declare that the car was still running fine and he had hit it big. Vic and his young assistant soon were building a reputation for good work and reasonable prices. Vic began to depend more on Meeks, taking him along when he chased parts and delivered customer cars. After work, young Bobby would come to Vic's

> "It was the most beautiful car I had ever seen and it was all mine." —**Bobby Meeks**

Bobby Meeks came to work for Vic Sr. at age 13 after moving to California with his dad from St. Louis, Missouri. He began as, a floor sweeper and matured into a skilled engine builder. Meeks and Senior enjoyed a big brother–little brother relationship and Vic looked after young Bobby until he became an adult.

The Mighty Midgets ruled supreme in the world of racing after World War II, and the center of the kingdom was Gilmore Stadium in Los Angeles. Known for featuring the best cars and the fastest drivers, Gilmore also attracted movie stars and high rollers of all sorts. More than just a race track, Gilmore was party central on Thursday nights.

GILMORE STADIUM
THANKSGIVING NIGHT
1936
3RD ANNUAL GRAND PRIX

apartment and hang out with Vic and Katie—when she had time away from the Kahns. Two of their favorite escapes were dining at the café on Sunset and Vine or watching midget car races on Thursday nights at Gilmore Stadium. Sometimes they just stayed home and listened to the radio, made popcorn, laughed and told stories. Katie began to see Bobby as a brother and the trio became a surrogate family.

As business grew, Vic decided he needed a better car, so he bought a 1931 Chrysler roadster. He tore the car down to its bones then rebuilt the engine and running gear to his own standards. After closing, he spent hours stripping the paint to the bare metal and refurbishing every portion of the interior. Finally, he painted the car green and cream. The finished product was a thing of beauty, and every morning he displayed it in front of the shop as a testimonial to the type of work a customer could expect from Vic's garage.

A Growing Concern

By the rainy season of 1934, Vic had exhausted the growth potential in his small shop and wanted to move slightly more uptown and try for a more affluent clientele. A business contact told Vic about a location for lease in a newer portion of Los Angeles at the corner of Pico and Western Avenue. It was a six-pump Texaco station with a large garage in the rear. The station owner had established a loyal patronage with newer cars and more disposable income. Vic took one look at the setup and decided to move the old shop. While packing, he turned to Bobby Meeks and said, "You going to stay working for me?" Meeks simply nodded.

Once in the new location, Edelbrock began to mature as a mechanic and as a business owner. His penchant for perfect workmanship and his seemingly endless energy began to pay dividends. The neighborhood lived up to Vic's expectations—the cars were newer, so the type of repair work changed considerably—customers now wanted tune-ups, brake jobs and transmission work. Jobs were more profitable, and Vic began to make ends meet. Katie was still working for the Kahns in their spacious two-story Beverly Hills mansion. She had grown fond of the Kahn family. She sometimes found herself at lavish events when one of the Kahn's show tunes like "Blue Lovebird" would find itself in a hit musical.

Katie's job situation still wasn't sitting well with Vic. He wanted his wife to be a homemaker. He worked long days and equally hard nights to put together enough money to make that plan a reality. Although just a teenage boy, Bobby Meeks had shown great improvement and skill as Vic's student. Certain rituals like after-work discussions about the day's happenings over a drink became gospel. Procedures took shape that would become part of the Edelbrock way.

One day, Vic decided he needed Bobby to help shuttle customers' cars around town, chase parts and get lunch. Meeks recalled, "I told Vic I wasn't old enough to get a license and he said, 'Don't worry, we'll figure it out, no problem.'" Vic took Bobby down to the local DMV and went in alone. When Vic returned he told the teenager to go in and do what he was told. A few minutes later, Meeks had his unrestricted license. When he asked Vic what had happened, Vic simply smiled and said, "You have your license don't you? Don't worry about what went on."

A couple of months later, when Bobby returned from parts chasing, Vic surprised the young boy again. He suddenly dropped his tools and told Meeks to watch the shop. Vic returned two hours later with a trailer that was loaded with fenders, wheels, and boxes with what looked like engine parts. The pile of sordid-looking debris was a completely disassembled and very worn 1927 Ford Model T Roadster. Vic announced, "Here is your first car, now put it together—after working hours." For months, Meeks stayed late and worked weekends trying to piece the Model T together, part by part. Always in the background but never pushing, Vic would offer advice. If a problem got too difficult, Vic would jump in and fix it, but always, demonstrating the process. Finally, the moment of truth came and the Model T was whole. Vic took the car to the back of the shop and painted it with black lacquer.

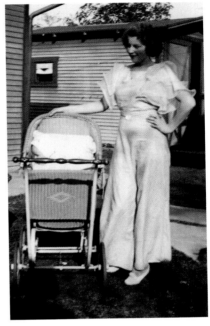

In the late fall of 1935, Vic and Katie's lives changed drastically: Katie was pregnant. Katie finally left her job and became a housewife. They bought a small California stucco house, not far from the shop, near Sycamore and Adams. It had two small bedrooms, a kitchen, bath, and living room, and had an attached one-car garage.

Vic began to work at a fever pitch. Katie would cook dinners of beef stew, chili, spaghetti, or Vic's favorite, chicken and dumplings. Meeks remembered, "She would come down to the shop about 7:00 in the evening and bring a pot of hot stew or something and we would drop everything and dig in. Katie would hang around and tell us about her day and joke and laugh when we told her about ours. Sometimes we would listen to the radio, Amos & Andy; Walter Winchell, Bob Hope, or Suspense. It was a fun time." As the months wore on, Katie struggled to keep pace with the growing business and Vic's long hours. It became more difficult for her to stay up late and hang out at the shop. Vic urged her to stay home and rest.

One day Vic came bursting from the makeshift office and told Meeks to lock up and get in the car. They hurried to the house, gently helped Katie to the car, and headed for the hospital. She was pale and in pain, but in good spirits. That evening, August 23, 1936, Otis Vic Edelbrock Jr. was born.

As his reputation and business grew, Vic Edelbrock Sr. took on more responsibility. On August 23, 1936, Katie gave birth to Otis Victor Edelbrock Jr., above. She then had to split her time between caring for the new baby and helping Vic Sr. run the shop. Many times Katie would pack up Junior and head for the shop in order to bring a home-cooked dinner to the crew. Vic Sr. rewarded his wife for her efforts with their first house top, at 2320 Sycamore Ave., in Los Angeles. Vic Sr. hated owing anyone, so when it came time to buy his family a house, he did it his way, and paid cash. Katie says it was prize money he earned racing midgets.

Childhood Days Filled with Happiness

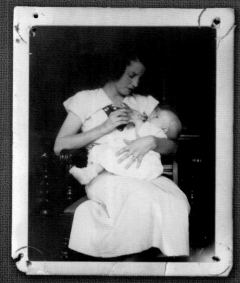

To this day, Katie remains a caring mom to her son. Although Vic Jr. weighed only seven pounds, five ounces at birth, he quickly proved that he could eat whatever was passed his way. Above, Katie, did her best to fill the ever hungry young Edelbrock. According to Katie, her son was always very close to his parents, shown top right with his mom and dad, and needed very little in the way of correction. The bottom photo is a rare picture of some of the Edelbrock family: (Left to right) Vic Sr's brother Ross with his son Bobby, Grandfather John Edelbrock (standing), Carl Edelbrock with his son Dennis, and Vic Sr. with son. *Opposite:* Senior and his son going for a bike ride. Far right, Katie shows off her young son with the pride of a new mom. Katie once said, "Vic Jr. was never any trouble, he was always a good boy." Vic Sr. loved his son and despite his hectic work load, always found time to play with and support his son. Junior repaid that love by always remaining close and wanting to emulate his father's high standards and moral business practices.

Childhood Days Filled with Happiness

Although he was raised as an only child, Victor Edelbrock Jr. was not spoiled by his parents. Katie says, "Vic's dad was strict but always allowed Junior to make his own decisions. I never did much in the way of handing out discipline, Victor was also happy and wanted to please both myself and his father."

In this candid look at Victor Edelbrock Jr.'s childhood, we see a happy boy enjoying his surroundings, a trait that continued into manhood. (Clockwise, from above) his first dog; first car; day at the beach; with Grandma Collins (Katie's mom) and cousin Rose Marie. Sitting atop one horsepower, something that would not last long. *Opposite:* Far right, even as a young cowboy, Vic Jr. was interested gaining knowledge by reading, something he still does today.

Vic Sr. driver, and Wes Collins as (passenger) chat with employee Duke Harding at Vic's Venice and Crenshaw location. The talk is about the fact that this vehicle had broken the stock-bodied roadster record at Muroc dry lake with a speed of 121.42 mph. Note that the front license plate carries the number 27, the same number carried on Vic's winning midget cars. This location was owned in partnership with Ray Haven, a friend and one of the key figures in introducing Vic Edelbrock Sr. to dry lakes racing.

Vic—now Vic Sr.—never strayed from the task of earning enough money and trying to beat down the blight caused by the Depression. Another firm personal rule emerged: buy with cash so there would be no payments to "cloud his sight." And every so often, when Katie least expected it, Vic would tell her to pack up the baby, and the three of them, plus Bobby Meeks, would close early and have a night out. During the Depression, a great meal in a suitable dinner house would cost about $1.50 with wine. If you went to one of the famous Clifton Cafeterias, you could dine on a turkey dinner with all the trimmings for under a buck. And if you didn't like the meal, Clifton's wouldn't charge for it.

By spring 1937, Vic's garage had become the place to take a car for reliable service. Customers told their friends, who told more friends, and so it went. Business was so good that Vic and Bobby could not always handle everything, so Wes Collins, Katie's brother, would drop in and lend a hand. The landlord walked into Vic's office one day and declared that he would not be renewing the lease, he wanted the garage for his own expansion. Vic was furious, almost coming to blows with the man. Now, he had to quickly find another garage and convince his customers to follow him.

Ray Haven, a friend of Vic's, approached him with a deal. Why not become business partners? Haven had a booming business with a six-pump Associated Gas station and a six-stall garage. The location was Venice and Crenshaw in West Los Angeles—a very busy intersection—and the neighborhood had a relatively good economy. Vic liked the idea that he would be close to Venice Boulevard again. He agreed to Ray's deal, and soon, Edelbrock was back in business. Haven was a car enthusiast with many friends who would drop by the shop—hot rodders and dry-lakes racers who captivated Vic with their tales of racing on the vast emptiness of the waterless lakes.

The Dry Lakes

The dry lakes had been formed over the centuries by torrential rainfall cascading from the mountains onto the desert floor, where the flood created a powerful polishing action as the wind drove the water across the sand. Imperfections were filled as the water moved and evaporated. The result was miles of hard, smooth roadbed close to Los Angeles where enthusiasts were free to develop their hot cars unimpeded by rules and regulations.

There were several lakebeds located in the Mojave Desert. El Mirage, Harper, Rosamond, Evans, Dale and Muroc (now Edwards Air Force Base). At more than 20 miles long and 10 miles wide, Muroc is the largest lakebed and the most popular for racing. Originally called Rogers Dry Lake, the name changed in the early 1900s after the Corum family founded the town. Muroc was Corum spelled backward. It was too hot to farm, so mining and making moonshine became the primary trades.

At the start of the 20th Century, artesian water wells were drilled at Muroc and very high quality water was obtained. During the days of Prohibition, whiskey makers found they could brew their concoctions in peace and not be bothered by the Feds, who considered the place inhospitable. Borax mining near the town of Mojave brought miners out from the East. However, unscrupulous mining companies would sometimes pay in stock options, then close shop and leave with the profits before the miners could collect. The successful mines could use only a certain number of miners, the rest ended up wandering the desert until they washed up in places like Muroc. For the racers of the 1920s and 1930s, Muroc offered the last outpost before venturing into the vast expanse of the dry lake. The Muroc Mercantile Company store offered some food staples and water from a pump well. Several doors down, there was a two-pump gas station, a garage, a part-time bar and livery stable as well as a blacksmith. Not much, but for the racers, Muroc, California, would become a holy land for the worship of speed.

According to sources, racing on the dry lakes began around 1919. Albert Drake's excellent book, *Flat Out*, mentions AAA-sanctioned records by Tommy Milton and Frank Lockhart in the mid-1920s. *The American Hot Rod*, by Dean Batchelor, pinpoints this same time as the start of serious racing at the lakes.

> "I went out with a friend of mine named Norman Thompson and, after checking wind direction, we measured out a mile with a tape measure. We drove pipe stakes in the lakebed and put a flag on top. We used two stopwatches to time the cars and wrote the times on a piece of paper." **—Earl Mansell**

FLAT OUT

Albert Drake

There are many who say that racing on the dry lakes of the Mojave Desert was the birthplace of the hot rod industry. One thing is for certain, the dry lakes provided year-round racing and limitless room for the hot rod racers to express themselves. The book *Flat Out*, shown above, by Albert Drake, tells the story of the early days at the dry lakes.

Dry Lakes Dust

The beds of California's dry lakes are part of the great Mojave Desert and were created by seasonal rains pouring onto the desert floor from the mountains above, forming a nearly perfect racing surface. The fame of the dry lakes is divided into two chapters. Before World War II, Muroc, the largest, was the hot spot. It was taken over by the government and became Edwards Air Force base. After the war, El Mirage took over as the place to race. Later runs were reduced to one or two cars at a time. Vic Edelbrock Sr. was a part of both chapters of lakes racing. His roadster bottom, broke countless records and he raced against the best of the best. One of his key rivals, Randy Shinn, above, used Edelbrock products but still wanted to beat the manufacturer.

Opposite: The sun could be a problem too. Vic Sr. in his roadster top, with Bobby Meeks hide in the back seat and Wes Collins in the passenger seat using an umbrella for shade.

Crashes, bottom, were a big part of the early days at the lakes. Two racers discuss a crash while the driver sits on a bumper holding a towel to his face.

ROSAMOND

"We had plenty of boys running, it was a good race, and nobody got killed." —Earl Mansell

One of the most interesting characters who raced in the early days of racing in California is a gentleman named Earl Mansell. Earl, who turned 93 years old in 2004, was a Sprint Car driver, below right, in the 1920s, as well as a promoter of racing events. He put together a Sweepstakes event at Muroc Dry Lake in 1927. The event featured cars powered by Model T four-bangers with Frontenac ohv conversions and Ed Winfield carburetors. The event hosted a big crowd of both racers and onlookers.

Speed runs at the lakes in the early 1920s were spontaneous, uncontrolled actions. On any given day, racers, spectators, thrill-seekers, and innocent amateurs would show up and camp out around the lakebed, and runs would be made in all directions. Races were set up by verbal agreement and safety was nonexistent. Crashes were commonplace. There were no medical personnel, no emergency transport—you were on your own. Homemade booze was plentiful and fistfights just made things even more interesting. Organization was sorely needed.

Earl Mansell was driving sprint cars in the mid-1920s when he discovered what was going on at Muroc Dry Lake, and he put together an organized racing event—complete with class divisions and prizes. Entry blanks were printed to announce the Southern California Championship Sweepstakes at Muroc Dry Lake on October 9, 1927. There were five classes comprised of roadsters, coupes, touring cars, a special flathead class, and a championship sweepstakes for the fastest car of the event. The entry fee was $3.00 per category. Cars could run with or without fenders and windshields, but all had to have hoods and turtle decks. Mansell went on to race sprint cars and midgets up and down the length of California.

Despite the attempts at organization with controlled events, during the late 1920s and early 1930s, running the dry lakes meant anything goes. The dust would blow so badly that only the leaders of the pack could see. Many crashes ensued, and as a result, side-by-side racing was eliminated.

The first officially sanctioned event at the dry lakes was held in 1931, the product of the Gilmore Oil Company and the owner of Bell Auto Parts, George Wight. About ten years earlier, Wight opened the first official speed shop for racers in California. He began with a junkyard and then

ENTRY BLANK
for
So. California Championship
Sweepstakes

Muroc Dry Lake
6 A.M., October 9th, 1927

I in no way hold promoters responsible in case of accident:

Name...

Address......................................

City...

Entries Must be in by 12 m. Thursday, October 6, 1927

	Events Entered Mark with X		Fee
1.	Roadster Race		$3.00
2.	Coupe Race		3.00
3.	Touring Race		3.00
4.	Special Flathead Race		3.00
5.	Championship Sweepstakes		3.00

In Case of Rain Races Postponed Till the Following Sunday

RULES AND QUALIFICATIONS
Event No. 1. Ford Roadsters
    With or without fenders and windshield. Must have hood and turtle deck.
Event No. 2. Ford Coupes
    With fenders, doors, hood and windshield.
Event No. 3. Ford Touring
    With or without fenders. Windshield removed if desired.
Event No. 4 Special Flathead Event
    Any flathead regardless of body which does not place in any above events. Winner of any above event entered in this race will have entry fee for this event refunded.
Event No. 5. So. California Championship
    Any Roadster, Touring, Coupe, with or without windshield or fenders.
    Three Judges to be selected later.
Mail Entries:

EARL MANSELL
1424 N. Fair Oaks   Pasadena, California

Entries Must Be in the *Mail* by Noon, Thursday October 6

moved to racing parts. Lee Chapel was another junkyard operator who had created a speed shop from a pile of used parts a few years after Wight. The two early lakes racers formed the Muroc Racing Association, developed rules for competition, and racing at the dry lakes improved. From the mid-twenties to 1941, all of the characters who would someday make up the speed equipment industry stood in the baking sun, covered with dust and grease, waiting their turn to streak over the hard-packed adobe of the desert. Other legitimate uses for the lakebed in those days included attempts at AAA-sanctioned speed records and testing by car manufacturers such as Studebaker and Dodge. Studebaker even tried an incredible promotion, attempting to run a car 26,000 miles in 26,000 minutes.

A Day at the Races

One of the most interesting stories about the lakes and the Hollywood folks concerns a match race for a considerable amount of money. In October 1932 a dinner party argument turned into a roaring adventure for a crowd of the beautiful people. One of the Marx Brothers, Zeppo, owned a Mercedes-Benz SSK roadster and he bet Phil Berg, who owned a Model J Duesenberg, that the SSK could blow the dress off of the Model J. A few glasses of wine later, a race had been set up to run at Muroc Dry Lake in October. The race would be fifteen miles and circle the lake. Berg and Marx hired big-name drivers: Zeppo hired Joe Reindt, an expert Mercedes man, and Berg signed Eddie Miller, who had finished fourth at the 1921 Indianapolis 500 driving a Duesenberg Straight 8 for the Duesenberg Brothers. A wager of $10,000 was made with another estimated $25,000 in side bets. Gilmore Oil Company got into the act as a proxy sponsor. The whole event was a tribute to the times. A galaxy of flapper girls, starlets in evening dresses, actors, and agents joined a crowd of two thousand onlookers who had made the trek to the desert. Whiskey bottles in hand, the onlookers went wild as the Duesenberg and Eddie Miller ate the SSK for lunch. It was all in great fun.

Setting Sights on Speed

Vic and Ray were very busy and worked side by side during the day. Afterward, many of the local racers would stop by to talk about their exploits on the street and at the lakes. Vic enjoyed the stories and began to get involved with the machines. He may not have known at the time,

Just before World War II, Vic Sr. became interested in midget racing. At first, he ran what they called a rail job, below left, then later he moved to the more popular and more competitive Kurtis Kraft chassis. Also before the war, George Wight started a speed shop called Bell Auto Parts. It is considered the first speed shop.

In 1931 Ford Motor Company stunned the automotive world when they introduced a revolutionary new engine, a V-8 cast with a one-piece iron block. The engine was the Ford flathead and would form the foundation for the hot rod performance industry. Vic Edelbrock Sr., left, seized the moment and created high-performance parts for the flathead including aluminum heads and manifolds like the Super, far right, and the Slingshot—his very first effort. Vic Sr. was master of the Ford flathead.

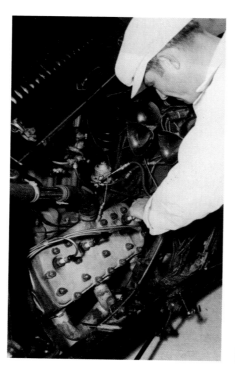

but his life was about to change forever. A friend and customer of Ray's worked in the movie industry as a stunt man. During the filming of a motorcycle stunt he crashed and was laid up with serious injuries. Now out of work, the stunt man needed money, he wanted to sell his 1932 Ford Roadster.

Vic wanted to test his mechanical ideas and try his skills in racing, so he bought the roadster and rolled it into the shop. As he did with everything important in his life, he thought out his entire plan, not saying a word until the right moment. He threw himself into the task of rebuilding the roadster and put together a flathead engine of his own design. Using a Winfield cam, he added a set of Denver cylinder heads produced by Ford Motor Company for use in high altitude. The Denver heads had more compression and a slightly different combustion chamber. He fabricated a set of headers, modified a manifold, and then topped his creation with three Winfield carburetors. When the roadster was ready, Vic headed for the lakes with Meeks and Wes Collins.

The difficult trip from Los Angeles to Muroc was an adventure. Edelbrock loved everything about the desert environment—sleeping under a tarp, eating cold beans, drinking warm soda pop, and waking in the morning to the sound of unmuffled exhausts barking in the still air. The atmosphere was crackling with sensation and passion. Here you became a racer—unbridled, wild, and free—the mind expanded without conditions. Everyone there was young and filled with passion, ready to become famous or infamous. Surrounded by those who would make an industry of incredible proportions in the decades to come, young Vic Edelbrock from Eudora, Kansas, pulled on a pair of white coveralls and a leather aviator's helmet and climbed into his 1932 roadster and roared into the desert.

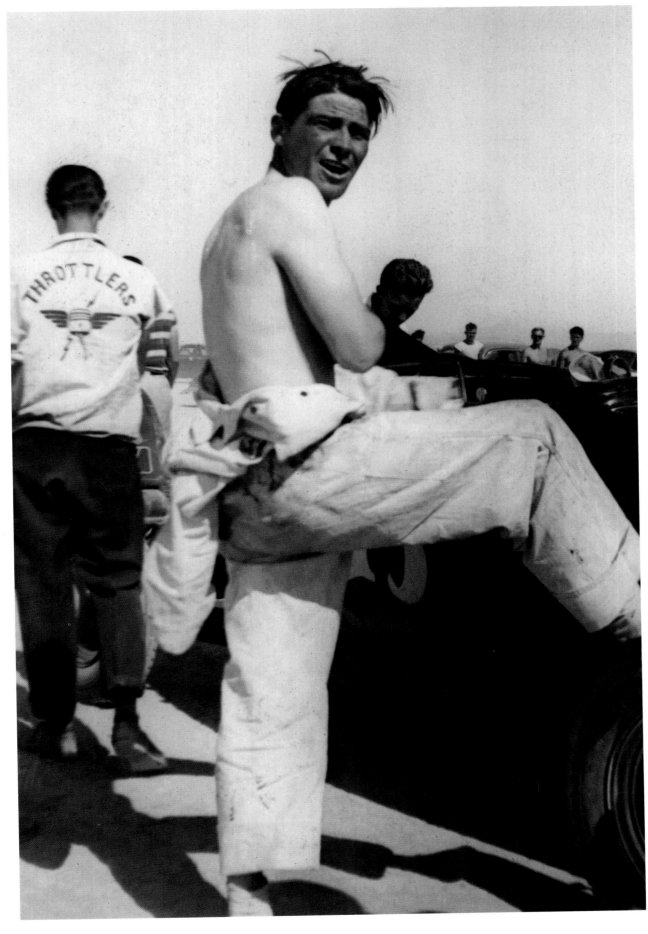

The Edelbrock name did not become part of the dry lakes scene until Vic had established himself as a first-rate mechanic and business owner. After moving his shop to a new location at Venice and Crenshaw, Vic Sr. joined the hot rod scene, buying a 1932 Ford roadster from a movie stuntman who had been injured in a crash. He rebuilt the car, using his own ideas. Only after he had completed the rebuild to his standards did he head for the lakes to make some history. Pictured in his racing gear, above, and getting some sun, left, Edelbrock broke many records, proving over and over that the racers needed his equipment to go fast.

THICKSTUN MANIFOLDS

Power · < Dual Carburetion > · Economy
FORD · MERCURY · Speed
PLYMOUTH · CHEVROLET · DODGE
AND OTHERS · ZEPHYR
2002 W. Washington - L.A. - RO. 6471

Before there was an Edelbrock manifold, Vic. Sr. worked with a fellow racer and manifold builder named Tommy Thickstun. Thickstun had developed a dual carburetor manifold that Edelbrock ran with a set of Arco heads. Above, a group (left to right) including Duke Harding, Pee Wee Gallant, Wes Collins, Vic Sr., Tommy Thickstun and Ray Haven check out the latest Thickstun manifold. When Edelbrock tried to convince Thickstun to make some changes in design, Thickstun refused, so Vic built his own design. Thickstun never found the success that Edelbrock would enjoy.

The roadster, top right, is a modified T built by the Spalding brothers using a Roots supercharger. The Spalding brothers would become famous as ignition specialists.

"Vic was so sharp that he picked up on what we were doing and he began building his own system something like the Lincoln V-12. He was a clever fox." —**Bill Spalding**

Vic threw himself into the emerging sport based on innovation, craftsmanship, and perseverance with a newfound love for performance and his inherent bent for perfection, His work ethic was so unrelenting and so meticulous that it cast fear in those who challenged him. In racing, a person was judged based on ability and courage.

Edelbrock became friends with Tommy Thickstun during a lakes outing. A pioneer in the racing business, Thickstun made high-performance intake manifolds for Ford flatheads. He asked Edelbrock to try one of his aluminum manifolds with a two-carburetor configuration. Vic accepted, added Stromberg carburetors as well as other components, and then, modified the combustion chambers. Later, he would work with other pioneers in the industry.

Tom and Bill Spalding started an ignition business in 1934. Using two sets of points, two coils, and two condensers, their system increased the rpm range of the flathead from around 4,700 to nearly 6,500 rpm. The brothers built and raced a modified T-body racer and were the first to average 120 mph at Muroc Dry Lake in 1938. Edelbrock respected the brothers, and had raced against the boys in what was called the "end of the day" race. This was a lakes custom, the three fastest cars in each class raced side by side at the end of the day. Vic found the Spalding brothers to be tough competition, which meant they built good products.

Edelbrock also met Wally Parks during his lakes racing days. The tall, slender kid came to California in 1922, and was considered a real player at the lakes, having earned his first timing tag (recorded speed) in 1933. Parks was a racer and an organizer who was so far ahead of his time that many wondered where he got his wild ideas. Wally Parks went on to found the National Hot Rod Association, but back in the 1930s he was just another kid with vision. Along with Edelbrock and the rest of the racers, Parks pioneered a California phenomenon: car clubs.

The idea of the clubs was to join forces with others to trade knowledge, socialize, and venerate the automobile. There was

One of the pioneers who guided hot rodding from its wild days on the dry lakes of California and the streets of Los Angeles into a respected industry was a tall, lanky kid born in Boyle Heights named Wally Parks. Parks helped create The Southern California Timing Association, he was the first editor of *Hot Rod Magazine* and he founded the National Hot Rod Association. Parks helped get racers off the streets and onto the race track. Parks was a member of the Road Runners, and he was a racer. Wally, left, behind the wheel of a wild looking roadster, ran the dry lakes and drove Bill Burkes Sweet 16 belly tank, below left, at Bonneville. Bottom, Wally Parks, (center) proved to be a good friend to Vic Sr.

no shortage of participants, and club names were colorful and provocative. The largest clubs included Road Runners, Gophers, Albata, Lancers, Idlers, Gear Grinders, Low Flyers, Sidewinders, Ramblers, Bungholers, Hollywood Throttlers, Knight Riders, Rattlers, and Centuries. As the number of clubs grew, so did the competition between them. Club members gathered at drive-in restaurants, garages, and gas stations to talk cars. Talking gave way to bragging and then challenging. Who had the most "go"? That was the question. Street racing became a major activity among the clubs. Unfortunately, when crashes and fatalities grew in number, the fun turned somber. The *Los Angeles Times* joined forces with the mayors and police departments of many surrounding communities condemning the clubs and street racing.

To the average citizen and parent, hot rodders were outlaws who should be put in jail. The police issued an ultimatum: stop killing people on the streets or lose the use of the dry lakes. Sensing that waging a war with the police was a futile endeavor, some of the clubs that were really interested in racing at the dry lakes joined together to try to stop the bad press and the carnage on the streets.

A group of club members decided something had to be done. Wally Parks, Art Tilton, and Jimmy Morgan enlisted others to create the Southern California Timing Association (SCTA) in 1938. The SCTA, unlike other lakes racing organizations, was incorporated as a non-profit organization. The founders collected dues for club memberships and developed bylaws, safety rules, regulations and codes of conduct. Classes were established for seasonal and club points championships. Within a year, nearly all of the California clubs would race under the SCTA membership umbrella.

Vic and Crew at the Dry Lakes

Prior to the beginning of World War II, Muroc Dry Lake in the Mojave Desert was the mecca for those trying to make a reputation as fast guys. Like gunfighters of the old West, racers would challenge each other to a speed showdown. Once Vic Edelbrock began racing his '32 roadster, he wanted to be the best, and in many races he was the best. However, half the fun of going to the lakes was hanging out and bench racing with his buddies. Vic, above, dressed the part of a racer, with a Stroker hat and white coveralls. He hung out with the likes of Wes Collins (with legs crossed, in photo at top right). In fact, Wes Collins (in aviator's cap, bottom right, was Vic's crew member for many dry lakes adventures. In 1940, Vic made the cover of the SCTA program, right, for his record-breaking runs in events before the war.

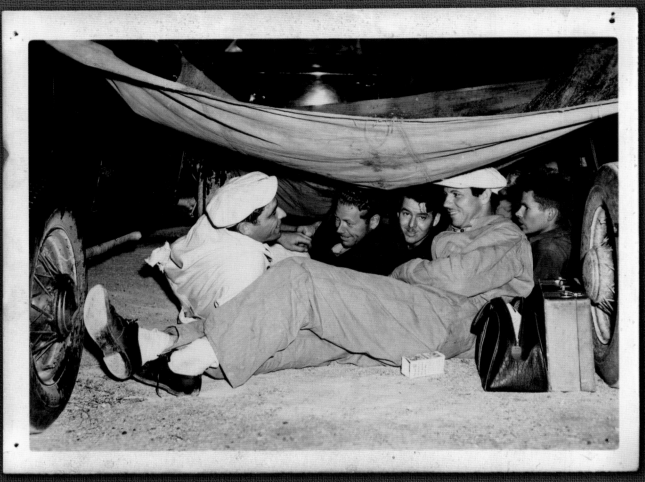

California Timing Association
INCORPORATED

Make Ford 18 Date 3/12/4
ich Edelbrock
Stoel

Ph. Rds. X Cps. Sdn.

QUALIFYING SPEED 9.68
115.25 Class 119.20
116.58 Class
118.52 Class aw 119.44

ROADSTER RECORD

Car clubs like the Bungholers, Knight Riders, Gear Grinders. Albata and the Road Runners were the heart of hot rodding in the early days. Every club had a club house, a home away from home. Above, Wally Parks, in a pith helmet, right, instructs Vic Edelbrock Sr. in the art of spreading tar on the roof of the Road Runners' club house. The guy on the right is holding Wally and Vic with a rope. Vic stayed a member of the Road Runners for years, and after World War II would drive his famed '32 (shown below with fenders and lights) to club events, sometimes with Katie and Vic Jr. along for the fun.

SCTA became recognized as the governing body for racing at the dry lakes. Wally Parks and Eldon Snapp were responsible for producing the newsletter, with Parks as editor. It was Parks who convinced Edelbrock to join the Road Runners as an active participant. This meant racing under the club banner, attending meetings, and helping with chores. According to Parks, Edelbrock never missed a club meeting, helped members work on their cars, and even volunteered to tar the roof of the two-story club house—nearly falling off the roof in the process. Vic started to bring Vic Jr. (who was then about three years old) to the meetings, to let him experience the sights and sounds of the hot cars. Junior was in awe of the noise, commotion, and attention. Guys would carry him around and provide a candy bar when Dad was not looking.

Racing set Vic Sr.'s imagination on fire. His reputation quickly spread as his 1932 Ford Roadster broke records at Muroc and Harper Dry Lakes. He appeared on the cover of the SCTA Racing News program in 1940 as a top-running record holder. Although he used a wide assortment of modified parts like a Thickstun manifold and Arco heads, Edelbrock figured he could do better, and secretly began to experiment on paper, developing manifolds and other pieces of equipment.

Vic Edelbrock Sr. came to realize that he was one of many dry lakes visionaries who were young and full of fire. He was surrounded by those who thought like he did, who created like he did, and who wanted to win like he did. The challenge was uplifting. He began to share the results of his labors with other racers, especially fellow Road Runners. He and Bobby Meeks would work late nights building speed parts for their friends and customers. Being a true racer, though, Edelbrock always kept something in reserve.

When he discovered some weaknesses in the Thickstun manifold, especially in fuel distribution, Edelbrock approached Tommy about making some changes, but he would have no part of it. This prompted Edelbrock to begin working in earnest on his own design, using a trial-and-error method to develop runner size and length, plenum chamber size, and carburetor location. One night, on the way home from a Road Runner club meeting, Vic told Meeks that he was going to look for a new shop. The new shop would not just be for racers but also for general repair, and he would make his own manifold.

Finally, Vic found a shop with four stalls—a lean-to behind a small three-pump Signal Gas station. The manifold design was in process, but took longer than expected. Edelbrock slowly pieced together the final plans and found a patternmaker for the new manifold design. Katie put up some of her personal savings to finish the project, something Vic would say he loved about her. "She is a perfect wife for a poor man who struggles," he admitted. A casting company was found, and the first Edelbrock manifold was cast. It was called the Slingshot, featuring a revolutionary Y-shaped design that would surprise a few people. And thus, the Edelbrock Corporation was born.

"After a club meeting one night, I had my 1933 Ford 5-window coupe, with a refined flathead V-8 engine that could usually hold its own. It had milled heads on a hand-ported block, a Jack Henry manifold with two 97s, and a much-lightened flywheel. We had no formality on who raced whom, but Vic and Wes Collins were there with Vic's '32 roadster, so we just paired off. We launched side by side in an even start. But the evenness quickly disappeared as Vic's roadster hauled away down the road, leaving me far behind in helpless pursuit. Never had I been so impressed with what appeared to have been an overnight upgrade in performance. I couldn't wait to ask what had been done to achieve this miracle in horsepower. The answer, Vic said, was that in reassembling the engine in the wee hours the night before, they had mistakenly lagged the stock Mercury 5-T camshaft gear 8 degrees, and exhausted from working late, had decided to install it as it was. The combination turned out to be a real winner, with a big boost in low-end power. I could hardly wait to perform a similar low-buck miracle." —Wally Parks

In 1940 Vic Edelbrock moved his shop to Oakwood and La Brea and bought his first family car, a Chevrolet sedan.

2 Dark Clouds and Pain

Vic opened his new shop at "Breawood Garage," named for its location at Oakwood and La Brea in Los Angeles. Bobby Meeks, who had gone to work at a machine shop while Vic relocated his business, returned to work at Breawood. The shop was an instant hit and business was soon booming, especially with the introduction of the innovative Slingshot manifold. Breawood Garage quickly filled with the sound of high-performance engines. Some of the hottest roadsters and coupes in town waited on the lot to show off. On the La Brea side, there was a small barbershop frequented by many movie stars. It was not uncommon for John Wayne, Ward Bond, and Clayton Moore (the Lone Ranger), along with other Hollywood cowboys to drop by Breawood Garage and check out the latest in hot cars. Most of the actors in those days were car enthusiasts and racing fans; some even raced, like Robert Stack, who ran at the lakes.

One day, Edelbrock showed up unannounced at the foundry that was casting his manifolds and discovered that they were casting other companies' manifolds as well. After he left, a red light went on in his mind and he decided to return for another visit. This time he found the patternmaker for a competitor carefully checking and documenting the port size and plenum angle entry of the Edelbrock manifold pattern. Vic went ballistic; he starting cussing, grabbed a hammer, and smashed the pattern the guy was working on, gathered up his own finished castings and patterns, and left.

Edelbrock immediately contracted with a new foundry, and cautioned the owner to never allow anyone to see any of his designs, or he'd better be ready to leave town. Vic began production on the Slingshot with the help of machine shop owner Lynn Saulter. Meeks joined in, doing some of the machine work at the shop using a drill press and a small engine lathe that Vic had purchased from Sears, Roebuck and Company.

After parting ways with Tommy Thicksun, Vic Edelbrock sat down at the family's kitchen table and designed his own manifold called the Slingshot, above. The Slingshot was a 180-degree manifold for the Ford flathead, and used two Stromberg 97 carburetors. The Slingshot went into production before the war. It was sold over the counter at Vic's Oakwood and La Brea shop. Katie actually helped fund the development of the Slingshot by giving Vic her own personal savings. All of the manifolds were hand-poured, right, and then machined by Vic and Bobby Meeks after regular working hours when the shop was closed. As Vic's reputation at the dry lakes grew, so did the orders for the Slingshot. Everything was going fine until December 7, 1941, when production stopped.

Despite the Depression, the war in Europe and an extra heavy workload, the new shop was a happy place. Katie continued to bring dinner when the boys worked late, and 3-1/2-year-old Vic Jr. enjoyed spending time with his dad and the boys. To help make ends meet, Vic took on any work he could get—even fixing a flat tire or two. To keep his company's name in racer's thoughts, he built a new race engine for the '32 that again broke records in the roadster class.

As sales of the Slingshot increased, Edelbrock's exploits at the lakes kept his name out front, and business slowly began to improve again in the summer of 1940. When aircrews began to train at Muroc Army Air Field, rumors started that fighter planes were conducting war games around the area. Part of the lake became off-limits when the Army Air Corps built a full-scale version of a *Mogami* class Japanese heavy cruiser. Fabricated out of aluminum tubing, it was a target for low-level skip bombing. As things at Muroc got more difficult, racing shifted gears to Harper Dry Lake.

No longer a kid, nineteen-year-old Meeks picked up a 1936 Ford Coupe, and with Vic's help, built a "shop engine." Word got out at the lakes and on the street that Meeks and his coupe were

Katie's Short Cut

Katie and some of her friends decided to give a baby shower to one of the girls on Mother's Day. Katie drove their family car, the '32 Roadster, to the event. Some of the husbands arrived early to pick up their wives and brought some whiskey. When asked if she wanted a drink, Katie accepted. After two small shots, things began to get fuzzy, because she was not much of a drinker. At the end of the party, Katie offered to drive a friend home. She fired up the roadster with Edith in the passenger seat, and headed home. When they got to Venice Boulevard, Katie decided to take a short cut around traffic by driving down the railroad tracks of the Pacific Electric Red Car. Bouncing along the tracks with Edith screaming, Katie stayed straight until an oncoming Red Car forced her to alter course. She avoided the train and arrived home safely, but not before cutting across a neighbor's yard and parking in the middle of her own front lawn. Katie marched into the house and went directly to bed. When Vic Sr. heard the tale, he was glad that she was safe, laughed to himself at the thought of his wife bouncing down the tracks, and then checked the roadster for damage.

Katie was a child of the Great Depression and therefore was always conservative with money earned by Vic Sr. Both believed in paying cash for whatever they wanted.

As a result of the success of the Slingshot and later the Super manifolds, Vic designed and built his own aluminum heads, based on information gathered from his racing experience. At that point, you could buy a power package, left, of manifold and heads.

Painless Dentistry

In late 1940 or early 1941, a young guy from Tulare, California named Ray O'Neal was in Los Angeles attending the University of Southern California. Ray was studying to be a dentist, but he was also a car nut with a very clean Model A Ford coupe. He wanted a hot Edelbrock engine complete with a Slingshot manifold. Vic built and installed the new engine along with a new transmission and then called O'Neal so he could pick up his Ford. The response left Vic in a tough situation. O'Neal could not pick up his car and asked if Vic could keep it overnight. Because the shop was full at the time, the only overnight parking was outside. But Vic did not want the beautiful coupe left in the open. A young employee named Peewee, who did odd jobs around the shop, volunteered to take the car home and watch it until morning. Vic did not see a problem, but told him to go straight home—no driving around. At 9:00 p.m., Vic got some bad news. The car had been hit broadside and was a total loss. Vic confronted Peewee the next day about the crash. It had been his fault and he would have to trade his super clean '32 Ford coupe for the wrecked Model A. Although he was upset about his Model A, O'Neal agreed to the deal. Vic worked on the '32, making it even better than it was and O'Neal was pleased. After he became a dentist, Ray O'Neal took care of the Edelbrock family's dental needs for years.

hot stuff. One evening, Meeks pulled up next to a hot-shoe street racer named Bob Hedman who thought he would blow Meeks's doors off with no problem. The two started drag racing down Washington Boulevard, but the cars were so close no one could tell who won. The next day, Hedman, who didn't know Meeks, was stunned when he walked into Edelbrock's shop and everybody started laughing. Asking what was so funny, he was told to go around back where he found Bobby Meeks's coupe—and a new friend.

By the end of 1940, Edelbrock Equipment Company and Breawood Garage were building

One of the untold stories about Vic Edelbrock Sr. was his uncontested loyalty to his friends. No example of this commitment is better illustrated than the story of his help given to Japanese-American hot rodders when they were rounded up and sent to internment camps.

complete engines and earning a reputation as a major player in the racing scene. When Road Runner club members won at the lakes, racers clamored for the new Slingshot manifold. Edelbrock became friends with several racers, including a group of young Japanese-Americans, and he helped them all to run faster. Henry and Frank Morimoto became Edelbrock customers and Tsuneo "Tunney" Shigekuni became a great friend as well as a customer. Vic spent hours at the shop tuning his car for the lakes while Vic Jr. played with Tommy, Tunney's baby brother. After Tunney beat Edelbrock at an SCTA meet, some serious joking ensued between the "Round Eye" white guys and the "Buddha Head" Asian guys.

At the beginning of World War II, many of the dry lakes racers were Japanese-American. Within days after Pearl Harbor, especially on the West Coast, Japanese-Americans were given orders to pack up and get ready to be hauled off to camps. One racer named Tunney Shigekuni, right and above, was a close friend of Vic Edelbrock. Tunney left his racing engine with Vic to care for until he returned after the war.

Nisei Racers

The war was hard on Japanese-American racers, because many of them were put in camps. A number of their records were erased, and if it had not been for fellow hot rodders, their cars would have been lost. One of the most famous "Buddha Head" racers was Danny Sakai, top right, who ran the lakes from the 1930s. Danny was killed in a motorcycle accident. Below right, Tunney Shigekuni, in white coveralls, was a member of the Road Runners and a close friend of Vic Sr., as well as one of his strongest competitors. Shigekuni returned to racing after the war, moving from the lakes to the track roadster circuit, but continued to use Edelbrock equipment. *Opposite:* Another famous Japanese-American racer, Yam Oka, a member of the Glendale Ramblers, held many dry lakes victories before the war. After the war, Oka left the dry lakes to go circle-track racing.

The Road Runners

Car clubs, especially in California, date back to the early 1930s. Clubs had a two-fold purpose. First, it was the joining of one's identity with others. It was belonging to a group with the same goals and interests. Secondly, it gave racers a chance to compare ideas and methods of engine building, acquiring the latest in speed equipment and just having fun. Clubs had wild and unique names like Outriders, Strokers, Gear Grinders, Mobilers and Road Runners. Vic Edelbrock Sr. was a Road Runner, as were Wally Parks, Dandy Shinn, Bill Kimball, Tunney Shigekuni, Ak Miller, Jack Henry, and many others. The Road Runners were no different than the other clubs; they had a clubhouse and went on runs or cruises together. They had picnics at the beach with wives and girlfriends. They went to the dry lakes and raced against other clubs. But most of all the Road Runners had fun. Shown on these pages are random photos of the Road Runners from the Bill Kimball collection and from a shoebox found in Vic and Nancy Edelbrock's garage. They still had a few original metal tacks and dirt from the dry lakes.

Membership Card for 1946
Club Affiliation *Road Runners*
This is to Certify *Bill Kimball*
is a member in Good Standing of the
SOUTHERN CALIFORNIA TIMING ASS'N, INC.
Los Angeles, Calif.
Date Issued: 5-27-46
Wally Parks
President
Randy Shinn
Secretary

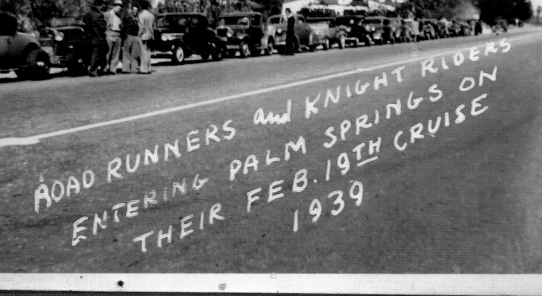

ROAD RUNNERS and KNIGHT RIDERS ENTERING PALM SPRINGS ON THEIR FEB. 19TH CRUISE 1939

AURORA SUNDAY BEACON-NEWS

U. S.–JAPAN AT WAR!

America Repulses Air-Sea Attack

For every single hot rodder, World War II was their most trying hour. All racing at the dry lakes and at most circle tracks ceased within months of the war's beginning. Gasoline was rationed, there were no tires or batteries, and automobile production in Detroit came to a halt. Racers would have to put down their wrenches and pick up guns to defend their nation in its time of peril.

On Monday morning, December 8, 1941, the *Los Angeles Examiner's* massive headline proclaimed, "U.S. AT WAR." There were maps showing the destruction caused by bombing raids at Pearl Harbor. On the West Coast, blackouts were ordered and military guards posted outside the Boeing and Lockheed aircraft plants. Neighbors roamed the streets with helmet and flashlight as Air Raid Wardens. Parents put blackout blankets over windows at night to prevent light from escaping.

By February 1942, a four-billion-dollar-a-year automotive industry ground to a halt. On orders from President Roosevelt, car production stopped, and every automaker began manufacturing arms and ammunition for the war effort. Ford Motor Company began to retool for building a GP (general purpose, or "jeep") vehicle for the Army, under contract to Willys. General Motors divided the wartime work between each of their divisions. Oldsmobile built automatic cannons and Cadillac built the famous M-5 tank. Pontiac manufactured cannon shells, torpedoes, 40mm field guns, diesel engines for boats, axles for the M-5 tank, and parts for army trucks. GM's Fisher Body Works made all types of tanks, bombers, and anti-aircraft guns while Buick built aircraft. When it came to tanks, Chrysler built the big ones and their De Soto division manufactured the B-26 Marauder bomber and aircraft engines. Packard built engines for Rolls-Royce, Warhawk, Hurricane fighters, Lancaster, DeHavilland Mosquito bombers as well as the famed PT boats of the U.S. Navy. American truck builders, including GMC, built the trucks and the big guns that were towed behind them.

Racing had all but stopped. Under the newly approved Selective Service Act, anyone who could pass the physical was drafted into the military. Everyone from eighteen to thirty-five had to register. If you were five feet tall, one hundred pounds, had correctable vision and most of your teeth, you were a candidate for the army. There were cases that were deferred, but within weeks after the attack on Pearl Harbor, a million young men volunteered for service. As the need for troops increased, the draft age was dropped from twenty-one to eighteen years old, and nearly all racers would fall into this age group.

There was real concern that this country could be invaded and bombs could fall on our cities. Edelbrock had set a record of 121.42 mph in his '32 roadster just three weeks prior to the bombing of Pearl Harbor, but now records were of little consequence. Racing continued at Harper Dry Lake during the spring of 1942, but its heart and soul faded as the war grew. As a married man with a child, Edelbrock was temporarily deferred, but he wanted to be part of the fight. As a superb welder, he quickly got work building warships in the shipyards of Long Beach.

In the mornings, Vic would go down to his shop, fill orders for manifolds, work on his customers' jobs, and manage the books. Meeks would come to work around noon and close the shop in early evening. There was no aluminum to spare for hot

"Vic lay on his back to weld overhead, all that hot metal dropping back on his body. He worked from afternoon to midnight. He would come home covered with dirt and burns and he could hardly open his fingers because they were so cramped from holding the (arc welding) torch." —**Katie Edelbrock**

In September of 1941, racing was still going strong at the lakes and Vic Edelbrock was continuing his record-breaking career. On September 28, 1941, Edelbrock, using his now-famous manifold, set the fastest V8 Roadster record of 121.42 mph. In December of 1941, as war broke out, Vic Edelbrock and Tunney Shigekuni, both Road Runners, finished first and second at one of the last events held on Muroc Dry Lake. Photos show Vic crossing the finish line at Muroc, left, and Vic and Wes Collins working on the roadster, below just prior to making a run.

The Bill Kimball Story

As research for this book turned to the gathering of photos to help substantiate the history of the Edelbrock family, a strange story emerged from the past and cried out to be told. The story involves a gentleman named Bill Kimball, and his gift to this project. The story of Kimball is one of the more poignant events in the Edelbrock family history.

A few years ago, Bill Kimball contacted Vic Edelbrock Jr. He requested a meeting, which was never scheduled, explaining only that he had some photos of the early days of the dry lakes and clubs—photos concerning the Road Runners.

Vic Jr. relates what took place at that meeting. Says Vic, "One day, totally unannounced, this man walks into my office on Coral Circle in El Segundo, and tells me his name is Bill

Kimball was never a superstar at the lakes, but he raced just as hard as those who were. Kimball always admired Vic Sr. for his abilities.

Kimball. He went on to say that we had never met, but he was a friend of my mom and dad's from the dry lakes days. He then told me he was dying of cancer and had only three months to live. He presented me with two scrapbooks of photos he had shot of the lakes and the Road Runners. The books were divided into photos before the war and those after. Kimball said he wanted me to have the albums, and after placing them on my desk, he simply walked out of my office and left. I was shocked, I didn't even have time to say 'thank you'. I later found out that Bill raced a '32 roadster against my dad, and was a photographer. Some of Bill's photos are in this book as a tribute; he deserves to be remembered."

"I was building a racing engine using hand-me-down equipment due to lack of money. When I needed to get some millwork done, I went to Edelbrock's shop, but did not mention my name, and I had grown up a lot in five years. I asked Vic to mill a set of competitor's heads and he told me that the combustion chamber design was wrong, and how I could improve it by using a grinding tool. There was no charge for the labor or the advice. I'll never forget his kindness and compassion for a totally anonymous, poor, aspiring racer who needed help." —**Thomas Shigekuni**

rod manifolds, because the war effort needed every scrap of metal available. With a stockpile of fifty Slingshot manifolds and little chance of additional castings, Edelbrock saw the writing on the wall. He vacated his shop and moved to a garage he had built behind his home.

Displacement

On March 3, 1942, Bobby Meeks joined the Navy. And, in an effort to conserve gasoline and rubber, the Office of Defense and Department of Transportation, placed a ban on all auto racing in the United States. Race cars were placed in storage, and even the mighty Indianapolis Speedway shut its doors. Edelbrock took a job at Todd Shipyards and worked many overtime hours because of the around-the-clock demand for military ware. When Len Saulter won a government contract to machine critical parts from newly developed exotic metals, Vic jumped at the chance to help, and released himself from the confines of a big company. The work was categorized as essential to the war effort and would keep Edelbrock from being drafted for the remainder of the war.

In the Los Angeles area, Japanese-Americans who had lived in peace since the late 1800s and had become entrenched in business, particularly in fishing and farming, were now regarded as the enemy. The same people who had landscaped American homes and put food on American tables were suddenly considered dangerous. People whispered that the fishermen were really Japanese soldiers in disguise, that the farmers were all spies, that they were going to turn on their neighbors and kill them at night. Old prejudices against blacks and Mexicans were readily turned on the Japanese, although the vast majority of Japanese who lived on the West Coast were second-generation American citizens. President Roosevelt signed into law Executive Order 9066 in February 1942 that moved more than 125,000 Japanese Americans into internment camps. These families were given less than two months to sell off or give away all of the land, goods, cars, and any personal property that would not fit into two suitcases.

Despite the fact that many of the Japanese-American racers were sent to camps and lost their personal property, at the war's conclusion they returned to racing and picked up the pieces. One of the most famous Nisei racing teams were the Oka brothers. After the war, Yam and Harry Oka turned from hot rods to track roadsters. Photo shows the brothers (left to right) Yam and Harry Oka, their driver, Tom McLaughin and Takeo "Chickie" Hirashima posing with the team's track roadster. Hirashima went on to make his mark as an Indy 500 mechanic.

In 1941, color, race, and religion didn't matter to the racers. Many Japanese-American names like Kamimura, Oka, Morimoto, Ishizawa, Sakai, and Shigekuni filled the record books and photo albums of the dry lakes racers. Unlike the majority of the population, the Caucasian racers supported their Nisei cohorts anyway they could by hiding, buying, saving, or storing their cars, engines and tools so their racing gear wouldn't be lost in the mayhem. As for Vic's pals—Tunney, Henry, and young Thomas—they were shipped to Colorado. The Shigekuni brothers would be gone for more than four years. Edelbrock was horrified that his friends were to be sent away. Tunney had stored his Edelbrock-equipped 1941 Mercury racing engine in the cellar of a neighbor's house. Concerned that the engine would rust on the cylinder walls and the valve springs would deteriorate in the damp cellar, Vic picked up the engine and kept it in perfect condition. The friendship endured long after the war. Tunney went oval-track racing and continued to use Edelbrock equipment. His son, Thomas, became an Edelbrock customer, a racer, a lawyer, and finally an author when he wrote a book about his camp internment.

The Home Front

Most of the other racers made it home after the war but their lives had been changed forever. The Depression had made them tough enough to fight a war, but the military gave them skills to survive and had shown them technology never seen before. The racers were quick to learn and take advantage of this new knowledge. They acquired new skills in welding, metal forming, and working with aluminum as well as other exotic metals. They were exposed to aircraft engine science, turbo charging, and hydraulics. These skills, created by the needs of war, would be taken home and put to many other uses.

"Vic Edelbrock was always a special hero to me. He was one of the most innovative, dedicated, and sincere people I have known in the auto performance industry." **—Wally Parks**

Racers in Uniform

Just about all of the young dry lakes racers were either enlisted or drafted by the end of 1943. Wally Parks, an SCTA officer who helped put the organization in mothballs until the conflict was over, served in the Army Tank Corps. In his off-duty hours, he built a hot rod Jeep. Two other young men who would play very important roles in the Edelbrock story, Alex Xydias and Dean Batchelor, also served in the Army Air Corps. Batchelor was shot down in Europe and spent time in a prisoner of war camp.

Ak Miller went to Europe and saw the worst kind of action as he fought for his life in the Battle of the Bulge. Bill Stroppe, Vic Hickey, and Fran Hernandez were all in the navy. Stroppe received a presidential citation for two inventions that saved many lives. Chuck Daigh was a paratrooper, and was wounded in battle. Like Hickey, Stroppe, and Hernandez, Tom and Bill Spalding were in the navy. The brothers would later become famous for ignition systems and record-breaking hot rods. Paul Nelson, who was a racer and longtime friend of Bobby Meeks, as well as the younger brother of famed drag racer Jim "Jazzy" Nelson, fought in some of the bloodiest battles of the war in Europe. Bob Hedman, who would become the King of Headers, fought U-boats as a member of the U.S. Coast Guard.

Some of the most famous drivers of the time served in the military during the war. National champion Rex Mays served in the air force. Famed

The two most defining moments in the lives of the pioneers of performance were the Great Depression and World War II. Noted dry lakes racer and journalist *extraordinaire*, the late Dean Batchelor (at left in photo above) shown with his buddy Ivan Damond, was shot down and spent time in a POW camp.

From 1941 to 1945, racers had to put away their cars for a more important task, defending the Nation. Times were tough but young men did their duty. For Katie's brother Wes Collins, above, (working on engine in photo above), the effects of war are devastating, and resulted in bouts of depression. Katie says, "He was never the same."

Indy car builder Frank Kurtis turned his shop in Glendale, California, into a defense plant that built Plexiglas canopies and gun turrets for fighter planes, under contract to Northrop and Lockheed. Kurtis also worked on designs for the navy PT boat. Bill Vukovich joined the army and became a tank mechanic. Walt Faulkner, a close friend of Vic Edelbrock, joined the Army with his old buddy Johnny Mantz, and served in the 9th Armored Division. Ray Crawford, midget and Indy car driver, flew a P-38 Lightning and became an ace in Europe, shooting down seven German fighter planes. Mike Nazaruk, one of the toughest guys to ever drive a racecar, was a hero as a marine in the Pacific Campaign. The Thin Man, Sam Hanks, later the 1957 Indy 500 winner and a National Champion, also served in the Air Corps.

Eventual two-time Indy 500 winner and Edelbrock driver Rodger Ward joined the Air Corps and went off to flight school. He then graduated as a fighter pilot with a lieutenant rating, flying a P-38 Lightning like Ray Crawford. Post-war midget and sprint car driver Walt James was a bombardier/navigator on a B-17 in Europe.

Danny Eames, another lakes racer, who in later years would manage and drive for the Dodge team in the Pan-American Road Race, become close friends with Vic Sr. Eames joined the seabees and served the entire war in the Pacific, seeing some of the worst fighting on Saipan and other island invasions.

Bobby Meeks joined the navy and was given the job of ammunition truck driver at a base in San Diego. At first, he could come home on weekend passes to work with Vic at the machine shop, but the gravy train didn't last long. Meeks shipped out on the USS *Ross*, a newly commissioned destroyer headed for the Pacific to support island invasions. While in the Philippines, Bobby's ship hit two mines, ripping it wide open. The crew stayed and fought rather than abandon ship. They were towed to a spot between two small islands where the crew began to make repairs, but a Japanese observation plane discovered them. For the next seven weeks, the USS *Ross* lost about a third of the crew while fighting off 274 air attacks. "Those days changed my life forever," Meeks said. "I just wanted to make it home alive."

Racers remained racers even during the toughest battles of the war. Wes Collins stationed in Burma, saw a lot of action but still took time to have a moment of fun. After the war, Wes became unable to cope and in the end, took his own life. His sister Katie and Vic Sr. had a very difficult time handling the tragedy.

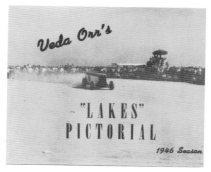

One of the great stories to come out of the war years had to do with a couple who were both red-blooded Americans and hard-core racers—Karl and Veda Orr. Veda, center, looks over a roadster, and Karl, right, sits on the rear tire of his famed streamliner that ran a model B four-banger with a Cragar ohv cylinder head. Karl was a member of the Road Runners, and he and Veda produced a newsletter during the war that was sent to racers in service throughout the war zone. It kept racers informed and helped prevent homesickness. During interviews conducted in 2002, Wally Parks, Vic Hickey, Ak Miller, and Alex Xydias remembered the letters. After the war, above, Veda produced a booklet called *Lakes Pictorial* that is now considered a treasure. Both Veda and Karl are gone, but their kindness and love for hot rodders will always be cherished.

The SCTA: During and After the War

Veda and Karl Orr had been dry lakes racers for many years. Karl had been racing the lakes since the 1930s, and after the war, he would own and operate a successful speed shop in Culver City, California. Veda was a record-breaking racer, the first woman to become a member of the SCTA, and the kind of person that always made a special effort to help. While the editors of the SCTA Newsletter, Alex Xydias and Dean Batchelor were serving their country, Veda put together her own newsletter, and mailed copies to the men in service. Club members from all over California wrote to her about the war from their viewpoint, and about their dreams of what they were going to do when they returned. Veda's mailing list grew to about two hundred during the war, and in 1946, she produced a booklet called "Lakes Pictorial." It was filled with pictures taken at the lakes from the years before and after the war, as well as racecar drawings by an artist named Dick Teague, who later became AMC chief designer. The forty-page booklet was a treasury of "early days" images of guys like Lou Baney, Stu Hilborn, Jack McGrath, Manny Ayulo, Sandy Belond, Ed Iskenderian, Phil Remington, Vic Edelbrock Sr., Tony Capana, Bill Burke, Tom and Bill Spaulding, and others.

For the members of the Road Runners and SCTA, their world would always be a shade darker after they found out that fellow racer and SCTA club secretary, Art Tilton, had lost his life when his plane went down. Wally Parks and his buddy, Eldon Snapp, returned to reinstate the official SCTA newsletter to provide information on clubs, members, events, and times run at the lakes. Local artist Bozzy Willis contributed drawings and cartoons.

The war affected everyone in many areas both home and abroad. Because of the pressure placed on every working American to produce goods for the war effort, there were long hours at the work place and little time for anything else. Home was a place to sleep and prepare for the next day's labor. Katie was a master at managing funds while still providing a comfortable home. Vic worked fourteen-hour days, filling orders for Slingshot manifolds, working in his backyard garage on his roadster and several other cars left in his care. Wartime rationing was a huge reality check. Gasoline was rationed, and rubber tires, spark plugs, and batteries were impossible to obtain. The foundry casting his manifolds could not buy aluminum at any price.

Katie made clothes for the family, toys for Vic Jr., and even her own undergarments, as silk and nylon were a luxury. Food products like sugar, coffee, meat, milk, butter, canned soups, and

"Katie, you make a wonderful wife for a poor man, you never waste a thing. Someday I'll make it all up to you, I promise." —**Vic Edelbrock Sr.**

canned vegetables were rationed too. Each family received a monthly ration book containing color-coded stamps with a numerical value, and everyone needed to be quick if they wanted to get what they needed at the store.

There was more to the war effort than just rationing. Families were asked to recycle everything that could be used in industry. Everyone was instructed to wash out and flatten every tin can used, even the tin foil from gum and cigarette wrappers was peeled off, rolled into balls and turned in for collection. Paper, cardboard, scrap metal, old stockings, bicycle tires, inner tubes, and rubber from any product—from hot water bottles to rain boots—was recycled. Victory gardens were another popular part of the war effort. Housewives like Katie would have their husbands dig up an area behind the house and then plant an assortment of vegetables. What was not

From 1945 to 1949, a one-time Associated gas station at 1200 Highland Ave. became ground zero for the Vic Edelbrock climb into history. After the war, Vic went back into the business of producing high-quality products. He also went back into the midget racing business, fielding two cars, above; an Offenhauser for the Blue Circuit and a V8-60 for the Red Circuit. Check out the business card, above—the telephone number is only four digits and the address has no zip code. Times were simple then.

used at harvest time would be canned for the winter. Despite the rationing and lack of money, Katie managed to put a few pennies aside every week to buy war bonds. These bonds would be cashed in after the war to help provide the family a foundation for a new course in life.

Vic and Katie had saved every penny they could—overtime money, war bonds—it was a nickel here and a dime there. Vic was on fire with a passion to get his own business up and running again. His experiences from making wartime tools would be turned into ideas for speed. Vic decided he needed a bigger and better location for the next shop, which would be for more than general repairs. All Vic's efforts would go into making Edelbrock a name to be reckoned with in the racing equipment business. In the fall of 1945, Vic found a location at 1200 North Highland Avenue in Hollywood. It was a six-car stall, divided in half with an office and an Associated Service Station on the end. He bought the entire complex and hired several employees, including Bob Bradford, who would play an important part in future business development. By March 1946, Bobby Meeks was discharged from the military and returned to work with Vic. The old gang was back in business.

There where those who said his touch was magic. Vic Edelbrock Sr. checks a problem at the San Diego track.

The war had jolted the American economy out of the Depression, and industry flourished as it turned from making war materials to producing products for the domestic market. In 1946 the Office of Defense Transportation lifted the ban on auto racing. The SCTA quickly regrouped and began running races on the dry lakes, except Muroc, which had become Edwards Air Force Base. It was a good time to be young. Automobile mania unleashed itself with a fury. Veteran racers returned from the war filled with new ideas and a hunger to get back to their sport. They brought with them a new crop of enthusiasts. Vic promised Katie that he would make up for all the tough times and deficiencies they had endured during the war by turning his business into a success. Vic had been secretly designing and developing a line of products during the war, including a new manifold called the Super and a design for high-performance aluminum heads for the flathead Ford. The new shop at 1200 North Highland in Hollywood now meant he could fulfill his promise of creating a line of speed equipment carrying his name. A typical small automotive complex of the time, the main stucco building had five stalls with an office, and huge sliding metal doors. In front, there was an Associated service station with two gas pumps and an outdoor lube rack. Vic converted two of the five stalls into a machine shop, which left the remaining three designated for customer service and installation.

Vic purchased new equipment for the machine shop that included a lathe, a drill press, and a milling machine, as well as all the hand tools and gauges required to build engines and install Edelbrock products. The workforce included good friend Bob Bradford, a fellow named Red, whose last name is lost in the clouds of time, and Bobby Meeks, who had just returned from the navy. Vic convinced Katie's brother, Wes, who was out of a job and also home from the war, to run the gas station part of the business. The first year was challenging and fatiguing, but Vic never deviated from his goal. By 1946, the shop was filled with dry lakes racers, midgets, roadsters,

History Would Be Made on Jefferson Boulevard

In the spring of 1949, Vic packed up and moved to larger quarters. For the first time, he was owner and builder of his facilities. The location at 4921 West Jefferson Boulevard in Los Angeles would remain Edelbrock Equipment Company until the late 1960s. The move allowed the expansion of the machine shop and room for the development of new products. A long list of new manifolds could be added to early models like the "Super", top left. The crew grew with the expansion and now included Bobby Meeks, Don Towle, Bob Bradford, Fran Hernandez, Murray Jensen, Girard "Pee Wee" Gallant and a young Victor Edelbrock Jr. Clockwise from above left, De-burring a manifold, Super manifold, the expanded machine shop, more equipment. *Opposite:* The 200-hp Clayton dynamometer was first installed at Highland, then moved to Jefferson where there was more room to work. Edelbrock was able to test and evaluate every product before it hit the racetrack. Although his was not the only Clayton in use, it did give Vic a leg up on the competition.

Of all the rivalries found in midget racing on the West Coast, none was fiercer than that between car owners Vic Edelbrock Sr. and Eddie Meyer. They were both in the business of making racing parts and they both wanted to win. The great Walt Faulkner, right, in Meyer's midget, also drove for Edelbrock.

and coupes—all waiting for Edelbrock equipment. The swirl of activity at the Highland shop was intense. Aluminum chips flew from the lathes and drill presses, Edelbrock's newly-purchased Clayton engine dynamometer announced itself with the bark of the open exhaust. Wherever you looked, racing machines stood waiting. Like a general, Edelbrock stood directing his men in the center of the battle.

When racing resumed at the lakes, Vic picked up where he had left off, beating the likes of Jack McGrath and other future superstars. But now, racing took on the added purpose of serving as a testing ground for his products, and a way to rebuild his reputation. As the Edelbrock Equipment Company became divided into four distinct subdivisions, Vic was well aware that his time must be spent wisely. Manufacturing became primary, which was followed by parts development for midget racecars. Then came building and supplying competition engines for the dry lakes and other forms of racing, and finally, the street performance parts business that was growing, as more and more young men wanted to build cars that performed well on the road.

Unlike Vic's previous shops, Highland was large and allowed plenty of room to congregate. The activities in the shop attracted many racers and the Edelbrock shop became a popular hangout.

"I liked the early days the best because all of the boys had to make their own parts and pieces. It was who had the best ideas, the most inventive mind, and creative hands that went the fastest. Vic Edelbrock was one of the people who looked for answers. It was guys like him who started our industry." —Robert Petersen

Accomplishments varied among the racers, ranging from consistent winners to backyard innovators to those who simply wanted lots of advice. And then there were those who would help to create a new industry in the near future.

By the 1950s, Vic Edelbrock Sr. was gaining ground on the performance industry. He had his own building on West Jefferson Boulevard in Los Angeles. His flathead products, top and left, were very popular at the drag strip, at the lakes, and on the street. His ad agency, Tilts & Cantz, produced ads, above, for major magazines.

> "Vic Sr. once told me that he really didn't want to grow too big, because he felt that he would lose control and not be able to stay on top of the development of new products." —**Robert Petersen**

Before World War II, Vic Sr. ventured into midget racing with an outdated "rail job" driven by Cal Niday, below. Also, after the war, Robert E. Petersen, far right, (with tie, talking to Vic Jr. in the sixties) began his rise to power in the auto publishing world. However, before Petersen, there was Ed Almquist, bottom, who published performance magazines in 1946.

Edelbrock set down the rules. During business hours, work was to come first. After work, anyone who was interested could partake in the day's bench racing session. Once again, bench racing became established as a ritual.

On the midget racing scene, Vic bought a new rail job car and ran a few races in 1946 with Cal Niday behind the wheel. The midget became a test bench to perfect his V8-60 product line. Business grew on all fronts at an astonishing rate. For the first time, Vic had a few dollars in his pocket, and Katie didn't have to sew driving shirts for the midget drivers to make extra money. She could now spend time in her comfortable two-bedroom house on Sycamore Street caring for her son.

A Speed Catalog

The speed shop was a new phenomenon that was growing all over the country, and advertising placements spiked upward. Before the war, Vic had only placed ads in the dry lakes racing magazine, *Throttle*, which lasted only a year before the war put an end to its publication. Ads in the *SCTA Newsletter* only reached a few hundred readers. Now, magazines like *Speed Age* were being distributed nationally. On the East Coast, a young man named Ed Almquist wrote a book called the *Hot Rod Speed Equipment Handbook* featuring Edelbrock equipment, including the latest manifolds and aluminum heads. Almquist became a pioneer in the automotive speed equipment business. After the publication of his book, he became an East Coast distributor of Edelbrock parts, and eventually developed a product line of his own.

One day, Vic said to his friend, Robert E. "Pete" Petersen, "Hey Pete, I'm getting so many letters, I don't have time to answer them, what do you think I should do?" Petersen told him to lay out a catalog; he would shoot the photos and get a printer. Edelbrock realized that this was a great idea. If he could send a catalog upon request, he could easily answer many of the frequently asked questions and create more sales by displaying all of his products. Working at night on his kitchen table, he fashioned his eight-page catalog with Petersen's help. Katie did the editing, with Vic having the final say in content. (Note: Throughout the years, nothing has really changed. Vic Jr. works with daughter Camee on the catalog, and also has the last say about content). Vic started sending the catalog to customers who wrote letters or came by the shop, but when Petersen stopped by a short time later, Vic said, "Pete, I'm getting so many requests for the catalog it's costing me money." Petersen told Vic that he should start charging for the catalog, so Vic started with twenty-five cents, then fifty cents, and finally a dollar, as the catalog grew in size.

The unceasing demands of his growing business caused Vic to be unaware of the telltale signs of a personal tragedy that was about to overtake him. After Katie's brother, Wes, was discharged from the army, he returned to California a different person. He never discussed what he went through during the war, but Katie knew it had devastated his spirit. At first, Wes seemed happy to be back. Bobby Meeks, now married to his wife, Elizabeth, and Vic and Katie would include Wes in family dinners or nights out to see a movie. Wes was part of Vic's racing crew whenever they ran the midget or headed for the lakes with the roadster. It all seemed uplifting. Wes showed up in a white uniform, black bowtie, and captain's hat every morning to run the gas pumps of the Associated service station in front of the shop. He loved talking to the customers. After work, he would join the crew for bench racing and a drink or two in the shop.

"It was the first time we could look ahead, and I loved staying home. I did a lot of canning. I remember a friend of ours took me to the San Fernando Valley to pick apricots. I was so excited that I picked bag after bag. When we got home, I canned enough apricots to last all year and then some. I think Vic got tired of canned apricots, but it was great to have the pantry full." —Katie Edelbrock

The First Catalog

Called "Edelbrock Power and Speed Equipment," the 7½ by 4-inch booklet featured a cover announcing highlights to be found inside. The sell lines touted Edelbrock Equipment as "For the Speedway or the Highway," and "Proven/Tested/Always Superior." When they read the cover, customers were reminded, "It Pays to Buy the Best."

Highlighted inside, of course, was the manifold line, consisting of two manifolds for the full-size Mercury and Ford flathead. The Super Dual manifold was listed for competition-only use and the Edelbrock Regular Dual manifold for street applications. The major difference between the two was in the runner design and the placement of the carburetor mounts. The Super had carburetor mounts located very close to the port openings. The street version had the carburetor mounts in the center area of the manifold. For midgets, the catalog proclaimed the Edelbrock V8-60 manifold offered the same design as the Super and offered maximum efficiency in the low rpm range as well as higher rpm. Rounding out the manifold section, Edelbrock offered the Zephyr Dual manifold for all models of Lincoln Continental/Zephyr V-12s.

The centerfold of the catalog presented both the standard size heads and the V8-60 heads for midgets. The standard heads offered compression ratios of 7¾, 8¼ and 8¾ to 1, and the V8-60 heads offered 9 and 9½ to 1. Now, Edelbrock could compete with all of the other manufacturers, including Eddie Meyer. Filling the remaining pages, Edelbrock offered stroked crankshafts, special racing pistons, adjustable tappets for Ford, Mercury, Ford 6-cylinder and Ford Ferguson engines. There were camshafts from Winfield and Harmon & Collins, balancing services, fuel lines, throttle kits, manual fuel pressure pumps, chrome carburetor stacks and steering wheels for racecars.

Prices in the first Edelbrock catalog provided something for everyone. Mercury and Ford aluminum heads were $69.50, camshafts ranged from $30.00 for a three-quarter cam to $40.00 for a race cam. A stroked and balanced crankshaft would cost a racer $85.00, and manifolds ranged from $32.00 to $44.50. Adjustable tappets cost $.85 each and a chrome carburetor stack would run $1.25.

Midget racing hit an all-time high between 1946 and 1950. Teams could run five and six nights a week, and make money in the process. Vic Edelbrock was fully involved in midget racing at his shop on Highland Avenue. He ran two cars, each carrying the number 2, above and below, one a V8-60 and the other a four-cylinder Offy. His driver Perry Grimm (top right with white pants) also had his own midget (2-USA) that he raced in Australia in the off-season. The reason behind running two cars was a matter of money. The Offy could run the very exclusive "Blue Circuit" (best teams and fastest cars) and the V8-60 could run the "Red Circuit" (teams with less money). Also, Vic made parts for the V8-60, so he could make money in two ways.

Slowly, Wes's mood changed, and he would leave work without saying a word to anyone. He suffered deep bouts of depression; perhaps in part due to burns suffered in an engine fire years earlier, or perhaps from his wartime experiences. He had come back from the war a changed man. Katie remembered, "I never knew what happened, but it must have been dreadful. He was a loving man and a good brother." One evening, Wes Collins ended his suffering with a single gunshot. Katie and Vic, along with the entire Edelbrock crew, were devastated.

At this time, Vic decided that his company would stand on its own and become a manufacturing business where a customer could buy, and have installed, all the products that Edelbrock produced. They would also build and test race engines. Vic was ready for new challenges, and little did he know that he was about to get his wish. That year he bought his first Kurtis-Kraft midget, a V8-60, joined the next year by an Offy. He raced both cars through 1947, but sold the Offy the following year because it required too much work to keep it running. During the next two years, Vic Edelbrock would make his name synonymous with speed, racing, and the expansion of the aftermarket performance industry. In that short span, he would own and race two new midgets, employing some of the most famous drivers in America. He would build engines for some of the fastest dry lakes cars around. With the help of Bobby Meeks and other racers,

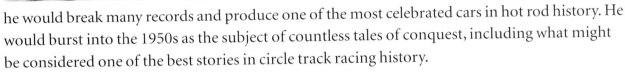

he would break many records and produce one of the most celebrated cars in hot rod history. He would burst into the 1950s as the subject of countless tales of conquest, including what might be considered one of the best stories in circle track racing history.

Speed and Safety

As the 1950s arrived, Edelbrock was only part of the explosion of activism that took place within the hot rod movement. Dry lakes racing had moved to El Mirage, and a racer named Bill Burke had introduced the use of World War II aircraft fuel tanks (the belly tank from a P-38 was the most popular) as streamlined bodies for racing cars. The lakes had become a battleground for manufacturers to vigorously promote their products. On any weekend, the desolate sands of El Mirage became a living, breathing, noisy, advertising domain to speed producers. Racers sported parts from Navarro, Sharp, Evans, Thickstun, Tattersfield, Weiand, Meyer, and Edelbrock.

Wally Parks was elected president of the SCTA, and when the National Safety Council went on record wanting to ban all forms of racing in the United States, the

One of the most interesting stories to come out of the early days is that of Bill Burke. He had served in the Army Air Force during the war and was introduced to aircraft belly tanks, used by fighter planes for an auxiliary fuel supply. After the war, Burke, above left, took the streamlined tanks from a P-38 fighter and converted them into aerodynamic race cars, his most famous, number 16, was dubbed "Sweet Sixteen."

"Vic spent hundreds of hours, many times after work, designing and testing his ideas for manifolds and combustion chamber design for his heads. He was brilliant when it came to flow patterns in the manifold runners and in plenum designs. We would test a manifold, then tear it apart and weld up a new version. As for the head design, Vic would take several sets of Denver heads to a friend of his and have the combustion chambers welded up, and then he would spend hours reshaping the chambers and then trying the design. Vic Edelbrock wanted every product he built to be tested and proven before his name went on the casting." —**Bobby Meeks**

Mighty Man, Tiny Cars

There was a period between 1946 and 1950 when midgets were racing on every bullring, fairground, and dog track up and down the length of California, seven days a week. Every driver of Indy 500 fame ran the mighty midgets, including Bill Vukovich, Jack McGrath, Sam Hanks, Johnny Boyd, Perry Grimm, Walt Faulkner, Rodger Ward and others. Most drove for Edelbrock at one time or another. Edelbrock was a mighty force in the world of the tiny cars, building engines for many of the teams, showcasing his own products and creating a winning image. Midget racing provided Edelbrock with extra income. Vic ran hard from 1946 to 1950 and used a variety of cars. Clockwise from top left, Vic climbs into his most famous midget, the V8-60 Kurtis Kraft that beat the Offys at Gilmore. Vic works on his 1946 rail job, a car he ran only a short time. Bobby Meeks (far right) checks out V8-60 mill as Don Towle works on a race engine; Vic Sr. (far left) works on the cockpit area of the car. *Opposite:* Perry Grimm takes a tumble after being clipped by another car. Left, Vic Sr. works on his favorite test engine.

This gent—Vic Edelbrock — has been watching his new Red Circuit midget, usually driven by Perry Grimm, cause nothing but trouble for the boys, especially at San Diego where No. 63 has won three consecutive main events. No. 63 is powered with a V-8 60 and is one of four new cars of its type now competing in the Red Circuit.

"When I picked up my engine, Bobby warned me not to jump on it until I had 500 miles. So I just started driving around until the odometer registered 500. Then I headed for Picadilli's Drive-In, a hot spot in Culver City, to show off my new machine. I wasn't there two minutes when the so-called King of the Street ambled up and chose me off. We raced right down Culver Boulevard and I blew up his dress big time. So he wants two out of three, and I do it again, and this time I really dust him off. The guy was so pissed that he didn't even come back to the drive-in. The next day, I get a phone call from Meeks telling me to get my ass down to the shop, Vic wanted to see me right now. When I show up at the shop, Vic tells me that I am working for him and I better clean up my act. He told me he didn't want me tarnishing his name and the reputation of his equipment by street racing and running with bad guys causing trouble. Vic knew that the cops had warned me, but since they couldn't catch me they would stop me at a drive-in and threaten me with jail time if they caught me racing. I just laughed. I started drilling holes and sweeping the shop. When I joined the Coupes Club I realized that it was more fun to race with the club than on the street. Besides, the clubs were formed as a way to buy insurance and get protection against lawsuits. If something happened, people would sue the club and not the person or equipment maker. Vic liked that idea. Everything went along fine until one day Bobby found out that my car had a couple of stolen parts. He went nuts and told me to get rid of that stuff or hit the road." —**Bob Pierson**

SCTA joined the National Safety Council. The group opposed street racing and required use of helmets and seat belts in all racecars. As a result, the Safety Council backed off its campaign for an all-encompassing ban. The next battle came with the previously excluded coupes and sedans. Banned from running in SCTA-sanctioned events, the closed-bodied cars became more popular after the war, and innovative racers like Bobby Meeks and the Pierson brothers were avid supporters. A group of racers, which included Bobby Meeks, formed the Coupes Club and began racing for the rival sanctioning body, the Russetta Timing Association. Russetta allowed coupes, roadsters, motorcycles, and belly tanks, without restrictions. The Coupes Club emerged into a "kick-butt" group of racers who soon ignited a speed battle between the roadsters and coupes. Backed by Edelbrock, Meeks gathered a tough, hard running group that included Don Towle, Bob Pierson, and Francisco "Fran" Hernandez. Fran worked for Fred Offenhauser at the time, but would one day play a pivotal role in the Edelbrock Company. Finally, the SCTA relented and allowed the closed-bodied cars into their ranks.

Bob Pierson

In 1942, Pierson came to Inglewood, California, from Centerville, Iowa. He and a friend bought two brand new flathead engines in 1947 from George M. Sutton, a local Ford Dealer, who also raced at the Los Angeles Mines Field (now Los Angeles International Airport). Pierson put one of the engines into a '36 Ford and went racing. However, when he was away in Colorado on military duty, his father sold the car out from under him to prevent him from racing. Pierson bought another '36 in Colorado Springs and drove it home. He took his other flathead engine to the Edelbrock shop for a total performance upgrade, and then dropped it in the '36. Pierson paid $354 dollars, out the door, ready-to-install. He estimated that he ran nearly four hundred street races in a year with that engine.

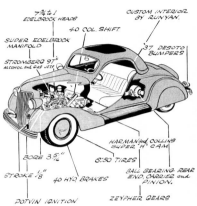

Construction Cutaway labels:

7¾ to 1 EDELBROCK HEADS

CUSTOM INTERIOR BY RUNYAN.

40 COL. SHIFT

SUPER EDELBROCK MANIFOLD

'37 DESOTO BUMPERS

STROMBERG 97's ALCOHOL and GAS JETS

HARMAN and COLLINS SUPER "H" CAM

BORE 3⅜"

6:50 TIRES

BALL BEARING REAR END, CARRIER and PINION.

STROKE 1⅛"

40 HYD. BRAKES

ZEYPHER GEARS

POTVIN IGNITION

Next to the rivalry between car clubs, the competition between the roadster owners and the coupe drivers was a hot subject. In the early days, the SCTA did not let coupes run with the roadsters. So, the coupe owners formed their own group, "The Coupes Club," and went to war with the roadsters. Bobby Meeks was one of the founders of the Coupes club and had this to say, "At one point, SCTA didn't let us run, so we went to the Russetta Timing Association, and soon we were running faster than the roadsters. The SCTA had to acknowledge us." Some of the fastest coupes running at that time included Bobby Meeks, the Pierson Brothers and Joe Torvick, left.

The Pierson Brothers Coupe

The most famous story of Bob and Dick Pierson that includes Edelbrock is the 2D car, a 1934 coupe that would become one of the most famous cars in hot rod history. Now known as the Pierson Brothers Coupe, it began as a $25 fender-flapping junker bought for Dick's school and work transportation.

Bob remembered that "the car was such a piece of junk that my brother and I started to tear it apart and try and fix the parts that were falling off. My parents told us, 'Don't make this one a hot rod.' I'm under the car, taking off brackets and parts, passing them out to my brother. When I rolled out from under the car everything I had taken off was gone. My brother told me he piled them on the trash heap for the following morning's collection. He said, 'We're gonna make a hot rod out of this one,' and I thought, this is going to be trouble." The top would get chopped, windshield laid back, the fenders would be gone and then they'd rework the nose. "We started building the car in Meeks garage, but when Bobby's dog knocked over a welding gas bottle, breaking the top off and sending it down the street like a rocket, Bobby's wife said, 'Take it someplace else.'"

The car was moved to T&T Engineering in Gardena, California. Tommy Backe did the welding and fabrication, and from time to time it went to Vic's shop for engine work. Everyday, guys like Bill Vukovich, Perry Grimm, Troy Ruttman and others, would tease Bob about his hot rod, telling him it didn't look much like a racecar. Pierson decided he would show them all a thing or two about hot rods and that's when he decided to put a Kurtis midget front nose grille on the car. So radical was this machine, they invented a new class (Class D) to allow it to run.

Hot Rod magazine wanted to do a story on the car, and Bob wanted to run it in the very first Bonneville speed trials in 1949, but Vic said no. When Pierson complained, Vic told him not to come back to work if he went to Bonneville. "So my brother and I took the car to El Mirage instead, and broke records at SCTA and Russetta events. Vic and Bobby [Meeks] really helped, and supported the car totally. Vic was such a honest man that he would

never think of trying to tell one of the racers using some other equipment that he could make them run better if they switched. But as the coupe started kickin' butt, the racers would come over and start talking to me about Edelbrock Equipment."

When the car first hit the track, it was primer gray, and Pierson decided to paint it red, white, and blue. Finding the correct colors for the white and blue paint was simple, but they couldn't find a red that Pierson liked. One day, he cut his hand and the blood went flying. When he went to wipe it up, the

In the world of hot rods, there are a number of cars that have retained their mystique throughout the years. Examples include Jim "Jazzy" Nelson's coupe, Art Chrisman's number 25 dragster, and Calvin Rice's first National Championship digger. One more car that should be added to the list is the awesome Pierson Brothers' '34 coupe.

The car started out as a pile of junk—discarded as useless. The brothers Bob and Dick Pierson took the pieces to a friend and began chopping and channeling the body, reworking the chassis,

sun hit the blood and Pierson knew that was the color he'd been looking for. "We had worked with a local auto paint dealer and asked if he could mix up a color for us. After about twenty-five samples, the dealer told me, 'You're costing me money with all these samples, so take your samples and don't come back.' Well, after that, I would sneak into the paint shop through the rear door while the owner was at lunch, and continue to mix colors. Somewhere between mix thirty-seven sitting on the bench and mix thirty-eight in the can, the owner walks in and

and turning the junk heap into a real hot rod. Next, the brothers went to Vic Edelbrock for power, and he provided the boys with a winner. Along with the engine, Vic sent Don Towle and Bobby Meeks to maintain the record-breaking flathead. The 2D became one of the most significant cars of the 1950s. Today, the Pierson Brothers coupe is totally restored to its original state and is owned by car buff and hot rod historian Bruce Meyer. Bob Pierson with the car, below, behind the Edelbrock shop on West Jefferson Boulevard.

starts yelling. He took the two samples and threw them in a can and said, 'get out and stay out, you got your last sample.' The mix was exactly the color I wanted."

That same day, Pierson won the check pool at Edelbrock's. According to the custom, the guy who won the pool would buy a bottle of booze for the bench racing session after work. Bob and his brother took the money to another paint shop, bought the white and blue, and painted the car instead. Later, when the Piersons started running hard, the car was too flexible and didn't want to handle, so Vic boxed and welded the frame himself, and designed and installed a complete roll cage. After that, the car ran as straight as an arrow. The Piersons broke records with the car for two years before selling it.

Alex Xydias—Mr. SoCal

Alex Xydias graduated from Fairfax High School in 1940 and began going to the lakes. Vic Edelbrock was soon a hero to him, because of his style and the way he ran his '32 roadster. With money saved from a paper route and odd jobs, Alex bought a 1929 full-fendered roadster for $65. Then he got a job in a defense plant. "Just before the war, I was making a little over 20 bucks a week, which meant I was rolling in dough, so I stepped up and bought a '34 Ford, and had Jimmy Summers build some super-looking rear fenders. I took it to Carson Top Company and had a removable top made—the hot setup for street machines."

After his discharge from the Air Corps in 1946, he was ready to make a lifelong dream come true—to have his own business. He called it SoCal Speed Shop, and handled nothing but parts, no mechanical work. "In the beginning, I sold a ton of chrome acorn nuts, carburetor stacks, and air cleaners, but nothing substantial. I got scared, and figured that I had made a mistake before things started to turn around. One thing that really saved me was the fact that hot rodders wanted to get rid of the Ford wire wheels and replace them with new Ford steel wheels. I made a deal with several local Ford dealers, and began selling all the wheels I could get. The second thing that took off was Stewart-Warner oil pressure gauges—they became a status item."

Over the next few months, Alex expanded his inventory to include heads and manifolds. Vic Edelbrock and Eddie Meyer both agreed to give Alex a 25 percent discount on their parts. Then he

added a line by Phil Weiand, a good friend of Xydias', who was working out of a two-car garage on San Fernando Road in Glendale. At dawn on Saturday mornings, Alex would jump into his pickup truck and make the rounds, picking up a one- or two-week supply of parts.

As business got better, Alex realized that there were only two ways to get recognized nationally—advertising in *Hot Rod* magazine and making a name at the dry lakes. He went to Bill Burke, the father of

Forever young and filled with energy—the best possible description of the life and times of Alex Xydias. Born a native of California, Alex exemplifies the pioneer California hot rodder. After serving his time as a gunner on a B-17, during World War II, Alex wanted to leave the war behind and go racing. He had gone to the dry lakes as a teen, but never really got to race. In 1949, when Wally Parks and the SCTA began running the Bonneville Salt Flats, Alex got hooked on streamliners. Alex built his first belly tank, below, from a P-38 tank in 1948. Power for the streamliner was provided by a Vic Edelbrock V8-60, identical to

the belly tank, and had Bill build him a chassis and body from a P-38 tank. Alex put a V-8-60 in the rear and was ready to go racing. He painted "SoCal Speed Shop" on the side of the car and set out to make a name for himself.

In 1949, the SCTA had decided to go to Bonneville. By now, Alex and long-time racer Dean Batchelor had become friends. Dean had read about the Auto Union (now Audi) and their streamlined Grand Prix car of the late 1930s, and a version driven

the engine used in a midget. Then Alex teamed with Dean Batchelor and created a true streamliner, the first purpose-built aero hot rod in 1949. The car shattered the class record by nearly 30 mph. Opposite: Top left, Dean in the car, Alex leaning on the body and Bobby Meeks (with pith helmet) reaching in the cockpit as the car prepares for its Bonneville record. Top right, Dean (in T-shirt) accepts the fastest car award. Alex (left, short sleeves in white shirt) looks on. Below right, the Hot Rod Magazine award stands in front of Dean and Alex's car, in 1950 after they set a record of 210 mph.

by Bernd Rosemeyer that had accelerated over 250 mph on the German Autobahn with the use of full-body streamlining. He set out to design a full-body, enclosed-wheel streamliner to run at the first-ever SCTA Bonneville Speed Trials. He designed a body to work with the chassis from the belly tank, and Neil Emery at Valley Custom Shop formed the aluminum panels. Dean, Alex, and some friends put the panels together and did all of the rivet work. Many of them had learned sheet metal fabrication during the war, so this car had a lot of aircraft construction.

Alex remembered, "At first we decided to run the V8-60, the same engine that had powered the belly tank. But when I took the idea to Vic, he saw more potential, and became emphatic that he build a full-sized Mercury 'Edelbrock' engine to back up the V8-60. We could then run both A-Class and C-Class. Vic felt so strongly about our chances that after he built that engine, he sent Bobby Meeks with us to tune them both, and to ensure that Edelbrock Equipment would show its best."

They ran the V8-60 first because they were familiar with it. With Dean driving on the first attempt, the two-way average was more than 156

mph, breaking the record held by a belly tank with a full-size flathead. Then they put the big engine in, and wheeled off for their second attempt. Their speed surpassed 190 mph, which was about 30 mph faster than any hot rod. "We were pumped, and so was Bobby. Edelbrock power was leading the way, and it was going to make great advertising. A year later, we broke the record at over 200 mph."

One advantage the Edelbrock Equipment Company had over many others was the fact that the employees who worked there were hard core and very respected racers. Racers like Bill Cantley, above, used Edelbrock equipment because it was produced by racers. Bill Likes, above right, raced many cars, including this roadster, and brought his experience to the Edelbrock shop, helping to develop better parts.

Pierson's reputation was that of a street-racing, fist-fighting hooligan. It was understood that he would clean up his act and quit street racing when he became involved with Meeks and Edelbrock Sr. Pierson was the Coupes Club vice president and a record holder in the Russetta Timing Association. Bob and his younger brother Dick would build another coupe that would become one of the most eminent Edelbrock-equipped hot rods of all time. Bob Pierson became an inner circle member of the Edelbrock racing family.

Ray Brown

A friend of Vic Edelbrock's, Ray Brown was also a fierce competitor in 1952 at the Bonneville Nationals, when he battled with Alex Xydias and his Edelbrock-powered Streamliner for world records. Brown began his career as a dry-lakes racer, hot rod kid, and overall car junkie. He became a noted engine builder and Bonneville record breaker and went on to be a successful businessman, beginning in the early '50s with Ray Brown Automotive, on Western Avenue in Hollywood. He built engines for some of the most renowned hot rods ever put together. Ray was a pioneer in the manufacture of aftermarket automotive seat belts. His company, Saf-Tee-Belt, sold do-it-yourself seat belts long before they became mandatory in passenger cars. He ended his long career after helping to make Superior Wheel Company one of the largest in the world. But when Ray Brown showed the promise of the Hemi engine, it spelled the end of the flathead era and the beginning of a new age of engine technology.

"In all the years I have been in the performance business, there were very few people who really influenced my life. Vic Edelbrock Sr. was one who not only taught me about the business, but made me a better person by his example." —**Ray Brown**

Fran Hernandez, left, was one of Vic Edelbrock's original key employees during the early years of the company. Fran was a racer and an innovator, and he was very close to Vic Jr. when the young Edelbrock was learning the skills of the trade. Although Fran once worked for Fred Offenhauser, he subsequently changed allegiance and carried the Edelbrock name proudly on his roadster, below.

Ray Brown's Hemi

In Ray Brown's senior year of high school at Hollywood High, he worked for Eddie Meyer Engineering Company on Robertson Boulevard in West Hollywood. Meyer was in direct competition with all manufacturers of flathead parts, thus Eddie and Vic really went at each other. Ray had a '32 Ford roadster that he would drive daily and also race at the dry lakes. Nearly every day, he drove past Vic's shop on Highland. Ray had seen Vic at the lakes and at Gilmore for the midget races. Vic had a reputation as a sharp mechanic, and Ray was fascinated by his ideas and the way he worked.

One bright Saturday morning, Ray dropped in at Vic's shop to buy three special cylinder head studs used to offset the generator on a flathead engine. They were fifteen cents apiece. While he was paying for the bolts, Ray spied a midget driver named Walt Faulkner, who had once driven for Eddie Meyer and now drove Vic's V8-60. Walt was just building his reputation as a hot driver on the West Coast, and he had a tough-guy image. "Walt started getting on my case about how much better Edelbrock's stuff was than Meyer's. The argument became heated, and all at once, Vic came bursting out of the office and gave me one of his famous glares. I felt a little twinge of panic. He said he had heard enough of my bullshit and I should hit the road.

"I apologized, telling Vic that I had really wanted to meet him, and I was sorry. Vic calmed down

and admitted he was very sensitive about their rivalry. He finished up by saying if I wanted to come by the shop, he didn't want to hear any more crap about Eddie Meyer. On my way home, I hated that I had acted so childish in front of a man and a company that I admired. With time, the heat of the first meeting subsided, and slowly we became friends. "

In 1949 Ray left Eddie Meyer and opened his own Speed Shop in Hollywood, building engines, tuning race cars, and selling speed equipment. At twenty years old, Ray had gained a lot of dry lakes and midget-racing experience. As the demand for parts expanded, he called Vic and asked if he could open an account selling Edelbrock Equipment. Vic

Ray Brown, another of the great pioneers of the performance industry, once held allegiance to Eddie Meyer, the arch rival of Edelbrock Equipment Company. But after some serious talk from Bobby Meeks, Brown joined the Edelbrock camp. Although very successful in business and a member of the SEMA Hall of Fame, Ray Brown is most remembered by the other pioneers of hot rodding as the guy who put the Chrysler Hemi into the vocabulary of the hot rodder. He and Alex Xydias staged one of the great duels on the salt during the 1952 Bonneville Nationals, as the two traded top speed records throughout the entire meet. In the end, Brown set a Class C record, and Alex set two records. Later, Ray Brown built Hemi engines for one of Bonneville's most famous cars, the Shadoff Special, owned and driven by Mel Hooper. The

agreed, and Ray literally raced to Vic's shop and picked up his first order.

"By 1950, I began advertising in Hot Rod magazine and started getting requests from all over the country, for both equipment and to build engines. One day, completely unannounced, Vic Edelbrock comes wandering into my shop, and we begin bench racing about business. He leaned over, lowered his voice, and gave me some of the best advice I had ever heard: 'Ray, you have got to manufacture and sell products, not labor, in order to be successful in business. You need to sell very high-quality products that last at least ten years.' He was so right."

car set a Class C record of 236.36 mph. The photo, below left, shows Ray Brown (right) talking tune-up with Bud Meyer, son of Eddie Meyer, and lifelong rival of Vic Edelbrock Sr., before Brown made the switch to Vic's camp. Shown below the Shadoff Special after their record run, getting ready to accept the fastest two-way flying mile award and the Maremont Trophy for engineering excellence. The team also set six AAA American National records. *Opposite:* Ray Brown's T-roadster powered by a V8-60, advertising his own engine-building business. Below left, Ray's 1932 roadster, number 99C, has been restored, and now resides at the Petersen Automotive Museum. Below right, Ray Brown's first belly tank that ran both a flathead and a Chrysler Hemi on display at a car show.

In 1951, Chrysler introduced the first 331 cubic-inch, Hemispherical head passenger car engine. Ray was pumped. It looked like something hot rodders could work with. Ray discovered that the engine could be destroked and sleeved down to 305 cubic-inches, and run in Class C at the lakes—a class that he was running at the time. He had both a belly tank and a streamliner. Ray bought two complete and ready-to-run engines in the crate for $700 apiece from a local Culver City Chrysler dealer.

"My plan was to complete the Chrysler and have it ready to run in my tank for the 1952 Bonneville Nationals. Alex Xydias was the strongest running C Class tank, and he was using an Edelbrock shop engine tuned by Bobby Meeks. I wanted to beat them at their own game. My flathead was making about 218 horsepower on the Wil-Cap dyno. When we put the Hemi on the dyno, the jump in power was astonishing. After some serious tweaking, readings were over 300 horsepower; I was ready for Alex, Vic, and Bobby. I thought we could run about 20 mph faster than they could, especially at Bonneville, with the extra length of the track."

But as the speed trials got under way, Ray's great game plan of blowing the competition into the salt with his unbeatable Hemi went right into the tank. The Alex Xydias-Clyde Sturdy SoCal belly tank and Ray's Hemi tank ran neck-and-neck the entire week of the event. "I was out of my mind—how could that flathead stay with my Hemi? I knew that they were burning valves because I caught them behind the hotel at night changing them. The battle got so heated that everyone would drop their tools and run to watch the record runs. There was a separation of .71 mph difference in our cars. I ran 197.88 mph and Alex ran 197.17 mph. On the one-way runs, the SoCal car ran a 198-mph, and I ran slightly over 200 mph, so Alex and I have been arguing for decades over who was the real winner."

Years later, at the SoCal Speed Shop 50th anniversary party, Vic Edelbrock Jr. told the crowd that Meeks had been lying all this time. They were running 40 percent nitro, which explained why they burned up so many valves. Bobby admitted to 10 percent. Ray admitted to running the same. Bobby just laughed and said no one would ever know the truth. After the battle at Bonneville, however, Vic Edelbrock knew the era of the flathead was over.

76 BONNEVILLE SPEED TRIALS

Racing automobiles over the crystalline surface of Utah's Bonneville Salt Flats became a reality in 1949. From that point on, the unlimited speeds driven over the flats became an important asset of the Edelbrock Equipment Company. Vic Sr. worked with many of the record-breaking teams. Don Waite, one of the company's most gifted employees, set a one-way speed record of 189.17 mph, and backed up the feat with a 186.09 mph average, driving the Waite-Bradshaw C Modified Roadster, above. The trio of Streamliners, right, were the subject of the October 1950 *Hot Rod* Magazine cover, and two of the cars, Alex Xydias (center) and the Kenz and Leslie 777 (bottom), used Edelbrock equipment.

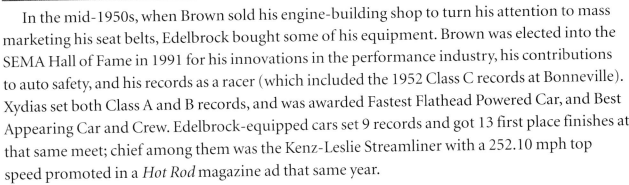

In the mid-1950s, when Brown sold his engine-building shop to turn his attention to mass marketing his seat belts, Edelbrock bought some of his equipment. Brown was elected into the SEMA Hall of Fame in 1991 for his innovations in the performance industry, his contributions to auto safety, and his records as a racer (which included the 1952 Class C records at Bonneville). Xydias set both Class A and B records, and was awarded Fastest Flathead Powered Car, and Best Appearing Car and Crew. Edelbrock-equipped cars set 9 records and got 13 first place finishes at that same meet; chief among them was the Kenz-Leslie Streamliner with a 252.10 mph top speed promoted in a *Hot Rod* magazine ad that same year.

A Sport Finds Its Voice

Robert Petersen was born in 1926, where his family lived in East Los Angeles, in Boyle Heights. He remembers the neighborhood as a great place to grow up. "All the mothers on the block would watch over the kids, and the food was excellent." As a teen, Petersen caught the car bug and began hanging out with the car guys—car clubs were just catching on. Petersen had no money, and no way of getting to the dry lakes unless Bobby Meeks would stop by and pick him up on the way. When the Petersen family moved to the Palmdale area of Antelope Valley, he was closer to the lakes. As soon as he was old enough, prior to World War II, Pete began racing at Harper and Muroc. When the family moved back to Los Angeles, Petersen got a job as a publicist at MGM Studios. After the

The Denver, Colorado, based team of Bill Kenz and Roy Leslie began racing Bonneville in 1949 with their twin flathead powered pickup truck, top right. In 1950, they came back with a streamliner, top left, and went over 200 mph. Kenz and Leslie were very close to Vic Sr., and later to Vic Jr., and used Edelbrock products on all of their race cars. Two men who helped Vic Jr. and the industry advance the goals of racers like Kenz and Leslie were Dick Day (center), publisher of *Hot Rod* magazine, and Robert E. Petersen (left), owner of *Hot Rod* magazine. The pair also helped Vic Jr. (right) when he took over the company from his dad.

Dyno Room Stories: Bench Racing

Bench Racing is an art form requiring many years to perfect. It is the way practitioners of motor sports chronicle significant historical events and pass them along to future genera-

Bench racing has always been the pastime of racers. Two of the best story tellers ever were NASCAR racer Benny Parsons (left) and the late Murray Jensen (right).

tions. Best done, it is a subtle blending of fact and fiction into believable narrative. Unwritten rules prohibit malicious falsification: to make any bench racing tale worthwhile and reputable, more than three quarters of the event must be related to some plausible trace of fact, no matter how distant. A certain amount of amplification is acceptable.

There are also rules of engagement related to proper bench racing. It never occurs during the workday, and it is banned when a deadline is looming. Bench racing is best accomplished when all is quiet, and evening loosens the tensions of a stressed mind. Like a great movie or play, bench racing can be best expressed amidst a decorous backdrop: tool boxes, work benches, half-completed engines. Smells, too, are part of the mood—the musty odor of gear oil, the stench of solvent rags, and the remnants of gasoline vapors seeping like sweat from the pores of a muscular race engine.

HOT ROD OF THE MONTH

Sitting in the driver's seat is Eddie Hulse, who, a few moments after this picture was taken, drove number 668, to set a new SCTA record for Class C roadsters. Hulse, a native Californian, nosed out Randy Shinn, a long-time top honor holder for the RC Class. Shinn's old record was 129.40 in a channeled Mercury T.

Keeping the Car Out Front by George Riley—Page 19

Vic Edelbrock Sr. is considered one of the pioneers of the hot rod industry, and Edelbrock products are accepted as a leader in the marketplace. In the beginning, telling the world about performance products was expounded by another visionary. Robert E. Petersen exposed the world to *Hot Rod* Magazine in 1949 with its first issue, featuring the Class C roadster of Regg Schlemmer, with Eddie Hulse driving.

war, he became part of a loose-knit coalition called the Hollywood Publicity Associates, handling various types of public relations work.

Wally Parks was president of the SCTA when increasing pressure from law enforcement and the National Safety Council about hot rodders and street racers forced Parks into action. He talked to Bob Petersen about becoming a safety spokesman for the SCTA. "Drive Carefully, Save a Life," became the motto. To give the hot rodders a better image, the campaign featured a car show called the Hot Rod Exposition, held at the Los Angeles National Guard Armory. Then, Petersen and another studio expatriate, Bob Lindsay, had an idea for a publication designed for the hot rod and racing interests of America's youth. The two young men made it happen with help from Bob's father, who had connections in the publishing field, Wally Parks, and a staff that included Richard Sobotka, Lee Blaisdell, Don Miller, Hugh Gilbert, John Lelis, and Andy Granatelli (of Indy 500 fame).

The first issue of *Hot Rod* magazine, dated January 1948, was actually released in December 1947, just in time to be sold at the first Hot Rod Exposition in Los Angeles. The car show was a huge success, and the magazine well received. The National Safety Council backed off their threat to close the lakes, and public opinion of the hot rodders turned from negative to at least neutral. *Hot Rod's* first cover featured a Class C roadster owned by Reg Schlemmer, driven by Eddie Hulse, and reported to be the first hot rod to race on the salt at the 1949 Bonneville Speed Trials. Within the issue's thirty pages were features on racing at the dry lakes and the tracks of Southern California. Full-page photos displayed some of the hottest cars, like Bill Burke's "Sweet Sixteen" belly tank, with driver Wally Parks. A piece called "Parts with Appeal" featured a cute girl, Jane Norred, holding a fuel pump. Ads in that first issue were mostly from California companies who made hot rod equipment like Sharp and Navarro manifolds. Winfield carburetors shared an ad with Roy Richter's Bell Auto Parts and noted custom car builder Jimmy Summers. There were speed shops like Blair's along with the Original Smithy Muffler Company, the Carson Top Shop, and the Douglass Muffler Shop. Puritan Homemade Candies and Hollywood Trophy Company rounded out the advertising package.

From its humble beginning, Petersen Publishing Company became a true automotive giant. Petersen bought out Bob Lindsay a year and a half after the first issue. Wally Parks became editor, and the early staff, which made the magazine a success from day one, stayed intact. This included Eric "Rick" Rickman, *Hot Rod's* ageless photographer, who used an airplane gun camera in the

early days to shoot action at the lakes. There was lovable Tom Medley and his alter ego, Stroker McGurk, the cartoon hot rodder who personified the hot rodder's creed: if you can't buy it, make it.

Petersen and his new magazine helped launch Wally Parks and the NHRA. After that, Bob and Wally organized the Hot Rod Safari, a team of racers who set up drag racing events across the country. By the third issue, *Hot Rod* was available in Arizona, Nevada, Utah, Michigan, Missouri, Minnesota, New York, Illinois, and Pennsylvania. The fourth issue, dated April 1948, would feature Vic Edelbrock's '32 Ford roadster and his exploits at the dry lakes.

The first time Bob Petersen met Vic Edelbrock was on a sales call. He wanted Vic to place an ad in an early issue of *Hot Rod*. As Bob put it, "He was so busy all the time there was no room for creating an ad. But just by looking around the shop at all the midgets, roadsters, and other race cars, I knew he needed to be advertising his products." Vic, like many of the shop owners and manufacturers of the time, advertised in racetrack programs to attract local customers. When *Hot Rod* expanded nationally, Vic finally agreed, but only after Petersen volunteered to help put together the advertisement. Edelbrock's first *Hot Rod* ad appeared in the May 1948 issue that featured Bob Pierson's '36 Ford coupe on the cover, and a full story inside. Pierson was one of the prime users of Edelbrock parts, and the engine had been built by Vic and Bobby Meeks. After the magazine hit the market, Vic's business started getting some action, so he bought a larger ad space in the September issue. Vic's second ad featured Edelbrock cylinder heads, photographed by Bob Petersen.

HOT ROD *Magazine*

Bob Pierson's '36 Competition Coupe AUGUST, 1948 25¢

It would take a book of many pages to tell how important the name Wally Parks is to the history of the performance industry. Wally was a founding member of the Road Runners club, a close friend of Vic Edelbrock Sr., and his son, and he was the prime mover in starting the SCTA. Wally was the first editor of *Hot Rod* Magazine and the creator of the National Hot Rod Association. Parks, in his 90s at this writing, continues to work tirelessly for the sport. Photos show Wally, top left, (with tie), talking to Vic Sr. Top right, the NHRA Safety Safari and, above, an early issue of *Hot Rod*.

Packaging Speed

In Los Angeles, the midget car racing craze spurred some hot competition among equipment manufacturers. Those who provided parts for the V8-60 flathead turned their attention away from the dry lakes and towards the mighty midgets, and no battle was more fierce than the

"When I first met Vic and we started working together, Junior was a little kid running around the shop, sweeping floors and and trying to help the guys work on cars. Later, when Vic Jr. took over the business, he became a real friend, and no matter what we needed for the industry to grow, or to solve problems, Vic Jr. was always there. I think the old man would be very proud of his son." —**Robert Petersen**

> "I idolized the man; I believe that he was the finest mechanic and engine builder I ever knew. It didn't matter if it was a dry lakes car or a midget, Vic was the best. He was miles ahead of the pack." —**Bob Pierson**

In the world of midget racing, Vic Edelbrock Sr. was a fierce competitor. As a car owner, he won many races, shown below standing next to his trophy case. He first used midgets of the rail-type design, bodies for the chassis shown at bottom. Later, Vic switched to the Kurtis Kraft brand built by Frank Kurtis. Vic wanted to win, and so did Eddie Meyer, his rival. Below right, the two men could put a stop watch on their cars without speaking a word.

one between Eddie Meyer and Vic Edelbrock. Vic had been producing V8-60 components for years, but when midget racing exploded, he, too, intensified his efforts. Now, Vic planned to go racing on a more serious level, he sold his out-of-date rail job midget, and stepped up to a Kurtis Kraft midget. The Edelbrock name was about to begin a new chapter in the history of racing.

Frank Kurtis had been building race cars in general, and midgets in particular since the 1930s, before he came up with a brilliant marketing plan to capture the market in 1946. Using an assembly-line shop operation to build the new KK midget, and because he counted on volume, prices were within reason. For $790, you could purchase a completely assembled car with either a V8-60 or an Offy engine. All parts were included, such as the chassis, body, tail, hood, radiator, radiator shell, grille, motor pan, belly pan, tail pan, seat, front axle, bumpers, gas tank, and springs. The kit price for a car without the engine was slightly lower, but most customers wanted their midget complete. Spare parts were also available, and suddenly it was easy to get started racing.

Kurtis' son, Arlen, remembered those times: "Vic bought an early car, and at first, my dad was just selling to local racers. He thought we could build twenty or thirty cars, if we were lucky. But, the midget phenomenon took off, and we were selling about thirty cars a month, ending up producing about five hundred to six hundred before it was over. We shipped whole cars and kits all over the country. There was such a demand for the cars, my dad told me that some drivers, Peewee Destarce for one, would buy a car, and order a second at the same time. They would race the first car for a couple of months, then go back East and sell it for a thousand more than they paid. Some drivers tried making a business out of buying and selling Kurtis midgets."

Vic Edelbrock was building and selling about three V8-60 midget engines a month, so it made sense to run a shop car to prove to customers that his equipment worked. With the new Kurtis chassis, Vic was ready to do battle. Every driver around knew that an Edelbrock car would be a hot setup, so they all dropped by the shop to see if a seat in the car was available. Major players included Walt Faulkner, Bill Vukovich, Danny Oakes, Mack Hellings, "Daring" Bill Zaring,

"He was an incredible guy to have on your side, and would work day and night until a problem was solved, and always offered us the best he had. When Vic opened his shop on Highland Avenue in Hollywood, I was amazed at how much work he did. The shop was packed to the roof with boxed-up manifolds and heads and midgets with famous racers walking around all the time. But through it all, Vic would always drop everything to talk to me, and offer a helping hand. He even gave me an unheard-of 30 percent discount to sell his equipment. It was great for guys like me. Vic outfoxed the industry; it paid to handle Edelbrock Equipment. He was a great friend to me, and one of the smartest guys who ever worked on an engine." —**Alex Xydias**

Perry Grimm, Andy Guthrie, and Rodger Ward. To add to the confusion, shortly after buying the first Kurtis in 1946, and installing a V8-60, Vic bought a second Kurtis the next year, powered by an Offy. Painted different colors, but both carrying the number 27, the Offy and V8-60 ran as a team, first with Bill Zaring and Mack Hellings, and later with Perry Grimm driving both cars in different circuits on different nights. The Red Circuit was the realm of the V8-60, and the Blue Circuit was the Offy's realm. The cars were painted colors to match their respective circuits. Danny Oakes, who substituted when Perry broke his hand in a bar fight, remembered his Edelbrock days. "Vic was a great guy to drive for, and a hell of a golfer. He would beat Perry Grimm and me all the time. When Perry broke his hand, Vic was mad, Perry was mad, and I was the happiest guy at the track, because I got to drive the car. I won three main events in that car."

Although he never made a single part for the Offy engine, Vic Sr. felt that he should run one of the high-priced little jewels just to prove that he could run in the elite "Blue Circuit" of midget racing. He wanted to race against the high dollar teams that were the blue-blood members of midget racing. The number 27 Offy and crew, bottom left, at Gilmore Stadium behind car, (left to right) a young helper, Vic Sr., Bobby Meeks and driver Perry Grimm. By 1948, Vic Sr. would sell the Offy and run just the V8-60.

When Midgets Were King

When the midgets were king of the dirt track racing world, California was the place to be. You could run every night of the week and make more money than most bank presidents. The men who raced were rough and tough and would race hard, fight hard and, in some cases, drink hard. Vic Sr. was part of the scene, and his cars were sought after by the hot shoes of the day. Some of the best drove an Edelbrock car. Shown here are some of the men who would stand on the gas in an Edelbrock midget. Clockwise from above, "Daring" Bill Zaring, "the man" Bill Vukovich, Vic's long-time driver Perry Grimm, Mack Hellings, quiet and fast Danny Oakes, with Vic. *Opposite:* The man who gave Vic Sr. his greatest victory when his V8-60 whipped the Offys at Gilmore—Rodger Ward poses with trophy queen. Top right, Walt Faulkner, who once drove for Vic Sr., and whose wife, Mary, babysat for Vic Jr. many nights. Walt ended up driving for Eddie Meyer.

"Vic Edelbrock was one of the first to have a dyno, and that made his products even better. But the bonus in dealing with Vic Edelbrock was that he would always take time to talk to you about his products, racing, and the overall business. It was great fun to hang around his shop." —Alex Xydias

Perry Grimm drove for Vic Sr. over a long period of time. He eventually gave up racing after several bad crashes and some serious injuries. Grimm drove the Offy number 27 and the V8-60 number 27 and later number 63, but it was Rodger Ward who stunned the world at Gilmore.

For about a year after Edelbrock started racing the midgets, he, Katie, and Meeks would run the midget trail nearly every week from up north to San Diego. Katie Edelbrock delighted in socializing with the drivers' wives. She became close friends with Esther Vukovich and Mary Faulkner who would baby-sit young Vic Jr. The trio made a ritual of Thursday nights at Gilmore Stadium and Vic Jr. became a regular at the races. Although only a kid, he was a hard worker, and delighted in doing the worst jobs, from cleaning mud off the car to washing parts. He loved every second with his mom, dad, and Bobby at the races.

Through the 1948 and 1949 seasons, Vic and the crew maintained their pace. Perry Grimm became Vic's number one driver, running the V8-60. Grimm, a Los Angeles native, had been racing midgets since the late 1930s, and had a reputation as an excellent driver. He ran in the Blue Circuit for AAA and the Red Circuit for URA. He also drove for John Balch, owner of one of the most famous hangouts and race shops in Los Angeles. Located on Vermont Avenue, the Balch Garage fielded many great cars. Balch helped make Los Angeles a hotbed of midget racing. As Vic Edelbrock's knack for building competitive engines strengthened, and Perry Grimm began winning main events on a regular basis with the V8-60, Vic decided to sell the Offy to Balch at the end of the 1947 season.

By then, business had become more hectic than ever. Edelbrock was building V8-60 engines as fast as time would allow. Manifolds and heads were selling well, and the racing side of the business was busy. They were building full-size flatheads for track roadsters, Bonneville teams, and street hot rodders. They were driving to four or five tracks a week, and filling orders from speed shops all over the country during the day. The ads in *Hot Rod* were paying off, and Vic bought Katie a house in Windsor Hills.

The Highland shop was completely jammed with equipment, the shipping department had boxes piled everywhere, and the catalog was creating business. The company needed a new home as well. Building his own plant with room to grow was the answer to Vic's dilemma. Vic and Katie scouted locations at every opportunity, and when they found a lot on Jefferson Boulevard in West Los

Orange Crate Racers

Vic Edelbrock Jr.'s passion for race cars, fast driving, and preserving the past goes back to his childhood, when his senses were filled with the sounds and smells of racecars. He would sit on a stool, listening to stories, bench racing with the guys who ran the lakes and the midget drivers who threw dirt high in the air as they raced wheel-to-wheel on tiny tracks. Since his early years, Vic wanted to race, and he continually tested the waters of limitations, because of his father's opposition. He raced bicycles, sometimes against his playmates, and other times against his own imagination. At age eight or nine, he pushed too hard, and organized a group of neighborhood kids into a racing organization. The organization, figured young Edelbrock, would change his father's opinion. The group built race cars from orange crates and handmade parts. Vic became the leader, and organized events on a seldom-used street with a downhill slope. Competition was stiff: there were crashes, skinned knees, and bloody noses. As a gesture to his friends, and to prove that he knew all there was to know about real racing, young Edelbrock began giving away his father's highly prized, brass dash plaques, engraved by the SCTA, with the winning speeds and records, won by his father at the dry lakes. Once discovered, Vic Sr. put an end to the racing and Junior managed to retrieve most of the trophies, but racing would have to wait.

"Vic Edelbrock wanted to be known as making a product of quality, not quantity. His products were always top of the line." —**Ed Almquist**

This 200 hp Clayton engine dynamometer was Edelbrock's first. It allowed Vic and crew to test every race engine they built to verify performance before going to the track. New product ideas were also run on this dyno with Bobby Meeks (left), Fran Hernandez (right) and Vic Sr. doing the testing; Vic Jr. would soon follow.

Angeles, they bought it outright. The plans for the new 5,000 square-foot building included space for manufacturing, shipping, a machine shop, offices, and a dyno. This new structure would have a special area for maintaining race cars—both the shop cars and those belonging to customers.

Work Day: From Highland to Jefferson

The move to 1200 North Highland in 1945, shortly after World War II, was significant in several ways. It marked the first time Vic Sr. was the owner of the building in which he had his shop, more room meant more business, and it was at 1200 North Highland that Edelbrock began racing midgets and reduced his activities at the dry lakes. Clockwise from above, the shop at 2921 Jefferson allowed for more equipment like drill press machines. Vic expanded the balancing department. Don Towle (left) and Bobby Meeks work on an aircraft project. It was at Jefferson (left to right) Vic Jr. as an employee worked side by side with Meeks, Perry Grimm, and Don Towle. Meeks (running balancing machine) said Jefferson was the turning point in the company's history. *Opposite:* The most popular race shop in Los Angeles, 1200 North Highland Avenue (note dyno for testing engines).

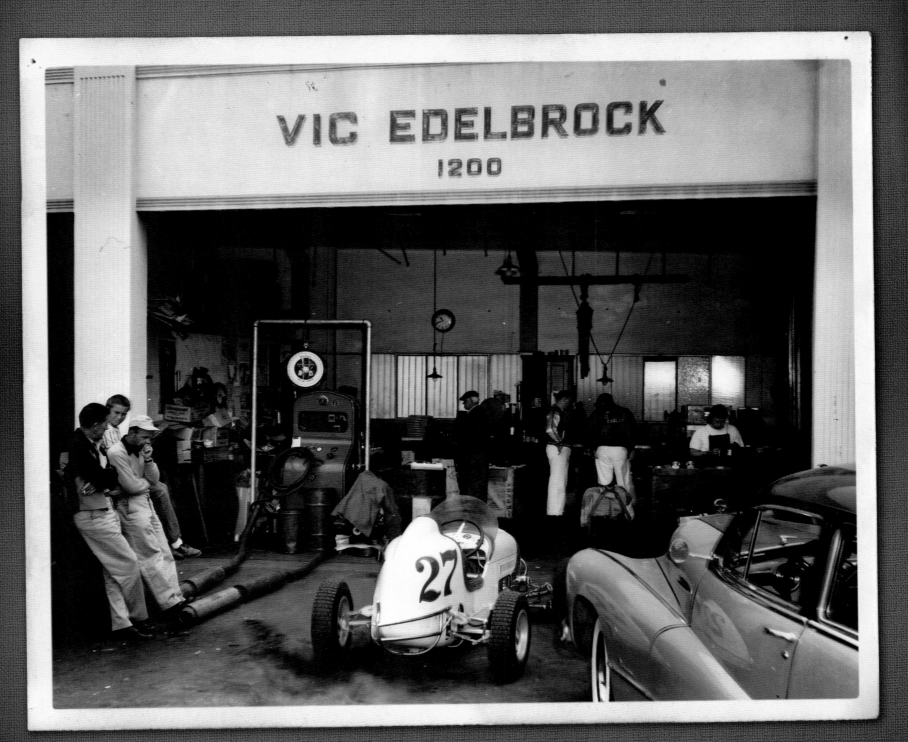

Bob Hedman

Bob Hedman's father was service manager at Hillcrest Cadillac in Hollywood, and as a very young child, he became aware of the automobile as a lifestyle, so it was only natural that he would be a car enthusiast from early on. "In 1938, at fourteen, I got my first car, a Model T. I was going to school with Ed Iskenderian's brother, Luther. We called him Doda. Ed was a little older, and he had already begun to experiment with grinding cams in a garage behind his father's house on Adams Boulevard in Los Angeles. Ed was a genius when it came to mechanical things, and Luther and I would bug him all the time about engines and building cars. He was great. By age fifteen, I bought a 1929 Model A roadster, and started running the dry lakes with the stock four-banger."

When Bob saved some money, he replaced the four-banger with a V-8, and wanted some header work done. Tommy Ikkanda had a Signal gas station, and did all types of mechanical work, including headers, in the back shop. Tommy cut the tubes, but he was too busy to put them together. He asked Bob if he could weld, and Bob proudly announced the results of the welding class he had just completed. Tommy told Bob to put the parts together, and when Bob was done, Tommy was impressed and offered Bob a job. Bob quit school and went to work, and his stock V-8 soon had a Thickstun manifold, Arco heads, and his own header system. "I painted Ikkanda Automotive Service on the side of the roadster, and at sixteen years old, thought myself to be a real racer. It took a late night street race with Bobby Meeks and his very hot '36 coupe to put things in proper perspective."

From time to time, Hedman would stop by the shop and bench race with Vic and Bobby. One Sunday, on his way to the lakes, Bob's car backfired and the engine burst into flames. Vic was just behind and stopped to help put the fire out. From that point, the two became friends. It didn't take long for Hedman to realize that Vic was way ahead of the crowd as a racer and a mechanic. "I started learning all I could from Vic Edelbrock."

Like most of the racers in his generation, Bob got caught up in the war, joined the Coast Guard, and ran convoys in the Mediterranean. While Hedman

A rare breed, Bob Hedman was born in Hollywood, California, and says, "I was one of the lucky ones. I was born in Hollywood, and I was already in place when the hot rod world was created." Hedman's introduction to the Edelbrock clan came about because of a street race. Hedman and Bobby Meeks tangled one night on the streets of West Los Angeles. Meeks was running the new Edelbrock Slingshot manifold, and he dusted young Hedman, who was running a Thickstun-equipped roadster. Hedman and Meeks became friends, and Hedman began hanging out and bench racing

was overseas, he got a letter from Tommy Ikkanda, telling him he had been sent to an internment camp near Bishop, California, and had lost his home and business. After the war, Bob went to work for a fellow named Archie Porter on Sunset Boulevard in Hollywood, installing Dual-Tone and Mello Tone muffler sets. There, he met a coworker named Sandy Belond, and they began making headers on their own and paying Porter for the material. Then, they started installing their headers, and Archie let them run their own, business alongside his. Sandy decided that he wanted to go back to owning his own shop as he had done before the war. He didn't have enough money, so he approached speed shop owner Karl Orr, who agreed to help by renting Belond a small shop and apartment in Culver City. He quickly got so busy making exhaust systems that he couldn't handle the shop alone and he asked if Hedman would start designing and building headers.

Before long, the two became partners, calling the company Sandy Belond/Southern California Muffler. Later, it was shortened to Sandy Belond Manufacturing. Howard Douglass, who had started

with the crew at the Edelbrock shop. Hedman began welding his own headers while working for a Japanese-American named Tommy Ikkanda. When Tommy was sent to camp during the war, Hedman went to work for a fellow named Archie Porter. After the war, he teamed with Sandy Belond, making mufflers and exhaust systems. Hedman then opened Hedman Hedders Company and when the Chevy small block hit the market, he joined with Edelbrock to become the official header of the Edelbrock line of Chevy products.

Douglass Muffler in San Gabriel, California, was one of the few making production-type aftermarket exhaust systems like Sandy and Bob. By the mid-1950s, Sandy sold Hedman the manufacturing end of the business, and Bob started Hedman Muffler and Manufacturing, which later became Hedman Headers. Bob dropped all installation work and concentrated on developing a full line of tube headers. Business grew so quickly, that for a while, they moved into a larger building every year. For many years, Hedman Headers were number one in the field.

As the header business grew, so did the manifold business. Edelbrock and Hedman began dyno testing new products. Soon Hedman Headers became the official Edelbrock test exhaust system. Every new manifold that Edelbrock developed was dyno tested using Hedman Headers for the exhaust system. When the Chevy V-8 came out, Vic and Bob worked together constantly. An employee of Hedman, Bill Million, was at Edelbrock's shop most of the time, working on exhaust systems and testing manifolds. Edelbrock created better manifolds, and Hedman created better headers.

Edelbrock began moving into the new facility at 4921 West Jefferson by the end of 1948. During the moving process, which took several months, a new member joined the close-knit circle at Edelbrock Equipment. Dry lakes racer Don Towle was a Coupes Club member who had worked at Flammer's Auto Parts in the machine shop, and brought to Edelbrock a substantial background in engine building and machine tool work. As the years passed, Towle would play a pivotal role in the development of the company. Next, Fran Hernandez came aboard. A schoolmate of Bobby Meeks, he was a top-flight machinist, a record-holding dry-lakes racer, and had worked for Fred Offenhauser, competing against Vic Edelbrock.

Fran would join Towle and Meeks in Vic's tight inner circle. They would work together like a family to outperform their competition. The new shop on Jefferson boasted three milling machines, three spindle drill press machines, a single spindle drill press, a Clayton dynamometer, a stock room, shipping room, race shop, and a real sit-down office. As the new shop became activated and the Highland shop closed down, Vic began to build his employee list to ten, including Bill Likes, another SCTA record-breaking racer, and the returning Girard (Peewee) Gallant, plus an eager fourteen-year-old Vic Jr., who worked after school and during vacations. Although he would occasionally drill holes in the wrong places, Vic Jr. loved being part of his dad's business. And the senior Edelbrock, although tough on his boy, was a very proud father. It was 1950, and Vic Edelbrock had attained many of his goals.

As mentioned time and again, the crew of racers who worked at the Edelbrock shop were the backbone of the company and its success. Fran Hernandez, top left, came from a background of dry lakes racing and his share of street racing on the wild side of Los Angeles. Fran drove his coupe equipped with the Edelbrock shop engine and a jolt of nitro in the infamous drag race with Tom Cobbs. Although Fran left Edelbrock for Ford Motor Company, he has always been considered one of the key figures in the Edelbrock company's first team. Bill Likes, manager of the machine shop when the company moved to West Jefferson Boulevard was a SCTA B-Class Roadster record holder and all-around fast guy. Top and above, is his roadster in street trim and then stripped down for racing. Likes joined Bobby Meeks, Fran Hernandez and Don Towle as racing spokesmen for Edelbrock products.

"Senior ran the dyno tests for me, and scared the crap out of me in the process. He had no mercy when he ran the tests. I would be yelling 'not so hard' and he would yell back, 'if it won't take the load on the dyno, why in the hell would you tow it 700 miles to Bonneville just to blow it up?'" —Don Waite

In 1955, the Chevrolet small-block was the new battle cry for racers. Edelbrock was ready, and introduced the X-1 Ram Log manifold.

4 The Sweet Smell of Innocence

I n the elusive search for more horsepower, early pioneers of racing experimented by adding various chemicals to their fuel tanks. For Vic Edelbrock, introduction to a potential power enhancer came from midget driver Ed Haddad. Ed had been given a nitromethane-based fuel sold by a company called the Dooling Brothers of Los Angeles. Manufacturers of aluminum midget slot cars, the Brothers used the fuel to power a 6.1 cubic-inch single cylinder engine used in one of their miniature cars. Haddad brought the one-gallon can of nitro to Edelbrock saying he didn't want any part of it, because it could blow up in your face. Edelbrock thought the threat of explosion was overrated. He had heard about the wonders of nitro and wanted to try it immediately.

On the dyno, Vic, Meeks, Towle and Hernandez added ten percent nitro to the V8-60 flathead engine. When they pulled the handle on the first test, they saw instant horsepower gains. "They just about broke the beam," Vic Jr. recalls. "The spark plugs were so hot they turned into 'glow plugs.' When they tried to shut it off, it kept right on running. They finally had to throw a towel on it to get it to quit." The engine needed a complete rebuild, but at this point, nothing would stop Vic Sr. from trying again.

As with everything he did, Edelbrock threw himself into the project with all of his energy. He ran countless dyno tests, checked parts for wear, and then recorded the results. He learned that the engine needed more fuel, a colder spark plug, and internal components that could stand up to the corrosive effects of nitromethane. After using several gallons of fuel, Vic realized that in order to make a breakthrough, he would need larger quantities. Fran quizzed the Dooling Brothers about their sources for nitro and learned of a place that sold fifty-gallon barrels. Vic ordered one hundred gallons the following day. Testing continued using various percentages of nitro; the end result was 40 percent more horsepower with 20 percent nitromethane. The Edelbrock team had their secret weapon.

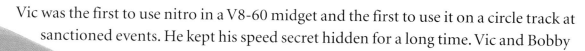

Vic was the first to use nitro in a V8-60 midget and the first to use it on a circle track at sanctioned events. He kept his speed secret hidden for a long time. Vic and Bobby had devised elaborate ways to keep their competitors in the dark about what was in the gas tank. They found that a certain chemical, when added to the fuel, disguised the distinctive smell of nitromethane. "Orange peel", as they called it, made the exhaust smell like burned oranges, and changed the flame from blue to orange. Spectators couldn't understand why their eyes burned when the Edelbrock midget passed by. Vic's V8-60 won races, set records and beat the Offys two times in a row before anyone knew about their secret weapon.

During this time period, nitromethane became the chemical of choice for revolutionary hot rodders like Tony Capanna and Joaquin Arnett of the Bean Bandits. Vic Sr. continued to experiment with other concoctions, but nothing worked better than Nitro. He even sold a carburetor kit that made a flathead nitro-ready. After his success on the circle tracks with the V8-60, Vic tried the fuel in other racing applications, and continued to dominate.

Goleta: The Day Drag Racing Began

Ninety miles up the coast in Santa Barbara, a young hot rodder named Bob Joehnck was making a name as a fast guy and serious engine builder. He had turned his two-pump Texaco service station with a one-stall garage into a well-known hangout for local racers and a top Edelbrock Equipment Dealer. Shipping products was difficult then, so Bob made a ritual out of driving down to the Edelbrock shop on Jefferson, spending the day collecting his monthly order, and picking up the latest speed tips. Bob recalled, "I would hang out while the guys pulled my order. Sometimes we would go to lunch, other times Vic Sr. would invite me into his office and talk. He loved filling me in on all the latest happenings in the world of hot rods. He always made me feel important. On one of these trips, I told Vic what we were doing about street racing and that we had found a place to drag race without having the citizens up in arms."

In a tiny suburb of Santa Barbara called Goleta, Bob Joehnck's car club, the Santa Barbara Acceleration Association, began planting the seeds of drag racing history. According to Joehnck, "The airport

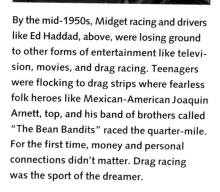

By the mid-1950s, Midget racing and drivers like Ed Haddad, above, were losing ground to other forms of entertainment like television, movies, and drag racing. Teenagers were flocking to drag strips where fearless folk heroes like Mexican-American Joaquin Arnett, top, and his band of brothers called "The Bean Bandits" raced the quarter-mile. For the first time, money and personal connections didn't matter. Drag racing was the sport of the dreamer.

"A guy came up one Sunday to take some pictures, and asked what we were doing and how far we raced. I told him we ran from a rolling start—a white line painted on the road—to a bridge, and when the cars got to the bridge, the winner would be the first car to bounce when it hit a rough spot between the bridge surface and the road. He asked how far and I said about a quarter-mile, and that's how it started, as far, as I'm concerned. That quarter-mile never changed. Everyone else can make up their own mind as to where a quarter-mile drag race came from." —**Bob Joehnck**

in Goleta was a U.S. Marine base during WWII and a huge parcel of land around it had been used as a Marine camp. At first, we would kind of go out and race on the roads adjacent to the runway. Nobody ever said anything. There was one road that ran off at an angle from the runway, and I thought to myself, maybe we could use it as a more permanent track. I asked the airport manager if we could use the road on Sundays to race some cars. He said, 'Sure, if you get some insurance.' One of my customers, an insurance salesman, got us a Lloyd's of London policy for fifty bucks. We measured off a piece of road, and started racing. We ran from a rolling start (a white line painted on the road) to a bridge. The winner was the first car to bounce when it hit a rough spot between the bridge surface and the road; this is what determined the distance. It was about a quarter-mile and that's how it started, as far as I'm concerned. At the time, there was no charge for admission, the boys would pass the hat, and we had a local hot dog vendor who would bring a portable barbecue and give us a percentage of the profits."

Street Racers Face Off at Goleta

Vic Sr. had done his share of street racing and enjoyed it, but he knew it was risky business. Fellow racers like Wally Parks, Ak Miller and Art Chrisman felt that racing on the street had to be curtailed and an alternative found. Although he was unaware of it at the time, Vic Edelbrock would be a part of drag racing history, even though he would just be trying to prove a point.

Tom Cobbs was a street racer from Santa Monica with a reputation as a "quick gun" in the San Fernando Valley. Even though he was heir to part of the American Tobacco Company fortunes, Tom built much of his own equipment. He was a rich kid with fast cars and a wide variety of friends. Several of Tom's "friends" had found their way into the path of Bobby Meeks, Don Towle and Fran Hernandez at the Edelbrock shop. They claimed that Cobbs was "the hottest around and could beat any junk coming out of the Edelbrock shop." The Cobbs vs. Edelbrock rumble had begun.

Dry lakes racer John Wolf remembers how the situation began, "The burr under the saddle of this story is that the guys doing the talking really didn't know Tom that well, and were trying to be part of the action." Cobbs remembers, "I had scared myself a couple of times street racing,

The dispute over the exact location of the origin of drag racing will go on forever. It will start fights in bars, and heated discussions in garages. The truth is it doesn't really matter. One thing is for certain, California played a very important role in the roots of drag racing. Two men can claim to be very close to the source; Bob Joehnck, above left with his roadster, the Santa Barbara engine builder who today believes that racing at the Goleta Airport comes close to being first. Second on the list is C. J. "Pappy" Hart, above, who held organized drag racing on a small airstrip in Santa Ana, California. Pappy always claimed that he didn't invent drag racing; he was just a part of the start. Top right, Jim "Jazzy" Nelson ran some of the earliest drag races and went on to become legendary for his abilities. Jazzy always used Edelbrock parts.

Before the Dawn of Drag Racing

At the dawn of the 50s, street racing had grown to epidemic proportions. Not only was street racing more prevalent, the cars were getting faster. Crashes and citizen complaints prompted the Mayor of Los Angeles to order the Police Department to go to war with the hot rodders. The flames of conflict were fanned by the *Los Angeles Times* newspaper, when reporters began writing incendiary stories with emotional headlines aimed at street racers. The campaign proved to be little in the way of a deterrent—the racers simply became more resourceful at detection and avoidance. Drive-in restaurants and local service stations were the focal points where car club members would meet and talk cars. It didn't take long for the conversation to get a hard edge. Who was the fastest? Who wasn't afraid of the cops? There was trash talk and the inevitable challenge. "Choosing somebody off" to settle the question of who was faster was common. If you were hip, there were plenty of places to race—the Los Angeles River bed, North Sepulveda, San Fernando Road, Ventura Boulevard, just to mention a few—but the cops were also on the prowl. Cooler heads suggested taking it to the dry lakes, but hot tempers and quick reactions would fade if a challenge went unanswered. You might be considered chicken.

Police Capture 31 Youths With 'Souped-Up' Jalopies

Pasadena Juveniles Offer to Aid Law if Given Race Tracts

'HOT-ROD' CAR—Sheriff's Dep. Norman Hoskins and youthful drivers examine motor of "souped-up" jalopy impounded after arrest of 31 Pasadena Junior College youths as they gathered at Sierra Madre and Villa Blvds.

It was no secret that the Los Angeles Police Department and the *Los Angeles Times* newspaper went to war against the hot rodders of the 1930s.

because we were going faster and faster. I wanted to race, but I wished we could find a better place. I was up for racing the Edelbrock guys, 'cause they had a reputation for being the best. I was a cocky kid and wanted to prove myself . . . no hard feelings." Bob Joehnck remembers, "We knew about the guys and the hot cars from Southern California. I heard that some of Tom Cobbs' friends had started bad-mouthing Vic in front of Bobby and Don. They passed it along to Vic, and it didn't take much to piss him off. All I know is, they wanted to race, and we let them."

Bobby Meeks tells a different version: "Vic overheard some guys as they were leaving the shop, they said that Cobbs could blow our doors off. Vic said, 'Have you heard enough of that bullshit? Let's do something about it.' He suggested that we take the shop engine, put it in Fran's '32 coupe, blow this guy off and be done with it. We did the engine swap, and made arrangements to run Cobbs at Goleta Airport. Although events have faded somewhat, I think that Bob Joehnck had something to do with setting it up. On a Sunday morning, we packed up the shop truck, hooked up Fran's coupe and headed north. We talked Bob Bradford into helping, and picked him on the way."

"When we got to the track, it was decided that Don would do the driving. The crowd was buzzing, they were ready to see the boys from down south get it on. As we got ready to run, Vic told us his game plan. If we won the race, Don was to drive directly to the tow truck, hook up, and we would all leave. If we got the job done, there was no reason to hang around. We were running unblown, and Cobbs had a blower, but we were running a load of nitro and nobody really knew our secret. Towle and Cobbs lined up, and they took off. Our shop engine was really strong and Don blew Cobbs off, but not before he bent the shift lever slamming the transmission from first to second. After the race, Don did just what Vic had told him, and we started hooking up. A bunch of Cobbs' crew came running over yelling for 'two out of three'. Vic just laughed, 'You wanted to race, we won, you didn't get the job done, so see ya.' Vic never said another word about the race, and we never said anything bad about Cobbs. He knew

> "Vic said, 'Have you heard enough of that bullshit? Let's do something about it.' He suggested that we take the shop engine, put it in Fran's '32 coupe and go blow this guy off and be done with it. We did the engine swap, and we made arrangements to run Tom Cobbs at Goleta Airport." —**Bobby Meeks**

he was a good racer, and just wanted to try us out to see who was best. Any racer would have done the same thing. For Vic, winning was enough, he had proved a point." Vic Jr., then 13 years old, had enjoyed watching his pal Don Towle beat Cobbs with his dad's engine and Fran's coupe. It was a team effort.

A Special Place

The streets and early drag strips weren't the only venues for speed. The big show was at Gilmore Stadium. Racing began in 1934 at Gilmore, and throughout the years it had become a mystical patch of sacred ground. Many drivers who would fill the history books of American racing, took the main event checkered flag at Gilmore. Some of these famous racers included Bob Swanson, Johnny Parsons, Sam Hanks, Cal Niday, Perry Grimm, Johnny Garrett, Bill Vukovich, Henry Banks, Danny Oakes, Bill Taylor, Duke Nalon, Johnny Boyd, Dickie Reese, Troy Ruttman and Ronny Householder.

Tom Shedden raced the dry lakes with Vic Edelbrock, and worked as a crewmember for many teams. Later, he became a driving force in the performance industry with companies like Cragar Industries. Tom went to Gilmore as a young kid, when it cost fifteen cents for kids to get in. "When we didn't have the money, we would climb over the back fence. In the 1950s, I was a crewmember helping Cal Niday with his midget. At the time, I worked for Sandy Belond, and we would call on Vic Edelbrock at his shop on Jefferson to sell him headers. He ran an Offy and V8-60 at the time. He and his guys were hard racers, and they made Gilmore nearly every Thursday night. Gilmore to me, was the epitome of midget car racing. The cars were always first-rate, and the officials policed the pits, making sure everybody wore whites. The drivers all had fancy outfits, and would wear colorful bandanas over their faces when they drove. They looked like wild west outlaws. I can still see the dirt flying and the smell of the cars. It was quite a show."

In the course of history, certain events have changed the flow of mankind's destiny. This may be a little strong for the fate of racing in California after 1950, but times were changing. Fans, who once flocked to Gilmore Stadium, far left, to witness the Mighty Midgets, were gone. By the 1950s, midget racing's popularity faded as drag racing took its place. The end of an era was reinforced by the death of Bill Vukovich, above, midget racing's most revered hero. Vic Sr. and Perry Grimm, center, enjoy NEHI refreshment during the Indy 500.

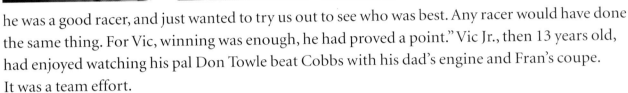

"Many of the tales told today seem to be larger-than-life events. But back when they actually happened, it was just a matter of racers getting together and doing what they did best—race. It was just having fun and settling up who was the best and the fastest. Nothing special."—**Don Montgomery**

A Victory at Gilmore Made You a Race Driver

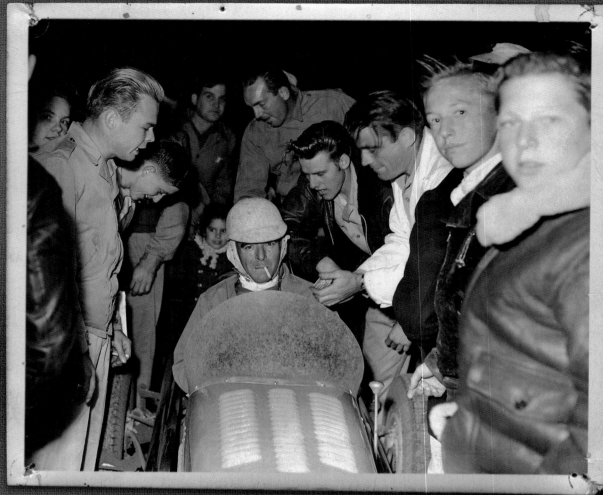

Midget racing did not die quietly. The average race fan, especially in the Los Angeles area, loved the mighty midgets, and although drag racing was coming of age, it would take a few years to drown out the roar of the midgets. Wednesday nights meant Gilmore and party time. Everybody loved Gilmore. Tom Shedden, retired head of Cragar Industries, says, "We would hop the fence and run all over the place watching the races. Kids like me loved the midgets and everyone wanted to grow up to be a racer."

Gilmore Stadium was built by the A.F. Gilmore Company and Earl Gilmore, in 1934, and was located at the corner of Fairfax and Beverly in Los Angeles. Gilmore made stars like young Troy Ruttman, above, and Danny Oakes, right, shown sitting in Vic Edelbrock's car after a win. Vic is in white. The Edelbrock number 27 midgets (there were two for a short period of time, one had an Offy engine, and the other a V8-60) ran nearly every night of the week, bottom left and right, sometimes winning and some times crashing but always running up front.

Opposite: Clockwise, Vic's number 63 with Bill Schindler, shown picking up a trophy dash win. A copy of the August 1949 Gilmore program. A group photo showing many of the Gilmore drivers, including Rodger Ward (third from left/front row) Walt Faulkner (far right/front row) and Bill Vukovich (back row, in helmet).

According to everyone who knew him, including his son, Vic Sr. loved midget racing. He built engines for the midget racers with such precision and care that orders poured in from all over the country. But, Vic Sr. held some of his most guarded secrets for his engines alone. Most of Vic Edelbrock Sr's success came with his long-time driver Perry Grimm, right. Perry, posing here with Vic Sr. and fellow driver Gib Lilly, drove both number 27 midgets (the Offy and V8-60). However, when Vic stunned the racing world by beating the Offy-powered midgets at Gilmore with his V8-60 flathead, the driver was Rodger Ward and not Perry Grimm.

THE TRIBUNE-SUN, San Diego 12, California, Wednesday, Oct. 23,

Grimm Rated One to Beat

Dominated Card Last Time Out

"Beat Grimm and Edelbrock and take it all" should be the theme for tonight's midget auto racing program over Balboa stadium's quarter-mile speedway.

Not since the season opened here back in May has a team enjoyed such respect as is now being accorded Driver Perry Grimm and Car Designer Vic Edelbrock by local midget fans.

Edelbrock built the swift No. 63 V-8 which Grimm drives and last week it led the field in every race in which it was entered. However, repeat triumphs have been a rarity this season—Cal Niday is the only driver to score two straight—and as a result the odds favor someone besides Grimm to visit the winner's circle tonight.

With a host of new cars primed for the program, a new one-lap record may be written into the books during time trials beginning at 7 p.m. Johnny Parsons says most of the kinks have been worked out of the new G. & K. No. 39 Drake. Danny Oakes has the wheel on Frank Brewer's rebuilt No. 3 V-8, and Bobby Barker has the V-8 No. 91, a "twin" of Grimm's mount, running in top shape. Any of those cars is capable of a "hot" night.

Fans who look for a long-shot favorite find a candidate in Bill Prereton, the slender chauffeur who does the driving for Elmer Ross, local car designer. Boomin' Bill was

"RABBIT" MUSIC

"Rabbit" is a newcomer to the midget auto racing clan from the east, and will be seen in action in Balboa stadium tonight.

unbeatable in the closing races at Bonelli stadium near Los Angeles and more recently won three consecutive main events at Bakersfield.

As always, Bill Vukovich, the point standings leader, ranks high

although it's been quite a while since he visited the winner's circle at the stadium. Vuki has given his No. 1 Drake Special another major overhaul and, if he qualifies for the main event, probably will be one of the boys to beat for first place.

In 1949, Vic Edelbrock moved again, this time to an even larger shop on West Jefferson Boulevard in Los Angeles, above left. He continued to race midgets and became somewhat of a hero to the midget drivers of the time. Top, Sam Hanks, who would win the Indy 500 in 1957, hung out at the Jefferson shop, and had fun teasing young Vic Jr., who was always asking questions. America's World Driving Champion, Phil Hill, above, once drove midgets at Gilmore, admitting that he drove a midget like "a cow sliding through a mud patch on her belly."

Alice Hanks, widow of former National Midget Car Champion and 1957 Indianapolis 500 winner Sam Hanks, said, "Gilmore for Sam was always very special. My first race there was Thanksgiving night a couple of years after the war. I was a new bride, and the wives would all sit together in the grandstand, because women were not allowed in the pits. The drivers' wives seemed so glamorous to me, but they took me in as one of their own. We would spend half the time watching our husbands race, and the other half watching the movie stars. The biggest social happening in those days was going to the Singapore Spa afterward. The drivers would spend half of their winnings on partying. Sam was an owner/driver, so he would pack up and leave after the races to get home and work, so I never got to party much. Sam and Billy Vukovich would get their money and go home to work on the cars. It was a big deal in those years. You had to earn a living."

Phil Hill, America's first World Driving Champion in 1961, was born and raised in Santa Monica, and knew the special nature of Gilmore long before he appeared on the world stage. Phil came to Gilmore with his dad before World War II. "After the war, I came with my friends. I had a 1924 Pierce that I had bought from a guy at a drive-in one night. We would come to the track every Thursday night in that thing. I loved the way the cars were turned out, and the uniforms the crews wore, it was very unique. And, the racing was always awesome. It was very important for a driver to win at Gilmore."

Phil continues, "I actually drove midgets, shortly after I started with sports cars. My baptism of fire came at San Bernardino one night, when a car owner who was a friend

"I was a green kid back then, running seven nights a week in anything I could get my hands on. When we ran Gilmore, I wanted to be a hero, because all of the great drivers would be there. I think I made a lot of guys mad before I learned to drive like a professional. But Gilmore always got my heart pumping." —Walt James

"Gilmore was very special to me. I came here as a young girl. I loved coming here. Movie stars would sit down front in the boxes, all dressed up, rooting for their pet drivers. The track was always fast and beautifully prepared. The drivers and crews wore white pants, and some of the big names had custom driving shirts handmade. It was a party atmosphere. I remember that the track photographer would shoot pictures of the crowd, and the following week the track would publish a crowd shot with a circle drawn around someone in the stands, and if you claimed the picture, you got in free for the next race. And, there was the Singapore Spa, a bar located across the street from the track. It was very exotic for the time, and nearly every driver and crew member would head for the Spa after the races. It was wild. Gilmore was a lifestyle within itself." —**Carmen Schroeder**

of mine told me that his driver was hurt, and I had to qualify his car. I protested, and reminded the man that I had never even warmed the car up. It didn't seem to matter. He pushed me into the driver's seat. It was a horrible, wet, slick night and when we went out onto the track, everybody started sliding and slithering around. I spun the car in the first turn and stalled the engine. The crew came running out with a push truck and they started me up. I had no clue what to do. I ran a couple of laps and then it was time to qualify. Because nobody could get a decent lap in, I qualified for the main event. In the pits, Walt Faulkner and Bill Vukovich were staring at me like I had the plague."

"Finally, the Gardner brothers came over with Faulkner and said, 'your driving style looks like a cow on an ice pond—you are really bad.' I protested by saying that the car wants to spin on me. Howard Gardner said, 'you're not close to spinning. You're just not doing the right thing at the right time. Watch Walt, and see where he lifts off the throttle, and you do the same.' After the second warm up, I started to get the hang of it, but they put me at the rear of the pack for the main event. Everyone had a great laugh at my expense. I did improve enough to run Gilmore a few times, without much success, I may add. But I loved that place and the drivers who ran there. They were all so good that just being able to be in the field with them was a huge honor."

Perry Grimm, below, enjoys a unique perk after winning the illustrious Gilmore Turkey night race. Once Vic Edelbrock's hired gun, he also drove for the famous Balch Garage located on Vermont Avenue, in Los Angeles. The Balch Garage was a hangout for drivers like Vukovich, Johnny Boyd, Allen Heath and Walt Faulkner.

Chasing the Offy

Gilmore Stadium had been a fertile ground for growing many reputations, and it would be the same for Vic Edelbrock. For most hot rodders, the 1950s was a time of explosive development for the sport, when many ideas came to fruition. Pioneers like Ed Winfield, Barney Navarro, Karl Orr, George Riley, Earl Evans, Phil Weiand, Alex Xydias, Lee Chapel, Roy Richter, Eddie Meyer, Tommy Thickstun, Jack Henry, Tom and Bill Spalding, Kong Jackson, and Vic Edelbrock, were joined by a new breed of thinkers like Stu Hilborn, the Chrisman brothers, Lou Senter, Lou Baney, Don Blair, Chet Herbert, Howard Johansen, Harry Weber, Ed "Isky" Iskenderian, and Paul Schiefer. It was a whirlwind of change.

By 1950, Vic Edelbrock had been a success in nearly every endeavor he had undertaken. He was a record holder at the dry lakes, he had developed a line of racing products second to none, and he had built winning race engines for hot rods, midgets, boats, and street-driven cars. His business had grown from a tiny shop behind a gas station to a 5,000 square-foot manufacturing building with his name emblazoned on the front. Many men would have sat back and said, "Look what I've done," but not Vic Edelbrock. What happened yesterday was old news, what was happening today was the focus.

Vic Edelbrock was at the peak of his game when he recognized the racing grind was taking its toll on him and the crew. The V8-60 flathead was the lifeblood of his business, and his shipping department hummed, sending off sets of V8-60 heads and two-carburetor manifolds in rapid-fire order. They were working every day and racing by night to the point of exhaustion—something had to give. Vic backed off and began to pick the races he wanted to run.

Perry Grimm, Vic's close friend and driver, had started midget racing in the late 1930s, and the effects of several industrial-strength crashes had taken their toll on him. He was tired, and recommended that Vic replace him with a rough-and-tumble, hard-living youngster named Rodger Ward, who had been driving Grimm's car for a few seasons. Ward took over late in the 1949, season and by the following year demonstrated his fearless driving style running the V8-60. He built

During the peak of the flathead years, Edelbrock Equipment was known all over the country. The name was established on the West Coast, but it was equally well known in the Deep South, with Whiskey Runners and dirt track racers. Midget owners on the East Coast wanted Edelbrock parts, and for hot rodders in the Midwest, the cry for power meant Edelbrock. Shown above, two veteran Edelbrock employees Bill Likes, left, and George Bishop, center, run some high compression heads through the machining process. Lou Senter, above right, one of the true pioneers, raced with and against Edelbrock during the flathead years. He said he used parts from other manufacturers in his time, but conceded that he always admired Vic Edelbrock Sr. as a true racer.

"For me, Gilmore was California, and it was just a little more of a show than at any other track. The drivers would always try harder, and to win at Gilmore was something you could talk about the rest of the season." —**Alice Hanks**

Beating the Offys: Rodger Ward and the V8-60

"Perry Grimm introduced me to Vic Edelbrock Sr. in 1949, when I was driving Grimm's midget. I soon realized Edelbrock was one of, if not the best, midget engine builders and mechanics I had ever seen. He had a way with setting the car up and tuning the engine that set Vic Edelbrock apart; he had the same approach as Clay Smith and other top Indy car guys. When Grimm gave up driving for Edelbrock, Vic offered me the Ford (number 27), and I jumped at the chance. We ran everywhere, and Vic had the V8-60 running as strong as I had ever felt a flathead run.

The Edelbrock crew kept after that car until it was nearly perfect. Vic Jr. was in charge of cleaning and polishing the car after every race; he would work as hard as the other guys making the car shine like a jewel. Vic told me one night that Fran, Bobby, and he had been experimenting with some fuel mixtures that would make flatheads run stronger. I told Vic, I didn't care what they did, as long as the car kept running like it was. We were winning, and that's all I cared about. I knew Vic wanted to win a main event at Gilmore Stadium with the V8-60 against a full field of Offys. The night that finally happened, Vic and Katie sat in the grandstands with Vic Jr., and the crew ran the show. Two things went on before I qualified: Bobby put in the latest trick fuel, and Vic had told the guys to reduce the tire pressure in the rear so the car could get a better bite off the corners. Because they had lightened the crankshaft by cutting down the counterweights, Vic was worried about the engine staying together and the low pressure twisting the inner tube and causing a tire failure. There was nothing to worry about. I won my heat race to put me on the front row in the main event. I noticed that the low tire pressure and the light flywheel got me out of the corners quickly, and the engine seemed to have power to spare.

"When we warmed up for the main event, I felt the car dancing. It was ready to go. At the green, I jumped on the throttle, and the car ran like magic. It was 'see ya later.' I took off, and that was that. My old buddy, Danny Oakes, finished second and his mechanic, Danny Eames, just shook their heads when

The greatest night of Rodger Ward's midget racing career and the pinnacle of Vic Edelbrock's dream to win at Gilmore with a Ford happened on August 20, 1950. On the famed clay of Gilmore Stadium, Rodger Ward, armed with a Vic Edelbrock V8-60 flathead Ford and loaded with a shot of nitro, planted his right foot down and history was made.

The Offys were beaten at their own home field. Rodger and Vic had whipped 'um and there was nothing more to be said. A few

it was over. Vic came tearing out of the stands with this giant smile on his face. He said, 'Man, you made me the happiest guy in the world.' It was a great win, and it ended up being the only time a Ford V8-60 won a main event at Gilmore over a field of Offys. There have been many excuses since: the track was

critics cried the track was too dry and too hard so Rodger got the jump. Ward answered by saying. "We won, fair and square."

To this day, the V8-60 Edelbrock–Ward victory stands as one of the great nights in midget racing. Clockwise from above: Rodger and one of the many, many trophy girls he knew. Ward (in the cockpit), Bobby Meeks, Vic Edelbrock Jr., and a friend, at the showing of the car restored. Rodger on the gas in car 27!

too hard for the Offys, the track was too soft, the Offys had a bad night. None of that stuff matters, we won fair and square, end of story." To prove that the Gilmore race was not a one-time fluke, Ward and the number 27 went to San Bernardino the following night and blew the Offys off again.

"I was just a kid, about 14, when my dad put Rodger to work at the shop, to keep him from getting into trouble. He put Rodger at a long bench, working with me, drilling holes and deburring manifold castings. During the day, when my dad was not around, Rodger would provide me with the facts of life, and intimate details on scoring with girls, and what was the best booze to drink. Plus, he offered a wide variety of other manly activities a boy reaching the full effect of puberty should know. Between Rodger, Bobby Meeks and Don Towle, I was given enough information to make me a card-carrying member of the racing clan very early in my life. My dad never said anything, but he must have known that the boys were giving his son a substantial education." —**Vic Edelbrock Jr.**

a reputation for hitting the party circuit as hard as the racing circuit, which made him an unpredictable driver. One night, he was untouchable on the track, and the next night, Vic would have to pick him out of the car at the end of a race because he had indulged too much the night before. He was also quick to mix it up with drivers in the pits after an on-track dispute. Vic Edelbrock didn't like the wild side of Rodger Ward. After hiring him as a full-time employee, he set him on the straight and narrow.

Edelbrock and his crew continued to improve the V8-60, experimenting with combustion chamber, valve pocket design, weight reduction, and fuel flow. Each time they ran the race engine on the dyno there was a spike in power. Their "secret weapons" included their nitromethane blend and working hand-in-hand with Ed Iskenderian, the Armenian camshaft master, whose shop was very close to Edelbrock's Jefferson Boulevard location.

The fun-loving, celebrated cam grinder remembered the frantic work going on as Edelbrock tried to extract power from the diminutive Ford flathead. "At the time, we were making a mushroom tappet camshaft for the V8-60. I asked Vic if he wanted to test the setup in his race engine. I suggested that he find the power curve, pull the cam, bring it to my shop, and I would grind off a few degrees of intake opening and closing. After many tries, we took off five degrees of intake opening and intake closing, with five degrees coming off exhaust opening and closing. We never needed the long duration we had started with. As the cams put out more power, Vic stopped telling me the results of the dyno tests. The engine gained mid-range torque without losing top-end power, which meant it would run hard off the corners and keep going strong down the straight. I think that Vic, Bobby, and Fran found a secret with the combination of cam, manifold, carburetors, and nitro. Vic was a very bright man and he knew that when he found some kind of advantage, it was best to never tell."

After Ward won at Gilmore against the Offys, he continued driving for Vic Edelbrock, but as his reputation grew, he moved onto the championship dirt cars and the tracks of the Midwest and East. In 1951 he took his rookie test at Indy and won the Indy 500 in 1959 and in 1962 driving the Leader Card Special built by A. J. Watson. Upon Ward's departure, Vic Sr. turned the midget-racing program over to Bobby Meeks and Don Towle, with Vic Jr.

The late Rodger Ward, above, sits in the restored midget that he drove when he beat the Offys at Gilmore Stadium. Rodger won the Indy 500 in 1959 and in 1962, driving the car below. Ward credits Vic Sr. for making his career a success.

Although Rodger Ward made history beating the Offys at Gilmore in Vic Sr.'s V8-60 midget, it was Perry Grimm, top right, who drove the most races for Edelbrock. Grimm won many main events, including a feature at the Rose Bowl, top left, in Pasadena, California.

continuing as chief maintenance man in charge of spit and polish. Vic Jr. was by now a familiar figure in the pits. Although the rules stated that crew members must be 21 years old, the 15-year-old was big for his age, and most officials turned a blind eye to his working in the pits. To fill Rodger's shoes, Vic Sr. hired Billy Cantrell, followed by Harry Stockman, who drove the car through the 1951 and 1952 seasons.

By the end of the decade, midget racing had faded and the glory days of the mighty Thunderbugs had dulled. The crowds of more than fifty thousand that once filled the Los Angeles Coliseum and the Rose Bowl would be no more. For the Edelbrock midget team, the colorful history came to a crashing end in the fall of 1952, at the Orange Show Stadium in San Bernardino. After Rodger left, Vic Sr. had stopped going to all of the races, but on this particular night he was there with Vic Jr. and the crew. Harry Stockman had qualified second fastest, with Allen Heath close by on the starting grid. When the green flag dropped, Heath and Stockman moved into the first turn together. Heath maneuvered his right front wheel near Harry's left rear and hit the brake, causing Harry's tire to ride up onto Stockman's front, flipping Harry completely over the fence.

Vic Jr. remembered it well. "We all went running over to Harry, who was crawling out by the time we got there. My dad told Bobby and me to get the car on the trailer 'right now.' Afterwards, Dad went hunting for Heath, and I tagged along. When we found him, Dad just said, 'Thanks, Allen,' then turned around, and walked off. Number 27 sat in the garage until Eddie Kuzma, a famous race car builder on Budlong Avenue in Los Angeles, finally repaired it. Dad took it home and stored the midget in the garage, where it sat for a couple of years before he sold it to Frank Pavese in Chicago."

Pavese retained number 27 on the car and Harold Wildhaber, his driver, ran it throughout the Midwest until the late 1950s.

"If it wasn't for Vic Edelbrock, I don't really know where my career would have gone. As a result of my driving his midget and winning Gilmore plus a bunch of other races, I received three offers to go back to Indy at the end of the 1950 season. When I told Vic, he said, 'Rodger, you've got to make the best decision for you.' I actually gave serious thought to staying on with Vic, because the car ran so good and he and Katie were the most wonderful people you could ever drive for. But, every driver has the dream to run Indy, and I couldn't resist." —**Rodger Ward**

When Frank fell ill, he gave the car to his mechanic, who raced it for a while, then sold it to a fellow named Mike Riley of St. Louis, Missouri. Mike ran the midget until the V8-60 was no longer competitive and then simply parked it until 1986. Then, with the help of racecar builder Johnny Pawl, the Edelbrock Corporation bought back the famous midget and Bobby Meeks restored the car to perfect condition. By 1989, the project was complete and number 27 was featured on the cover of Petersen's *Circle Track* magazine. Today, the car sits in Vic Jr.'s collection and, according to him, "will never leave the Edelbrock family again."

The Business of Sport

For Vic Edelbrock Sr., the 1950s were much more than just a few tales of racing adventures. The high-performance pioneer was ready to strike out into new frontiers and create innovative, groundbreaking products. Across the country, drag racing caught on like a wildfire. C. J. Hart's drag strip in Orange County was a commercial success. Lou Baney and Lou Senter ran a drag strip in Saugus. Paradise Mesa drag strip near San Diego opened shortly thereafter, and more followed, dotting the California landscape.

The year 1951 proved to be not only a milestone in the growth of commercial drag strips but signaled the start of the National Hot Rod Association (NHRA), an organization envisioned by Wally Parks, then editor of *Hot Rod* magazine. With support from the magazine and publisher Robert Petersen, Parks became NHRA's first president and Ak Miller stepped in as vice president. The organization would shepherd the sport into prominence, first in the United States, then worldwide.

Working a great deal with Ed Iskenderian, who was also aware of the value in this new sport, Vic Sr. gravitated toward drag racing. The pair continued to develop the flathead, Isky perfecting his 404 racing camshaft and Edelbrock enhancing his manifold and creating more efficient

The tale of the number 27 midget that won Gilmore has taken many turns. The car was sold by Vic Edelbrock Sr. to Frank Pavese of Chicago in the 1950s, top left. Many years later, the car was discovered in St. Louis and bought back by Vic Jr., top right, shaking hands with owner) and taken to Torrance, California, where it was totally restored under the watchful eye of Bobby Meeks. The car now rests in the Vic's Garage in Torrance. Above one of the true pioneers of the Performance Industry, Ed Iskenderian, in roadster, grew up in the hot rod business along with Vic Edelbrock Sr. The two men helped each other become legends in the world of fast cars.

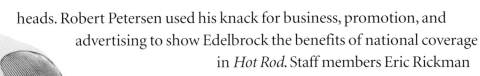

heads. Robert Petersen used his knack for business, promotion, and advertising to show Edelbrock the benefits of national coverage in *Hot Rod*. Staff members Eric Rickman and Racer Brown crafted illustrated articles featuring Edelbrock-equipped cars in California, the Midwest, and the East Coast. Hot Rod magazine was making Edelbrock Equipment a household name.

With sales growing, Edelbrock began a covert sponsorship arrangement with several of the strongest runners. He and his crew began working with some of the hot shoes of the day. The Edelbrock name became linked to racers like Joaquin Arnett of the Bean Bandits, and Vince Rossi, Tom Lisa, and Bob Corbett, the trio known as the Spaghetti Benders. The name Edelbrock Equipment Company, alongside a banner for Iskenderian's 404 camshaft, was emblazoned on the doors of one of the most famous drag racing cars of all time—the Fiat Topolino coupe of Jim "Jazzy" Nelson. Running a load of nitro, Nelson was the first car to break the ten-second ET barrier for a quarter-mile. How the car ran so quick was a well-kept secret, but Jazzy's brother Paul shed a little light. "We used to tweak the chassis so both rear tires would plant at the same time, and with the same load. My brother played with the clutch so he could really get the car off the line without lighting up the tires. Although they did run nitro, he never told me what Vic and Bobby used to do to the engine. I think not knowing everything makes the story even better."

The Edelbrock crew built engines for other forms of competition, such as boat and sports car racing. Don Towle was a Champion SK Class boat racer, and with Bobby Meeks, they competed in national events with an Edelbrock engine. Then, despite an overwhelming workload, Vic Sr. took on America's latest craze, the sports car. Cars with names like Allard, MG, Jaguar, Porsche as well as many "Specials" were pitted against Ferrari for action-packed events. Powered by an Edelbrock-equipped flathead, the "Baldwin Special" was raced in Palm Springs, Santa Ana and Torrey Pines. Built in Santa Barbara by Willis Baldwin, the car was featured on the cover of *Road and Track* in May 1950. Now owned and driven by Jim Herlinger in the vintage car races, it still runs the original 284-inch Mercury flathead with Edelbrock heads, manifold, and three Stromberg 97 carbs. Years later, Tom Carstens, a good friend of Vic Sr.'s, would use one of Edelbrock's small-block Chevy test engines in his HRM sports car.

The awesome Fiat Coupe of Jim "Jazzy" Nelson, top, made drag racing history. The Edelbrock Equipment Company made its name making parts for the Ford flathead, center, and the use of those parts was not limited to just one area. The cover of the May 1950 issue of Road and Track, above, featured the Baldwin sports car powered by Edelbrock Equipment.

The Team Grows

Murray Jensen joined the team in the early 1950s, and played an important role in the history of the Edelbrock dynasty. Like Bobby Meeks, Jensen, who worked on special assignments for

Edelbrock, came from Manti, Utah. His father came to California to find work in 1935. "I was drafted at age eighteen and sent to Europe, saw quite a bit of action, got shot up a few times, and was pretty much scared to death most of the time. Guys spent their free time dreaming about the cars they would build after the war. I was no exception. The service did wonders for my education. I had gone to aircraft mechanics school, learned a tremendous amount about exotic metals, actual engine building, and the theory and practice of hydraulics. By the time I got out of the service, the hot rod movement had really grown. First I got a job as a tune-up man in a service station, and later got involved with people who were racing. That led to building flathead engines and tuning hot rods."

Jensen's wife, Helen, was a friend of Wanda Towle, whose husband Don was working at Edelbrock. It was 1952, and Jensen was having trouble building an engine. Towle offered to help figure out why the supercharged flathead was burning pistons. Jensen went to the Edelbrock shop, where Towle and Meeks helped Jensen out. After that, Murray stopped by all the time. A few months later, Towle told Jensen that they were looking for an apprentice to build racing engines, and that he should talk to Vic. Jensen remembered, "I wanted that job so bad I could taste it, so I set up an appointment." Vic asked, "Do you know how to paint? Do you know how to sweep floors, mow lawns, pull weeds?" Jensen answered yes to all the questions. Then Vic said, "You know, there might be times when business is slow and you may have to do some of these jobs so I don't have to fire you, is that okay?" Again, the answer was yes. Vic finished with, "Good, you're hired; the pay is $2.00 an hour and a 48-hour week. We do everything perfect here, especially when it comes to our customers, and you do things the way you are told."

Jensen started out building boat and V8-60 midget engines. The crew at the time consisted of Bobby Meeks, Bill Likes, Don Towle, Fran Hernandez, Bob Bradford, Girard Gallant, and sometimes Bob Pierson. When not in school or playing sports, Vic Jr. was also hard at work in the shop. Meeks and Towle ran the engine building and manufacturing with, Hernandez taking

Murray Jensen

"There was a lot more to working at Edelbrock's than just a job. Everyone did their best to produce the finest products and reputation. It's a family. My wife wanted a sewing machine so she could save a few dollars making her own clothes, but we had no extra money to buy the machine. One day, during a bench racing session, I mentioned that I felt bad about not being able to afford it. It was near Christmas, and about a week later, without saying a word Vic, comes in the shop with a top-of-the-line sewing machine and hands it to me.

"When I wanted to go drag racing with a 1934 Ford Altered, Vic Sr. helped me build the engine, and then had Jazzy Nelson help me with the chassis. Jazzy was famous for the quickest coupe in the world, and most of his secrets were in the chassis set up, so Jazzy tells me to go hide and he would handle the setup. I was never beaten at the drags in that car. But here's the kicker: Vic told me to make a list of every single part, nut, and bolt I took from inventory to build the engine, and mark each price. After the car was running, I came into Vic's office with my list to ask how much he would he take out of my weekly check. He laughed, as if he had heard the funniest joke of the day, and said, 'Jensen, stick that list up your butt.' He never took a dollar from me.

The performance industry is a better place for having had Murray Jensen as a member.

"When an order from Ford Motor Company came in for five hundred manifolds, the office guys—I think it was Bob Bradford or Bob Fleckenstein—were going nuts. It was the biggest order we ever had. Vic comes out and says, 'I'm not going to shortchange the rest of my good customers just so we can satisfy Ford Motor Company. Send them fifty, and they can wait for the rest until we fill orders of our own customers.' Vic was loyal to his friends and good to those who worked for him. For me, the most significant kindness showed by Vic Sr. manifested when my wife Helen was in the hospital for surgery. I was worried that I would never be able to pay the bills. When the bills came, Vic Sr. simply added a check to my pay envelope that covered the hospital costs and enough to buy a bowling ball and shoes. He wanted me on the company bowling team of Bobby, Vic Jr., Ed Pink, and himself."

Many people think of Edelbrock as a company that built its reputation on speed equipment for racing cars. This is true, but the company was also famous for fast boats.

Above left, the Edelbrock number 27 midget after a race in San Diego with (left to right) Harry Stockman, Vic Jr., Fran Hernandez, Bobby Meeks, Vic Sr., and a local helper. Above right, Henry Lauterbach and his Wa Wa I, an Edelbrock flathead-powered hydro boat. Henry would also drive Wa Wa II, powered by a Chevy.

care of the machine shop. Hernandez, a terrific machinist, took Jensen under his wing, and within a few weeks he was assembling short blocks. Meeks or Towle checked every move that Murray made for at least one year. When they finally gave him the freedom to build engines on his own, things did not go according to plan.

The first engine Jensen built was for Henry Lauterbach, a big customer who raced boats in Florida. It was the first time they had ever built an engine using a dry sump oil system. They planned to ship the engine without the oil pump, and Lauterbach would hook up the complete system on his end. A couple days after Lauterbach got the engine, he called Vic and started yelling that the engine blew a minute after they started running it. When Vic found out Murray had built the engine he told him to build another one and ship it to Lauterbach. After getting the second engine, Lauterbach was on the phone again complaining that the second engine blew and he wanted another replacement. This time Vic said, "Henry, there is nothing wrong with the engines we're sending you. Whatever is going wrong, you're doing it back there. We aren't building you any more engines until you figure out the problem." Sure enough, Lauterbach had been hooking the dry sump system up backward, pumping the oil pan dry, and blowing the engines. It made Jensen feel good that Vic had backed him up the way he had.

"We began getting involved with drag racing and Vic decided to set up programs for some of the top racers of the time, giving them technical help and providing parts and equipment for some. I started building engines and working with guys and teams like Jazzy Nelson, Don Waite, the 'Spaghetti Benders' and others. Bobby Meeks and I would go to the races nearly every week." —Murray Jensen

Eventually, nearly every racing engine that left the shop had Murray Jensen's name as builder. Vic added a building next to the main shop on Jefferson and they started a balancing business as a separate division of the Edelbrock Equipment Company. Because Edelbrock was one of the few places in Southern

BALANCING & SERVICE DIVISION

Edelbrock

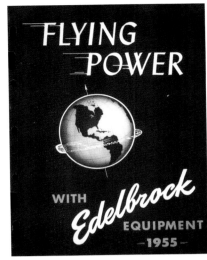

FLYING POWER

WITH *Edelbrock* EQUIPMENT -1955-

With the move to West Jefferson Boulevard in 1949, Vic Sr. became both owner and builder of his shop for the first time. Edelbrock stayed in this location through the late 1960s. The business grew fast, and expanded to include a balancing division, left. The Edelbrock catalog, above, was getting larger.

California doing this type of work, business came from racing, aircraft companies and other manufacturers who needed parts and pieces balanced.

By 1955, the company was concentrating on a program to develop Edelbrock Chevy V-8 manifolds. Jensen had an intense interest in induction systems, which gave him opportunities to work directly with Bobby, Don and Vic. As time passed, Jensen's knowledge grew, and eventually he spent most of his time working on carburetors, testing manifolds, and developing Vic's ideas on new products such as a progressive linkage system for multiple carb set-ups. He also helped design some of the manifolds of the day.

Jensen's path changed in 1958 when he got an offer from Fran Hernandez. After leaving Edelbrock in 1957, Fran worked with Chrysler, developed an automatic transmission for drag racing, then went to Peter DePaolo Engineering who was under contract with Ford Motor Company. Ford was developing an advertising campaign for '58 Fords featuring a drive around the

"I loved going to the shop every chance I could get, and like all kids, I sometimes got into trouble—kid stuff—with my dad and the guys. Before we were totally moved into Jefferson, there was still construction going on and the trash was being taken to a lot next to the building and piled up to be hauled away. I talked Dad into allowing me to drive the skip loader and dump the trash in the lot. I was crazy to drive anything, so I couldn't wait to get home from school and jump on the loader. As time went on, I got faster and faster. On the backside of the building there was 1500 square feet of flat concrete, the future parking lot with a chain-link fence at the back and a driveway that dropped about eight feet into a dirt alleyway. One day, I decided I was Rodger Ward and came flying across the parking lot toward the driveway with a load of trash. I ran into the fence, bounced off, and hit a retaining wall at the bottom of the driveway. I lost the load of trash, got scared, and went flying back to the main building to park, and promptly ran the dump bucket into the side of the shop. My dad grabbed me and told me I should find something different to work on. Driving would have to wait." —**Vic Edelbrock Jr.**

world in eighty days, a take-off on the film. Hernandez offered Jensen a spot on the team at a thousand dollars a month, an unheard-of salary at the time. Urged by his family to take the job, Jensen went to Vic and told him he felt it was the best thing for his family. "Vic was not happy about my leaving, but said to come to work when I returned. I was gone six months, and my wife saved nearly all of the money so I opened a couple of service stations in Pasadena. I was embarrassed for having left Vic, and I didn't think I should go back." Jensen eventually did return to the Edelbrock Corporation in 1968.

The Small-Block Chevrolet V8

The new engine was 265 cubic inches with a bore size of 3¾ inches and a stroke of 3 inches, which gave an over-square to bore ratio of 8-to-1. The block, with five main bearings, was produced by a new method called green sand casting. John Dolza was responsible for developing the precision process that allowed the section thickness to be controlled more accurately. Wall thickness in the casting went down to 3/16 inch.

Other innovations included lower block weight, interchangeable cylinder heads, and a high-turbulence, wedge-type design for the combustion chamber which was cast—not machined—to shape. The use of flat-top pistons gave the engine an 8-to-1 compression ratio. The manifold formed the entire top enclosure of the engine, eliminating the separate valley cover.

The valve train was equally revolutionary. The rocker arms were stamped steel and completely independent of each other, with no rocker arm shaft. The push rods, made from welded steel tubing, were hollow and allowed oil flow from tappets to rocker arms without using oil galleries in the cylinder heads. The pistons, an autothermic design (an aluminum piston in which steel or alloy inserts are cast to control expansion of the piston skirt), allowed the counter-weight to be close to the piston pin, shortening the overall height of the engine. The exhaust ports were designed short, for minimal heat rejection to the water jackets. The new small-block would be used in the 1955 Chevrolet lineup, but it was a sensation before it was even presented to the public.

The 265-inch small-block Chevrolet opened the door to a whole new market for the Edelbrock Equipment Company.

The Corvette and the Small-Block Chevy

Losing ground to Ford Motor Company, General Motors wanted something new, startling and revolutionary. The job fell on the Chevrolet division to take away Ford's lead in the market, and in 1953 the Corvette arrived: a stunning new roadster powered by a six-cylinder "Blue Flame" in-line engine producing 150 horsepower. The vehicle was sensational at first, but Chevy engineers already knew the Corvette needed more of everything, including power.

One of those engineers was Zora Arkus Duntov, who years ago had created the Ardun overhead valve conversion for the Ford flathead with his brother Yura. As early as 1952, Duntov saw the potential for performance. He was so convinced that the youth performance market would explode that he wrote a letter and addressed it to the Chevrolet Research and Development director, Maurice Olley. Dated December 16, 1953, the letter would later become a manifesto. Entitled "Thoughts Pertaining to Youth, Hot Rodders and Chevrolet," Duntov predicted the high-performance industry, and pushed Chevrolet to become part of the movement.

A new engine under development would be revolutionary rather than evolutionary. It was the responsibility of Chief Engineer Edward Cole, who would later be called the father of the small block. Cole eventually was promoted to President of General Motors. Despite all predictions, no one could have foreseen that the perfect design of the small-block would create a multibillion-dollar industry and capture the attention of the world.

It didn't take long for racers and engine builders to hear about the new engine, but only a few were chosen to receive pre-production models. Ed Cole made sure that Smokey Yunick and Junior Johnson were involved from the start. Vic Sr. was anxious to be involved and his opportunity came from an old friend, ex-midget racer Ronnie Householder, who worked at Chevrolet.

The Chevrolet small-block V8 engine, introduced in 1955 as a 265 cubic inch option to the Blue Flame 6-cylinder standard, changed the face of hot rodding and the history of the Edelbrock Corporation. Vic Sr. was one of the first engine builders in the country to have the new engine.

From left to right: Vic Jr. talks with Zora Duntov, the father of Chevrolet performance. The controversial Smoky Yunick (center), who also got one of the first V-8 engines. Vic Jr. talks with Junior Johnson, another early Chevy builder, left.

Although Vic Edelbrock created many parts for the Chrysler Hemi and its tiny brother, the De Soto Hemi, much of the direction was centered on boats and street applications. However, Vic Sr. did work with Ed Pink, above center, on his top fuel dragster.

Ronnie contacted Barney Clark at Campbell-Ewald, Chevrolet's ad agency, who set up a program to send three engines to Edelbrock for research and development. Vic had to decide how he would improve the small-block's performance, what products to develop first, and how much energy should be taken away from his business for the Chevy. Vic knew that other manufacturers would also get an engine, if they didn't have one already.

Ed Pink, today a master engine builder, first went to Edelbrock as an eager beginner—with the coming of the Chevy small-block, they were all eager beginners. Vic and his crew jumped in and started to create a new line of products for this hot new market. He knew the challenges, and if he didn't live up to his reputation he could lose a lot of ground. Straight out of the crate, the first small-block was completely disassembled and every part checked, measured, balanced, cleaned, and then reassembled and run on the dyno for a baseline. Notes on every moment the engine ran were taken. Senior had an uncanny ability, just by listening, to determine what an engine needed in order to pinpoint a performance curve. He would work for hours in his office or at home at the kitchen table, sketching, figuring and designing, then tearing up the drawings and starting over. "Chevy One" became not only the focus of Vic Sr., but the entire Edelbrock crew, who spent much of their own time researching every piece of information they could acquire to find the secrets that would put them one step ahead of the rest.

Even before the small-block, the automobile industry was rapidly changing. Chrysler had introduced their incredible 331 Hemi in 1951, and later as both a 241 Dodge and 271 DeSoto. Ford hit the market with an all-new overhead valve, inline six cylinder in 1952, and in 1954 replaced the flathead when they introduced the Y-block OHV V8. All of these new power plants provided new markets for Edelbrock, and the first products included a Quad-Jet manifold for the Dodge as well as a Ford stroker kit, manifolds, dual-quad, and triple carburetors. Vic Sr.

Vic Sr. was given three Chevy small-block engines very early in the development stages of the V8. He created a three, two-barrel carburetor manifold, top and above, for the street and for boat racing. The result was a kick-ass hydro, above left, that blew the window off all of the hot boats with bigger engines.

considered the flathead to be his bread-and-butter seller, and as the new engines broke into the performance market, sales of Ford flathead products continued to be strong. *Hot Rod* still featured Edelbrock-equipped roadsters from around the country. The flathead may have been doomed, but it was still kicking hard in the mid-1950s.

There were other pressures as well. The pace of business in the Balancing Division was frantic and engine orders were overwhelming the crew. Vic Jr. began to take on more responsibility and Vic Sr. hired his old friend and ex-driver Perry Grimm for extra help. Tests continued on Chevy One, but contrary to popular conjecture, Vic Sr.'s reasons for being excited about the 265-inch engine didn't have much to do with hot rods or race cars, but its application to boat racing. For years, Edelbrock had been building a reputation in the 266 class of hydroplane boat racing—their standard flathead and V8-60 engines were considered the best in the business.

The new Chevy would work perfectly for the class. Vic had been working with boat builder Henry Lauterbach in Florida, who built and maintained boats for a hard-running racer named Bill Ritner out of New Jersey. Soon, Henry would be issued Chevy Two.

Vic Sr. worked at a fever pitch as he welded tubes into shape, cut cardboard, and brought his ideas into reality. The first venture into the performance world of the new Chevy small-block would be

"With the coming of the Chevy small-block, Vic would now have to create products for a whole new market, using his own bank roll. If he didn't live up to his press clippings, he could lose a lot of money. What made Vic Edelbrock Sr. such a tremendous pioneer was the fact that he never blinked, never wavered, never stepped aside from a challenge. He was so sure of his ability and his crew that he just jumped in and started creating his new line of products. His Chevy development would be as great as the flathead, and just as revolutionary. He was a genius when it came to designing engine components." —**Ed Pink**

Harvey Hartman, shown above in the 1950s, turned Vic Sr.'s product ideas into a reality. Today, Harvey's sons, Mark and Randy, produce patterns for Edelbrock manifolds, cylinder heads, and more.

a manifold featuring three two-barrel carburetors. The manifold had to conform to the stock heads and port configuration, which put limitations on the design. Knowing that gentle curves and tapered radius would help accelerate the air/fuel mix, he spent hours designing runner length and diameter, with emphasis on the shape. Once the initial design was ready, patternmaker Harvey Hartman created a pattern and it was sent to Buddy Bar Foundry for casting. Vic Sr. was proud of the new Edelbrock manifold and one of the first production units was installed on a '55 Chevy two-door that he used as a test vehicle.

Vic figured that multiple carburetors would give him better fuel distribution, mix and flow. However, running three carburetors presented a challenge. Opening all three carbs at one time would cause the engine to stumble. To solve this problem, Vic Sr. developed a progressive linkage for the new combination. It's a solution that is still used today.

During this time, Vic Sr. had sent the word out to a group of camshaft manufacturers that he was looking for a cam to meet his specifications for his small-block Chevy program. All work would be strictly confidential. Among the makers were Jack Engle, Cliff Collins, Ed Iskenderian, Kenny Harman, Clay Smith, and the very secretive Ed Winfield, who by this time in his life had become somewhat of a recluse. With an assortment of camshafts in hand, Vic and the crew began setting baselines and running various combinations. Vic Jr. was delegated to run every camshaft

When the small-block Chevy came onto the performance scene in the mid-1950s, Edelbrock Equipment Company was issued three engines to develop and create new products for the racer. Vic Jr. was issued the task of testing his dad's products on the company's Clayton dynamometer, left. Vic Jr. was not only the boss' son, but a member of the crew who developed products.

Corvette Breaks Through

Those who lived through the 1950s remember the time as one of eager anticipation, the loosening of rules, and a freedom to experiment with new ideas. Car enthusiasts dove headfirst into the new wave of freethinking laissez-faireism. Long-standing barriers crumbled. Hot rodders and dry-lakes racers mingled with drag racers. Circle-track-hard liners, began to accept those who chose to race in a straight line. And the old stuffed shirt, stodgy sporty car racers were dropping their teacups in favor of American beer. All of this hybridism was especially prevalent in California, the Mother Lode of the car culture. One shining example of this amalgamation took place in the mid '60s and involved road racers, a leading car buff magazine, a hot-rodder-turned-journalist, a master photographer/racer, and a giant auto maker. Tossed into this mix was the man who took America's sports car, the Corvette, to world-class status. The legend, Zora Duntov, shared his mythical powers for creating high-performance with all who raced cars. It was no secret that during the 1950s, Chevrolet's Ed Cole and GM design wizard Harley Earl were both vocal cheerleaders for the Corvette, and wanted an American sports car to kick some butt. Since the introduction of the 265-inch small-block V-8 in 1955, Corvette had been out on road courses, banging fenders with Europe's best. They had run Sebring and on the sand beach of Daytona. Corvettes could be found at local sports car events as well as those drawing national attention. Some very good drivers had taken the wheel of a Corvette, including John Finch, Walt Hansgen, Indy driver Ray Crawford, Dr. Dick Thompson, and even Duntov himself had broken a few records. Corvettes went hill-climbing, and drag racing; several went to the salt flats of Bonneville.

In 1956, after observing the results of the Corvette racing efforts, two California hot rodders, both employed at *Hot Rod* magazine decided to take matters into their own hands and go road racing with a Corvette, hot rodder style. The two were William "Racer" Brown and Bob D'Olivo. Brown was a dry-lakes racer, engine builder, and the technical editor for *Hot Rod* in the early '50s. D'Olivo was the

magazine's chief photographer and a close friend of founder Bob Petersen. Between the two of them, they had a plentitude of experience and the magazine's blessing to do whatever was necessary to add excitement for the reader. At a dinner party attended by Duntov and other Chevrolet managerial types, the two hot rodders openly challenged the executives to allow them to take a shot at building a road racer, hot rod style, and see what develops. Shortly after the dinner meeting, a 1956 Corvette was delivered and the two hot rodders got serious. The object of the project was to rework the car, race it in various events, and document the results in magazine articles. At that time, a Corvette could be ordered with factory-available options aimed toward the road racing aspirations of a customer. Parts on the option list included: heavy-duty shocks, brakes and springs. D'Olivo added his own ideas on the suspension, coupled with special

stabilizer bars, a factory-limited slip differential and a reworked transmission. Racer Brown worked his magic on the stock engine, calling on Vic Edelbrock Sr. to do the blueprinting and balancing of the engine parts, and to offer his own brand of advice. Racer and Vic had worked together on many projects, and although Edelbrock was more famous for other types of race engines, Brown trusted Vic's insight for a road racer. When the Corvette was ready, it began competing in two different sports car organizations: Cal Club and SCCA, with two drivers; Bill Pollack and Dick Thompson.

The end result of the efforts of "two hot-rodders-turned-sports-car-builders" was the stuff movies are made of. Their car won the SCCA National Championship for B Production models with Dick Thompson driving. It was the first championship for the Corvette.

Two hot rodders, William "Racer" Brown and Bob D'Olivo, proved that they could cross over from hot rods to sports cars by building a Corvette and winning a championship. Shown here after winning

the B Production championship, driver Dick Thompson, and (leaning on the car) William "Racer" Brown. Photo taken by the other half of the team, Bob D'Olivo.

Boat racing has always been big at Edelbrock Corporation. Don Towle drove race boats, as did Vic Jr. and his daughter Camee. But in the early days, the team of Bill Ritner and Henry Lauterbach, left, made Edelbrock a famous name in the water.

through a series of tests on the company's Clayton Dynamometer. After every run, he would diagram the torque curve with drafting tools and document the specs for duration and lift.

After days of testing, Vic's old friend Ed Iskenderian was chosen to develop the camshaft. The two worked closely on every aspect of designing a perfect product, including lobe configuration, duration, and lift. The design that worked best was one Iskenderian called the Bigelow cam, because the profile was originally developed for a racer named Bigelow, who ran a six-cylinder in-line Chevy. It was strange that the profile for the six and new V8 could be the same. Eventually, the E4 cam for the street and the E2 cam for competition were also added to Vic's catalog. Developed using Chevy One, the new Edelbrock manifold was ready for market.

The second Chevy test engine was built by Bobby Meeks and the crew, then sent to Henry Lauterbach and Bill Ritner for their hydroplane. Vic Sr. sent Meeks with the engine to do the tuning for the first event, and he remembered it was not a routine trip. "The first race we ran was was an international event in Florida, with boats coming from as far away as Italy. The engine was sent to Henry's shop in New Jersey, installed in the boat, and towed to Florida. During the trip, the crew drove through a huge rainstorm and the engine got really wet. When I got to the race, the engine wouldn't start and we had to pull it apart, rework the carburetors, and clean up everything." They finished just minutes before the first heat race. Henry Lauterbach hit something in the water and broke off a piece of the prop, finishing second. They changed the prop, and in the next heat, Henry set a world record. The small-block was running so strong that

The Ford flathead was losing its grip on the hot rod world by the mid-1950s. Tony "The Loner" Nancy tried to hang on with his Edelbrock-equipped blown flathead roadster, shown on the cover of December '57 *Hot Rod*, above. But the small-block Chevy could not be denied. Edelbrock engaged in "Chevy mania" and produced all types of manifolds including a Ram Log six carburetor model and a dual-quad version, above. Edelbrock attracted racers like Carroll Caudle, above right, to help develop new products.

Henry said, "Let's run the 7-Liter International Class. I think we can whip their butts." They changed the prop again and won the International Class with another world record.

Chevy Three was built and given to Tom Carstens, an old midget racing buddy of Vic Sr.'s who had become involved with sports car racing. Carstens had purchased several HRM sports cars that had been used in the Kirk Douglas movie, *The Racers*. He installed Chevy Three into one of the cars and began campaigning up and down the West Coast.

By 1957, the Chevy small block had become a phenomenon. From hot rods to drag racers and stock cars to sports cars—the engine was everywhere. Nearly every manufacturer in the performance business was turning all efforts to the Chevy. At the factory level, Chevrolet was building a reputation as the performance leader in the industry. Duntov's memo had been right on target and he took over a leadership role with the Corvette, installing the V-8 for a limited run in 1955. A dual-quad setup, for street and competition, hit the market in 1956. It was a brilliant move. Ed Cole had envisioned the small-block V8 as competition for the Ford Thunderbird, and it was leaving the 'bird in the dust. At the drive-in, the classic roadster and Ford flathead—the Fundamental image of the hot rodder—was taking on a new look. The '55, '56, and '57 Chevy Bel Air and other two-door models would become classic hot rods of the time. The street kids would lust for them, and the performance industry was torn between the death of the flathead and the born-again energy of the small block. The Chevy was in the battle for the long haul; only the Hemi could challenge it for brute performance. But the small-block would simply outnumber any other competitor. The flathead hung on for a time, as witnessed by the December issue of *Hot Rod* magazine featuring Tony Nancy's #22 blown, Edelbrock-equipped Jr. roadster. The small block grew to 283 cubic-inches in '57 and Chevrolet offered fuel injection. Vic Edelbrock promptly designed a Ram Log manifold with six carburetors for the 283 that produced 285 horsepower — over one horsepower per cubic inch.

Boat racing has always been big at Edelbrock Corporation. Don Towle drove race boats, as did Vic Jr. and his daughter Camee. But in the early days, the team of Bill Ritner and Henry Lauterbach, left, made Edelbrock a famous name in the water.

through a series of tests on the company's Clayton Dynamometer. After every run, he would diagram the torque curve with drafting tools and document the specs for duration and lift.

After days of testing, Vic's old friend Ed Iskenderian was chosen to develop the camshaft. The two worked closely on every aspect of designing a perfect product, including lobe configuration, duration, and lift. The design that worked best was one Iskenderian called the Bigelow cam, because the profile was originally developed for a racer named Bigelow, who ran a six-cylinder in-line Chevy. It was strange that the profile for the six and new V8 could be the same. Eventually, the E4 cam for the street and the E2 cam for competition were also added to Vic's catalog. Developed using Chevy One, the new Edelbrock manifold was ready for market.

The second Chevy test engine was built by Bobby Meeks and the crew, then sent to Henry Lauterbach and Bill Ritner for their hydroplane. Vic Sr. sent Meeks with the engine to do the tuning for the first event, and he remembered it was not a routine trip. "The first race we ran was was an international event in Florida, with boats coming from as far away as Italy. The engine was sent to Henry's shop in New Jersey, installed in the boat, and towed to Florida. During the trip, the crew drove through a huge rainstorm and the engine got really wet. When I got to the race, the engine wouldn't start and we had to pull it apart, rework the carburetors, and clean up everything." They finished just minutes before the first heat race. Henry Lauterbach hit something in the water and broke off a piece of the prop, finishing second. They changed the prop, and in the next heat, Henry set a world record. The small-block was running so strong that

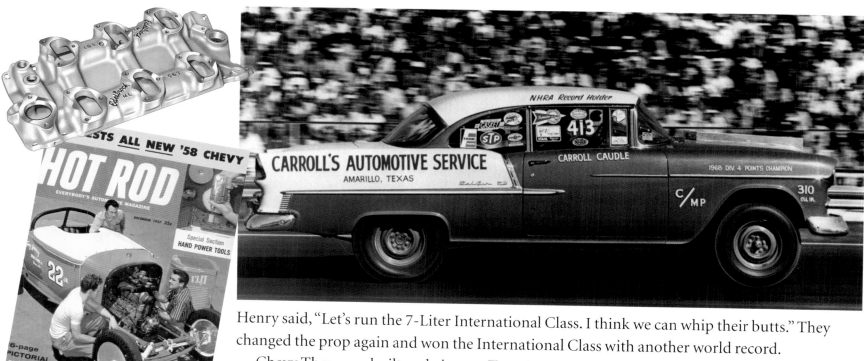

The Ford flathead was losing its grip on the hot rod world by the mid-1950s. Tony "The Loner" Nancy tried to hang on with his Edelbrock-equipped blown flathead roadster, shown on the cover of December '57 *Hot Rod*, above. But the small-block Chevy could not be denied. Edelbrock engaged in "Chevy mania" and produced all types of manifolds including a Ram Log six carburetor model and a dual-quad version, above. Edelbrock attracted racers like Carroll Caudle, above right, to help develop new products.

Henry said, "Let's run the 7-Liter International Class. I think we can whip their butts." They changed the prop again and won the International Class with another world record.

Chevy Three was built and given to Tom Carstens, an old midget racing buddy of Vic Sr.'s who had become involved with sports car racing. Carstens had purchased several HRM sports cars that had been used in the Kirk Douglas movie, *The Racers*. He installed Chevy Three into one of the cars and began campaigning up and down the West Coast.

By 1957, the Chevy small block had become a phenomenon. From hot rods to drag racers and stock cars to sports cars—the engine was everywhere. Nearly every manufacturer in the performance business was turning all efforts to the Chevy. At the factory level, Chevrolet was building a reputation as the performance leader in the industry. Duntov's memo had been right on target and he took over a leadership role with the Corvette, installing the V-8 for a limited run in 1955. A dual-quad setup, for street and competition, hit the market in 1956. It was a brilliant move. Ed Cole had envisioned the small-block V8 as competition for the Ford Thunderbird, and it was leaving the 'bird in the dust. At the drive-in, the classic roadster and Ford flathead— the Fundamental image of the hot rodder—was taking on a new look. The '55, '56, and '57 Chevy Bel Air and other two-door models would become classic hot rods of the time. The street kids would lust for them, and the performance industry was torn between the death of the flathead and the born-again energy of the small block. The Chevy was in the battle for the long haul; only the Hemi could challenge it for brute performance. But the small-block would simply out-number any other competitor. The flathead hung on for a time, as witnessed by the December issue of *Hot Rod* magazine featuring Tony Nancy's #22 blown, Edelbrock-equipped Jr. roadster. The small block grew to 283 cubic-inches in '57 and Chevrolet offered fuel injection. Vic Edelbrock promptly designed a Ram Log manifold with six carburetors for the 283 that produced 285 horsepower — over one horsepower per cubic inch.

Boat racing has always been big at Edelbrock Corporation. Don Towle drove race boats, as did Vic Jr. and his daughter Camee. But in the early days, the team of Bill Ritner and Henry Lauterbach, left, made Edelbrock a famous name in the water.

through a series of tests on the company's Clayton Dynamometer. After every run, he would diagram the torque curve with drafting tools and document the specs for duration and lift.

After days of testing, Vic's old friend Ed Iskenderian was chosen to develop the camshaft. The two worked closely on every aspect of designing a perfect product, including lobe configuration, duration, and lift. The design that worked best was one Iskenderian called the Bigelow cam, because the profile was originally developed for a racer named Bigelow, who ran a six-cylinder in-line Chevy. It was strange that the profile for the six and new V8 could be the same. Eventually, the E4 cam for the street and the E2 cam for competition were also added to Vic's catalog. Developed using Chevy One, the new Edelbrock manifold was ready for market.

The second Chevy test engine was built by Bobby Meeks and the crew, then sent to Henry Lauterbach and Bill Ritner for their hydroplane. Vic Sr. sent Meeks with the engine to do the tuning for the first event, and he remembered it was not a routine trip. "The first race we ran was was an international event in Florida, with boats coming from as far away as Italy. The engine was sent to Henry's shop in New Jersey, installed in the boat, and towed to Florida. During the trip, the crew drove through a huge rainstorm and the engine got really wet. When I got to the race, the engine wouldn't start and we had to pull it apart, rework the carburetors, and clean up everything." They finished just minutes before the first heat race. Henry Lauterbach hit something in the water and broke off a piece of the prop, finishing second. They changed the prop, and in the next heat, Henry set a world record. The small-block was running so strong that

The Ford flathead was losing its grip on the hot rod world by the mid-1950s. Tony "The Loner" Nancy tried to hang on with his Edelbrock-equipped blown flathead roadster, shown on the cover of December '57 *Hot Rod*, above. But the small-block Chevy could not be denied. Edelbrock engaged in "Chevy mania" and produced all types of manifolds including a Ram Log six carburetor model and a dual-quad version, above. Edelbrock attracted racers like Carroll Caudle, above right, to help develop new products.

Henry said, "Let's run the 7-Liter International Class. I think we can whip their butts." They changed the prop again and won the International Class with another world record.

Chevy Three was built and given to Tom Carstens, an old midget racing buddy of Vic Sr.'s who had become involved with sports car racing. Carstens had purchased several HRM sports cars that had been used in the Kirk Douglas movie, *The Racers*. He installed Chevy Three into one of the cars and began campaigning up and down the West Coast.

By 1957, the Chevy small block had become a phenomenon. From hot rods to drag racers and stock cars to sports cars—the engine was everywhere. Nearly every manufacturer in the performance business was turning all efforts to the Chevy. At the factory level, Chevrolet was building a reputation as the performance leader in the industry. Duntov's memo had been right on target and he took over a leadership role with the Corvette, installing the V-8 for a limited run in 1955. A dual-quad setup, for street and competition, hit the market in 1956. It was a brilliant move. Ed Cole had envisioned the small-block V8 as competition for the Ford Thunderbird, and it was leaving the 'bird in the dust. At the drive-in, the classic roadster and Ford flathead— the Fundamental image of the hot rodder—was taking on a new look. The '55, '56, and '57 Chevy Bel Air and other two-door models would become classic hot rods of the time. The street kids would lust for them, and the performance industry was torn between the death of the flathead and the born-again energy of the small block. The Chevy was in the battle for the long haul; only the Hemi could challenge it for brute performance. But the small-block would simply out-number any other competitor. The flathead hung on for a time, as witnessed by the December issue of *Hot Rod* magazine featuring Tony Nancy's #22 blown, Edelbrock-equipped Jr. roadster. The small block grew to 283 cubic-inches in '57 and Chevrolet offered fuel injection. Vic Edelbrock promptly designed a Ram Log manifold with six carburetors for the 283 that produced 285 horsepower — over one horsepower per cubic inch.

Tom Carstens

Vic Sr. met Tom Carstens in the mid-1940s when he came to the Edelbrock shop in search of horsepower. Vic was known for his race-winning flathead engines and Tom wanted one built for his #44 midget. He had recruited rookie driver Allen Heath and needed an edge over the competition. Tom didn't know it then, but that request became the catalyst for a great friendship, one that would extend through four generations of the Edelbrock family. It just took a good prank and a race in San Diego to make Vic and Tom true friends.

Even though Carstens had won many races, including the '47 WMRA Championship, Edelbrock's midget could still beat him. Vic insisted that both V8-60s were the same, but Tom knew something had to be different. After months of putting up with Tom's accusations, Vic decided he had heard enough, and secretly swapped engines. At the next race in Balboa Stadium, Carstens qualified for the main event and finished mid-pack with Vic's engine. The Edelbrock team, with Tom's powerplant, had won again. Vic casually lifted the hoods of both cars after the race and asked Tom, "See anything unusual?" It wasn't long before Tom realized that Vic had done the swap. That was all it took, the two racers were now the best of friends.

Vic Jr. was just a kid when Tom bought an Allard J-2 in 1950. The sports car was delivered in a crate to Vic Sr.'s shop on West Jefferson. There, Tom prepared the chassis for racing while Vic installed a modified 331-inch Cadillac engine. Young Edelbrock stood in wonder as the strange-looking car took shape. Carstens' #14 Allard became a legend, with driver Bill Pollack negotiating the twists and turns of tracks like Golden Gate Park, Torrey Pines, and Reno. On the famous 17-mile drive in Pebble Beach, they beat Phil Hill in the ex-Tommy Lee Alfa Romeo 8C2900B in '51. In 1952, the August issue of *Auto Speed & Sport* magazine reported how Pollack drove to victory beating the "up-and-coming driver" Phil Hill in a 2.56-liter Ferrari. It was the beginning of a remarkable streak for the Allard, a car that's still remembered for its black paint job, red wire wheels, and white sidewall tires. Carstens was fond of saying, "The tires make the car go faster." He was correct,

because in the early '50s, almost all tires were synthetic. However, Tom's racecar had pure rubber tires, purchased earlier for his Packing Company's fleet of cars. It was a sad day in 1953 when the Allard's winning record ended. Pollack was having brake problems near the end of the Pebble Beach race, but managed to hold on for third. Afterwards, he took an Allard engineer for a test drive to show him the brake problem, when an axle broke—throwing the car off-course and wrapping it around a tree. The occupants were unharmed, but the car was a wreck.

In 1955, Vic Sr. was fortunate to receive three of Chevrolet's brand-new small-block engines, and one of these revolutionary engines would go into Tom's HWM sports car, previously used in a Kirk Douglas movie called *The Racers*. Driver Bill Pollack re-visited Pebble Beach and other tracks he'd seen before. Tom's HWM-Chevrolet "Stovebolt" continues to compete in vintage road races today.

After a lifetime of racing, Tom Carstens passed away in the late 1990s. Vic Jr. recalls, "Tom was like a second father to me after my dad passed away. His steady advice and support was invaluable and will never be forgotten." Tom was a car guy, an accomplished seaplane pilot, a successful businessman, and an avid sportsman. He taught Vic Jr., his wife Nancy, and all three daughters how to fish and shoot cannons. During a visit to the Carstens' cabin in British Columbia, Canada, Vic's two oldest daughters went salmon fishing with Tom. It turned out to be a bad day for catching fish but not for the Carstens boat. Camee and Christi each caught a thirty pound salmon, much to the chagrin of the fishermen who looked on.

Tom was a great teacher, loyal friend, and a really fun guy to have around. He and his wife Sadie convinced Vic and Nancy to lease a cabin adjacent to their own on Quadra Island. To this day, the families still celebrate the Fourth of July with loud, unscheduled cannon blasts. The ammunition is always a Carstens-designed concrete-filled juice can that flies dramatically into the ocean after a roaring blast that can be heard two mountain ranges away. It's a perfect tribute to Tom Carstens.

Vic Jr. and Tom Carstens, top, show off the day's catch. Carstens raced his number 44 midget, center, using Edelbrock equipment, but always believed that Vic Sr. was keeping secrets from him.

Father and Son

Victor Edelbrock Jr. was coming of age in the 1950s as his father's company took shape as a force in the high-performance industry. Edelbrock Equipment Company, like Vic Jr., was filled with energy, awkward enthusiasm, and wide-eyed excitement. The young man loved his mom and dad, was totally enthralled with race cars and working around his dad's shop with the guys. Those years were a time for Vic Jr. to be with his idols and work with his dad—the biggest hero of all. Bobby Meeks considered him a younger brother. The rest of the crew recognized that the kid's energy and wonderment was more than a passing fancy. Junior was hooked; he could not get enough of hot rods and race cars, their sights and sounds, and the heroes who drove them.

Vic Sr. never wanted to favor his son over his full-time employees. The only concession given was cleaning and polishing the midget—it was Junior's job alone. He was never allowed to get out of line with the guys in the shop or the racers that hung around. Katie Edelbrock recalled, "We raised Victor strict, but I can never remember when Vic Jr. did not want to go to the shop and be with his dad. He loved that place and wanted to work so badly that it got him into trouble. He was always bugging the boys in the shop to let him

The Young Bomber

Along with the contract for aircraft parts came work with exotic metals like chrome-moly steel, aluminum alloys of all types, and magnesium. Vic Sr. bought huge canisters of talcum powder and placed them next to the machines working with magnesium to prevent fires from the highly combustible shavings. If a fire ignited, you could cover it with talcum to smother the flame because water on the fire would cause an explosion.

At this time, Fran Hernandez was teaching Junior the basics of machine work. A potential setback in Vic Jr.'s future at the Edelbrock Equipment Company came when he decided to take the magnesium shavings outside and experiment. "If I dropped a match into piles of magnesium dust, I got a bright, white-hot flash fire. Better yet, if I added cold water to the fire, I got a big-bang explosion, which scared the living crap out of the crew. The more dust, the bigger the blast. However, a side effect of the blast was the removal of large chunks of concrete from my dad's brand-new parking lot. He was not amused, and I ceased my newfound activity shortly after I became expert at it."

The Jefferson building included Vic Sr's first real office. He had always shared his office with part of the shop or in a trailer next door. Now he had a place to think and be alone with his ideas. However, he still invited the crew in after work for cocktails and bench racing.

do something with the machines. His dad wanted Victor to learn life's lessons on his own. So, as long as he behaved himself and did his school work, he was allowed to come to the shop."

"My dad always gave me a choice," Vic Jr. recalled. "When we first moved into our house on Overdale, I started hanging out with kids going in the wrong direction. My dad sat me in a chair and said, 'If you keep on going the way you're going you'll be in serious trouble. You can continue what you are doing, or you can come back to work every day at the shop, but it's going to be one or the other, you can't have both. What's it going to be?' Well, I agreed to work, and every day after school I would hitchhike from Audubon Junior High down to the shop and work a few hours, then go home with my dad. It was the best choice I ever made. It straightened me out and that was the end of my rebellious period."

"The original building on Jefferson covered about 5,000 square feet—a far cry from the four-and-a-half stall gas station on Highland. On the right, just as you entered was Dad's pride and joy, his first paneled office. It was the first time he had given himself a real perk. Edelbrock Equipment Company now had a sales office run by Bob Bradford, a real bookkeeper in Walt Saulter, and a stock room filled with product.

"I could now sharpen my own drill bits, much to the surprise of my dad, Bobby, and Don, who had not paid much attention to my progress. This may not seem like much, but sharpening a drill bit to drill perfect holes is a remarkable accomplishment for anyone, more so for a fourteen-year-old. I moved on to drilling holes—bolt holes, water holes, spark plug holes—in head castings. The shop had contests to see who could drill the most heads in one day without screwing up. I once drilled sixty heads in an eight-hour shift, which made the guys sit up and take notice." **—Vic Edelbrock Jr.**

Like His Father—His Own Person

There is no question that Vic Jr. loved his dad and wanted to walk in his footsteps. Shown here are the many similarities between father and son. Clockwise from above: Vic Jr. jumping his Indian TT Warrior dirt bike; Vic Sr. aboard his full-dress Indian; a motley crew of midget racers with Vic Sr. (right) and Vic Jr. (second from right in white-shirt); a very young Jr. sitting behind the wheel of his dad's rail job in 1945. *Opposite:* Clockwise, Vic Sr.; sitting in the number 63 midget; Vic Jr. in a mini-midget built by Bill Stroppe; Vic Jr. and his 1966 Corvette; Senior with his 1955 Ford Thunderbird.

From the very first days in business, Edelbrock included other manufacturers in its catalogs and believed in the "one-stop shop" concept. Many products, like the Mack Hellings air cleaner, above, were included in the Edelbrock catalog and ads, right.

"We hadn't gotten to the point of having a shipping department, so the stock room was filled with racks to hold the heads and manifolds as they came out of the machine shop. When orders came in, the pieces would be pulled from inventory, put into boxes, and shipped. There was no such thing as Federal Express or other shipping services. We would take a part, wrap it in newspaper, make up a cardboard box, stuff in the part, add more newspaper, address the box, take it to the post office, and ship via good old parcel post. We used postage stamps. My dad would buy $500 worth of stamps and after we weighed the packages we would slap on stamps."

On Jefferson, Vic Jr.'s first real job was cleaning the two bathrooms and sweeping up outside the machine shop. Vic Sr. and Bobby Meeks would often check the boy's work and point out the places he had missed. It didn't take long before the odd jobs didn't satisfy Vic Jr. and he grew frustrated and asked for more. Running machines and drilling holes became the boy's next objective. Not everyone was a cheerleader for young Vic Jr., or "Squirt," as he was called. Bob Bradford was a very conservative man and thought that a boy Vic Jr.'s age should not be running machines and actually processing parts. It was very tough to gain his approval, and for a long time Bradford had his doubts.

"For a time, I wandered away from hanging out with my dad and the guys at the shop in favor of a bunch of wild kids my own age. As always, my parents offered me the chance to make a choice. Dad, Fran, and several other racers had bikes. After work on Saturday and most Sundays, they would go riding in the hills behind our house. I wanted to go, and it only took once and I was hooked. My dad let me buy a brand-new Triumph motorcycle. There was an abandoned golf course up in Baldwin Hills and we would use the sand traps as part of a hare-and-hound trail that ran all though the hills. We also used the oil fields that dotted the hills, blasting down dirt roads, flying between the derricks. Back then, Bud and Dave Ekins were my heroes at the Catalina Grand Prix, and I would make believe I was racing with them. I rode that bike every chance I could, and soon I forgot about running wild with other kids. I was having too much fun and I realized that my dad and the racers were the ones I wanted to be like." —Vic Edelbrock Jr.

Bobby Meeks, above, started work at Edelbrock as a teenager and retired many years later. Edelbrock shipping, left, was photographed by *Hot Rod* magazine with several boxes stacked neatly to impress the readers. Standing at attention behind the counter (left to right) are Gene Arseneault, Lyle Ikeuchi Jr. and Vic Jr.

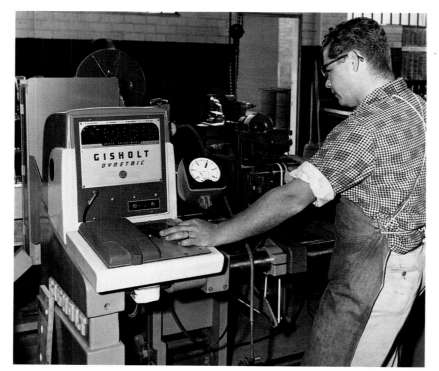

Without Don Towle, above, building the company would have been much more difficult. Towle was a racer, a machinist and a manager. He stood with Vic Jr. after his dad passed away. And, Vic Jr., above right, learned well and could do all the jobs in the shop by the time he was in high school.

"Dad put me on a bench with Rodger Ward, and I got my first lesson in drilling holes and a verbal sex education at the same time. After Rodger went back East to race, I went under the wing of Fran Hernandez. Fran had come from Offenhauser to work for my, dad and he was both a great racer and an outstanding machinist. On Jefferson, Fran ran the machine shop. At times I would get pushed aside when I asked questions or asked to be shown something. It was nothing personal, the shop was busy and it was hard to stop and show some kid how to do something that he would probably screw up anyway. Fran was different. It could have been the fact that he was Mexican-American, and in the fifties in Los Angeles, life was hard for Mexican-Americans. He understood what it meant to be pushed aside. Fran wanted me to learn all I could, and treated me as an equal."

The Apprentice

Just about every racer in America knows Edelbrock as a manufacturer of speed equipment, but few know that in the first few months of operation at Jefferson, the Korean War was raging and the performance business took a sharp drop. Vic Sr. worried that the new shop might not support itself and fell back on his experience gained during World War II. He won contracts with Lockheed, Douglas, and North American to machine various parts for aircraft, which saved the company and kept the crew employed.

Vic Sr. allowed his son to work in the machine shop. They had landed a contract to machine a special landing-gear part for the Northrup F-89, a plane made famous fighting the Russian MIG-15 fighters over North Korea's Yalu River, sometimes called MIG Alley. The part required precision drilling and milling. The material was very tough and tolerances extremely close. Fran taught Vic Jr. to do the job completely by himself. It was a boon to the young man's confidence level.

By 1953, Jefferson had become a very busy place. A new catalog illustrated just how much growth the company had experienced. The pages were splashed with a full line of racing heads and manifolds, including V8-60 heads. There were different manifolds for Ford, and Chevrolet six-cylinder engines; also a new triple carburetor, competition manifolds for Ford and Mercury, and aluminum heads for the Lincoln V-12.

Now a customer could buy Edelbrock pistons (as suggested to Vic Sr. by Lou Baney), aluminum fly-wheels, stroker crankshafts—reground camshafts from Ed Winfield, Clay Smith, Harmon & Collins—and special racing cams from Ed Iskenderian. The catalog also featured a full line of accessories, including methanol conversion kits, air cleaners, chrome velocity stacks, pressure pumps, and old standbys like acorn nuts and chrome air cleaners. The building next door housed a complete machine shop with balancing and dynamometer services. Murray Jensen remembered the variety of products and jobs. "We did everything and anything we could to make a buck. We built engines for guys running on the street, and they would come in to get a quick tune-up, then go race somebody over Mulholland Drive and come back for a different setup."

Under apprenticeship to Fran, Vic Jr. soon began making fixtures, milling castings, and doing most machine shop jobs. "I began absorbing information like a sponge. My dad officiated over my education, and he insisted that, along with learning machining skills, I continue sweeping floors, cleaning restrooms, and taking my turn shipping parts. One advantage of being Vic Edelbrock's son was the fact that I could participate in all of the shop traditions, from after-hours bench racing to stopping all work when the midget engine was fired up."

As for racing, Vic Jr. was close to all the action, from the midget races to the drag races. He was even allowed to go to Bonneville. Each adventure unveiled something new. "It was an amazing experience to learn the tricks of the trade and some of my dad's secrets by watching Don, Bobby and Fran. I was now accepted at the shop, not just by my dad's crew, but also by those who visited and conducted business at the shop. I started having people like Jazzy Nelson, Ray Brown, Ed Pink,

Dyno Room Stories: The Turkey Herder

At Edelbrock, the dyno room has always been the focal point for bench racing. Even before it was an actual room, Vic Sr. and those who sought his wisdom gathered around the

Murray Jensen was the butt of many dyno-room pranks, but he was also very good at dishing up a bad joke or two on his fellow workers.

machine. With cocktail or beer in hand, he would conduct the evening's ceremonial ritual of research from experiences of the day and colorful banter aimed at those who had screwed up. Despite the growth of the company and the changes brought on by technology, the dyno room at Edelbrock is still at the center of the operation. No product will ever see the light of day, nor carry the Edelbrock logo, without first running the gauntlet posed by the room. To accurately record all of the dyno room happenings that have transpired over the years would take more pages than the Bible itself. To say nothing would be an even larger transgression.

Ray Brock, one-time publisher of *Hot Rod* magazine, called the Edelbrock dyno room a temple in which the liturgy of speed was offered.

Murray Jensen was somewhat less demonstrative than his fellow workers, but always ready to take part in any dyno-room shenanigans. He was, on occasion, the brunt of a laugh or two and the instigator of many of the most hysterical jokes. In his youth, Murray had worked on a turkey ranch, herding the birds from one pen to another. Armed with this information, the dyno-room crew once named a carburetor "the Turkey Herder" after Murray, complete with a decal portraying a turkey's head protruding from the center of a four-barrel carburetor. But the guys just couldn't leave well enough alone. Jim McFarland bought a live, twenty-pound turkey and put it in the dyno room before Murray arrived one morning. When Jensen showed up the rest of the crew took cover as he entered the dyno room and confronted the turkey. When Murray saw the turkey roosting on one of his ready-to-run race engines, he decided to shoo it off immediately. The turkey would have no part of the plan, and began to fight back. The battle lasted for half an hour. It was not a pretty sight. According to Murray, "That son of a bitch shit on every part of that engine. It took me the rest of the day to clean it up. I looked him in the eye, and thought 'you are going to look good sitting on a table full of dressing and waiting to get carved.' Lucky for me I worked all those years herding turkeys." McFarland and the crew laughed themselves sick.

Dyno Room Stories: Hap's Blanket

Fire played a major role in Bobby Meeks's favorite dyno room tale. Next to the dyno cell was a drinking fountain. Next to the drinking fountain was a drip bucket holding excess

Hap, the shop dog, was never aware of the part his blanket would play in great history of stories played out in the Edelbrock dyno room.

runoff from the fountain. The bucket had also become home to soggy cigar butts, rancid coffee, spit, and fungi of various species. Hanging on the wall near the bucket and drinking fountain was a wool blanket belonging to a shop dog named Hap. The blanket was Hap's bed after hours, and it was not only filled with dog hair and drool, it had not been washed in anyone's memory. During a test of an experimental race manifold, a backfire caused a serious ignition of raw fuel. Without hesitation, either Bobby Meeks or Murray Jensen (neither admitted culpability) grabbed Hap's blanket, dashed into the burning holocaust, and covered the engine in order to smother the blaze. The blanket, rich with years of dirt and grime, burst into flames, prompting another crew member to grab the bucket next to the fountain to douse the fire. The result was a smoky room filled with one of the most disgusting odors ever released. It took weeks before the normal smells of gasoline and motor oil could reconstitute the air.

Don Waite came to Edelbrock after Vic Jr. had taken over and the company had grown into a corporation. However, Don had been involved with Vic Sr., going back to the dry lakes days and at the first drag racing events.

Don Waite, and Ed Iskenderian looking over my shoulder, watching me work and passing along a suggestion or instruction."

As Vic Jr. learned the art of balancing pistons and rods, he began to lobby the guys to let him build an engine on his own. It took a while—Meeks and Towle were very tough, they didn't want anything to reflect on the quality of work coming out of the shop. And Junior couldn't run to his dad for sympathy because Vic Sr. was an even tougher boss. Finally, Vic Jr. began to stand his ground against the pressure from guys in the shop. His confidence level showed them he was ready to take the next step and they agreed to let him build an engine for a customer.

"At the time, my dad was popping out midget engines like cordwood, and he was very involved with some of the top runners. But he always had a soft spot in his heart for the guys who did not have big budgets or name drivers. One of these budget racers was an auto shop instructor from Manual Arts High School in Los Angeles. The guy loved midget racing and he had bought an old rail job built in the late forties. My dad was helping him with engines, not charging full price for parts, and also doing some of the machine work on the side.

"One day Dad told me that I was going to put together the engine for this guy's midget and go to the race. I couldn't believe it was happening, and my excitement showed as I ran around telling anyone who would listen. Of course, Bobby would watch over my every move. It didn't matter; I actually put in the rods, crankshaft, rings, pistons, camshaft, and set the valves. I torqued the heads and installed the manifold and carburetors. I checked and rechecked every step. We even ran the engine on the dyno. What a sound—my first real racing engine for a customer!

"We stuck the engine in the car and my dad let me go along down to San Diego. I was still too young to get in the pits unless the officials knew me, so I had to sit in the grandstands. Not being one of the hot shoe drivers, the guy didn't make the main, but ran the semi-main and when the dust settled, he took the checkered flag. I was jumping up and down telling everybody that it was my engine in the car. The guy was happy because it was a rare win. When I got home, my chest was stuck out a mile and I was strutting around. My dad and the guys would just smile. I was learning."

Fame

In the 1950s, many Hollywood stars and television personalities were involved in the hot rod scene. Racers since their youth, actors such as Robert Stack and Lee Marvin were joined by newcomers such as James Dean, a hot rodder in *Rebel Without a Cause* who created a persona for entertainment luminaries to replicate. It was only natural that those interested in hot rods would gravitate to the Edelbrock shop on Jefferson.

However, there was another customer base that fascinated Junior as a teenager. Edelbrock Equipment was one of the first performance manufacturers to become popular in South America—especially in Argentina where they did quite a bit of racing. It differed from the United States because much of the South American racing was done point-to-point, similar to European rally racing. The hero was world champion Juan Manuel Fangio. A Grand Prix race was run in Cuba and the Carrera Pan Americana in Mexico was getting world news coverage. Racing in Spanish-speaking countries was very popular.

"Most of the racers in Argentina raced flathead Fords, although a few ran six-cylinder Chevy engines," Vic Jr. explained. "My dad made parts for both, and the drivers would come to the United States, and show up at the shop. They were as famous as movie stars and had postcards printed with their pictures, like American baseball cards. My dad would get ready for their arrival as if we were expecting royalty. Then, several cars would pull into the lot and the

"It always impressed me when someone famous would come into the shop. John Wayne came by often, Dad had known him for a long time; he and Bobby Meeks had worked on Wayne's cars when Dad had the Breawood Garage. Lawrence Welk, above left, (in tie) was a very stylish bandleader who hosted a popular TV show that opened every week with the sound of a champagne cork popping and bubbles flowing. Although he gave all the appearances of being a conservative gentleman on TV, he loved hot cars and asked Dad to put together a high performance Hemi engine for his Dodge sedan. When he came to pick it up, Welk brought my dad a bottle of champagne and a cake.

About the stars, Vic Jr. says, "Lawrence Welk and John Wayne may have been big Hollywood stars but the racers from South America were bigger stars in their country. We would ship a truck filled with parts (above) to those guys a couple times a year. They were heroes; they even had postcards with their pictures on them."

Not many people know that Edelbrock shipped tons of speed equipment to South America for racers who ran in the long distance events and rally races. Even the World Champion Juan Fangio ran an Edelbrock manifold with the name ground off so no one would know that it came from Edelbrock.

Argentineans would exit the vehicles with theatrical drama, interpreters in tow. They would spend the whole day with my dad, picking out parts and pieces, checking the work being done on the dyno, arguing prices, and sometimes ordering whole engines."

The visitors would sit around after closing, have a few drinks, and tell jokes none of the Edelbrock men could understand. The racers from South America considered Vic Sr. as big a hero as any engine builder in their home country. They always paid in cash and usually ordered big. The South American buyers not only went for the assembly packages but they ordered heads and manifolds, carburetors, camshafts, chrome pieces, and flywheels. Once the pieces were pulled from inventory, Vic Jr. remembered. "We had to package the entire order and take it to Long Beach to be shipped to South America. My dad took a picture when we were ready to go to the boat dock. We had to rent a stake body truck, and it was filled to the top with product. That was big business back then."

Victor Edelbrock Jr. was growing up fast, and his life was filled with the excitement of fast cars and racing. He wanted to be a hot rodder; he liked being part of the new breed of teens joining the ranks of racers. His father was famous, and he

"My first real hot rod was a 1946 Ford Convertible. For Christmas Dad built me a special short block with our own pistons and stroker kit. Then he let me, with Bobby and Fran helping, put together the rest of the engine. He even made a special four-barrel manifold. When I was just about done, all I needed was a fuel pump, and I borrowed the shop pickup to run down to the parts house to get one. On the way back I saw a girl, a hot number, who worked near our shop and drove a Studebaker Champion—the type that you couldn't tell if it was coming or going. Anyway, she was walking toward her car and I was all set to give her a big wave and a whistle when the fuel pump fell over and I reached down to catch it. The road jogged to the right and I stayed straight—right into the side of the Studebaker. I told my dad I had a little accident when I got back to the shop, and when he saw the damage I got one of his famous stares that said, 'Don't ever do that again!'"—**Vic Edelbrock Jr.**

wanted to take advantage of the prestige and privilege surrounding the name Edelbrock. Privilege must be earned, and young Edelbrock would have to wait a few years and get past the bumps in the road of his teen years before recognition came his way. Vic Jr. wanted to race, but his parents didn't want their son to take the risk. "My dad had told me, 'No drag racing,' because he had spent years building a reputation and he didn't want me screwing it up. At the time, Lou Baney and Lou Senter were running Saugus Drag Strip and they let my friends and me in for half price because of my dad. One day, several of my buddies were heading out to Saugus and I was going along just to watch. The last thing Dad said before I left the house was, 'Don't run your car!'

"It didn't take long before the guys called me chicken shit, and to stop the taunting, I made a pass. I ran a disappointing 84 mph and then I let a racer named Don Rackemann drive—he ran quicker and faster. On the way home, I was thinking if I hadn't run my car, I wouldn't be feeling like a failure. My dad was upstairs in the den watching Jalopy Derby on television, when I came into the house. He looked up at me, a big smile on his face, and asked, 'How fast did you go?' I couldn't lie; I told him 84 mph. 'Ok, give me your keys, no car for 30 days, and no more drag racing.' From that point on I gave up on running my car at the strip, but I hadn't promised not to street race."

Vic Jr. graduated from Dorsey High School in 1954 and prepared for college. Because of his size and athletic ability he had earned a full football scholarship to the University of Southern California. In the fall he began a schedule of business courses and a football career for the famed Cardinal and Gold. However, he was chosen for the practice squad and that left little chance of making the starting lineup. "I was getting the crap beat out of me by the really big guys and had no chance of playing in actual season games. Just being on the practice squad was not really earning my way, so I turned in my four-year scholarship and decided to pay for my education." He earned a degree in business that permitted him to take a more serious role in his

Moonshine

Years after Vic Jr. had taken over the business, Ralph Seagraves, who ran the Winston program when it first came to NASCAR, told him that Vic Sr. was one of the most famous men in the Southeast. He made the flathead equipment that the guys running moonshine needed to build engines that could outrun the law. When those same guys started racing on weekends, they used Edelbrock equipment. Vic Jr. remembered hearing his dad and mom talking about the boys Down South. Bobby and Don would joke about the 'good old boys' and their 1939 and '40 Ford coupes with forty-gallon tanks in the trunks that could blow the doors off any cop in North Carolina. "My dad actually went to North Carolina once to see one of his best dealers, a circle-track racer named Buddy Shumann, who built engines in a barn behind his house. The place was buried deep in a wooded piece of land way out of town. The barn was filled with race cars and moonshine cars, and nobody but Buddy's friends and kinfolk ever set foot inside the place. Buddy had a storeroom filled with manifolds and heads, piston sets and rods, Isky cams—everything my dad had in the catalog, Buddy had in that storeroom." Buddy Shumann was typical of the hard racers that lived Down South. He thought Edelbrock made the best parts and they wanted to run the best. That visit by Vic Sr. was the start of a relationship with the stock-car racers that is still strong today. Before the moonshiners faded into the folklore of the South, rumor had it that the Feds were using Edelbrock equipment in their chase cars.

The spacious trunk of the 1939 Ford Coupe could hold sixty four-quart bottles of contraband whiskey, making it the most popular delivery vehicle for the early moonshine racers.

Vic Jr. on his 1951 700cc Triumph Thunderbird.

Vic Jr. earned a scholarship to the University of Southern California for football. Right, Vic Jr. in his freshman year, when his team beat Stanford. He decided to give up his scholarship and pay his own way for the rest of his term. Like his father, Vic Jr. believed in paying his own way. Katie, above right, was always proud of her son, whether he was on the football field or working in the family business.

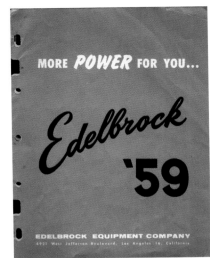

A senior at Dorsey High School in 1953, Vic Jr. poses with his mom and dad at graduation, left—unaware that he'd be working at Edelbrock when the 1959 catalog was printed, above. There would only be a few short years before his dad would pass away, thus pushing Vic into a leadership role at a young age.

father's business, but it was his love for the shop and his drive to learn all there was to learn about the automobile engine that would place him front and center in what would be the greatest period of growth yet for the performance scene.

By 1959, the Edelbrock Equipment Company had grown to one of the largest manufacturers of speed equipment in the country. It had dealers all over the United States, Europe and South America. The catalog now featured a full line of their own accessories, a selection of manifolds, and other equipment. Six-carburetor manifolds were available for the Chevrolet big block and small block, as well as for Ford, Pontiac, Buick, Oldsmobile, Chrysler, Cadillac, and even the Edsel. There were three two-barrel manifolds and dual-quads for all the majors. And the full line of Ford and Mercury flathead manifolds and heads were still available. Vic Edelbrock Jr. had moved to the front office and was putting his college education to good use. He concentrated on developing advertising, working with the magazines, and cultivating more speed shops around the country. Vic Jr. had a vision of growth and he wanted to expand his ideas, but a conflict grew between father and son. Vic Sr. never left any doubt as to whose business it was, and he kept a firm hand on his son's enthusiasm, college education notwithstanding. Vic Jr. wanted the company to grow quickly, but his father fought to retain control, and there were plenty of arguments about it.

"I was progressive and wanted to grow quickly. My dad, on the other hand, wanted to keep things status quo and enjoy the fruits of his labor. He liked playing golf and bench racing after work. He and Mom had a good life and he was happy with the business as it was. We needed to incorporate and set up lines of credit. Dad still wanted to pay cash for what he wanted. The disagreement got a little heated."—**Vic Edelbrock Jr.**

5 Passing the Torch

When two strong-willed personalities continually test each other, the lessons are often learned the hard way. Vic Edelbrock Jr. had paid his dues, sweeping floors, cleaning restrooms, and listening to bench racing stories. By the time he graduated from USC in 1958, he had a keen sense for business and a youthful enthusiasm that would run headlong into his father's perspective on how things should be done. Vic Sr. was an intense man whose education had come from the school of hard knocks. With sheer determination, he had built a business, and through fierce competition, he had earned respect. Vic Sr. was a man of his word, who came from a time when a handshake was a contract, not a document you learned to draft in college. Surprisingly, the emotional conflict and strategic battle that followed would prove positive for both father and son.

There was no doubt that Vic Jr. would follow in his father's footsteps. He loved the day-to-day operations on the shop floor and envisioned the day when his own ideas would shape the Edelbrock Equipment Company. Vic Sr. didn't mind his son's eagerness, he just didn't agree with his ideas, especially when it came to promoting the business. What worked in the past would work in the future, he saw no reason to change. Although proud of his son, the process of letting Junior become part of the business was tougher than any competitor he'd ever raced.

Vic Edelbrock Sr. had reached a comfortable plateau. His parts were in demand and trusted employees like Bobby Meeks, Don Towle, and Bob Bradford handled many of the daily business details, allowing more time for designing products. Everything was paid for and there was money in the bank. He owned a fashionable home and a weekend retreat at Lake Arrowhead in the San Bernardino Mountains. Vic Sr. could now enjoy a golf game without concern about work. Even though he never went to college, he knew that his son would need a formal education to meet the challenges ahead. He understood the meaning of a university degree, but did not approve of

Not one to exhibit social excesses, Vic Sr. did enjoy a good time and a cocktail on special occasions. In March of 1960, Vic Sr. and Katie (left) took Vic Jr. and wife Nancy (right) to one of Hollywood's hottest night spots, Frank Sennes' famed Moulin Rouge on Sunset Blvd. in Hollywood.

the party mentality that went along with living on campus in a fraternity house. Vic Jr. accepted his father's rules by living at home and working at the shop during his free time, but all was not lost. He joined the Delta Tau Delta fraternity and enjoyed every aspect of college life.

Vic Edelbrock Jr. had always idolized his father, but as he was reaching manhood—no longer "the Squirt" at over six feet tall—he wanted to be viewed as an equal. It was the age-old struggle between the dominant ruler and young challenger. Vic Sr. had faith in his son and slowly relented, but his reserved nature and desire for perfection made him cautious. Junior would be limited to small steps toward his goals. Much like his father, he would rather demonstrate his ideas in action rather than talk. To fulfill his dream of being a pilot, he joined the ROTC in college and worked every spare minute at the shop to maintain his position. When Congress made it mandatory to serve two more years to earn combat wings, Vic Jr. gave up his chance to fly. He knew it would take him away from the business too long. Vic Sr. understood his son's desires and a pattern emerged in their confrontations: he would throw a fit over something, then back off, allowing Vic Jr. to gain ground. The crew in the shop soon caught on to the mock battles and enjoyed watching from a distance.

"It was hard for us not to think of Junior as a kid running around, getting in the way and pestering us with his endless questions. Things really changed when he went to USC. He was very smart and he wanted to show his stuff, but Senior liked things the way they were. They would have a closed-door meeting where things would get pretty hot. After a fight, Senior would bark and snap around the shop for a while, and then the next thing you know, him and Junior were back best of pals." —Bobby Meeks

The airplane has been a part of Vic's life since childhood. During college, Vic joined the ROTC to fulfill his dream of becoming a fighter pilot. When Congress passed a new law making it mandatory to serve five years instead of the original three years before combat wings could be issued, Vic gave up the dream in favor of his duty to his dad and the running of the business. Left, Vic gets ready for a flight in a T-33 trainer from an airbase in Laredo, Texas. Vic finally fulfilled his wish, earning his pilot's license in 1968. Today, he pilots Edelbrock's turbo-prop Commander and flew as a guest in a Blue Angels F-18 Hornet.

Sweet Thunderbird of Youth

When it was suggested that Vic Jr. take his mother on a mission to collect a new 1955 Ford Thunderbird in Colorado, it signaled the first real change in Vic Sr.'s attitude toward his son. It would be Vic Jr.'s responsibility to return both to home safe and sound. Vic Jr. remembered, "Dad ordered the car through his friend Roy Leslie, a famous land speed racer at the Bonneville Salt Flats. Mom and I flew to Denver and then drove back to Los Angeles. We had a great time; everybody was eyeballing the car because there were very few around at the time. Mom and I talked about my ideas to work with my dad and make the business better. She reminded me that my father had struggled to establish his own set of rules and standards, and it was troublesome for him to change, but he would if just given time. She suggested that I take things slow and give my father time to adjust to the idea of his son going from childhood to manhood. I promised to be less aggressive and let things happen naturally."

Vic Sr. immediately began developing manifolds for the Thunderbird Ford Y-block V8, and he and Don Towle, and Bobby Meeks started drag racing the car. Vic Jr. forgot the promise to his mother, and pushed his dad to let him drive the car instead of Don, but Vic Sr. cringed at the idea. "I had to be satisfied as a member of the pit crew. The goal was to beat Dick Jones and his Paxton supercharger-equipped Thunderbird. Dad was a disciple of the normally aspirated engine, and he figured he could build a strong-running engine without the use of a blower. He believed blowers were for engine builders who couldn't figure out how to get horsepower any other way. Soon Don could stay right with the blown 'Bird running nearly equal times. One evening, Jones beat us two or three times in a row. At that point, my dad suddenly decided he would let me drive the car, I guess he'd heard enough of my nagging. I got my doors blown off by a school buddy of mine in a '55 Corvette. In fact, his dad owned a famous Southern California drive-in called The WichStand at Slauson and Overhill. My dad was very unhappy about my loss, because it tarnished the Edelbrock name. I was never allowed to race the car again."

In 1955 Vic Edelbrock Sr. purchased a Ford Thunderbird to be used as a test car for the development of manifolds for the Y-block engine. When the first tests were conducted, a close friend named Dick Jones showed up at the drags with an identical T-Bird using a supercharger to boost power and beat Vic's machine. After several meetings

Vic Sr. gave the '55 T-Bird one last chance to win. He talked to Bill Stroppe about a super trick transmission fluid that locked up the torque converter more quickly for a better ET and top speed. "At the next race, Don and my dad tried the new speed secret, but about halfway down the drag strip the transmission blew up. My dad said, 'Enough is enough.' He had the guys repair the T-Bird and parked it at the shop, eventually selling the car."

with Jones, Edelbrock decided to try some trick transmission oil given to him by Bill Stroppe. At Saugus Drag Strip, Don Towle ,below, blew the transmission to pieces. *Opposite:* The T-Bird at Bakersfield with Don Towle (foreground) and Bobby Meeks (facing) wrenching on the engine.

The airplane has been a part of Vic's life since childhood. During college, Vic joined the ROTC to fulfill his dream of becoming a fighter pilot. When Congress passed a new law making it mandatory to serve five years instead of the original three years before combat wings could be issued, Vic gave up the dream in favor of his duty to his dad and the running of the business. Left, Vic gets ready for a flight in a T-33 trainer from an airbase in Laredo, Texas. Vic finally fulfilled his wish, earning his pilot's license in 1968. Today, he pilots Edelbrock's turbo-prop Commander and flew as a guest in a Blue Angels F-18 Hornet.

Sweet Thunderbird of Youth

When it was suggested that Vic Jr. take his mother on a mission to collect a new 1955 Ford Thunderbird in Colorado, it signaled the first real change in Vic Sr.'s attitude toward his son. It would be Vic Jr.'s responsibility to return both to home safe and sound. Vic Jr. remembered, "Dad ordered the car through his friend Roy Leslie, a famous land speed racer at the Bonneville Salt Flats. Mom and I flew to Denver and then drove back to Los Angeles. We had a great time; everybody was eyeballing the car because there were very few around at the time. Mom and I talked about my ideas to work with my dad and make the business better. She reminded me that my father had struggled to establish his own set of rules and standards, and it was troublesome for him to change, but he would if just given time. She suggested that I take things slow and give my father time to adjust to the idea of his son going from childhood to manhood. I promised to be less aggressive and let things happen naturally."

Vic Sr. immediately began developing manifolds for the Thunderbird Ford Y-block V8, and he and Don Towle, and Bobby Meeks started drag racing the car. Vic Jr. forgot the promise to his mother, and pushed his dad to let him drive the car instead of Don, but Vic Sr. cringed at the idea. "I had to be satisfied as a member of the pit crew. The goal was to beat Dick Jones and his Paxton supercharger-equipped Thunderbird. Dad was a disciple of the normally aspirated engine, and he figured he could build a strong-running engine without the use of a blower. He believed blowers were for engine builders who couldn't figure out how to get horsepower any other way. Soon Don could stay right with the blown 'Bird running nearly equal times. One evening, Jones beat us two or three times in a row. At that point, my dad suddenly decided he would let me drive the car, I guess he'd heard enough of my nagging. I got my doors blown off by a school buddy of mine in a '55 Corvette. In fact, his dad owned a famous Southern California drive-in called The WichStand at Slauson and Overhill. My dad was very unhappy about my loss, because it tarnished the Edelbrock name. I was never allowed to race the car again."

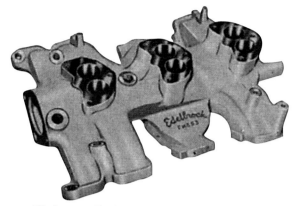

Vic Sr. gave the '55 T-Bird one last chance to win. He talked to Bill Stroppe about a super trick transmission fluid that locked up the torque converter more quickly for a better ET and top speed. "At the next race, Don and my dad tried the new speed secret, but about halfway down the drag strip the transmission blew up. My dad said, 'Enough is enough.' He had the guys repair the T-Bird and parked it at the shop, eventually selling the car."

In 1955 Vic Edelbrock Sr. purchased a Ford Thunderbird to be used as a test car for the development of manifolds for the Y-block engine. When the first tests were conducted, a close friend named Dick Jones showed up at the drags with an identical T-Bird using a supercharger to boost power and beat Vic's machine. After several meetings with Jones, Edelbrock decided to try some trick transmission oil given to him by Bill Stroppe. At Saugus Drag Strip, Don Towle ,below, blew the transmission to pieces. *Opposite:* The T-Bird at Bakersfield with Don Towle (foreground) and Bobby Meeks (facing) wrenching on the engine.

One nagging issue kept surfacing, Vic Jr. still wanted to race, and he had his eye on the T-Bird. This became a sore subject between Vic Sr., his son, and some of the crew. Bobby and Don were both racers; they wanted to see what the kid had. Fearing the wrath of Senior, they kept their thoughts to themselves. The discussion quickly ended when Senior parked the T-Bird at the shop and covered it with a tarp.

The 'Bird That Wouldn't Fly: A Lesson Learned

It didn't take long for Vic Sr. to buy a new 1956 Thunderbird after selling the '55. Once again, Vic Jr. and his mom were sent to pick up the car, but this 'Bird never went to the drag strip. It was used to test prototype manifolds and then it hung around as a shop car for about a year. Vic Jr. recalls his surprise when, "Just before I graduated from USC, my dad gave it to me as a Christmas gift! I got my dad's approval to build an engine, using our new three-carb manifold, with a longer stroke and a bigger bore. It was one fast little T-Bird, and I had a lot of fun with it, but there's one particular night that I'll never forget."

"It was May and I decided to take a break right before final exams and USC graduation. I was driving to my parents' place at Lake Arrowhead with a good friend of mine, Sim Hixon, who would later be my Best Man in my wedding. We stopped at a local bar called The Mountain Kitchen where we knew the bartender. Things got a little out of hand. We each drank about eight martinis, then jumped back into the T-Bird to continue the trip up the mountain. This was not a smart move, and something that would never happen again. After passing through a little town called Blue Jay, the road got very tight and twisting. Sim had a Jaguar, and this was the perfect opportunity to brag about how great it handled. I started running harder and harder, proving to him that my T-Bird could outrun his Jag anytime. Of course, we were both feeling no pain.

"As I went into a tight turn, I lost it and went straight off the road. Two trees about thirty feet down the hill were the only thing that stopped us from going another 300 feet down to the lake. One tree smashed the hood and the other bashed in the deck lid. We were stuck in the middle, piled on top of each other, with a water ski between us. Both of us had survived without a scratch and our cigars were still lit.

"Just as we scrambled to the top of the hill, a local Lake Arrowhead Sheriff showed up. We both knew him and he just shook his head and said, 'Boys, what did you do?' A young couple stopped and offered to take me to a telephone. They gave me a pack of gum for my breath, which I chewed, wrapper and all. I called a tow truck and we hauled the car to the road. I reconnected the battery, started the engine, and drove to my parents' house. It was dawn when we finally arrived. Mom was in a state of shock and dad was fishing out on the lake. When he came home I told him I had crashed the T-Bird. To say that my parents were upset would be a major understatement and my dad was especially angry. Then, when they saw the car and the place where I'd gone off the road, they were just thankful that their only son was still alive. After that, my dad never said another word about that night."

The Higgins Boat

Racing cars was something Vic Sr. did not allow his son to do, but messing around with boats was a different story altogether. The Edelbrock Equipment Company had been involved in boat racing for many years. From the early flathead days into the 1950s, Edelbrock was a name well-known on the water. Don Towle, one of Vic Sr.'s most trusted employees, was an SK Boat National Champion. And with a summer home at Lake Arrowhead, it seemed natural for the son of Vic Edelbrock to be involved in some form of boat racing.

Vic Jr. bought his first boat in 1957, and it was the start of many years of fun on the water. "My dad and I found a Higgins V-bottom with a Y-block Ford but I bought it without the motor, because my dad wanted to drop in a small-block Chevy. Bobby and my dad built a 283-inch small block with a ⅛" overbore. They did all the basic stuff and at first, the boat ran all right. Then we found out that the boat needed to go faster. My dad simply said, "Bring it down to the shop." Vic Sr. had decided that it was time to get serious.

"I put the boat in Dad's shop on Sunday afternoon and when I got to the shop on Monday, the engine was out and parts had been ordered. They were expecting a stroker crank, high compression pistons, and a new cam to match our new six-carburetor manifold. When we finished, I had about 343 cubic-inches and it ran like a rocket ship. Soon, my Higgins was the fastest V-bottom on Lake Arrowhead." Vic Jr.'s next stop

would be the boat drags near Bakersfield. "First time out, I raced this guy in a flat-bottom with a Chrysler Hemi and open exhaust. I blew his pants off. He got so mad that he pounded his boat with his fists. He had just lost to a fully-dressed V-bottom with a big windshield and a giant steering wheel."

Next came water ski racing. Every summer, the owners of the Lake Arrowhead Marina took a group of ski racers to Lake Mead for an annual race that featured only V-bottom racers. Vic Jr. remembers, "My good friend Rick Michel was willing to be the observer, so I hooked up with a skier and we won the first time out—we won twice that day. When we got home at about two in the morning I was so pumped about winning that I put the huge trophies in my mom and dad's breakfast nook. At about six o'clock in the morning they had their big surprise and they were excited. That morning marked the start of a long-term relationship with boat racing that would affect my life in ways I never imagined." Although fiercely competitive when racing, Vic Edelbrock Jr. was actually shy. He enjoyed partying with his fraternity brothers, but social affairs were another story.

Fast boats and Edelbrock speed equipment have been part of the family since Vic Sr.'s time. Vic Jr. continued the tradition, making boat racing an integral part of his life. He began racing boats in his teen years. Boat racing created the Fun Team and totally engulfed the family into water sports. Above right, Vic Jr. gets ready to run his Marathon boat "Sizzler" at Salton Sea. Above left, Fun Team members Mike Toll (wearing black hat), Vic's college buddy Rick Michel (standing left) and Vic (in boat) play at Salton Sea.

A New Partnership

In his senior year, Vic Jr. and his frat brothers took part in a USC tradition called "Songfest." The largest college event of its kind, Songfest was held at the Hollywood Bowl and it raised money for Troy Camp, a camp for underprivileged children in Los

"Thank goodness I was raised in the automobile business, because I knew the basics of business and what performance was all about. When Vic and I first got married, he was a very shy fellow and would kick the dirt and stumble around when he would meet a stranger. I had to fix that right off the top."—**Nancy Edelbrock**

The old saying "opposites attract" may be the key to a solid marriage for Vic and Nancy Edelbrock. In college, Vic was a football player, racer and hell raiser and Nancy was gentle, sophisticated and well-spoken. Above, at a college party, the couple shows off a "Vic cup" earned for being a good party couple.

Angeles. All of the sororities and fraternities had to audition for the chance to perform on stage. The Delts and Kappa Alpha Theta made the final cut, and rehearsals began. Nancy Crook, whom Vic Jr. had seen around campus, was assigned a spot directly in front of him. After some small talk, Vic recalls, "I remember she had a great car. It was a midnight blue 1946 Ford coupe, nosed and decked, with a ¾ cam and Belond glass packs exhaust, and a hot flathead that her dad had built. He always had hot rods on display in his showroom."

Nancy Edelbrock remembers the start of her relationship with Vic a little differently. "We had seen each other at parties and talked casually. A sorority sister of mine, Carol Briggs, was dating Bart Porter, who was a fraternity brother of Vic's. Carol and Bart fixed us up on a blind date after Songfest rehearsal one evening. The four of us double dated. Vic was very nice—quiet and polite. I thought he was very handsome; tall, well dressed, and seemed to be a fun person. Our first date was terrific fun and he asked me for a second date several days later and I accepted. When the time came, I waited downstairs at the Theta House for my Prince Charming, but he never came. I had been stood up, and I decided that I could find better things to do with my time than hang around waiting for Vic Edelbrock Jr. to show up.

"The next morning Vic was on the phone, very apologetic and claiming to be totally embarrassed. It seems that he had gotten caught up in a party with his fraternity brothers and forgot his date with me. He asked for a second chance, and for some reason I relented, but told him the next time would be the last time. We began dating on a regular basis, and before long we were together constantly with no desire to date other people. One evening, shortly after Vic had begun working full time for his dad, we went to the Seven Seas on Hollywood Boulevard—the most 'in' place of the time—a hangout for movie stars and social climbers. We danced the night away."

Vic Edelbrock Jr. and Nancy Marie Crook were officially engaged on Christmas 1958, and were married at Our Savior's Chapel on the campus of the University of Southern California on March 21, 1959.

"Things became semi-serious when Vic asked me to wear his fraternity pin. Back then it was a precursor to becoming engaged. A pinning is celebrated with some touching ceremonies. For the ladies of the Theta sorority, pinning was a romantic experience. I wrote a poem about how we had met that did not reveal our identities, and arranged to have a candle ringed with flowers and the poem delivered to a dinner where all sorority members were present. The president read the poem and the guessing began. With the candle burning brightly, the bouquet was passed to each member, all giggling in anticipation and suspense. When the candle came to me and I blew it out, they all knew.

"The second tradition took place when Vic's fraternity came to the Theta house for a gathering to sing songs and celebrate the couple being pinned. The ladies held candles and as the whole group sang 'You're My Delta Tau Girl,' we kissed and all the candles were extinguished. It was all very romantic. Afterwards all my girlfriends starting crying and Vic's fraternity brothers were slapping him on the back. And Vic, the racer, the football player, the man of the world, had a tear running down his cheek. It was all great fun and something that has lasted for both of us through the years." —**Nancy Edelbrock**

Above, Vic and Nancy shared many good times during their college years. Vic (center) Nancy (left) and Rick Michel (right) ham it up at a party in Lake Arrowhead. A beautiful bride, Nancy Crook left, married Victor Edelbrock Jr. on March 21, 1959, in Our Savior's Chapel on the campus of the University of Southern California. Nancy was born in Evanston, Illinois. Her father decided to move his family (wife Alice Mary, son Frederick Jr., and Nancy) to Hermosa Beach, California, after World War II. In the fall of 1954 Nancy Crook was accepted at Stanford, but transferred to USC. She was a natural leader and became president of her sorority, president of the National Art Fraternity, and a Helen of Troy member for her academic achievements. Nancy would prove to be a wonderful partner and loving wife for over forty-five years.

Joining the Perfect Partnership

The groom gets ready for his big event, above, as several of Vic's friends try to spruce-up the husband to be. On March 21, 1959, Vic Jr. began his partnership with the lovely Nancy Crook. It was the perfect combination. Vic Jr. was shy and reserved and Nancy was skilled in the art of meeting people and putting them at ease. Vic Jr. was filled with new ideas, and Nancy was ready to stand with him no matter how difficult life's path became. The happy couple joined with their parents for a photo, above right, before cutting the cake. Vic's mother Katie pins on the customary boutonniere, below left, before the wedding service begins. Below right, (left to right) Vic Sr., Nancy, Vic Jr., and Katie pose for a family portrait. *Opposite:* Vic Jr. and Nancy kiss after the service and, right, Nancy feeds her new husband some cake. Below right, on her wedding day Nancy could have been mistaken for the cover girl on *Bride* magazine.

Above, always ready for fun, Christi (right) and Camee (left) wait for someone to give them a ride. Above right, family has always been important in the Edelbrock tradition. Gatherings like Camee's second birthday brought the family together. (From left to right around the table) Nancy's mother Alice Crook, her father Frederick, Nancy, Christi, birthday girl Camee, Katie, Vic Sr. and long-time friend of Vic Jr., Rick Michel. The significance of this family photo is the fact that it would be the last time Vic Sr. would attend a family event. He passed away in November of 1962.

The wedding was followed by a short honeymoon in Carmel, California. The newlyweds didn't have long to wait for their first challenge. On January 27, 1960, their first child, Cathleen Ann Marie was born. The new mother, who had joked for years she had never been given a clever nickname, promptly took the first letter from each of her daughter's given names and added an extra E. Camee is a play on letters and not on camshafts as most would believe, and the nickname would stick for life.

Christina Lee Edelbrock joined the family crew on April 11, 1961, and Katie and Vic Sr. were now grandparents to two girls. With the girls Vic Sr. lost his hard edge and his soft side came bubbling out. He and Katie would occasionally spend Sundays and holidays with the kids, playing in the swimming pool and cooking outdoors. It seemed that Senior was finally enjoying life without stress.

Racing Ahead

The 1960s began with promise for all the Edelbrocks. The Chevrolet small-block ram log manifold was the hottest item going, the new catalog was bulging, and the list of speed shops handling Edelbrock Equipment was growing. The Jefferson shop had grown to a two-building facility offering dynamometer testing, balancing, a complete machine shop, and 24-hour order fulfillment via air freight. Magazines were virtually camped out at the shop, doing stories and shooting photos because Edelbrock was one of the few manufacturers capable of testing products, building engines, and offering a total research and development program for new ideas—all under one roof.

The 1960s produced many heroes, men like Vic Sr.'s pal and ex-whiskey hauler Junior Johnson, who became a legend after winning the Daytona 500. California produced its share of heroes, like Santa Monica's Phil Hill, who had gained fame racing and fighting on the bull rings of the jalopy and midget circuits, won the Indy 500 in 1963, driving J. C. Agajanian's "Calhoun," a roadster built by A. J. Watson. In 1967 Jones was back, this time driving for Automotive Icon and Andy Granatelli's revolutionary Pratt and Whitney turbine car. Parnelli ran the field into the ground and looked like a sure winner until the engine failed with only a couple of laps to go. Riverside's Dan Gurney set the Formula One world on its ear when he won the 1967 Belgian Grand Prix driving his own V-12 Eagle racer. Mario Andretti finished out the decade by winning the Indy 500 for Granatelli in 1969.

Drag racing's NHRA grew into a governing body as strong as USAC or NASCAR. Everything got faster and more technical with the advent of nitromethane. Top Fuel drivers became media personalities. Free spirit and revolutionary thinker of the time Ed Pink became famous as an engine builder. Pink had caught the eye of Vic Edelbrock Sr. years before. Vic Sr. would always ask his pal Ralph Guldahl Jr., who spent weekends at the races

Dyno Room Stories: The Big Bang

Curt Hooker's favorite dyno room prank is one called the Big Bang. Most of the time, the Big Bang met the standards set by the crew for good gags, but there were those rare moments when circumstances enabled it to work beyond all expectations. One such occasion involved a company called Traco in Culver City, not far from the Edelbrock plant. Traco was the partnership of Jim Travers and Frank Coon, two famous Indianapolis 500 engine builders.

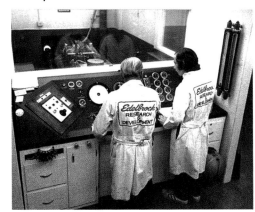

Considered by Bobby Meeks and Murray Jensen to be just a kid when first hired, Curt Hooker matured into a superb prankster, specializing in "big bangs."

Travers and Coon were not only big hitters in the racing engine business, they had become famous as the co-crew chiefs on Bill Vukovich's winning 1953 and 1954 cars and his last ride in 1955. After giving up Indy, they set up shop building everything from sprint car motors to boat power plants, with a few USAC Indy cars and NASCAR Winston West machines tossed in for good measure. Traco had their own dyno, but one time it was blown out of commission when an engine let go and the ensuing explosion tore the room into shreds. The Traco people called Edelbrock to ask if they could send over a race engine to be run on Edelbrock's dyno as a favor. Vic agreed. The engine was set up and the dyno engineer from Traco started his tests. As the engineer ran the engine up to full power and maximum load, Curt Hooker dispensed the Big Bang by dropping a steel flywheel onto the cement floor directly behind the guy running the test. The result was a near heart attack as the poor fellow envisioned another explosion—the Big Laugh followed.

California has produced its share of champion race drivers, and many have become close friends with Vic Edelbrock Jr. over the years. Photo at far left shows (in cap), Parnelli Jones, 1963 Indy 500 winner who also happens to be a neighbor of Vic's (left). Dan Gurney, left, kneeling next to one of his Eagle race cars, used Edelbrock manifolds on his Chevy Indy 500 engines in 1981.

"In the early 1960s we all were entering a very steep learning curve; everyone started going faster, and there was a tremendous amount of experimentation in every aspect of the sport. We were building stronger engines. The chassis builders were learning how to make the cars handle better and safer. At first, the drag racers remained a close-knit family and there was an open environment with everybody sharing information. As the decade progressed, the atmosphere began to change.

"The hemi produced more speed and quicker times, and engine builders like Keith Black began creating engines for teams with sponsor money, or at least rich backers. In 1962 I moved to a new shop in Sherman Oaks and began building only racing engines. It was part of a racing complex owned by Tony Nancy. Across from my shop was chassis builder Kent Fuller and the famous aluminum-body race car builder Wayne Ewing.

"A customer could come in and get a chassis, body, leather interior, and engine without leaving the lot. The drivers were getting very professional. They were not just hot rod kids racing on the street at night and drag racing on weekends. In late 1966 dry-lakes racer Lou Baney put together a deal with Ford Motor Company to use their 427 cubic inch SOHC engine in a dragster and I did the engines. At first Tom McEwen drove, then Don Prudhomme. It was very intense racing and we didn't share information with anyone. Things had changed." —**Ed Pink**

moonlighting as a reporter for local drag racing papers, "How did Eddie do?" When times were tough for the young engine builder, Pink would sometimes arrive at his shop in the morning and find a 55-gallon drum of nitro sitting in the driveway. There was no note, but he knew who was responsible.

As the interest in drag racing grew, the factories got more involved, creating a new style of car, or at least funneling money to those who would create the new cars called FX—Factory Experimentals. These would evolve into today's Funny Cars. After Fran Hernandez left Edelbrock's employ, he was hired by Ford Motor Company and became an early creator of factory-backed drag racing machines. Art Chrisman built many cars for the Bonneville Salt Flats, and together with his brother Lloyd and uncle Jack created a family name synonymous with drag racing. Art was an old-school racer who liked flatheads and respected Vic

Edelbrock Sr. even though he didn't use his parts. "Nothing against Edelbrock," Art remembered, "but I used Sharp heads and manifolds. I liked them, and I got a really good deal. Vic Sr.

Drag racing convinced many dry lakes racers to switch from the desert to the quarter-mile. Drag racing also developed its own brand of characters. Right, two of the most beloved journalists who helped Drag Racing grow, the late Gray Baskerville (with glasses) and Ralph Guldahl Jr. (with camera). Baskerville was the Hemingway of *Hot Rod* Magazine and Ralph was noted as the guru of Top Fuel dragsters. One of the most famous dragsters in drag racing, far right, the Chrisman Brothers digger driven by Art Chrisman (kneeling).

Don Garlits takes on Norm Weekly in a match race at Pomona, California, above left. When drag racing went wild in the 1960s, Edelbrock never cultivated a reputation in the Top Fuel dragster ranks, but two of the biggest names in building engines for Top Fuel dragsters have a long history with the company. Ed Pink, top, was taken on as a friend by Vic Edelbrock Sr. when first beginning his engine building company. And Keith Black, above considered one of the greatest engine men of all time, butted heads with Vic Sr. in their early boat racing days.

was very particular whom he gave a hot parts deal to. He wanted guys who were hard racers and who would work close with his guys, Bobby and Don. We were into doing our own thing."

Tony Nancy was a hard-running, independent racer who built his own equipment and ran the most famous upholstery shop on the West Coast. Nancy described drag racing during the 1960s as "a giant leap forward in all aspects. The cars in Top Fuel and Top Gas were getting faster, and new classes like Factory X were catching on. Chassis builders like Woody Gilmore and Kent Fuller were creating honest-to-God racecars, not backyard handiwork stuff. Tom Hanna and Wayne Ewing built car bodies that were works of art. Tires improved, Goodyear and M&H began molding purpose-built tires for dragsters, West Coast engine builders like Ed Pink and Keith Black were getting as famous as Indy car engine builders. Everything got more professional. NHRA was growing and the racers from the East came West ready to kick some ass. Don Garlits, Chris Karamesines, Connie Kalitta, Neil Leffler, Joe Schubeck, Pete Robinson, Eddie Lenarth, Gordon Collett, and others wanted to make their reputations by beating the West Coast guys. Drag strips like Long Beach, Bakersfield, and Pomona became the West Coast version of the OK Corral. During the 1960s, it was nothing to have a 64-car Top Fuel field at a Saturday night race. Times got hot. There was rock and roll, a lot of fuel, big speeds, low ETs, touring, fighting, chasing the girls, and wild times after the races. Action was all part of the scene. Those days are gone now, but for the guys who were there, the 1960s were special."

"When the speed equipment business took off in the late 1950s, Vic Edelbrock Sr. was the most respected guy in the speed equipment business. His products were outstanding." —**Art Chrisman**

NHRA Pro Stock, A New Goal for Edelbrock

Drag racing changed dramatically from 1950 to 1970. Wally Parks and the NHRA had taken a leadership role in the promotion of national events, with the AHRA presenting a challenge in the East and South. Tires, along with improvements in clutch design, a wider choice of parts, and additional classes, made the sport more competitive. Edelbrock began focusing on producing manifolds for a new breed of racer. Pro Stock, top right, featured drivers like Bill "Grumpy" Jenkins (foreground) and Paul Blevins, both using Edelbrock manifolds. Super Stock, another new class, spotlighted drivers like "Jungle" Jim Liberman (who became famous as a Funny Car driver) who also ran Edelbrock manifolds. In turn, new cars like the exotic digger of Pete Robinson above, were getting ready to make a statement.

Dragsters were changing their look as well. *Opposite:* Tiresmoking, fuel-burning lightweight diggers like the Ed Pink car, top, took the place of the shorter wheelbase cars like the Art Chrisman, Frank Cannon "Hustler I" below left. Below right, Vic Edelbrock Jr., left and Nancy, center worked to make winners out of racers who used their products, as in the case of Paul Blevins.

"When I took over, I had the full support of my mother, my wife, and of Bobby Meeks, Don Towle, Bob Bradford, and the rest of the crew. They all wanted me to succeed—their jobs depended on the fact that we keep growing. I also got a significant amount of support from my dad's old friends. Guys like Tom Carstens, Paul Schiefer, Bob Hedman, Bob Joehnck, Ed Iskenderian, Bob Pierson, and Ed Pink, all the guys who loved my father were on my side and that made me feel very good. But, when it came to the day-to-day struggle of keeping the business running, it was Bobby Meeks, Don Towle, Bob Bradford, Nancy, and my mom." —**Vic Edelbrock Jr.**

A Sad Transition

In midsummer of 1962, Vic Sr. and Katie were planning to tour Europe. Two weeks before their planned departure, Vic Sr. went to the doctor for a nagging sore throat and trouble swallowing. A lifelong heavy smoker, he dismissed the problem as an irritation. His doctor found his tonsils were inflamed and a small growth was attached to one side, so Vic checked into the hospital for tests. The trip to Europe was cancelled when the doctors determined surgery would be needed to remove the growth. Afterward, Vic Sr. no longer displayed his trademark constant energy. More tests revealed what looked like a tumor in one lung.

"You have to remember this was 1962," Vic Jr. recalled sadly. "They didn't have all of the high-tech detection machines they have today, so some of the decisions were based on guesswork. During surgery they discovered something on his lung, but also that he had lymphosarcoma. There wasn't much they could do, so they closed him back up and sent him home. My mom, Nancy and I were standing in the hall of the hospital when Dr. Epstein came out of the operating room, and the look on his face told the story. It was the worst moment in my life. I had never seen my mother so devastated. My heart was pounding and my mind just would not accept the fact that my father was that sick. He had always been so strong, and he had always been my hero."

One of the more popular manifolds designed by Vic Edelbrock Sr. was the Ram Log, using six carburetors. Introduced in the mid-1950s, the Ram Log was available for Ford, Chevy, Buick, Pontiac, Oldsmobile, and the Chrysler Hemi, like the 392 CID, above, built for Don Towle's SK boat.

Vic Sr. returned home and tried to find a cure in Mexico, but nothing worked and he became more tired. By November 1962, Vic Edelbrock Sr. had become a shadow of himself. He hardly ate, and his once-strong body had become emaciated, but his mind and his passion never waned. His son recalled that toward the end of Vic Sr.'s days, "we were making manifolds for the 392 cubic-inch Chrysler Hemi aimed at the boat racing market, but Towle was racing with a Pontiac. Keith Black was building engines for boat racing and he wanted us to make a ram-type manifold for the hemi. Dad agreed and built the manifold, and Keith bought six or eight right off the first run. He would sit in the balancing shop and talk to my dad while work was being done. Keith had begun his rise to power as a premier engine builder, with the 392 Hemi as his specialty. He was building them for the SK Class boats, and nearly every boat that raced in the SK Class had a KB Hemi. We delivered six manifolds to Keith and he installed them on his customers' boats for race testing. The tests didn't satisfy Black, so he yanked the manifolds and returned to his old setup. My dad told him, 'Keith, they'll work. I'll show you.' Both men were perfectionists, and strong in their belief in themselves, and I think there was a real conflict between them. Dad was very agitated and he told Bobby Meeks and Don Towle to remove the Pontiac from Don's boat and go out and find a Hemi. They actually bought three engines at a junkyard for fifty dollars apiece.

"During this time, my dad had not yet taken a downturn with his cancer. In fact, at this point he still believed that his sore throat was a very bad case of tonsillitis. At any rate, he worked long hours looking at every aspect of the hemi to find a solution to making his manifold work. Finally, he discovered the problem in the engine's piston design. Realizing the problem, my dad went to a noted piston maker and asked to have a set of cast pistons made, with unfinished domes. He then machined the pistons to include his ideas. The domes were changed to better fit the configuration of the combustion chamber. Next, my dad went to his old buddy Ed Iskenderian and asked Ed to grind a camshaft to his design. When the engine was assembled, Bobby and Don ran it on the dyno. The first pull produced a reading of 430 horsepower. But, on the second pull, a piston disintegrated under the load. To solve the problem, the cast pistons were exchanged for forged pistons with a higher tolerance for pressure.

"When the new pistons were machined and the engine tested, readings of 430-435 horsepower were no sweat. With the powerful combination confirmed, it was time to have some fun. Dick Jones, of Champion Spark Plugs, and the man who had beaten my dad's '55 T-Bird at the drag races, was running a Hemi in his SK race boat with the same setup as Keith Black, only the engines were coming out of the famed Traco shop of Frank Coon and Jim Travers. But, like Black, Traco was only getting about 400 horsepower out of their Hemi engines. My dad told Bobby and Don to call Dick Jones and have him come over to the shop for a

Boat racing has played a very important part in the history of Edelbrock Equipment Company. Vic Edelbrock Jr. took up the challenge of racing boats in his teens and continued for many years. He and his family have been involved in everything from water ski marathon racing to offshore Unlimited events. The company has also helped many racers, including the late Leroy Penhall, top left), with (left to right) Vic Jr., Bobby Meeks, and Don Towle. Penhall, above, ran Edelbrock equipment in his boat "Sizzler" for many seasons.

"One of the saddest days of my life was the day, at Vic's house, he told me that smoking had made him really sick, and that he had some serious health problems. He had tears in his eyes and you could see the pain in his soul. He wanted to live and see his son take the business over. I think he would have liked to see his grandchildren grow. He was a hard working, serious man, but he had a heart as soft as rain water." —Robert E. Petersen

Vic Edelbrock Sr.: Visionary and Friend

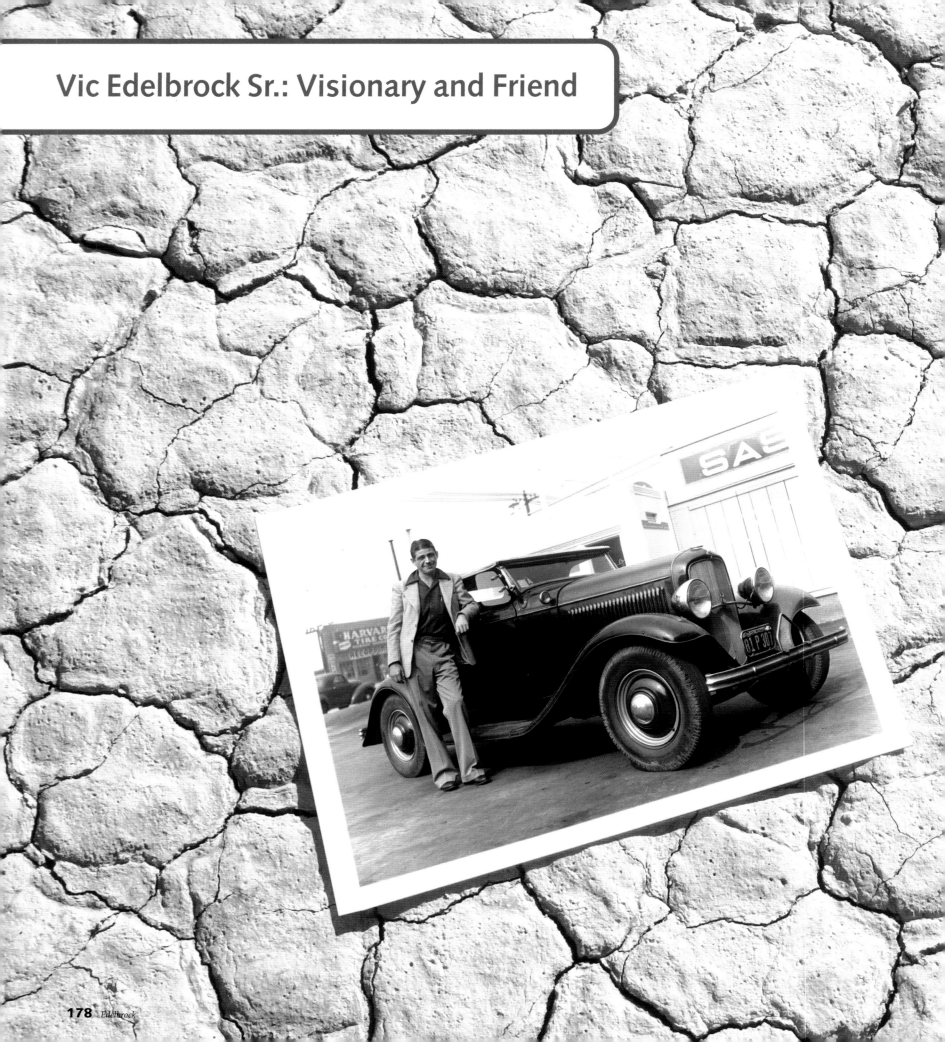

"In my judgment Vic Edelbrock was head and shoulders
above most everybody when it came to car building, and I suspect
that if he had put his mind to it he could have won the Indy 500.
Edelbrock was always fair; he always paid what he owed.
When I was down and out, he helped. Whenever I would do something
stupid on the track he would put his arm on my shoulder and tell me
that those things happened and we would get them next time.
To this day, I say that if it wasn't for Vic Edelbrock
I would never have become a famous race driver."

RODGER WARD

"It took years for me to get over Vic Sr.,
and the only thing that helped me go on was the fact that
we had to keep the business moving and do our job.
To this day it still hurts when I think about that day."

BOBBY MEEKS

"He was always so full of life.
He helped me whenever I needed advice
and as my header business grew and his business grew,
we became closer friends."

BOB HEDMAN

"The industry had lost a great innovator, but I had lost a great friend.
It hit me that we would never sit around at the shop after work and
bench race with a few cocktails in hand. . . . Never again, would I come
to my shop of a morning and find a barrel of nitro sitting by the door."

ED PINK

"When you were his friend, it was for keeps.
He was always the same guy who we all saw running the dry lakes.
He was a racer right down to his soul."

TOM MEDLEY

Vic Edelbrock Sr. spent a great deal of time designing manifolds that would work well for boat racing. The proof of his labor can be found in many examples, including his Chrysler Ram Log used on the APBA champion SK boat, above, driven by Don Towle. Above right, both Don Towle (right) and Bobby Meeks (left) worked in the field covering both boat racing and drag racing events.

couple of drinks. He also told them to leave the Hemi on the dyno. When Jones showed up, my dad said, 'Dick let's have a VO and Coca-Cola and then I want to show you something.' After a couple of drinks, Bobby and Don took Jones to the dyno and showed him the Hemi. Dad and the guys knew that Jones had just blown his race engine sky high trying to get more than 400 horses. When Jones saw my dad's engine, he couldn't believe it. He didn't even know my dad had a Chrysler in the shop.

"My dad fired up the engine and pulled 435 horsepower easy as could be. Jones about had a heart attack. This was the spring of 1962, and my dad made a deal with Jones to run the Edelbrock combination at the annual Fourth of July race at Long Beach. Dick agreed, and also promised to keep the deal a secret. Then my dad told Bobby and Don to put a Hemi in Don's boat and win the July race.

"By the time July came around, my dad had become very weak and had to watch the races from the back of the shop pickup truck. But, he was there and wanted to see his engines run strong. The competition was divided into two heats, and when the action started, Don Towle won the first heat, with Dick Jones second. In the number two heat, Jones won with Towle second. It was total vindication for my dad and a symbolic moment in our family's history. That would be the last race my dad would ever attend. Keith Black came running up, asking my dad what he did. I'm not sure if he ever told him about the pistons. And, I don't remember if Black

"Vic Sr., was a tough, rugged man and he didn't take losing very well. He was not morose, nor was his anguish uncontrollable. He wanted to fight the illness with all of his heart in a logical manner. Senior's long time friend, Tom Carstens, joined Vic Jr., and myself in the struggle. We began to research as much as we could find out about the disease and what alternative treatments were available. We talked to doctors in Mexico—Tom and Vic Jr. took him down for treatments. He remained courageous, despite the fact that the pain was horrid. As the end came near, his last words were those of caring. He wanted to make sure that Katie, Vic Jr., me, the grandchildren, and the crew would be taken care of and the bills would be paid." **—Nancy Edelbrock**

ever ran an Edelbrock ram-log manifold. Now Keith is gone and my dad is gone too. But on that July 4, a classic battle between two great engine builders created a life-long memory."

It had always been the elder Edelbrock's wish that his son take over the business with the full support of his mother, Meeks, Towle, and the rest of the crew, along with the support from his dad's old friends such as Tom Carstens, Paul Schiefer, Bob Hedman, Bob Joehnck, and Ed Iskenderian. "Don't ever get yourself in a position where you lose what is there," warned Senior in his dying days. Despite the terminal illness, father and son would still get into heated arguments with their voices raised until Katie would start crying and beg them to stop fighting. Vic Sr. would say, "Katie, calm down, we're not fighting, we're discussing."

As most people prepared for the Thanksgiving season, the end came for the man who wouldn't quit. The last days were indelible to Vic Jr. "Dad just kept getting worse, and we took him back to the hospital. Mom spent hours sitting on his bed comforting him. At the time I didn't know it, but they talked about what was going to happen to the business, and about me. Dad passed away on November 11, 1962. My life would never be the same."

Innovation

It was Junior's turn now. Katie sat Vic down and told him his dad wanted her to give him a chance to run things. However, if she saw that the business was going downhill, then she should sell.

As Junior began the transition to leadership, Meeks, Towle, Bradford, and Katie Edelbrock looked after the day-to-day details of keeping the business running. By the winter of 1963-64, the Edelbrock Equipment Company's second-generation leader had proven himself as tough as his

"My dad decided to fight the problem in his own way. He had me take him to a doctor in Tijuana, Baja Mexico, who claimed to cure cancer. I don't remember the treatment, but I think it was an early form of Laetrile. At first, my mom and I figured that getting him out of the hospital and allowing him to fight the problem his way was a good thing. But, nothing seemed to work and he just kept getting more tired." —**Vic Edelbrock Jr.**

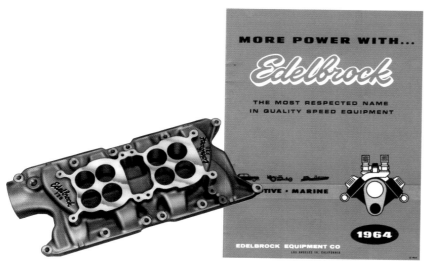

As the 1960s introduced society to a wilder side of life, the Edelbrock catalog, with Vic Jr. making the decisions, posted a continuing list of new and improved products like the F-28 Dual Quad manifold, above, for the Ford small-block. Vic Jr. was well-qualified to run the family business. He had learned every job from cleaning restrooms and sweeping floors to drilling holes and building engines. Above right, Vic Jr. (in t-shirt) worked at his dad's shop from his early teens through his college years.

father. Drag racing and street performance were now the markets to be addressed. The Chevrolet small-block was turning into a golden goose. Vic Jr.'s personal concepts worked their way into the company philosophy. A more aggressive advertising campaign was introduced and new product ideas emerged to expand the inventory.

Long-time engine builder Bob Joehnck suggested in a casual conversation that Edelbrock manufacture a single four-barrel aluminum manifold for the small-block Chevrolet similar to the factory model, only with the Edelbrock name on it. Joehnck recommended a manifold that would take a square-bore carburetor—either a Carter AFB or a Holley. However, in 1964 Holley was not in the performance game yet and only made OEM and replacement aftermarket units. At first, Vic Jr. said no, because at the time Chevrolet already made an aluminum manifold for the 327-cubic-inch V-8. After thinking about it over the weekend, however, he changed his mind.

"Back then we didn't use any set formula in creating a new manifold design," Vic Jr. remembers. "Dad had developed his own method, and as I was learning the business he passed the information along to me. He would figure out what the plenum chamber under the carburetor should be and had devised a formula with his patternmaker to create the correct taper, length, and shape of the runners. Luckily, our long-time patternmaker Harvey Hartman continued to make our patterns after my dad passed away. Without Harvey, things would have been much more difficult. He told me a lot about my dad and helped me understand his way of doing things. Harvey was part artist and part creative

"When I would come to the shop, I started noticing that Vic didn't act the same. He was tired all the time and would spend a lot of time in his office, by himself. You could see something was wrong. Unfortunately, he was a very heavy smoker, as were many of the old-time racers and engine builders. They were all men who had gone through World War II, where smoking was a way of life. After his operation, I went to see him a couple of times, but my heart would about break when I saw him and how Katie and Vic Jr. were suffering along with him. When he passed away, there was a huge void in my life. He was one of the best guys and the most honest man I had ever met." —Ray Brock

genius when it came to manifold design. We didn't give him a blueprint, just a rough outline. He would then create drawings on flat pieces of wood for the top, side, and overall view of the runners and the plenum design. Next, Bobby, Don, and in the case of the small block, Bob Joehnck all started making changes. A little more taper here, increase the radius there—all seat-of-the-pants concepts developed from years of experience racked up by the guys. Harvey would finally carve wooden patterns to come up with a set of cores. At our final meeting, as everyone voiced last-minute ideas, Harvey would make changes almost as fast as the guys could think."

"After Senior died, my Vic had a tough time because he didn't want to change things overnight. Something else really bugged me about the way the guys in the shop referred to my husband. The guys had been calling Vic 'Junior' since he was five years old. I looked at this 6-foot 3-inch strapping ex-football player and concluded that he doesn't look like a junior to me, so I put my foot down and told the crew call him Vic. I knew from day one that Vic loved his business second only to his family, and I understood there would be times when the business would take his time away from the girls and myself. It was something the two of us understood and accepted. It was sometimes painful, but necessary." —**Nancy Edelbrock**

When the patterns were ready for casting, Bob Joehnck asked if he could have a couple hundred of the new manifolds cast with his name embossed in the casting instead of Edelbrock. Since it had been his idea to create the manifold in the first place, Vic Jr. agreed, especially since a hundred-manifold order was huge at the time. Listed in the Edelbrock catalog as C-4B, Single Quad Hi-Riser for Chevrolet 283- and 327-cubic-inch engines, the new manifold featured a sweep-around port design and offered a 20-horsepower gain between 3000 and 7000 rpm. The real advantage was that the do-it-yourself mechanic could run the Edelbrock aluminum four-barrel manifold with a straight throttle hookup for street use. Sales showed rapid growth for the new product.

Edelbrock followed up with the dual-quad ram log manifolds that fit the small-and big-block Chevrolet and the small-block (260–289 cubic inch) Ford. Edelbrock already had a good-selling ram log manifold for six carburetors, but the linkage on the carburetors was a tedious setup. Edelbrock began testing a dual-quad manifold made by Mickey Thompson, who was marketing a dual quad, log-type manifold. Mickey's manifold produced excessive fuel "standoff" that at 5,000 rpm inhibited performance. So, Vic Jr. took his dad's existing 6-carb Ram Log intake, modified it to accept two 4-barrel carburetors, and into production it went—a 1960s big-seller.

This gave rise to the Model X-C8 dual-quad ram log manifold designed for two AFB Carter carburetors. Ads of the time claimed it was equal to 8½ Stromberg 97 carburetors and that it was available for the small- and big-block Chevy and small-block Ford. The dual-quad was a gamble, but when NHRA introduced a new class of drag racers called Modified Production, the situation changed. Most of the cars running the class were 1955-57 Chevrolets and Corvettes that required a high feed, high-performance manifold. The Edelbrock dual-quad was the answer. Orders for the dual-quad came in from all over the country, supply fell short of demand, and for the first time

Relenting to serious pressure from Bob Joehnck, Vic Jr. developed the company's first single 4-barrel manifold for the Chevy small-block, called the C-4B, above. In preserving the traditions of his father, the X-C8 Cross-Ram came from Vic Sr.'s Ram Log six-carburetor model of the 1950s.

"I had hung out with Bobby, Fran and Don Towle for years. And had become part of the tradition at the shop of sitting around in Vic Sr.'s office at day's end, having a couple of shooters of VO and bench racing. One thing always stuck in my mind about those days, and that was how serious Vic Sr. was about his work. He could look at the big picture and see his business from many angles. He was very involved in midget racing at the time, but he still managed to devote a large number of hours to helping me build my De Soto Hemi for Bonneville. In fact, he knew the days of the flathead were numbered and he wanted to expand his knowledge of what was new." —**Don Waite**

in the company's history they had a backorder problem. A speed shop in central New Jersey ordered 200 manifolds, then Honest Charlie Card in Chattanooga, Tennessee, who had one of the most famous catalogs in the business, ordered 200 more. Just a few years earlier an order for 20 manifolds was cause to break out the champagne. It wasn't just the company that was growing. On December 17, 1965, Carey Beth arrived, to increase the Edelbrock daughter inventory.

The speed equipment market was expanding in all directions. Young speed shop entrepreneurs began selling aggressively and giving discounts as volume exploded. Edelbrock's Hi-Riser single quad and the dual quad manifolds were selling well and the small-block Chevy was providing a solid base for much of the product line. Great as all this seemed, the company was about to crest a hill and begin a long, straight, flat-out run.

Packaging Performance

Located in Hayward, California, Vic Hubbard's Speed & Marine shop had been one of the first speed shops to carry Edelbrock equipment. By the mid 1960s, they were locked in a fierce battle with other West Coast shops for sales supremacy. Among the leaders were San Francisco–based Champion Speed Shop, Mickey Thompson's shop in Long Beach, legendary Blair's Auto Parts in Pasadena, and Ansen Auto Engineering in Los Angeles. Drag racing was now a solid motor sports segment and all the speed shops either raced or sponsored cars running every weekend up and down the California landscape. Nitromethane was the main reason speeds climbed

After taking over the business, Vic Edelbrock Jr. enjoyed the support of both friends and family as he struggled to direct the future of the company. His family was his inspiration. Nancy below center, did an incredible job raising (from left) Camee, Carey, and Christi. Below right, the girls (from left) Camee, Christi, and Carey returned the love of their parents by wanting to spend their fun times with mom and dad.

Vic Jr. absorbed much from Tennessee's Charley Card. Honest Charley was one of the first to take advantage of mail order, and worked with one of the very first computer systems in the country to reach customers with his catalog (below).

HONEST CHARLEY SPEED SHOP
Box HR 1904, Chattanooga, Tenn.
Sorry No C.O.D.'s without deposit.

weekly. Dragsters were kicking down records every week and fuel dragsters easily powered through the quarter mile in excess of 200 miles per hour.

For the speed shops, the adage "Win on Sunday, sell on Monday" never rang truer. Everyone wanted a bigger piece of the sales pie, and it took a sharp mind to outsmart the competition. The scales were about to be tipped when two Holley carburetor reps paid a friendly vendor visit up in Hayward. Jerry Light had taken over the Vic Hubbard machine shop back when the flathead was still king. A loyal Edelbrock dealer for many years, Light considered the Edelbrocks friends as well as business associates. When San Francisco area Holley sales rep George Bay dropped in on Jerry with Holley Technician Les Gough, it was more than a typical business call. Although Holley was strictly an OEM aftermarket manufacturer, the guys in the field were gearheads with lots of new ideas. Light called Edelbrock with a proposal of testing Holley carburetors with Edelbrock manifolds. Vic Jr. invited the trio down to Los Angeles and Light felt so strongly about the idea that he overcame his fear of flying and boarded an airplane for the first time to make the one-hour flight.

They brought with them a mixed bag of carburetors so Edelbrock could run tests on the company dyno. Included were a couple of #3310 units used on the first 396 cubic-inch big-blocks for the Chevrolet Chevelle SS; the #1850, #1849, and #2818 used on Fords; a three-barrel Chrysler 1000 CFM carb once used at Daytona, and a carburetor designed for the Edsel. Sizes ranged from 500 cfm to the Daytona monster. Ten test combinations were performed with the new Edelbrock C-4B single four-barrel and the dual-quad X-C8 ram log manifold version. Meeks and Joehnck helped Vic run the tests on a blueprinted 327 cubic-inch shop engine hooked to a Clayton dynamometer. *Hot Rod* magazine's tech editor caught wind of the experiment and sent staff member Jim McFarland and photographer Eric Rickman to cover the story during the tests.

The results were incredible and the story groundbreaking. The Edelbrock/Holley saga hit the pages of *Hot Rod* in February 1966 revealing that the

Dyno Room Stories: Firefighters

The story most embraced by the younger members of the dyno room crew—Curt Hooker and Robert Jung—and avoided by the senior members is known simply as the Shoot-out.

The new young guns of the dyno room, Curt Hooker (standing) and Robert Jung, love the stories from the early days, but feel the pressures of today's highly technical demands.

It involved Bobby Meeks and Murray Jensen. It was a hectic day in midsummer with temperature readings over a hundred degrees with temperaments about the same. The crew was running a small-block Chevy, equipped with the Edelbrock Tunnel Ram with two carburetors. During one of the runs the engine backfired, creating a large fireball. Murray, who was on the throttle at the time, grabbed a wall-mounted fire extinguisher and ran headlong into the dyno cell. At the same instant, Bobby Meeks uncorked a second extinguisher and charged into the cell from the back door. Without hesitation or thought, both men fired at the engine, missing by a foot or two and discharged the two extinguishers into each other's faces. In the meantime, the fire had blown itself out. Bobby and Murray, faces covered with foam, just glared. A muffled laugh could be heard throughout the shop.

The AMC manifold, below, used in the Trans Am racing series, was a new innovation. The company's blower manifold, bottom, was created for the hard core racers like Mickey Thompson, below left.

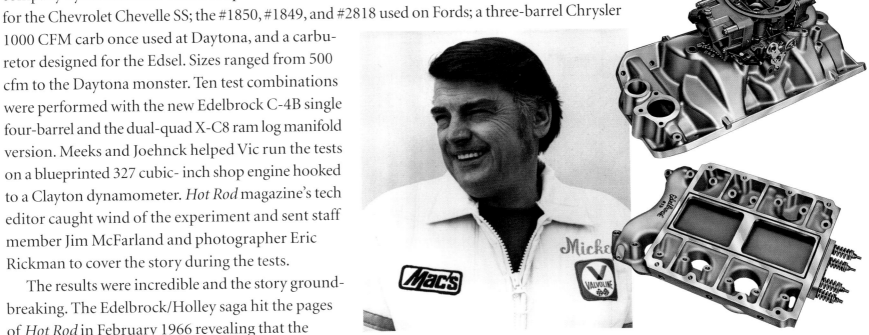

In the early 1970s Vic Edelbrock Jr. joined forces with Holley/Colt Industries. The two companies began packaging and combining sales under the Edelbrock + Holley= Performance logo. Edelbrock manifolds like C-3BX, above, and Holley carburetors were marketed as a package. The concept was revealed at a NHRA forum, top left, by an Edelbrock panel consisting of (left to right) Jim McFarland, Murray Jensen, Bobby Meeks and Vic Jr. Top right, Murray Jensen (right) explains the Edelbrock/Holley program at a seminar at the NHRA Nationals at Indy.

#3310 on a C-4B single four-barrel was the performance package to beat all. The #3310 was installed on 200 of the 396 cubic-inch Chevelles and Holley had only 200 more forecast for the following year.

Vic Jr. remembers what happened when the Holley story was published. "When McFarland's article hit the newsstands, the racers went wild and interest in the combinations sent Holley into a panic. Nancy and I were about to leave for the AAMA (Automotive Aftermarket Manufacturing Association) show in New York when I got a call from Stan Jurseck, the National Sales Manager for Holley, who told me that I better get my butt up to Holley Headquarters in Warren, Michigan, after my show. The next thing I knew I was standing at attention in Stan's office and he said, 'What the hell do you think you are doing with this story in *Hot Rod*? We only scheduled two hundred #3310s for the entire year and we got orders for 200 in an hour and half.' I started laughing and shaking my head, thinking, what is wrong with this picture. We were selling their carburetors faster than they can make them and they were complaining. I was about to hit the road back to California when Holley President Bob Burns got into the picture, and we struck an agreement to begin selling Holley carburetors and Edelbrock manifolds as a package. Ralph Johnson, a brilliant Holley engineer, was sent to our shop and began creating a line of high-performance carburetors with our crew. *Hot Rod* wrote more follow-up stories and soon the Holley/Edelbrock blend took hold. We even shared a full page ad in Hot Rod with the tag line 'Edelbrock + Holley=Performance Plus.' We had arrived at a crossroads."

Vic Jr. saw the package idea as a sure-fire way of increasing sales and profit, and wanted very much to expand on it. He provided his customers the opportunity to order Iskenderian cams, Hedman headers, Hurst shifters, Spaulding ignitions, Schiefer flywheels and clutches, Holley carburetors—parts that worked well with Edelbrock manifolds. Edelbrock Equipment was essentially now assuming the role of a warehouse distributor so speed shops could purchase most of their inventory in one order at Edelbrock. Vic Jr. had simply amplified an idea that his dad had toyed with after World War II.

Packaging in the performance industry was still a relatively new idea in the late 1960s. Nevertheless, Vic Jr. was convinced that it was the future, and the man he admired as a practitioner of this new form of salesmanship was Charley Card, a performance industry guru from Chattanooga, Tennessee. His catalog filled with homespun humor, "Honest Charley" was a pioneer in mail order and catalog promotion. Charley got his nickname when he owned a coffee shop. He operated it alone, using the honor system, allowing customers to pay their own bills and make change from the cash box on the counter. He later built his image around the nickname. He was one of the first to use an IBM computer to run billing invoices. He and his wife, Grace, would always wear white jumpsuits at conventions emblazoned with the names "Honest Charley Hisself" and "Grace Herself." Charley's philosophy was, "Never go anywhere without your name showing."

Another promotional tactic of Charley's was to attend a race like the Indy 500 or the NHRA Nationals and pass out cards offering a free catalog. When the coded card was mailed back to Chattanooga, he could measure how successful each event's promotion had been. He promoted discount prices that made others in the performance industry upset. Vic Jr. felt that Charley Card helped make the performance industry what it is today.

Murray Jensen had left Vic Edelbrock Sr.'s employ in 1957, and after that, dropped in only occasionally for a visit. When his service station partnership dissolved in 1968 he decided to get his teaching credentials at UCLA. On the way to the exam that was required for his credentials, Jensen stopped by the new location on Coral Circle in El Segundo. "They were in the process of moving, and Bobby Meeks told me, 'You're not going back to school, you're going to work. Grab an apron

Dyno Room Stories: the Do-It-Yourself Racer

The dyno room has been home for traveling race teams, and both stock car and drag racing engine builders have spent many hours testing race engines there. But when racers have time on their hands, things are going to happen. Back in the 1970s most of the top NASCAR teams would filter by the Edelbrock dyno when they were on tour in California. One of their favorite tricks was to run a race engine up high on the rpm range, set the throttle, and tell the Edelbrock crew it was time for lunch, leaving the engine running wide open while they went out for burgers. The reasoning? They claimed that since the engine would be running flat out for 500 miles, it could run at least 30 minutes through lunchtime. The great Benny Parsons and legendary engine builder Waddell Wilson would put an engine on the dyno, let it run full-throttle, and institute a joke-telling contest.

One-time crew chief for Benny Parsons, the great engine man Waddell Wilson was a regular at the Edelbrock dyno room.

But the famous weren't the only ones who came by. Curt Hooker remembers a first-time customer who wanted to buy some dyno time. The customer had purchased some Edelbrock equipment and wanted to test the engine that he had built himself. The engine was a big block Chevy constructed for use as an all-out racing power plant. Hooker and crew suggested that they be allowed to check the engine and run through their usual list of tests before putting it under a load. It was customary to check as many clearances and settings as possible, even removing heads and pan, to ensure that all was well. At this suggestion the customer flew into a rage, claiming his engine didn't need any checking. "Just run it!" he demanded. On the first test, as the engine reached maximum rpm and load, it exploded all over the dyno room, with parts, pieces, and oil painting the walls. The customer never uttered a single word, just cleaned up the mess and left the building.

"Back then, Hubbard Speed and Marine did a lot of sales and machine work on regular stock automobiles. Their speed equipment and racing division was a separate division. Jerry Light was an innovator, much like Vic Sr., and he was always looking for more parts and better parts to sell to his customers, especially drag racers, street rodders, and marine engine builders." —Mike Rao

The late Murray Jensen began his career with Vic Edelbrock Sr., then left for a number of years and returned to the company after Vic Jr. had taken over control. Murray's great love was the strange world of air and fuel. He was a master of the carburetor. Jensen, above, became so expert at carburetor tuning that his services were in demand by NASCAR teams from Daytona to Riverside. Murray was friends with drivers like the late Dale Earnhardt Sr., Benny Parsons, Richard Petty, and others. Above right, if any single factor played large in the success of the company during the turbulent 70s it was the tremendous effort by Vic and Nancy. Together they worked in the field covering races, going to industry shows and visiting dealers.

and go see Vic.' He hired me on the spot to test and build engines." Jensen would later make his mark as one of the most famous carburetor experts in the racing world, and in 1972, take the name Edelbrock into NASCAR, after the sanctioning body permitted aftermarket manifolds on stock car engines. With Jensen back in the Edelbrock clan, new product development was stepped up and became a top priority in the late 1960s. Bench racing remained the birthing ground for new ideas, just as Vic Sr. had done in the 1940s. When the guys would gather in the shop at the end of the day, ideas would pour out with the help of a little Canadian whiskey. The computer had not yet taken over and bench racing was still the pathway to discovery.

As the decade drew to a close, Vic Jr.'s reputation as a businessman was rising. While the flat-head inventory faded away, the new boss was fulfilling his vision of a marketing strategy to aggressively develop and buy larger ad spaces with greater frequency in automotive enthusiast magazines. Kal Peskind, the man behind an innovative advertising campaign for Iskenderian Racing Cams, became part of this strategy. "Kal and I began to develop new ads and a new logo, the one we still use today. He was a brilliant, creative guy, and he would churn out promotional materials, ads, and magazine articles, but I would always have to go to his house." Unfortunately, Peskind had suffered a nervous breakdown just before he agreed to take on the Edelbrock account, and when he recovered he became a recluse, working out of a studio behind his house.

"Carl Schiefer came into my office one day and said, 'Vic, you got to get your ass out of your cocoon on Jefferson Boulevard and start attending the national drag races, seeing your warehouse distributors firsthand, and begin hitting every trade show and meet every dealer you can.' I took his advice." —**Vic Edelbrock Jr.**

Vic Jr. was willing to do all the footwork. "He worked for us for ten years and I can't remember him ever coming to the building. If I had a check for $10,000 to pay ad billings, he would say, 'send someone over with it' and that would be that."

Vic Edelbrock Jr. is by nature a shy person. When he took over the company he had no choice but to get out of his office and beat the drum for his products. When SEMA put on an industry show, Vic bought a display booth, far left. Vic (seated, with sports coat), sales manager Gene Arseneault (standing), and Nancy tout products. In the early 1970s, Nancy, left, talked up the new Tarantula manifold for the company.

Specialty Equipment Manufacturers Association (SEMA)

No amount of brilliant advertising could circumvent government regulatory agencies, and it was no secret that state and federal bodies were thinking about controlling automotive emissions. The Air Pollution Control Act had made everyone aware that air pollution was a problem. In Los Angeles, banning the use of outdoor incinerators didn't do much to alleviate the smog, but then Congress passed the 1970 Clean Air Act that set standards for stationary sources of pollution. In the distant future, mobile pollution sources would also be pinpointed. Aftermarket speed equipment manufacturers could be next on the government's list.

Since the days of the dry lakes speed equipment, pioneers had always been an independent and free-spirited group, each individual keeping his secrets to himself as long as he could. Bobby Meeks observed, "You couldn't let the other guy find out your secrets or they would steal your ideas in a heartbeat. Ed Winfield wouldn't let anyone in his shop." Now the growth of the industry brought with it new business problems and legal concerns: credit ratings, racing equipment approvals, safety issues, and more. Some form of organization was needed, and there was little in the way of clear-cut regulations or specifications for components.

Several factors brought organization to the blossoming industry. The subject of bad accounts had been addressed back

"We were cookin', the business was growing, my family was growing, and Edelbrock had regained its name as a leader in the market. We were into ski boat racing, drag racing, the salt flats, and just starting to experiment with the boys Down South. They still couldn't run aftermarket manifolds, but they were looking to the future. As for the life-style of the 1960s, we watched it on TV, or talked about the crazy happenings, bench racing after work over a cocktail. We didn't have time for anything but work. Nancy and I began to travel to shows, and to visit our dealers." —Vic Edelbrock Jr.

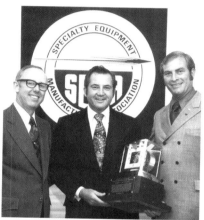

Above, Robert E. Petersen (center) was presented the "Man of the Year" Award from SEMA by its President Vic Edelbrock Jr. (right) for his support in helping the industry combat the new Emissions Regulations imposed by the government in the 1970s. National Transportation Safety Board head Doug Thoms (left) helped amalgamate laws that allowed the performance industry to continue. Vic Edelbrock Jr. served as SEMA President and Chairman for two terms beginning in 1971. He took the job very seriously and dedicated his efforts to promoting change in manufacturing practices and safety concerns. His duties included working with the members shown above right: (top row, left to right) Don Smith, Roy Richter, Hank Weldenhammer, Robert Carren and Vic Edelbrock Jr. (bottom row, left to right), Bob Spar, Dean Moon, Els Lohn, and Harry Weber.

in 1958 when Roy Richter, Els Lohn, Harry Weber, Fred Offenhauser, and several other manufacturers formed an organization called the Speed Equipment Manufacturers Credit Association. In the early 1960s the Revell Toy Company's vice president of public relations Henry Blankfort wanted to use manufacturers' logos on model cars and suggested that the equipment makers form an association. That way, Revell would be able to deal with many manufacturers by contacting only one source. The Specialty Equipment Manufacturers Association (SEMA) was created in 1963. The initial directors and officers included Roy Richter, Ed Iskenderian, Willie Garner, Bob Hedman, John Barlett, Phil Weiand Jr., Al Segal, Dean Moon, and Vic Edelbrock Jr.

Ed Elliott was the first staff member in Los Angeles and Ed Iskenderian was the first elected president. That year they served nearly forty charter company members, and others in the industry were soon to follow. In the future, SEMA would defend the industry against regulations stemming from the Pollution Control Board, and address safety issues in drag racing. Vic Edelbrock resigned from the board in the early '60s to devote his time to business when he believed the fledgling organization was no more than a social group, but later told president Willie Garner, "If you ever need my help just ask and I'll come running." Vic later changed his feelings. Within a couple of months Garner called. "Vic," he said, "there's this fellow named Eric Grant and he is running something called the California Air Resources board and he

"Nancy worked very hard, helping me and taking care of the girls, she stood up to all the pressure and never complained once, no matter how difficult the task." —Vic Edelbrock Jr.

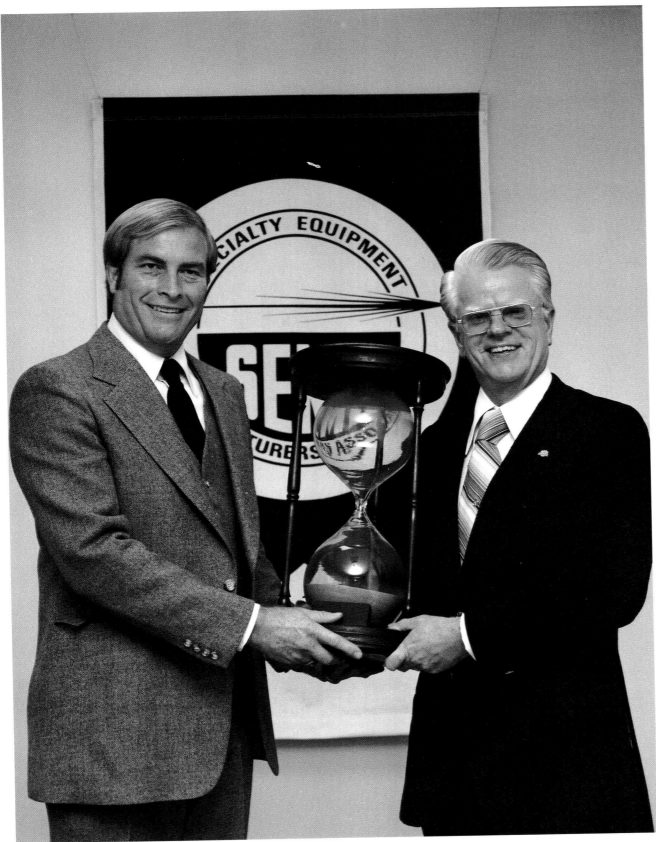

(Left) Honoring a great pioneer of the speed equipment industry, Vic Edelbrock Jr. presents Roy Richter the "Person of the Year" award at the annual SEMA banquet. Richter took over ownership of Bell Auto Parts, considered by many the first speed shop, when its founder George Wight passed away. Richter also continued manufacturing parts under the name Cragar, which became an industry giant. Richter played a very important part in the SEMA organization according to their records, he joined Els Lohn, Harry Weber and several others to discuss what to do about "deadbeat" customers. From that very first meeting, the SEMA organization was formed. Roy was also part of meetings with Revell Toy Company when they wanted to use manufacturers' logo decals on their model kits. From that point, Richter was a leader in creating a national trade show so SEMA members could show off their new products. Vic Edelbrock Jr. served with Roy Richter as one of the original directors of SEMA along with Willie Garner, Bob Hedman, John Bartlett, Phil Weiand Jr., Al Segal and Dean Moon. Richter and Vic Jr. shared many of the same goals for SEMA. Vic received his share of honors for his two terms in office including induction into the Hall of Fame in 1989.

Above, with Camee behind the wheel of the family Stevens ski boat, the Edelbrock women enjoy a day on the water without dad. Christi rides behind Camee and Carey. Right, Vic takes delivery of his first airplane, a Cessna 206, in 1967.

tells me that if we don't get our act together we're going to be in trouble." Vic Jr. was once again deeply involved at SEMA.

Moving to a New Era

Meanwhile, Vic had a major problem closer to home. The company was growing too fast and the Jefferson Boulevard location was becoming cramped. He knew the problem was critical, but because his mother still owned the property and a large portion of her income came from the rent, the idea of moving the company was a touchy one. Moreover, she enjoyed being a part of the company that she and Vic Sr. had built. Katie also feared that moving would throw the company into a tailspin because it would mean borrowing money. But something had to be done about the lack of space. Vic investigated an expansion of the Jefferson Boulevard facility and plans were drawn that included the construction of a second floor and expansion of the shop. When submitted to the City of Los Angeles Planning Commission, the red tape of big city politics that followed was an infuriating experience that eventually drove the Edelbrock Equipment Company out of the city.

The new location was found by chance late in 1967, just before Vic earned his pilot's license and placed an order for a new Cessna 206. A few weeks after deciding not to build within Los Angeles, Vic was notified that his plane was ready to be picked up. Just before he and old friend Tom Carstens left to transport the 206 back to California, a tornado hit the Cessna plant and caused severe damage. Vic's plane had been spared, but the company advised him to postpone the trip. With his appointments already cancelled, Vic could easily slip out and go property hunting. He hopped into the company truck, leaving his personal car parked in its usual location. "To this day, I can't explain the feeling I got leaving the shop. Something was pushing me and I ended up on the San Diego Freeway. As I went past the Los Angeles Airport I saw a sign for El Segundo Boulevard and something made

The move to Coral Circle, above left, in 1968, was a much needed expansion for Edelbrock. Shown under construction, above, the 20,00 square foot building became home for the company, providing space for offices, inventory and a state-of-the-art testing facility.

me take that exit ramp. The truck was leading me along and after I turned on Douglas Street there was a sign, 'Property for Sale,' complete with phone number and location map."

The lots offered were owned by a subsidiary of Standard Oil Corporation. Edelbrock followed the map on the sign, drove down to Coral Circle, and discovered a nice, flat piece of ground that would be easy to grade. After much negotiation, a parcel slightly over one acre was settled upon for $2.00 a square foot. "I concluded that the lot would be perfect and made a tentative agreement pending my mother's approval, but when I informed her of my plans she went through the roof. Afraid that she would not be able to rent the Jefferson building, Mom didn't want me to leave her in the cold. 'What kind of son would leave his mother without an income?' she told me."

Katie Edelbrock had met a man named Bob Higgins and the two planned to marry. Higgins had worked as a designer of interiors of high-rise buildings, and had spent many years in the construction business. This proved to be a saving grace for the business, son, and mother. "Although Bob and Mom were not yet married," noted Vic, "he was a big influence in her life. Bob quizzed me in front of Mom about the new property, building costs, and how long did I think it would take to pay off the loan. I answered, two to three years, but had no idea. He agreed that it was a sound idea and calmed Mom into submission."

They agreed that a tenant for the Jefferson building would be found before the company moved or else Edelbrock Equipment would continue to pay Katie until the building was filled. The new property was purchased and old friend and contractor Mike Toll agreed to start building without delay. By the end of 1968, Edelbrock Equipment Company had a new home at 411 Coral Circle, El Segundo, California. The 20,000 square feet provided enough space for inventory and offices, the balancing service would be under the same roof, the machine shop was enlarged, a polishing room added, and a state-of-the-art dyno facility was created.

With the 1970s came the battle to save the air and the performance industry. Vic Edelbrock Jr. would lead the crusade.

6 Winds of Change

The sixties will forever be known as the "muscle car" era, when automakers embraced the performance market and filled the showrooms with street machines that delivered up to 400 horsepower. The cars were ideal for enthusiasts or "gearheads" who enjoyed personalizing their rides by making them faster or better looking. The aftermarket industry answered the call by offering products for all makes and models. Automakers played the horsepower card to the limit. Customers could walk into a showroom and buy a twelve-second quarter-mile rocket from a list that was mind-blowing. Dealers offered cars like Chrysler's 426 Hemi and the 440 Six Pack. General Motors sold Z-28s, 460 horsepower Corvettes, Pontiac GTOs, Olds 4-4-2s, and big-block engines could be paired with lightweight bodies by special order. Ford gave Mustang customers a choice of eleven different powertrain combinations in 1969; these included the 290-hp Boss 302 and the 375-hp Boss 429. Even American Motors went along for the ride with the customized SS/AMX and the ram-air powered Hurst S/C Scrambler. Three two-barrel or two four-barrel carburetors were often standard issue.

The horsepower party would not last long in the 1970s. The performance industry, Detroit factories, and everyday hot rodders would soon be dealing with emission restrictions, gasoline rationing, and reduced speed limits. "I Can't Drive 55!" bumper stickers would appear across America. Rumors about "anti-tampering" laws raised even more concerns. The world of the performance enthusiast looked bleak as the government cracked down. Random roadside inspections of smog control devices started in California in 1966, and more emissions-related laws would follow. Now labeled as "gas guzzlers", the street machines of the '60s became the subject of heated debates.

One fact was clear, the performance industry would need to make a few changes. Vic Edelbrock believed that the best defense is a good offense. Armed with the courageous spirit of his father and a university degree, Vic Jr. met the challenges head on. He had succeeded in overcoming the

The late '60s and early '70s were both an exciting time and a period of change for the performance industry. On the wild side, American Motors, above, had a fling at the horsepower craze causing Ford and GM to show concern. On the down side, emissions control and the gas crunch would create new challenges. Jim McFarland, above right, came to work at Edelbrock in the late '60s, and helped put the company ahead of the curve on emissions programs.

shock of losing his father and prevailed against inexperience and industry gossip that claimed he was a spoiled playboy out to squander his father's money. Those trying to undermine Vic Jr. must have been unaware of the fact that he was a family man with three daughters and a wife as strong-willed as himself. This team would prove tough to beat, even with the decade that lay ahead.

Vic knew that a strong work force was key. After three years at *Hot Rod* magazine and a brief time at Schiefer Manufacturing, Jim McFarland came to work at Edelbrock in 1969. Texas-born McFarland would wear many hats, including overseeing the development of new products, advertising, promotion, and magazine editorial coverage. He was a very influential figure in dealing with the government and its policies concerning emission-control regulations. That same year, Curt Hooker came to Edelbrock as a car-crazed high school student, and was assigned the same chores that Vic Jr. had done. Curt recalls, "I was scared stiff of Vic when I first went to work, but he treated me the same as all the guys. I swept floors, cleaned restrooms, washed his car, and filled his mom's car with gas." Eventually, Curt worked his way to the dyno room under the strict apprenticeship of Bobby Meeks and Murray Jensen. The late 1960s brought Carl Schiefer, a brilliant public relations person and son of Paul Schiefer, owner of Schiefer Manufacturing. Carl had many innovative ideas that included the Edelbrock/Hang Ten sportswear line in the mid-1970s. Ralph Guldahl Jr., son of a U.S. Open golf legend, joined the team in 1973, and helped to set up Edelbrock's first in-house advertising agency.

"When Vic would tell me to sweep the shop floor, I would always sweep toward the dyno room and the engine shop. It was my ultimate goal, that's where I wanted to be. I would be sweeping, and watching all of the famous drag racers running their engines and telling stories. But I had to prove myself before the guys would let me near the place. I did every job Vic would give me. I put instruction sheets in manifold boxes and put installation kits together, anything that had to be done. Finally, after saving all my money, I built a drag race car of my own, and once the guys saw that I was learning on my own and how bad I wanted to do the job right, they started helping me. Bobby, Murray, and Don all helped me, and then Vic told me to put down the broom and get a haircut, and start helping in the dyno room." —**Curt Hooker**

Since the days when Vic Sr. called Bobby Meeks, Don Towle, Murray Jensen and Fran Hernandez his key employees, there has been an unspoken rule to carry the company name into the racing world. Employees not only work for the company they are the company. Left, the late Murray Jensen was a larger than life figure in the world of NASCAR racing and he passed the tradition along to the next generation, Curt Hooker (right) who built all of Vic Jr.'s ski boat engines along with other engines for the dyno department. Ralph Guladahl Jr., below left, (with Edelbrock hat) worked for the company as a PR director for many years and now oversees Edelbrock car collection. The Wally Award being held by Ralph and presented by Wally Parks (right) made him a member of the NHRA Hall of Fame.

There were times when business in the high performance market was slow and for a young man taking over a company from his dad, Vic Jr. had to face many obstacles to keep the business afloat. One solid source of income was the balancing shop, where the crew balanced everything from automotive parts to farm equipment and aircraft pieces. Bob Fleckenstein ran the balance shop for a long period and produced much revenue for the company. Bob (center) is shown with a couple of customers and a box of aircraft parts.

As the old ways changed to match the times of the 1970s, the company's foundation still rested in the hands of familiar names. Don Towle was head of manufacturing with a young Wayne Murray as apprentice. Bobby Meeks handled product development along with Edelbrock's drag racing customers. Bob Bradford took care of tooling, and Murray Jensen returned in 1968 after a ten-year absence. Don's son, John Towle, who came to work after school in the Jefferson days to sweep floors, eventually took charge of the sales department. Many others played important roles in the Edelbrock story, including Gene Arseneault and Bill "Super Sales" Smith as head of sales, Bob "Bobbo" Fleckenstein in balancing and later in the tech department, ex-sprint car driver Lee Leonard, Ted Frye, Don McCain, and Jerry Mallicoat.

Vic Jr. was expanding the company in all directions and part of this strategy included improving the company's capabilities. At 20,000 square feet, the new Coral Circle building gave every department room to grow. A specially-built dynamometer room was part of the new construction. It was home for a state-of-the-art Heenan & Froude GE-490 EH dynamometer capable of handling up to 1000 horsepower with an operating range up to 14,000 rpm. This addition put Edelbrock a big step ahead of other manufacturers. A flow bench was also installed for measuring flow capacity of cylinder head ports and manifold runners. First developed by Carl "Ax" Axtell, Edelbrock was the first aftermarket manufacturer to use the machine for testing automotive parts. Originally, Axtell put together his flow bench to test motorcycle heads on engines he built for racing in the early '60s. Ax admired Vic Sr's work and later became close friends with Bobby Meeks

Moving the company to the Coral Circle location provided the room to increase production. Vic Edelbrock Jr., left, wanted to express his ideas through a new line of manifolds, but there were hurdles to overcome. The state of California and the federal government threatened to put an end to the performance industry. Edelbrock came up with ways to increase business in these tough times, including developing manifolds that gave better mileage and lower emissions, Below, Bill "Grumpy" Jenkins (second from left) was one of the many winning racers who came to Edelbrock to run tests using their state-of-the-art dyno facilities in El Segundo with the team of Jim McFarland (left), Murray Jensen (right) and Curt Hooker (third from right).

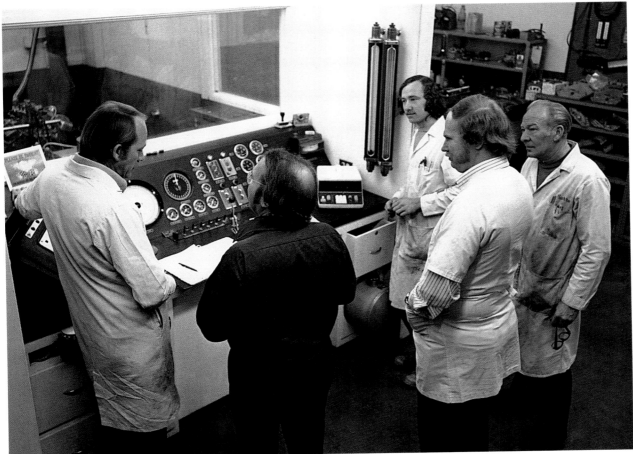

Top left, Edelbrock was the first in the automotive aftermarket to use a flow bench to test prototypes. The tests on manifold designs were so tough that many thought it was overkill. Here, Gene Thompson at the flow bench tests a new design. Carroll Caudle, above, and his Modified Production '55 Chevy, top right, were a hot combination. Caudle had taken a late '50s Chevy fuel-injection manifold and fabricated it to accommodate two four-barrel carburetors in a row, not opposed like the Edelbrock dual quad Ram Log. Vic changed the design slightly and developed a Tunnel Ram from Caudle's design.

and Don Towle. Even though Ax was a very reclusive man who never gave away his secrets, he took a shine to the Edelbrock crew because he believed they were the real thing. He knew the score and appreciated the fact that they did not, as Ax puts it, "bullshit like other engine guys of the times." The flow bench was soon adopted by all engine builders and parts designers as an essential testing tool.

The street performance outlook may have been bleak due to the government intervention, but the racing market was going gangbusters. When the 1969 Edelbrock catalog hit the market, the choices for racers were many. The two-plane 180-degree manifold was joined by the single-quad Hi-Riser, dual-quad, triple-carb, and the new Tunnel Ram. Glowing testimonials included in the catalog came from many hard-running racers, including Dyno Don Nicholson, Bill "Grumpy" Jenkins, John Peters, Paul Blevins, Bo Laws, the Sox and Martin team, Dick Arons, Dick Landy, Joe Sherman, and the fuel dragster of Ed Pink.

At the 1970 NHRA Winston World Finals in Tulsa, Oklahoma, Vic and Nancy were intent on talking to as many racers as possible. After the races, Edelbrock and a group of manufacturers that included Schiefer Manufacturing, Lakewood Industries, and Milodon Engineering hosted a cocktail party with an open bar. Most of the top racers came to bench race and watch some of the big hitters flip quarters for hundred dollar bills. It was here that Vic learned about a new manifold design that Carroll Caudle was testing on his '55 Chevy.

With one of the hottest cars in Modified Production, Caudle was an NHRA record holder and Street Eliminator champion with his own engine-building business. He had taken a late-fifties Chevy fuel-injection manifold, cut off the top, then fabricated a flange and mounted two four-barrels in a row—not opposed like the Edelbrock dual-quad ram log. The engine produced horsepower at higher rpm and would rev to higher rpm.

An NHRA record holder and Street Eliminator champion, Caudle had an engine building business in Texas. He had taken a late 1950s Chevy fuel injection manifold, cut the top off, fabricated a flange and mounted two four barrels in a row—not opposed like the Edelbrock dual-quad log ram. The manifold made horsepower at the top and the bottom ends of the power band.

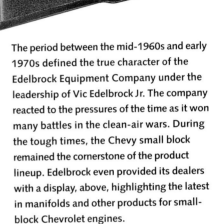

Edelbrock

THE MOST RESPECTED NAME IN HI-PERFORMANCE EQUIPMENT

AUTOMOTIVE ● MARINE ● DRAGS

SPORTS CARS ● STOCK CAR RACING

HI-RISE MANIFOLDS ● CARBURETORS

TUNNEL RAM, RAM LOG MANIFOLDS

VALVE COVERS ● MOTOR MOUNTS

LINKAGE KITS ● FUEL BLOCK KITS

✳ ✳ ✳

1969 CATALOG

The period between the mid-1960s and early 1970s defined the true character of the Edelbrock Equipment Company under the leadership of Vic Edelbrock Jr. The company reacted to the pressures of the time as it won many battles in the clean-air wars. During the tough times, the Chevy small block remained the cornerstone of the product lineup. Edelbrock even provided its dealers with a display, above, highlighting the latest in manifolds and other products for small-block Chevrolet engines.

Edelbrock and the NHRA—Pioneers in Horsepower

The relationship between the NHRA, Wally Parks, and the Edelbrock Equipment company goes back to the very beginning of the industry. Vic Sr. and Wally Parks were part of the dry-lake racing club called Road Runners and great friends. When Vic Jr. took over, the bond stayed strong. Clockwise from above, Bobby Meeks (left) receives a special award from Wally Parks, acknowledging Edelbrock for its sponsorship of NHRA events. Bobby Meeks laughs with Bob Glidden and wife Etta (with hats) after another victory using Edelbrock products—Glidden was one of the best Pro Stock competitors in NHRA history. Bobby Meeks (left) offers a handshake to a young "Dandy" Dick Landy after another victory. The highlight of NHRA's/Winston World Finals is the golf tournament—striking a pose: (left to right) a Winston official, Ralph Guldahl Jr., Miss Winston, Bobby Meeks, and Vic. *Opposite:* Clockwise from top left, Bill "Grumpy" Jenkins gets a " job well done" pat on the back from Bobby Meeks. "Dyno" Don Nicholson was one of the top Pro Stock drivers throughout the '70s. Fun-loving Wally Booth, who drove this AMC Gremlin, was one of the Edelbrock crew's favorite racers. The fantastic Freight Train of John Peters, which used Edelbrock manifolds.

Thanks for
all your help
The Freight Train
John Peters

Motorsports

Evolution in the world of motor sports during the 1970s matched the trends developing in the nation. There were great gains, new trends, spectacular beginnings, and appalling conclusions. The greatest spectacle in racing, the Indianapolis 500, was dominated by '63 winner Parnelli Jones and partner Vel Miletich, who together with driver Al Unser Sr. won in 1970 and 1971, driving the Johnny Lightning car. The team came close again in 1972, with Unser finishing second behind Mark Donohue, and Unser's teammate, Joe Leonard, taking third. In 1970, Ontario Motor Speedway opened in Ontario, California. The state-of-the-art two and a half-mile superspeedway could host Indy and NASCAR events, and it featured an infield road course and drag strip. The big crowds and major motor sports events never materialized, and after a decade it fell victim to financial strains due to taxes, unemployment, and the oil embargo.

Drag racing took a turn for the better in 1971, when Don Garlits brought the rear-engine dragster design to the mainstream and proved this was safer and faster than the old front-motor cars. By mid-decade, most fuel dragsters were rear-engine models. Funny Cars and Pro Stock cars became top draws at NHRA National events. Great cars now came from all over the country. Speeds increased and times decreased. By the end of the decade, fuel dragsters would run over 250 mph with elapsed times in the five-second range.

Over in road racing, the Can-Am series hit its peak during the 1970s. The unlimited sports cars drew big crowds at Riverside, Watkins Glen, Laguna Seca, and Elkhart Lake. The appeal was screaming thunder from gargantuan power plants, and aerodynamic body packages sleek enough to allow these cars such speeds that, as they passed, fans could hear a wake of turbulence crack like a rifle shot.

A new form of racing was catching on in Southern California. In the mid-sixties a four-wheel enthusiast and auto dealer Brian Chuchua created "The National Four-Wheel Drive Grand Prix," a wild and crazy romp through the Santa Ana riverbed. By 1970 the event was being covered by national magazines and drawing big names. At the same

time, a white-haired florist and pioneer off-road devotee Ed Pearlman and a group of hard-core off-roaders had formed an organization called NORRA (National Off-Road Racing Association) and had begun racing in Baja California. The big draw turned out to be a contest to see who could get from Tijuana to La Paz the fastest. Off-road racing had arrived, and with it came movie stars like James Garner and Steve McQueen, and racers like Mickey Thompson, Parnelli Jones, and the Mears gang.

When enthusiasts see the Edelbrock logo they usually think of drag racing or street performance. Both are true but there has been much more to the name over the years. Top Fuel dragsters,

Mickey Thompson took over in the mid-1970s and NORRA became SCORE (Short Course Off-Road Events), and races were now staged in Nevada and Arizona deserts as well. Thompson started closed-course events and began running at Riverside International Raceway in front of paying spectators. Suddenly, performance parts manufacturers were selling speed equipment to stadium racers, and there was a gluttonous appetite for tough, Baja-proven aftermarket equipment. A cottage industry was born.

off-road machines and, bottom, even the Indy 500, when Dan Gurney used Edelbrock manifolds on his Eagle Chevrolet-powered racers.

Vic introduced himself to Carroll and asked about the new design. By the end of their conversation, Caudle had offered to send the manifold to Vic after the season ended. True to his word, the manifold arrived at Edelbrock and testing began. Meeks and Jensen began making changes, and what emerged was the Edelbrock TR-1 Tunnel Ram featuring individual runners joined to an enlarged plenum chamber, with each port passage going directly to an intake port.

Vic recalls, "We used two in-line Holley 660 cfm carburetors and our own casting for the base because we wanted to improve on the re-worked factory manifold that other racers were using. Carroll didn't agree with all of the changes we made and we had a falling out of sorts, but over the years we reconciled our differences." The TR-1 also had new round ports that were positioned about one and a half inches above the plenum floor. We made a few changes to the manifold after the first version, and the Edelbrock Tunnel Ram became a race-winning success.

Edelbrock-equipped cars were running hard and setting records in the early '70s, and the distinctive Edelbrock logo was gaining recognition. Vic and Nancy had been attending races since the late 1960s, but increased the schedule in 1970 on the advice of Carl Schiefer and "Honest Charlie" Card. Starting with the Winternationals in Pomona, California, Vic and Nancy Edelbrock, Bobby Meeks, Murray Jensen, and Carl Schiefer hit the drag race circuit to promote Edelbrock. There were very few tents available in those days, so Vic would rent a motor scooter and Nancy would hop on the back, her purse filled with tools, carburetor jets and other miscellaneous tune-up items. They spent the days rocketing through the pit area from racer to racer, answering questions and talking about product.

By the mid-1970s, Edelbrock had a tent and display tables to showcase their products. Nancy took on the role of keeping the racers in line while they were waiting for Vic. At summer events, their two oldest daughters helped by handing out decals and contingency forms to racers. When sponsors, local officials and VIP guests attended NHRA events, Wally Parks would ask Nancy to accompany the wives in their suite. Nancy's outstanding education combined with racing knowledge served the association well as she explained the fine points of drag racing and

Decals displayed by champion drivers meant that your product worked best. When Pro Stock racing became the rage, two of the most notable names ran Edelbrock products.

Bill "Grumpy" Jenkins, top left, and the team of Ronnie Sox and Buddy Martin, top right, carried Edelbrock signage. The Pro Stock drivers favored the Tunnel Ram, center. Before the Tunnel Ram, the Ram Log manifold was used, especially in modified production. Above, the colorful decal used for Ram Log manifold.

Above, "Working the races," is what Vic and Nancy called riding their scooter at the NHRA National events from team to team, talking up their products. Nancy carried a bag containing tools, carburetor jets, timing lights and decals. Above right, Vic and Nancy (center) receive an award for their support of the NHRA.

became the unofficial tour guide of NHRA. Nancy was earning her stripes as a woman figurehead in a male-dominated sport.

Vic and Nancy Edelbrock's number one priority was to "get the name out there." But Vic was reserved and had trouble breaking the ice with new racers. However, he felt comfortable when he could approach a racer and say, "Hey, you want to run a decal on your car?" If the answer was yes, he would whip out a mason jar filled with water, immerse the decal and then apply it to the car. He even carried a towel to wipe up the water. Soon, the familiar Edelbrock logo was everywhere.

The Tarantula

If any single issue haunted Edelbrock during the decade of the '70s, it was the introduction of the Tarantula manifold in 1971. It was a revolutionary design, but also the subject of a bitter legal battle. It all started with Warren Brownfield, the owner of a cylinder head business called Air Flow Research. Brownfield had conceived a radical new manifold design. While still developing his thoughts, he met with Edelbrock, who was interested in his idea.

Vic helped Brownfield move his business closer to the Coral Circle plant, and even invested in his cylinder head porting business. When Warren's porting business slowed, Vic offered Warren a position at the plant as an engineer and he began working with Jim McFarland on the rough concept of his manifold design. A prototype fiberglass-Devcon-aluminum manifold of Brownfield's single-plane design was created and tested. The prototype performance was lacking, so McFarland, Meeks, and Jensen

"One time a guy grabbed a Victor Jr. manifold off the display table and ducked out the back of our display tent. With myself and the girls yelling 'Stop!', we chased the culprit, but he got away. It was great fun. We then felt sorry for the person who would resort to stealing in order to race." —**Nancy Edelbrock**

Vic introduced himself to Carroll and asked about the new design. By the end of their conversation, Caudle had offered to send the manifold to Vic after the season ended. True to his word, the manifold arrived at Edelbrock and testing began. Meeks and Jensen began making changes, and what emerged was the Edelbrock TR-1 Tunnel Ram featuring individual runners joined to an enlarged plenum chamber, with each port passage going directly to an intake port.

Vic recalls, "We used two in-line Holley 660 cfm carburetors and our own casting for the base because we wanted to improve on the re-worked factory manifold that other racers were using. Carroll didn't agree with all of the changes we made and we had a falling out of sorts, but over the years we reconciled our differences." The TR-1 also had new round ports that were positioned about one and a half inches above the plenum floor. We made a few changes to the manifold after the first version, and the Edelbrock Tunnel Ram became a race-winning success.

Edelbrock-equipped cars were running hard and setting records in the early '70s, and the distinctive Edelbrock logo was gaining recognition. Vic and Nancy had been attending races since the late 1960s, but increased the schedule in 1970 on the advice of Carl Schiefer and "Honest Charlie" Card. Starting with the Winternationals in Pomona, California, Vic and Nancy Edelbrock, Bobby Meeks, Murray Jensen, and Carl Schiefer hit the drag race circuit to promote Edelbrock. There were very few tents available in those days, so Vic would rent a motor scooter and Nancy would hop on the back, her purse filled with tools, carburetor jets and other miscellaneous tune-up items. They spent the days rocketing through the pit area from racer to racer, answering questions and talking about product.

By the mid-1970s, Edelbrock had a tent and display tables to showcase their products. Nancy took on the role of keeping the racers in line while they were waiting for Vic. At summer events, their two oldest daughters helped by handing out decals and contingency forms to racers. When sponsors, local officials and VIP guests attended NHRA events, Wally Parks would ask Nancy to accompany the wives in their suite. Nancy's outstanding education combined with racing knowledge served the association well as she explained the fine points of drag racing and

Decals displayed by champion drivers meant that your product worked best. When Pro Stock racing became the rage, two of the most notable names ran Edelbrock products.

Bill "Grumpy" Jenkins, top left, and the team of Ronnie Sox and Buddy Martin, top right, carried Edelbrock signage. The Pro Stock drivers favored the Tunnel Ram, center. Before the Tunnel Ram, the Ram Log manifold was used, especially in modified production. Above, the colorful decal used for Ram Log manifold.

Above, "Working the races," is what Vic and Nancy called riding their scooter at the NHRA National events from team to team, talking up their products. Nancy carried a bag containing tools, carburetor jets, timing lights and decals. Above right, Vic and Nancy (center) receive an award for their support of the NHRA.

became the unofficial tour guide of NHRA. Nancy was earning her stripes as a woman figurehead in a male-dominated sport.

Vic and Nancy Edelbrock's number one priority was to "get the name out there." But Vic was reserved and had trouble breaking the ice with new racers. However, he felt comfortable when he could approach a racer and say, "Hey, you want to run a decal on your car?" If the answer was yes, he would whip out a mason jar filled with water, immerse the decal and then apply it to the car. He even carried a towel to wipe up the water. Soon, the familiar Edelbrock logo was everywhere.

The Tarantula

If any single issue haunted Edelbrock during the decade of the '70s, it was the introduction of the Tarantula manifold in 1971. It was a revolutionary design, but also the subject of a bitter legal battle. It all started with Warren Brownfield, the owner of a cylinder head business called Air Flow Research. Brownfield had conceived a radical new manifold design. While still developing his thoughts, he met with Edelbrock, who was interested in his idea.

Vic helped Brownfield move his business closer to the Coral Circle plant, and even invested in his cylinder head porting business. When Warren's porting business slowed, Vic offered Warren a position at the plant as an engineer and he began working with Jim McFarland on the rough concept of his manifold design. A prototype fiberglass-Devcon-aluminum manifold of Brownfield's single-plane design was created and tested. The prototype performance was lacking, so McFarland, Meeks, and Jensen

"One time a guy grabbed a Victor Jr. manifold off the display table and ducked out the back of our display tent. With myself and the girls yelling 'Stop!', we chased the culprit, but he got away. It was great fun. We then felt sorry for the person who would resort to stealing in order to race." —Nancy Edelbrock

The Smokey Yunick Connection

One of Vic Edelbrock Jr.'s most prized possessions is the famed 1969 Trans-Am Camaro built by the late Smokey Yunick, owner of Daytona Beach's The Best Damn Garage in Town. In the early 1970s, Edelbrock was making inroads with the good old boys Down South and eventually Vic and Yunick met up. Jim McFarland had written articles on Smokey, so they already had a friendly relationship.

Vic remembers that Yunick called McFarland, saying he had a manifold they should look at. Vic thought it was worth a look. "Smokey had a prototype and we ran tests on our small-block Chevy test engine, but couldn't get the thing to run good. We tried everything we could think of, but something was wrong. When I told Smokey, he went through the roof, saying in part, 'you sons of bitches don't know shit, and if you don't want the thing, I'll take it to Offenhauser, and they'll make it!' I told Smokey we'd work with him and build the manifold, but I wanted to put his name and phone number on the instruction sheet, so if there were any problems Smokey could answer them. He agreed, and we produced the Smokey Ram, a trick-looking piece with some very special features. It had laid-over ports, thus significantly reducing fuel/air temperatures and increasing mixture density. And, although the manifold had many features of the Chevy Trans-Am dual four-barrel cross ram, Smokey's manifold used a single four-barrel."

The 1972 Edelbrock catalog offered the Smokey Ram with a disclaimer that the manifold was intended only for the small-block Chevy race engine and not recommended for street use. About 500 Smokey Ram manifolds went flying out the shipping room doors in the first couple months. Shortly thereafter, the commotion started, and calls came in to Smokey's garage about problems with the manifold. Smokey complained to Vic: "Edelbrock, get my phone number out of that instruction sheet right now. Those people are driving me nuts."

As Vic must have anticipated, buyers ignored the "race only" label and ran the manifold on the street. When Vic quizzed Smokey about what he had done during his testing of the manifold, Yunick

admitted that he had designed a special set of headers, modified a Holley carburetor and Racer Brown had made a special cam. When all of Smokey's secrets were used the manifold worked like a charm. But Vic had to make a hard decision. "It was a great manifold, but its reputation with its earlier problems turned sales downward, and within a year, we dropped the Smokey Ram from the catalog. Smokey and I agreed to split the pattern costs, but he would pay half from his royalties on sales. After we dropped the manifold, Smokey wanted the patterns, but I wouldn't do that because his half of the pattern costs wasn't paid for. I offered to make the castings, letting him machine them and sell them under his name, no problem. He got very angry, started cussing, then

said he'd think it over and call me back. He never did. Later, in his book, he told his side and made me out to be a bad guy. Then a few years ago, at the PRI trade show, Smokey presented me an award for my dad's pioneer work in the industry saying many good things about Dad and me. I guess he got over the past."

Edelbrock built and sold "The Smokey Ram manifold" in a deal with famed race car builder Smokey Yunick. Smokey labeled the manifold "race only" and kept some of the performance set-up secrets to run the manifold off of the instruction sheet. Most buyers ignored the "race only" warning and ran the manifold on the street. As a result, the street engines didn't run well, and customers complained. The instructions were changed, but complaints were something Smokey didn't want to deal with. In the end, Smokey told Vic to "shove it" and the manifold was dropped after two years.

RESTRICTED AREA

In the old days, Vic Sr. would draw a manifold design on a sheet of paper, take it to Harvey Hartman, and the two would create a wooden pattern. By the 1970s, manifolds were designed a little differently. The C-3B Chevy manifold, top, and the Chrysler small-block, above, were created by engineers (pre-computer age) and although Hartman still created the patterns, fiberglass prototypes like the one for the Tarantula, above right, held by Bobby Meeks, were tested on the dyno before a final design went into production.

began working with Warren to change the original design and continue testing. Weeks later, McFarland discovered and corrected a problem that had been overlooked by everyone, including Brownfield, who disagreed with some of McFarland's changes. Afterward, the manifold reached its full potential and went into production. All this forged ahead without any formal business arrangement.

When Edelbrock introduced the Tarantula single-plane single-quad manifold, it was a breakthrough manifold that featured "twisted," or laid-over, runners that were based on flow capacity and not just geometry, resulting in a less restricted path from the carburetor to the cylinder head. In turn, the mixture velocity offered the high speed associated with race engine manifolds. The construction of the Tarantula's plenum chamber and the design of the ports and entries into the heads enabled the isolation of cylinders in firing, thereby obtaining very good torque characteristics. The low-end torque was not quite as good as a dual-plane manifold, but better than a dual-plane at high rpm.

"I really wanted Warren to work with us, I respected his ability very much," Vic Jr. said. "My mistake on the production of the TM-1 was that I never really nailed down a signed agreement on the rights and/or royalties concerning the design. Warren and I had talked about things, but nothing got signed. At the time, I was a little naive about the law and design rights. When the Tarantula went into production, Warren believed that he should be compensated for more than he and I had originally discussed because it had turned out to be such an innovative design. Warren felt that he was right in his demands. I felt that because we had made sufficient improvements to make the design work, the current arrangement was fair. Warren did not agree. Warren stormed off and retained an attorney."

Vic Jr. felt that the Edelbrock team's improvements on Warren's original idea essentially made it a new product. "I also felt that if we could not hold a patent on the part, then anybody could have copied the design once it was produced. We would be unprotected from other manufacturers taking this idea and making a manifold of similar design. However, when the proceedings began, I learned about a factor called trade secrets, and Warren's 'overlaid port design' fell into this category. My lawyer advised me to settle out of court. There was a judgment, and Warren received payments over a number of years. We moved on, began to produce the Tarantula, and it was a major turning point in our business, a lesson well-learned, and I would be more careful in the future."

In 1971, Edelbrock celebrated thirty-two years in the performance parts business. The blue-and-black catalog showed that a substantial number of customers were engaged in drag racing, and a growing list of endorsements was rolling in. The Single-Quad Hi-Riser manifold was now available for most popular engines, with the all-new C-3BX for the Chevy 307 and 350 small blocks leading the way. The big news was the introduction of the Tarantula single-plane TM-1 manifold. Still strong was the Tunnel Ram for racing—a new version appeared for Chevy small-blocks, the American Motors 290-343 and 390 cubic-inch engines, and for Chrysler's 273, 318, and 340 cubic-inch engines. There were also "Rat Roasters" competition manifolds for the Chrysler Hemi using both Carter AFB and Holley carburetors in NHRA and AHRA Super Stock competition. The name "Rat Roasters" came from Chrysler Corporation engineers who were taking a pot shot at Chevy's Rat motor.

Edelbrock produced the Rat Roaster, above, a manifold for the Chrysler Hemi to blow off the Chevy Rat motor. Top, 1971 catalog.

The Edelbrock Chrysler Manifold

It was the pinnacle of the muscle car era, Detroit was pumping out high-performance cars at an absurd rate, and automakers were building on their performance image. At the time, Bob Cahill was Chrysler's marketing/public relations expert. He had developed a working relationship with Vic Edelbrock during a sponsorship program for their Super Stock and Pro Stock racing teams. Sox and Martin, Herb McCandless, and Dick Landy ran Edelbrock decals on their cars in exchange for sponsorship money.

"Until the day I retired, one tradition was never altered: every manifold was tested until there was no doubt it worked. This was something that harked back to the old man."—**Don Waite**

The Pro Stock racing team of Sox and Martin, shown running the NHRA Winternationals in Pomona, California. They began making a name in the mid-1960s running in the FX Class with the AHRA. The Factory Experimental cars were illegal in NHRA competition. The three-two barrel manifold (below) for the Chrysler "Six Pack" was the first Edelbrock O.E. manifold made to be assembled on new cars.

When Chrysler decided to bring their racing image to the street, Cahill offered Vic something even better, and he jumped at the chance. Edelbrock would provide the manifold for the awesome "Six Pack" 440 engine that would be available on the Dodge Super Bee, Dodge Challenger, Plymouth Road Runner and Super Bird. Even better, the manifold would carry the Edelbrock name. Up to this point, the only other aftermarket part used by the factory and allowed to retain its original nameplate was George Hurst's four-speed shifter.

Vic had been given an unprecedented opportunity; one that would help change the course of the company. Chrysler Corporation purchased between 1500 and 2000 manifolds with the Edelbrock name in the casting. It was the largest single order in Edelbrock history. Cost factors and the decline of muscle cars forced Chrysler to go back to factory cast iron after two years, but what a ride it had been.

Thanks for the
memories!
Happy Birthday
Love,
Linda

Above, George Hurst and Wally Parks discuss the Hurst 4-speed shifter being used
on all four speed Chrysler Corporation
cars in the early '70s. Consider the joys of
covering an NHRA Drag Racing National
event. Bobby Meeks, left, was the Edelbrock
Technical man for many years. His perks
included a pose with Miss Hurst Shifter,
Linda Vaughn.

The C-3B

In 1969 Holley's 1000 cfm carburetor originally created for Chrysler's NASCAR program aroused Vic's interest. He called Holley and they asked Ralph Johnson, a brilliant engineer, to develop a street race version. What emerged was Holley's part number R-3916-1AAS—a 950 cfm wonder with an enormous 1-piece secondary throttle blade. The carb needed a manifold, and it got one. Edelbrock debuted a new high-rpm 2-plane high-rise 180° design with improved runner taper and dimensions compared to the existing C-4B. Naming it was obvious: Model C-3B. To ensure secondary throttle plate clearance, a notch was cut into the plenum divider. Tests of this duo on the 1967 *Hot Rod* magazine test Camaro at Irwindale drag strip produced stunning results: high-rpm power along with quick recovery between shifts. Edelbrock's January 1969 *Hot Rod* magazine ad claimed that, running this package, Joe Sherman's 1967 stock-bodied Camaro with a Bob Joehnck-built 350 turned a 10.82 e.t. at 129.53 m.p.h. at Lions. Edelbrock carried an exclusive on this 3-bbl "package" and received orders considered large for the time. Twenty-five percent of the original order went to Jerry Light of Vic Hubbard Speed & Marine of Hayward, California. Before the year was out, Edelbrock placed another large order with Holley.

Designed as a 2-plane manifold for the street rod builder, the Edelbrock C-3B made using the Holley "Toilet Bowl" carburetor practical.

Edelbrock/Holley Relationship Continues

Edelbrock's relationship with Holley Carburetors had established a new performance criterion. They made the idea of matching parts an industry trend. However, Vic wanted a top-flight, professional group of sales representatives, like those working for Holley, to promote his products by calling on distributors and speed shops around the country. He wanted Edelbrock products in the display cases and on the walls of every shop possible. These representatives had to treat his customers as respected friends. With that in mind, he proposed to Holley that their staff of more than forty sales reps also handle Edelbrock products as part of their normal sales calls. Vic presented the project as a win/win deal for both sides. Although a much larger company, Holley bought the idea and they forged an agreement. Holley representatives were to become the exclusive sales force for Edelbrock products within the continental United States.

Now, Edelbrock's staff had increased, with sales people systematically working the performance world, calling on major shops as well as mom-and-pop garages. By 1972, the Edelbrock/Holley program was in full swing. Sales increased and the sales personnel split commissions. Holley paid the sales staff as employees and Edelbrock paid an additional commission. This concept was the beginning of the Edelbrock business plan.

One of the advantages was that sales reps could help customers and speed shop owners match the right manifold with the correct carburetor. Vic knew, based on his dad's experience, that even a tremendous product could be compromised if not correctly matched with other parts of the package. When Colt Industries bought Holley, the new management changed the reps pay to salary only. Vic was not aware of the recent changes. Sales kept growing and the company's name recognition grew. When Vic finally heard what had happened, he quizzed Colt executives about the new program. He was told that the staff loved the program and that his sales would continue to climb. Vic wasn't convinced. He decided to pull his line of products from the Holley sales reps, and the day he did this, fifteen reps walked out to form their own national rep agency. In a few weeks, Holley's former sales staff established Performance Marketers Inc. (PMI) based in Dallas, Texas. Edelbrock sales manager Bill Smith determined the new group was serious, but he remained concerned that the break with Holley and Colt Industries would cause a disruption in service for Edelbrock customers. He suggested they come up with a quick business plan.

Top view of the Holley 3-barrel carburetor.

Vic Edelbrock Jr. considered Bill Smith, far left, to be a super sales manager in the performance industry. Bill was instrumental in putting the deal together that allowed Performance Marketers Inc. to represent Edelbrock Corp. after Colt/Holley Industries was no longer involved. Vic says, "Bill could sell air-conditioning units to Eskimos." Murray Jensen, left, once said, "Vic's marketing skills are far more advanced than anyone gives him credit for. Holley should have stayed partners with him." In the early 1980s, emissions regulations caused a drop in factory compression ratio numbers. Edelbrock designed the Torker II, below, to work well with 9- to-1 compression ratio engines being produced by Detroit.

On October 1, 1974, PMI began representing Edelbrock. The increase in sales was nearly instantaneous, and several of the original PMI team still represent Edelbrock today with their own company.

The Edelbrock/Holley relationship came to an end when the Holley 6619 carburetors caused serious problems. Holly had designed the 6619 600cfm carburetor to go with Edelbrock's Torker II manifold for the just-introduced Chevrolet Blazer. The problem was that the carburetor was made of zinc, which conducts heat, and because of the Clean Air Act of 1970, car manufacturers increased the thermostat settings from 180 degrees to 220 degrees. This caused the carburetors to leak internally and go dead rich in the fuel mixture, and the engine did not want to run.

At that time, Vic approached Carter AFB about getting back into the carburetor business. Carter agreed and Edelbrock engineers calibrated the carbs for the market. Carter placed a full-page ad in *Hot Rod* magazine, and the main feature was an official endorsement from Vic Edelbrock. Holley could see the writing on the wall, and quickly, went into the manifold business under their own brand name.

Holley's ability to mass-produce parts and fund a serious advertising campaign sent a shockwave through the newly formed sales rep agency. Compared to Edelbrock, Holley was a corporate monster with a giant slush fund for promotion supported by the Colt Industries distribution system. First efforts included the Street & Strip Dominator series, included dual-plane and single-plane, single-carburetor versions, a high-rise series, and a tunnel ram with two four-barrel carburetors for Pro Stock racing. Holley even went after the NASCAR Grand National race teams.

According to PMI's Mike Rao, Edelbrock feared that Holley had the resources to grab a major share of the manifold business. Vic stepped in and offered a simple slogan: Competition is Good.

Charity Event

Among Vic's favorite Daytona events in those days were the charity fund-raising dinners hosted by Junior Johnson's wife, Flossie. "Every year Flossie and some of the other racing wives would choose a woman who had lost a husband in racing and honor them with this dinner—all of the proceeds going to help pay bills, raise children, save a home from fore-closure. Flossie would take over the house of one of the women helping and the ladies removed the furniture, replaced it with long picnic tables and bench seats. Then the cooking would start. Flossie was known worldwide for her biscuits, and once she started whipping up hot biscuits, the smell would drive a man crazy. Then toss in fried chicken, corn on the cob, fresh baked pie, and cold beer; it was little wonder why everyone dipped into their pockets to help a racing widow. She would have her dinner around 6:30 p.m. The same evening they would have the Hall of Fame induction at a Daytona Beach hotel, then a midnight breakfast given by NASCAR at the church. It was here that Seagraves introduced Nancy to Senator Barry Goldwater, her political hero at the time. Vic recalls that "I ate at all three events, so breakfast was short following the long day.

"The event was held in an old church. Not much praying, but a lot of storytelling went on. By the time everybody was ready to eat, it was 11:30 p.m. so the ladies offered the traditional chicken and, if you were so inclined, replaced it with flapjacks, cornbread, fried eggs, and ham. I actually think that the France family was behind the church event and they continued the tradition for a number of years."

Edelbrock had long been the leader in the manifold business and had gone head-to-head with the best in the business. He contended that the company had become a little complacent, and now Holley was giving them a wake-up call. Vic Edelbrock would stay with what had been successful since day one: better products and better technical service. The proven performance concept created by Vic Sr. relied on the premise that if the customers didn't feel a kick in the seat of their pants, the product wasn't worth selling.

The NASCAR Connection

As early as 1971, R. J. Reynolds Tobacco Company had begun sponsoring NASCAR Grand National racing and helped racing survive during the oil embargo. Ralph Seagraves handled Reynolds public relations during this period; he was a gregarious, dapper dresser, quick with a joke, and capable of controlling any room he entered. Seagraves convinced the Winston cigarette brand to become involved with both NASCAR and NHRA. Seagraves told Vic Jr., "Your daddy was a legend to the boys Down South. They would use his stuff to build moonshine motors and later they built track racers. They all loved him—the Pettys, Junior Johnson, everybody who had run shine in the old days got parts from California." Ralph spent hours in private sessions with Vic, offering suggestions on how to better promote his products. He opened up his personal notebook, providing consultation on new methods of advertising and tracking ad influence, even allowing Vic the insider information on Winston's latest ideas.

Whenever Vic Edelbrock Jr. talks about Ralph Seagraves, right, his faces lights up and he becomes very animated. Vic says, "Ralph Seagraves was very kind to Nancy and me, and he introduced us to NASCAR racing, and would always take care of us at Daytona. He took us to the best parties and made sure we met all the important people. He was a great man."

When Seagraves discovered that Vic and Nancy had never been to the Daytona 500, he decided to provide the Edelbrocks with the time of their lives. Vic remembers what great pleasure Seagraves got catering to their every need. "Ralph was the master of public relations—he oversaw every detail and wouldn't allow us to do anything. He took care of our room, meals, entertainment, and race credentials.

Edelbrock Equipment Company became involved with NASCAR racing in the early 1970s through the efforts of Ralph Seagraves. Vic and Nancy would make the Daytona 500 one of their premier events of the year. Above, in later years, Vic took his daughter Camee (with Vic at the starting line at Daytona). Vic says, "In those days, racing was only part of the fun at Daytona. The good old boys really knew how to party. Everybody would show up at the R.J. Reynolds party: Cale Yarborough, Benny Parsons, the Pettys, the Allisons, Junior Johnson, even Big Bill France would pop in for some great times."

We were special guests in the Winston Suite, and he made it a point to introduce Nancy and me to every corporate heavyweight that arrived." For several years, Seagraves showed the Edelbrocks all the tricks of gaining entry to major player hangouts. When this man showed up, doors flew open and people took notice. Seagraves later enlisted Nancy to spend time with the VIP's wives in the suite and explain auto racing, much like Wally Parks had done at NHRA events.

But racing was only part of the fun at Daytona. Vic and Nancy attended the parties, too. "We would show up on Tuesday of race week, and Ralph instantly took us in tow, and off we would go to an R. J. Reynolds–sponsored event every night. Food and drink were always plentiful. We'd be served catfish dinners, hush puppies, gravy and biscuits, fried chicken; you could gain ten pounds just smelling the kitchen.

All the drivers were at the Winston parties—Cale Yarborough, Neil Bonnett, Dave Marcus, Buddy Baker, Harry Gant Jr., Benny Parsons, Richard Childress, the Pettys and Allisons. While the drivers talked about the old days, Ralph would be talking business, and with his help, Vic was promoting his own business at the same time. "Within a four-year period, Ralph Seagraves helped us get our foot in the door with NASCAR, the France family, and many of the drivers and car owners. He was always trying to help us promote our products."

Those 200 mph Billboards

NASCAR/Nextel racing has become the most watched motor sports series in the United States. With the success comes tremendous advertising value. Fans of NASCAR buy and use the sponsor products that the drivers and teams endorse on their cars. Edelbrock has actually been involved with stock car racing since the 1950s, when Vic Sr. would build flathead engines for the moonshine runners and weekend racers. Today, many of the drivers past and present call Vic Jr. a friend, including (clockwise from directly above) Rusty Wallace, Bill Elliott, the legendary number 43 Richard Petty, Jeff Gordon and Bobby Labonte. *Opposite*: Clockwise, Darrell Waltrip, Sterling Marlin and Cale Yarborough.

NASCAR great Ned Jarrett, above, once had Vic Edelbrock Jr. on a radio show he hosted in Daytona before the 500. From that humble beginning, Edelbrock is now on the fender, top, of nearly every car at every NASCAR event.

One day, Ralph grabbed Vic and took him to a downtown Daytona restaurant. Inside, Ned Jarrett was doing a radio show. Ralph told Vic, "You've got to get on the radio." Vic sat down with Ned and they did a twenty-minute stint talking about the old days—Vic Sr.'s involvement with the racers and moonshiners and building flatheads in California and shipping them down south. "It was great stuff and I could never have bought that kind of publicity. Ralph was the most giving man I have ever seen in the PR business; whenever we look at our success with NASCAR we think of Ralph."

A New Regulatory Environment

When emissions laws first began to emerge in the mid-1960s, they went virtually unnoticed by Detroit, the aftermarket industry, and car enthusiasts. When Congress enacted the Clean Air Act in 1971 and established the Environmental Protection Agency (EPA), everybody was forced to pay attention because the new agency targeted air pollution caused by the internal combustion engine. Some feared that the high-performance vehicle was going to be in trouble. Detroit was not technically prepared, and the first control systems were added on—and not designed into—the existing engines and transmissions. These temporary fixes were the automakers' answer to the new laws, and the driving public suffered as catalytic converters and unleaded gasoline became the norm in 1975.

Dyno Room Stories: Manifold Bolt Roulette

For many years, no engine test could be performed on the dyno without Vic Jr. pulling the throttle. The crew would set up a test engine and warm up the oil, then hunt down the boss, who would drop whatever he was doing and sprint down to the dyno room and run the test. Vic Jr.'s standing rule serves as the backdrop for a final dyno room bench racing classic. Jim McFarland, who was at the bottom of many of the jokes and pranks surrounding the legacy of dyno team bench racing stories, tells the story in his own words.

"Some of the early design Edelbrock Tunnel Ram manifolds had plenum chambers that connected to the base with bolts inside the plenum. Consequently, attaching the plenums to bases while one of these manifolds was installed on an engine ran the risk of dropping one or more of these bolts into a runner and, further, into the engine. Of course, when stopped, some of an engine's intake valves are open and some are shut, so the seriousness of dropping a bolt into a manifold runner depended upon valve position. If the valve was closed, judicious use of an extended magnetic tool could fish the bolt out as it rested on the backside of an intake valve. However, if the valve was open, the problem of bolt retrieval went from medium to 'Where do you plan to work next?' because the solution involved removal of a cylinder head. It was also common to partake in a cocktail or two during evening dyno sessions, frequent event during twilight test programs.

"During one of these evening test sessions, it happened that Vic Jr., Bobby Meeks, Murray Jensen, Don Towle, and I were completing some verification testing on the then new small-block Chevy Pro Ram I. Four cap-screws were used to attach its plenum to the base. The machined sample casting was being installed with the engine on the dyno. Murray and I would install the parts and Vic would perform the dyno tests. Needless to say, there was an abundance of joking, needling, and trash talk exchanged among the participants in any of these sessions, flavored by the length of time into the cocktail hour. With everyone gathered in the dyno cell and around the engine, Murray dropped one of the plenum bolts into the manifold. In an attempt to minimize the situation,

since the bolt luckily landed on top of a closed intake valve, I fished out the bolt and decided to install it myself amid considerable harassment from Murray and the others. In my hurry, I managed to drop the same bolt into the same intake port and on top of the same intake valve.

"Since I'd previously handed the magnetic tool to Meeks after fishing out Murray's bolt, he moved everyone aside, retrieved the bolt and proceeded to berate both Murray and me for our clumsiness. Then, with all eyes on Meeks, he dropped the bolt into another intake port. But as luck would have it, the bolt landed on another closed valve. Now it was Towle's turn. Setting aside his bourbon and seven, Don announced to everyone his higher level of mechanical skills, further diminished those of Meeks, Jensen and me, and dropped his bolt into the manifold.

"That leaves one person who hadn't demonstrated his ability to thread a 5/16-inch cap-screw into the manifold's base from inside the plenum. Vic had

watched this entire scene with amusement, providing plenty of digs and degrading remarks about the ineptitude of the staff he'd entrusted to run his dyno facility and engineer Edelbrock products. Then, with 5/16-inch cap-screw in hand and a brush-aside of his bumbling employees, Vic mounted the dyno stand, reached into the plenum chamber and dropped the bolt through an open intake passage and into the engine. At that instant, had there been a fire or similar emergency requiring immediate evacuation of the dyno cell, Meeks, Jensen, Towle, and McFarland would have likely perished from an inability to move. Severe laughter can paralyze, and we were prime examples of that problem. The next day, Murray and I disassembled the engine and removed the bolt. From that day forward, all Tunnel Rams were completely assembled prior to installation on dyno-mounted engines. The infamous bolt, had it not been lost, would likely have been bronzed and displayed on a plaque in Vic's office. As it turned out, the memory of that night became bronzed instead."

Vic Edelbrock Jr. (foreground) worked with the dyno room team members, like Murray Jensen, (shown working on engine) until the business grew to the point where it was impossible for him to spend the time doing so.

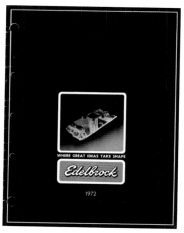

With the 1972 Catalog, above, Edelbrock was in the fight of its life: Emission controls were threatening the industry. The car, a Chevy Camaro, was nicknamed "Step 'N Fetch It" and provided a test bed for manifold design. It was even a good will vehicle as Vic Jr. allows National Highway Chairman Doug Toms, top, to take a ride. Vic Jr. took his turn at driving "Step 'N Fetch It", above right, as he puts out the chute after a 120 mph run at Lions Drag Strip in Long Beach, California. The photo was used for a magazine cover to promote the company's products.

At that time, manufacturers were using their own methods of controlling emissions, including the Positive Crankcase Ventilation System, the Evaporative Charcoal Canister System, and the Exhaust Gas Recirculation System (EGR). There were also "fixed idle" carburetors and "fixed distributor advance settings." Nearly every method took power out of the engine. In 1968 the L71 version Corvette, equipped with a 427 cubic-inch big-block, produced 435 horsepower. When fitted with the L88 option and given a few tweaks, horsepower readings could reach 500. By 1972 the 427 was replaced by the 454 big-block, and horsepower plummeted to 270. The once-popular 350 cubic-inch small-block dropped below 170 horsepower by mid-decade, and in 1975 the big block was gone altogether. At decade's end, the Corvette would struggle to make a comeback using unleaded gas and a catalytic converter, but the rules had changed, and it was time to move on to another adventure.

Early in the decade, Jim McFarland had pushed the idea that Edelbrock should expand on its research and development wing and increase its testing facilities for emission controls. He was instrumental in convincing Vic to make cars available to test products under actual conditions in the field. One of his first projects was converting Vic's 1967 Camaro into a "mule car" or, as it was known more picturesquely, "Step 'N Fetch It." The Camaro got a trick suspension package, roll bar, street/strip racing slicks, and full safety harness. Used for testing manifold and carburetor combinations, engine configurations, ignition systems, headers, camshafts, transmissions, even competitor's products, the test car would prove on the track what the crew tested on the dyno. It embodied the tradition that Edelbrock products were proven before they were sold to the public. There would be many mule cars in the future, but the practice began with "Step 'N Fetch It."

Mr. Edelbrock Goes to Washington

"My two terms at SEMA came at a very exciting time. The 1970s became the decade of change and a challenge to the survival of the industry. I was elected in 1971 for what would become two terms. My business was very secure, and I saw a need for SEMA to react to situations on the horizon. Emissions controls were going to change things for the worst. I surrounded myself with a great staff, formed Emissions, Noise, Safety, and Public Relations Committees (something that SEMA had not done to that point), added representation from retailers, warehouse distributors, sales representatives and media. We could then attack problems from many angles. Success on many fronts came because staff and members did much of the work; I simply acted as coordinator. One element of the job I really liked was the face-to-face conversation—it was fulfilling when I went out into the field and talked about our cause.

"A highlight came when I went to Washington, D.C., to speak to a Senate committee hearing. Representatives from the big 3 automakers from Detroit offered their arguments on the impending emission controls laws first. I was about tenth on the list, and by that time some of the senators left because they didn't want to hear about performance. I explained in detail that SEMA was just as concerned about safety and emissions as the government, that we were not a bunch of knuckle-draggers with greasy fingernails stripping down engines and running amuck in the streets. SEMA members were trying to develop performance and safety products that would benefit the industry. We also represented the majority of performance-related companies in the country who employed thousands of workers. If the government legislated us out of business then it would hurt the economy of the entire country. And if both sides didn't work together, then the performance industry would revert to becoming a bunch of outlaws, hopping up their cars as part of a counterculture instead of a law-abiding group of voters. This was the first time anyone had ever presented our side of the story at this level of government. Dale Houge had prepared my speech, and I gave it with all my energy, as it all went into the Congressional Record.

"Back then, the big 3 automobile manufacturers wanted to control everything. They wanted customers to bring their cars to the dealer for all servicing and they did not want any changing of parts or adding of specialty equipment. This defensive stance by the car companies was in retaliation for the feds putting the emission laws into effect so quickly. Had they gotten their way it would have been chaos. The automakers convinced Congress to delay the hydrocarbon and carbon dioxide (HC and CO) emissions standards until 1978, but then Congress initiated fuel mileage standards, or the Corporate Average Fuel Economy standards (CAFE) through the Energy Policy Conservation Act. I must have done some good, because from that point on whenever I went to Washington, D.C., Dale and I would have countless meals with congressional staff members. This was a good thing, because while senators and congressmen form ideas, it is the staff and the little guys who work out the details.

"Our next challenge was aftermarket wheels. President Nixon appointed Doug Thoms to head the newly formed National Highway Transportation and Safety Bureau. Thoms understood what performance equipment was all about and he was willing to work with the industry to solve problems, but as soon as we sat down in our first meeting, he issued a warning by telling us about helmet specifications. At one point, the helmet industry had flooded the market with cheap imported helmets, the public filed complaints, and the government reacted. Those helmet companies involved in racing had no problem meeting government standards, but the phony companies did not comply, and the feds yanked them from store shelves. In short, they put them out of business.

"At our meeting Thoms told me point blank, 'Vic, we have a situation with aftermarket wheels.' At the time, there were some really bad wheel manufacturers making knock-off performance wheels that were failing on the highway. Thoms issued a warning—either work with SEMA and create a specifications program for safe wheel standards or his department would step in and do it for the industry. He added, 'If we do it, it may not be as friendly as this meeting.' I went to the membership, explained the situation, and everyone agreed to set standards without government intervention. Although it took several years, we began a wheel program that became the blueprint for the SEMA Wheel Specification program in place today."

Because of his substantial background in the media, McFarland claimed many professional drag racers and NASCAR drivers as friends. Over the course of his twenty-year Edelbrock career, he played a direct role in the development of new products and Specialty Equipment Manufacturers Association (SEMA) programs, the formation of a research & development team, and production of the company's catalog and its advertising programs, while maintaining strong relationships

Vic Edelbrock Jr. served two terms as SEMA president in the 1970s as well as being a member of the original board of directors in 1963. Vic was an extremely active president and made some outstanding promotions, right, while in office. He worked on emission programs, wheel safety issues and even spoke in front of a Senate committee hearing in Washington. Vic says, "It was very tough to work as president of SEMA and run a business at the same time. But we did some well needed great work."

Says safety, pollution & noise are industry problems . . .
Edelbrock names Duffy 1st VP At SEMA Ball

LOS ANGELES—"Safety, air pollution and noise are three of the most important areas we must concern ourselves with in the coming months and years," newly sworn-in SEMA President Vic Edelbrock told the 280 members and guests attending the President's Ball and Reception here recently.

"This," he said, "is why, as my first official act and with the approval of the board, I have added new committee chairmen in those areas. As Safety Committee Chairman we have George Hurst of Hurst Performance. Heading up the Emissions Committee will be Al Reed of TRW. As Noise Committee Chairman will be Bob Carren of Perfection American."

APPOINTED as chairmen of previously-established committees were: Finance—Harry Weber, Membership—Richard De-

Continued on page 3

Honoring past SEMA presidents with commemorative plaques for their service to the association and the industry, is Wally Parks (l.), president of the NHRA. Holding their plaques are (l. to r.): Dean Moon, Els Lohn, Willie Garner and Roy Richter. Receiving plaques in absentia were Ed Iskenderian and Bill Casler.

hp np high performance news & products
Trademark®
THE NEWSPAPER OF THE HIGH PERFORMANCE AND CUSTOM INDUSTRY
A Stanley-Action Newspaper
Volume 3, Number 9
September, 1971
Monthly Circulation: 50,310 BPA Verified

with the enthusiast magazines. He would prove to be a key employee for Edelbrock and an essential voice in the upcoming legislative battle brewing over performance parts and emission controls.

The Rise of SEMA

The performance industry had always been a collection of maverick idea makers who rarely agreed on anything. Now those independent souls were being forced by outside influences to join together for a common good. Insurance companies were trying to portray the speed equipment industry as a reckless and lawless bunch roaming the streets in hopped-up cars. On another flank, the federal government was starting to chip away at the performance aftermarket's revenue streams by attacking horsepower improvement parts.

The formation of SEMA was the direct result of these growing threats to the fledgling marketplace. SEMA's executive director, Eric Grant, was former director at the California Air Pollution Control District and understood better than most the new emission control regulations. Vic Edelbrock Jr. was elected president at a crucial time in the history of SEMA; he took over in 1971 and would serve two terms, succeeding one-term president and close friend, Roy Richter, owner of Cragar and Bell Auto. Richter laid claim to owning one of the oldest speed equipment business concerns in the industry. Bell Auto was founded in 1930 by his father-in-law George White. And in SEMA history, Richter's name is associated with many of the group's milestones. He was part of the initial meetings to form SEMA back in the early 1960s. Richter lobbied to create a national association and a SEMA trade show in the

"By creating our own specialized equipment we could control product quality closer than ever before. As the product line expanded and demanded more precise machine work—we bought CNC machines and several custom screw machines, which led to new standards for quality control." **—Wayne Murray**

1960s. His other accomplishments included heading the first Wheel Committee to set standards for aftermarket wheels, and working on many of the safety programs begun by SEMA in the late 1960s. Vic's presidency was the sixth in the short history of SEMA. Aside from his predecessor, Richter, Ed Iskenderian, Dean Moon, Els Lohn and Willie Garner had all served as well. As a result of their leadership and the growth of the industry, SEMA's organizational structure now had a board of directors with members representing retailers, distributors, and manufacturers.

Building a Team for the Battle

As Vic took the leadership role in SEMA, the atmosphere was akin to the late 1940s and early 1950s in Los Angeles, when the Police Department and the Los Angeles Times tried to discredit hot rodders. SEMA had to take up the fight and hit back with vigor. When Vic took over as president, he wanted to hire Dale Hogue as legal counsel. SEMA needed $35,000 to pay Hogue's salary, so Vic went to Dick Day at Petersen Publishing Co., who in turn went to Robert E. Petersen, and asked him to step up. Petersen, who had been friends with Vic Sr., didn't hesitate, and put up the money. This was a major step for SEMA.

Edelbrock surrounded himself with a staff of knowledgeable people who not only knew the industry, but also were willing to fight as hard as he did to save it. Edelbrock employee Jim McFarland, one of the most informed experts on emissions, was an advisor to Vic on emission issues. Lou Baney was hired to help build up the membership; Lou was a people person respected by everyone in the performance market. Baney, who would succeed Grant as SEMA's executive director, could sell anything; he had owned and raced Top Fuel dragsters, worked in the automobile dealership business, operated drag strips, had even raced the dry lakes.

Baney in turn hired one-time fuel dragster driver Don Prieto, who was editor of Petersen Publishing's *Hot Rod Industry News*, the industry's official magazine. As SEMA's staff communications director, the quick-witted Prieto could be very determined in a fight, and proved himself when he helped defeat critical negative legislation to the speed equipment industry. "I got the job, and soon found myself up to my eyelids working with manufacturers, and seeing firsthand the business side of the industry," remembered Prieto, "We produced the SEMA show and worked with Petersen Publishing's ad people, headed by Dick Day, selling ads and booth space."

Don Prieto is well known in the industry as "the hot rodder's hot rodder". He is also known for his work with Vic Jr. during the '70s. Prieto was the builder of a clean air engine created from aftermarket hot rod parts.

Working with aftermarket products, like this Carter carburetor, right, Edelbrock Equipment Company went all-out during the early days of the emission wars to prove their products as well as other manufacturers' products could produce power and run clean.

The First Clean Air Project

Prior to coming on board with SEMA, Prieto took the lead on the Clean Air Engine project. With the blessing of his publisher Alex Xydias, he set out to build a high-performance engine using only aftermarket speed equipment parts, and then prove it to be clean-burning. Lawmakers contended that aftermarket parts could never replace OEM factory parts, and that hot rod engines were air polluters. Hot rodder Prieto surmised that if he built a performance engine using only off-the-shelf aftermarket parts and then tested it to new emissions-control standards, that it might prove the lawmakers wrong. He approached SEMA Executive Director Eric Grant who was also a factory representative for Clayton Manufacturing Company and asked if Clayton would be interested in running their new Key Mode Engine Evaluation System test to meet the new air quality standards. At the time, Clayton, makers of engine dynamometers, wanted the government to see the potential of its emissions measuring systems, so they jumped at the chance. The project car would be Prieto's personal 1957 Chevy Nomad, and he would feature the results in *Hot Rod Industry News* magazine.

At the same time, Vic Edelbrock Jr. had already seen the handwriting on the wall. McFarland was aware of all of the new emission-control laws that were emerging from state and federal rulings, and how they could change the way the performance industry was doing business. Edelbrock, McFarland, Meeks, and Jensen were already designing and testing emissions-friendly manifolds, as well creating a full spectrum of emissions tests. The beauty of the Edelbrock research and development program was their use of the air flow bench. Through testing they designed a manifold that kept the fuel in suspension longer than original equipment manifolds. The result was a cleaner, more complete burn of the fuel mixture, resulting in cleaner emissions.

In 1970 Congress established the Environmental Protection Agency and gave them power to regulate motor vehicle pollution. By 1971, new cars had to be equipped with emissions reducing equipment. By the mid-1970s, Southern California established the Air Quality Management District. Vic realized that his company had better come up with answers to emissions problems or find a new line of work. Left, testing at the Coral Circle plant.

While president of SEMA, Vic was engulfed with dispelling the negative attitude toward the performance industry from not only the federal government in general, but from the state of California in particular. California, through its Air Resources Board, would enact the most stringent pollution standards in the nation—tighter than even the federal guidelines. "The first step was to tune up the stock engine, run a baseline emissions test, and record the results," explained Prieto. "We also listed the 1966 figures for government standards and those of California. I then totally disassembled the engine and rebuilt it using all hot rod equipment, including a Racer Brown camshaft, Edelbrock manifold, Hedman headers, an aftermarket ignition, and two different carburetor choices (Holley and Carter). The engine also had forged pistons, custom rods, racing piston rings, and basic machine work such as honing and balancing."

Edelbrock paid for all of the machine work. Jim McFarland procured most of the parts and pieces. Prieto built much of the project engine at the Edelbrock facility. The Edelbrock manifold played a very important part in the project because it validated all of the design and testing the company had been doing secretly to meet emissions standards. The end result of Clayton's Key Mode Engine Evaluation System test was amazing. They had constructed an early model Chevrolet small-block using hot rod parts and were not only able to meet 1972 emissions regulations, but the engine ran cleaner than the new engines coming out of Detroit at the time. An unequivocal success, the project made the cover of the December 1971 *Hot Rod Industry News*. The performance industry had started to fight back against unfair legislation. One of Edelbrock's first moves as SEMA president was to put Jim McFarland on the Emissions Control Committee because McFarland and the crew were already engaged in emissions testing at Holley's emissions lab that included work with Holley components. McFarland had even gone so far as to invite members of the Air Resources Board to the shop.

Texas-born Jim McFarland, below, came to Edelbrock in 1969. Jim knew early on that emissions controls would play an important part in the survival of the performance industry. On Vic's watch as SEMA President, the Feds tried to impose a bumper height regulation, but SEMA fought hard to win over the lawmakers and the rule was never really adopted.

Winning Them Over

Shortly after Edelbrock became SEMA president, the state of Wisconsin attempted to pass several laws dealing with swapping out stock tires and wheel sizes with aftermarket products, and restricting rear bumper heights to stock measurements. The state was trying to ban cars that were raised 12 to 15 inches in the rear. Don Prieto remembered being called into Vic's office. "He basically told me he was throwing me to the lions. He sent me back to Wisconsin to see what

could be done about the situation. I flew back east and sat down with speed shop owners and the local lobbyist and discussed what could be done.

"I quickly discovered that the state had a hidden agenda: to rid the state of hot rodders who were putting their cars on a rake. Back in those days, the hot setup was putting little tires in front and huge tires on the rear, thereby standing the car on its nose. Putting a car on a rake in some cases exposed the rear-mounted gas tank, and lawmakers hit the panic button. Our problem was trying to prevent the state governments from arbitrarily passing laws to outlaw certain parts and pieces. After much discussion, it was concluded that the state cannot simply outlaw products at their discretion, but must construct certain parameters that will allow for the replacement of components, factory OEM, or aftermarket, as long as they meet the specifications of OEM—original equipment manufacturers. If an aftermarket wheel is as strong as the factory wheel it is replacing, then it should be legal. The same holds true for other products. As for the bumper law, there was an already established federal bumper height requirement, so we said, as long as the bumper height is within the federal limitations, then it should be legal. We put our case in front of the Wisconsin Transportation Committee and their decision was not to write rules into law that would be hard to implement. We had won a victory of sorts."

The experience was good for SEMA, and no sooner had Prieto returned to California than the state of Oregon tried a similar tactic. This time, he took a representative from the wheel industry, an expert member of the SEMA Wheel Committee named Jim Kavanagh. The local wholesalers had hired their own attorney to help. Together they beat back this second attack. They maintained that if an aftermarket product was as good or better than the factory original, then the replacement should be allowed. Throughout his terms as president, Vic fought hard to make SEMA stronger and better able to protect the industry.

Jim McFarland, below left, helped Don Prieto of *Hot Rod Industry News* build an engine from aftermarket parts that was cleaner than a factory stock engine straight from Detroit.

Vic Edelbrock Jr. knew that the industry had to meet emissions standards or the government would step in and prevent products like manifolds from running on the public highway. Not everyone agreed, but he wanted his company to be the leader, so the company built their own emissions lab, right, before the Feds forced the issue.

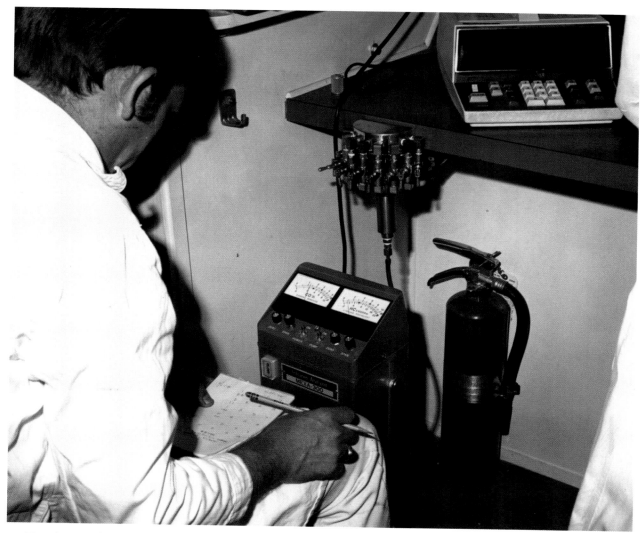

During Vic's terms, SEMA also met with an organization of police chiefs from around the country to discuss various problems, a step that helped improve the relationship between the speed equipment industry and government. SEMA convinced them to work with lawmakers and aftermarket parts manufacturers in writing and enforcing laws pertaining to equipment changes. If rules were written in conjunction with SEMA specifications as well as those of the manufacturers, then many problems could be avoided in advance, making life easier for law enforcement officers.

The Second Clean Air Project

Replacement parts and noise issues were not the only problems Vic had to battle during his terms as president of SEMA. Emissions issues were a constant problem, and Vic was always up for a challenge. His interest was a carryover from his dad, who loved testing new ideas. So when Dale Houge and Don Prieto came up with an idea to help lobby the federal government regarding the clean air act and its repercussions on the industry, Vic jumped at the chance to give it his blessing.

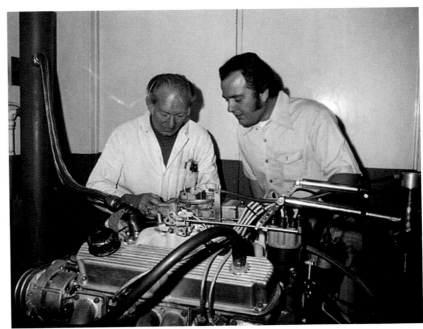

Once again Prieto was in the middle of things. "Our plan was to get various aftermarket manufacturers to supply parts, then buy three different cars. The engines of the cars would be rebuilt using mixed parts chosen at random from the aftermarket manufacturers and then they'd be tested. By this time Vic had built an emissions lab with a seven-mode testing system. He opened up the lab and allowed us the services of Bobby Meeks, Murray Jensen, and Curt Hooker. When McFarland filled them in on the project, they all jumped at the chance. We bought a Dodge, a Chevy, and a Ford, and proceeded to ask all of the manufacturers, including Edelbrock, to help fund the project. Because it would be a major undertaking, something that had never been done before, no time limit was set. First we rebuilt all of the engines and gave them a baseline test to get emissions readings in stock configuration."

Testing has always been the key to success for the Edelbrock line of manifolds. Murray Jensen, above left and above (with shop coat), worked tirelessly throughout the 1970s and 1980s, testing ideas to make Edelbrock manifold and carburetor combinations produce power while maintaining legal emissions control standards. The hard work paid off as the company survived the gas crisis and won the battle to make performance parts legal in all fifty states.

The team began adding intake manifolds, ignition systems, headers, and carburetors. The program lasted about eighteen weeks, with each manufacturer being responsible for their particular parts and installations. Prieto still marvels at the teamwork. "What was so amazing about the test, and what makes the performance industry as strong as it is today, was the fact that the players in the test were all competitors. There were Doug Thorley Headers and Hedman Headers used along with Black Jack Headers. Edelbrock manifolds were used along with Offenhauser and Weiand. Holley and Carter carburetors were used along with Mallory and Accel ignition systems. Plus, all of the work was done by a bunch of racers and hot rodders. Greats like Art Chrisman and Brad Anderson pitched in and helped. Everyone worked together for a common goal. Vic Edelbrock and his crew allowed all of the engines to be tested on their equipment. Vic paid his crew and all the expenses to conduct the tests. Each test procedure took one full day, and not only did Vic supply the manpower and the lab, he bought lunches, dinners, and paid for the gas to run the engines. After all the tests were complete and all of the parts had been swapped and

Vic gets an award, above, from Wally Parks (left) and Carl Olson (right). Carl was a National Top Fuel champion, above right, before working with Vic Edelbrock at SEMA. Olson worked on programs dedicated to driver and race car safety issues.

endless combinations matched, the data was accumulated and given to a group of independent engineers. They extrapolated the information and the results proved that the three cars, regardless of combination and equipment, proved to be cleaner with aftermarket parts than when they were tested in stock configuration. But the best news for the industry was that no single part hurt emissions.

"Vic would poke his head into the dyno room at all hours, day or night, ready with a check if anything was needed, Prieto remembers. "In many ways, if it had not been for Vic Edelbrock, Jim McFarland, and the fact that Vic had hired Lou Baney and Lou forced me to do battle, the problems could have been worse. Vic had the ability to see down the road. Some of the manufacturers didn't want to deal with the Air Resources Board; they stuck their heads in the sand and just sold parts. When I first started working at SEMA, someone told me 'SEMA has cancer, and the government is the cause.' Many believed that the speed equipment industry would not survive."

In early 1975, Vic Edelbrock was in the final year of his presidency of SEMA when Don Prieto resigned to take a job in Washington, D.C., with the Automotive Parts and Accessories Association (APAA). Carl Olson, a thirty-two-year-old NHRA Top Fuel champion driver stepped into the vacated spot. Precise, mild-mannered, and well-educated, Olson had a smooth, articulate demeanor. Quick to smile, he was always ready to offer assistance, a trait that had certainly played a part in his being voted Driver of the Year in 1972. Well-known for his racing deeds, Olson captured the envy of many by winning the Last Drag Race at Lions Drag Strip in Long Beach as well as two other prestigious contest—the Smokers Championship in Bakersfield, California, and the Winternationals in Pomona. He had also served on the SEMA Technical Committee in 1967, focusing on the racing portion of the SEMA Specifications Program. Olson soon became the Technical & Legislative Director for SEMA. Because of his prior service, Olson had no problem

Fire! As a blower lets go on a Top Fuel dragster the driver is protected by a fire suit, helmet, on-board extinguisher and other safety features. Men like Wally Parks, Carl Olson and Vic Edelbrock Jr. have spent much of their time trying to make drag racing a safer sport.

understanding the need to refocus the SEMA Specifications Program toward the street rodder and the related products purchased over the counter.

The specifications program originated in drag racing when SEMA and NHRA worked together to improve safety after a rash of explosions caused some catastrophic injuries to drivers, spectators, and officials. The NHRA became the enforcement arm of the program, and steady progress was made with containment of clutches and flywheel explosions, roll cage improvements, and upgrades of safety harnesses, fire suits, and helmets. By the time Vic Jr. left office in late 1975, the committee had made significant progress on many products, including the initiation of an industry-wide aftermarket wheel specifications program accepted by manufacturers and acknowledged by lawmakers.

Edelbrock's administration also worked to reverse federal and state officials' perception that the performance industry was incompatible with the emerging world of emissions controls. SEMA's staff began working with attorney Dale Houge, who explained the inner workings of lobbying and dealing with lawmakers in power. Carl Olson's duties were mainly advocacy work with a wide variety of governmental agencies. The threat to the performance aftermarket industry from unsympathetic governmental agencies began in the early '70s, and continued through the 1980s. SEMA was able not only to represent member companies but to preserve the very right of the industry to exist. "It took tremendous effort to convince the government that what they were doing or about to do, was unfair, unreasonable, and downright un-American," recalled Olson. "SEMA, Vic Edelbrock, and other leaders such as Phil Weiand, Bob Spar, Holly Hedrick, Roy Richter, Els Lohn, Willie Garner, Wally Parks, Lou Baney, Dick Wells, Bob Burch, and Russ Deane, had to re-educate the ruling bodies of government to at least sit down and conduct a dialogue regarding how aftermarket parts could be tested and certified as replacement parts."

In order to set up a formal certification program, emissions standards had to be met. Because Edelbrock's company had been working on this problem for years when he became president of SEMA, his major effort was to develop a procedure by which all performance aftermarket components could be certified for use in emissions-related systems. Technical and engineering aspects of the emissions control battle were worked out by Jim McFarland, leaving Carl Olson to go to Washington and debate the cause with officials. One positive aspect of the battle during the 1970s was that it forced parts makers to spend money on research, development, and new tooling. So dire was the battle that even usually contentious and competitive nonconformists joined forces to fight unfair laws. "Without the combined effort we would all be doing something else for a living," concluded Olson. "SEMA turned the war between the performance industry and the lawmakers into an ongoing cease-fire."

A Continuing Fight

Despite Vic Jr.'s unifying approach, the industry lost many weaker members who could not afford the costs of developing new products, or who simply thought the government was tyrannical in its attempt to control small business. But Vic's conversations about saving the industry were not limited to government officials; he spent time out in the field talking to the people selling the products. Not only were the government agencies pressuring the performance industry, the economy during the 1970s was weak: interest rates, unemployment, and gasoline prices were all high. The designated industry cheerleader was also worried that his own business could become a victim of the times. He had found it difficult to run a business and be president of SEMA at the same time. In those days, there was a saying, "Get your competition to become president, then they can't spend as much time doing business."

When Vic spoke to an assembled crowd of warehouse distributors, shop owners, and manufacturers at Vic Hubbard's Speed Shop in Hayward, California, he asserted that parts makers could not only create products that would be better than OEM and meet the regulations of the feds, but they could still make money. Not many believed him—especially the California people—but to keep interest high, the SEMA show moved to Anaheim, an awards program was founded including the Paul Scheifer Award, and the Hall of Fame was established honoring the pioneers of the business. At the same time, a push to expand membership was paying off as the organization started to grow.

According to the crew at Edelbrock Equipment, Vic Jr. coped with the gas crisis and fought for products offering better mileage. Below, Vic holds the 1978 S.P.2-P. manifold designed for RV use and increased mileage. Bottom, a gas saving winner was the Streetmaster manifold. It sold very well when other companies hit a slump.

HOW TO GET BETTER MILEAGE FROM YOUR BIG CAR

In 1975 Vic Edelbrock Jr. stepped down, but remained on the board of directors. In 1976 Lou Baney left, and Dick Wells took over as executive director. Russ Deane had stepped in as the legal voice in 1974, and helped SEMA win a Clean Air Act amendment that provided for the acceptability of a voluntary parts self-certification program, maintaining the industry's right to produce and sell emissions-related parts. More important, this milestone victory ensured that automakers would be unable to void emissions warranties solely upon the basis that performance equipment was used.

Edelbrock Corporation was setting an example for other manufacturers. "I was damned if I was going to let anything stand in the way of us overcoming the challenges of the day," Vic Jr. recalled. By 1973, they were already making products that were meeting emissions standards, including a manifold for RV-type vehicles covering Chevrolet, Dodge, and Ford. They also offered manifolds equipped with EGR (Exhaust Gas Recirculation Systems) adapters for O.E.M. emissions equipment and the Streetmaster series produced from the Tarantula manifold. There was a line of small engine manifolds, (Vega, Corvair, Volkswagen) with emphasis on emissions and economy. In the late 1970s, the company developed the S.P. 2-P. manifold and the aftermarket automotive industry's first electronic sequential fuel injection system (EFI).

The year 1978 marked forty years in the performance business for Edelbrock Equipment Company. Edelbrock could point to a long list of satisfied motor sports customers. On the drag strip there was Don Nicholson, Bob Glidden, and Wally

The gas crisis of the 1970s forced Edelbrock to quickly solve problems regarding emission and fuel mileage. For the first time ever, Edelbrock produced a direct replacement for factory manifolds. The E.F.I. system, far left, was a first for the industry in 1978. For the RV market and four-wheel drive enthusiasts, Edelbrock produced the S.P.2-P.

A milestone for the Edelbrock Corporation took place in 1978. The company celebrated 40 years in the performance industry. Many of the pioneers who began as competitors of Vic Edelbrock Sr. back in 1938 failed to endure. One of the reasons for the Edelbrock success story has been the ability to adapt to changing conditions. When the gas crisis put fear in many manufacturers, Edelbrock developed a counter-attack by introducing gas saver-type manifolds. The S.P.2-P. manifold, above, offered emissions-legal performance and reasonable mileage for RV and off-road vehicle users.

Throughout the years, Edelbrock Corporation has been involved in many types of racing. Vic Sr. was a champion on the dry lakes. He was also very successful as a midget car owner after World War II. In the 70s, Vic Jr. teamed with drag racing stars like Don Nicholson, far left, and Winston Cup racers like Bobby Allison, left. Edelbrock products became so popular an Edelbrock manifold was used in the famed International Race of Champions series.

Booth; in Winston Cup racing, names like Benny Parsons, Bobby and Donny Allison, Darrell Waltrip, and Richard Petty ran Edelbrock, as did Roger Penske. Edelbrock manifolds were the official choice of the International Race of Champions (IROC) series. It was not all roses and checkered flags, however; in 1978 the company was dealt a big hit when jobbers, speed shops, and distributors pushed the panic button during the gas crunch and the emissions control law fight. Manifold sales dropped, and Vic Jr. spent hours on the telephone convincing his buyers that Edelbrock products would sell.

Curt Hooker, then the dyno room rookie, shed a bit of light on how Edelbrock reacted to the oil embargo. "Vic was a wild man during the gas crisis. He hated waiting in gas lines. Whenever he needed gas he would come find me in the dyno room, hand me a bunch of gasoline credit cards and tell me to take his car and his mom's car and fill them up. I would have to find a station, get in line, and wait. One day Vic had to wait in line for about an hour, and when he got to the pumps the attendant told him the pumps were closed. Vic went ballistic. A couple months later the company installed gas pumps in the rear of the building and Vic sold gas to employees at his cost. No more waiting in line."

"The easiest thing you can do when you own a company carrying your own name is to be nice to those who work for you. My dad always felt his employees were part of his family and I have continued that feeling, although nowadays it is more difficult. Just saying, 'Good morning, how are you?' as you walk through the shop makes the people doing the labor know the company cares. It makes the worker want to do a better job. And, when all is said and done, making a quality product is what keeps us in business and the crew working." **—Vic Edelbrock Jr.**

The Fun Team

The Fun Team name was born out of their well-earned reputation of having fun while water ski racing. But long before the name was coined, the idea of having a good time with race cars percolated in Vic Edelbrock's childhood mind as he accompanied his father through the pits of bullring racetracks up and down California. Wide-eyed, he watched, listened, and absorbed the excitement.

While most kids could only dream of race cars, they surrounded Junior on daily basis. Take for example a trip to Bonelli Stadium, (later Saugus Speedway) located in the Santa Clarita Valley north of Los Angeles in the early 1940s. The youngster was with his father and the Edelbrock race crew of Meeks and driver Walt Faulkner. Racer Bill Stroppe, who was sponsored by Art Hall Lincoln Mercury in Long Beach, showed up with a Kurtis-Kraft midget, powered by a V8-60 using Edelbrock equipment and a child's version of a midget with a Briggs and Stratton engine. The car had been built as a promotional tool. When young Edelbrock saw the car he worked up the courage to ask Stroppe if he could drive it. Stroppe, who loved kids, laughed. "Sure, no problem," he answered, believing if a kid wanted to race, let him race.

Before the midgets qualified, young Edelbrock jumped into the tiny car and had great fun spinning around the infield while his dad worked on the race car. Vic Sr. was stunned to see his son in the car. Junior had neglected to ask his father's permission.

The following week, the team went to Huntington Beach racetrack, and another father had brought another mini-midget to the track so that his son could join in the fun. Stroppe saw it as an opportunity to race, and the track announcer picked up on the idea. A match race was inaugurated, complete with a ten-year-old trophy girl to kiss the winner. Vic Jr. took the honors despite nearly smashing into the wall when he forgot to turn because he was too busy watching his opponent. He earned the kiss after the race.

Vic Edelbrock Sr. once told his wife Katie that he would be glad when his son grew tall and wouldn't fit in a midget. Before that day happened, Vic Jr. got his chance when he drove a mini-midget, built by Bill Stroppe, during intermission at Huntington Beach Speedway. Note Vic Sr. in the background with his arms folded.

The next week at Huntington Beach, a rematch was set up and the other car, aided by some nitro in the tank, ran away from Vic Jr. The telltale smell of the exhaust tipped off Vic Sr. and Meeks, and they added a little mix of the volatile chemical to Junior's engine for the second race. Vic Jr.'s car ran out in the lead at first, but eventually the engine began detonating because the crew had not changed carburetors, and the second race was lost as well.

It was well known that Edelbrock Senior did not want his son to drive a real race car. It was a great relief to his father when Junior, at age fifteen and six foot two outgrew the midget cockpit. Several clandestine forays into drag racing, trying to convince his father that it was a reasonably safe endeavor, also failed.

Boats, on the other hand, were a different story. "I really believe that ski racing for me was a spin-off of the fact that Dad didn't want me to race cars. I had aspirations of running at the drag races, but Dad jumped all over that idea because he thought if I competed using his equipment and got beat, it would be bad for our reputation. It was a no-win situation. For some reason, when I started water ski racing, he didn't view it as a threat."

The Young Man and the Sea

Boat racing has always been a major contributor to the overall success of the family business and wove itself through the years into many segments. Although his father's passing brought a sharp refocus of young Edelbrock's time, from dreaming up racing adventures to concentrating on taking control of the Edelbrock Equipment Company, the urge to compete was never far from Vic's consciousness. After purchasing a V-bottom Higgins, he entered ski racing at Lake Arrowhead and Lake Mead.

"By pure coincidence, Len Marks, a long time friend of Don Towle's, asked if I would like to drive with him in a marathon race at Salton Sea," recalled Edelbrock, "I jumped at the chance because it is a little like endurance racing with cars: you run for long periods of time, over many hours, usually 500 miles, to determine the winner. This particular event was run over a two-day duration, and I was to relieve Len at the first pit stop on Saturday. After my stint in the boat, I was so excited that I wanted to drive Sunday, but another driver for Sunday had already been arranged."

To compete the following year, Edelbrock built a Rayson Craft hull with a big-block Chevy and started his first marathon in San Diego. Halfway through the event, he was leading, but a broken throttle bracket brought him into the pits, and by the time it was repaired, it was time to swap drivers. Old friend Butch Peterson took over, and just as he began to close in on the leaders, the boat flipped. After the boat was repaired, the next race took place at Salton Sea, and after Peterson took over the rudder broke. Unable to fix it, Peterson believed he could keep going by using the cavitation plates as a rudder, but the crew was wary. Amazingly, he was soon running as fast as he did with the rudder, and the team ended up third. According to Edelbrock, Butch Peterson was a magnificent boat driver, one of the best he ever knew. Two years later, in 1968, after the races had shifted to Lake Elsinore, Vic Jr. and Len Marks won the 500-mile, two-day marathon.

The Lost Racers
The Edelbrock Rayson Craft was converted to a race boat in the early 1970s, which brought a young, tough and

Throughout the history of Edelbrock Corporation, boat racing has played a major role in both product development and reputation building. Vic Sr. never wanted his son to drive race cars, but relented when it came to boats. From playing around on Lake Arrowhead, to water ski racing and offshore boat racing, Vic Jr. did it all. After a victory at Lake Elsinore, above left, Vic collects his trophy (left to right): Vic Jr., trophy girl, Don Towle, Bill Michel and Nancy Edelbrock. Above, Vic Jr. in number 45 goes head-to-head with friend and rival Butch Peterson in San Diego.

"I nearly flipped the offshore boat a couple of times because of a lack of concentration. Nancy and I began thinking, do we really need this in our lives? I was taking a real beating due to water conditions." —Vic Edelbrock Jr.

Star-Quality Boat Jockeys

In 1965, Chevrolet introduced the Mark IV, a 396 cubic-inch big block. GM public relations manager Bill Yeager approached Edelbrock to consider using a 396 in an SK-class race boat application. Bill Dunsmore and Tony Maricich owned the boat. Edelbrock agreed, and the crew developed a dual 4-bbl. Ram Log manifold, and initiated a series of dyno tests to establish a package including camshafts, valve train components, carburetors, and other parts. After testing, the engine was fitted into the boat hull and the finished product was taken to Florida to run the American Power Boat Association (APBA) Nationals, where it was the only 396 Chevy entered. The boat won—Chevrolet was ecstatic and Yeager overjoyed. The following year, Yeager called again saying he had a problem he needed help with—nothing that would take much time.

"I had no reason not to accept, and gave my word we were ready to help," recalled Edlebrock. "Bill had gotten involved with a Michigan boat builder who had built a racing boat for a couple of astronauts who wanted to run the Salton Sea 500, and had several major sponsors in the effort. The boat was powered by two 396 big-blocks, and Chevrolet would feel better if we put the engines in tune for the race." The boat drivers were Gordon Cooper and Virgil "Gus" Grissom, two of the original Mercury Seven Astronauts. Tapped to fly a rocket to the moon, in the early 1960s these men were revered celebrities. More than mere mortals, they were heroes headed for other worlds.

The Edelbrock crew met Cooper and Grissom in the fall of 1966. No one could anticipate that only a few months later, on January 27, 1967, Grissom and fellow astronauts Ed White and Roger Chaffee would die in a terrible fire during a test of Apollo I. The first astronauts were not only brave beyond measure, but each possessed a special "can-do" character, a throwback to the wild days of barnstormers. Cooper and Grissom used fast cars and fast boats as relief valves for blowing off stress. Both owned Corvettes, and Grissom was close friends with 1960 Indy 500 winner Jim Rathmann.

The Salton Sea 500 was conducted over a two-day period with pit stops so boats could be fueled and

drivers changed. However, Cooper and Grissom both wanted to be aboard the entire race, so their boat was equipped with dual steering and fuel tanks large enough to run nonstop.

"The boat and trailer arrived on a Tuesday afternoon and we discovered the engines were not remotely close to race ready," Edelbrock said with a sigh. "In fact, there was no manifold, carburetors, wiring, headers, and marine water pump systems. Yeager told me that the boat had to be in tech inspection on Friday or the guys would lose their sponsors. I suggested that he was cutting things a little close."

The problems started with trying to unload the boat from the flatbed semi. It was too heavy, and the unloading ramp buckled and would have wrecked the boat had the crew not done a quick support job using 4-by-4s. Edelbrock and his men worked all

night Tuesday straight through into Wednesday without stopping. About mid-afternoon, two brand-new Cadillac convertibles came flying into the parking lot and screeched to a halt in front of the shop. Grissom and Cooper jumped out, laughing hard.

Moments later, a herd of television crews from ABC, CBS, and NBC followed by reporters, photographers, and spectators pulled into the lot. There was a lot of pushing and shoving as the news people vied for space and tried to setup interviews. Cooper and Grissom went off to one side so the crew could work. As the day wore on, the TV crews and spectators moved away from the shop, and Edelbrock and his men started to make some progress. Late in the afternoon Cooper took off, leaving Grissom behind. Around six p.m. Grissom said, "Hey, what do you guys need to keep your spirits up?" Vic said something to

In 1965, Chevrolet was ready to introduce the Mark IV— 425 horsepower, 396 CID big-block. The Chevrolet PR department asked Vic Jr. if he would be interested in working on a boat project involving two of America's astronauts, Gordon Cooper and Gus Grissom. He jumped at the chance. The result was a great friendship between two American Icons and

Edelbrock Corporation. Below (left to right), Grissom, Vic, and Cooper. According to Vic and the crew who worked on the boat, Grissom and Cooper were super guys and helped the project by keeping take-out food and great jokes in constant supply. Vic says, "They were both great to work with, and proved to be real racers."

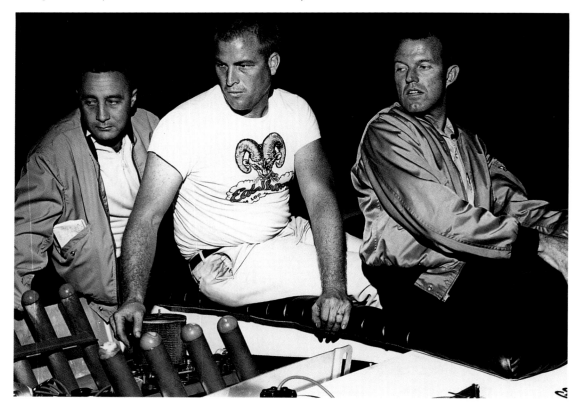

> "The time I spent with Cooper and Grissom was something I'll never forget. When Gus was killed, all of us were hit hard. He was a great hero, but he was also a real racer, and the kind of guy everyone liked to hang out with." —**Vic Edelbrock Jr.**

him and Grissom took off in a cloud of dust. About half an hour later, he was back with a carload of V.O., beer, food, chips, and other goodies. After a brief party, the crew went back at it for the rest of the night, with the only breaks being the men taking naps in shifts.

Cooper and Grissom showed up early Thursday, still with the press in tow, but by now panic was starting to set in and the humor of the moment was wearing thin. If they didn't get the boat to the Salton Sea and have it pass tech inspection by Friday afternoon they would lose their sponsors and have to pay a lot of bills out of pocket. About noon, the phone rang and someone asked to speak to Grissom. He got on the phone and told the caller not to worry, everything is under control. At the same moment, Vic lit one of the engines and it blasted off. Grissom held the phone up so they could hear and then said, "You hear that? Everything is okay."

The crew finished tuning and tweaking, and then the boat and trailer were hooked up to a truck and the whole flying circus—TV crews, the Edelbrock gang, and the two stars of the show—headed for the Salton Sea. Once there, the next challenge was getting the boat up to race performance. They began running practice sessions, with performance improving in every segment. The racers and crews were based in Brawley, a small town just south of Salton Sea. The road from town to the lake was typical of desert roads in the area—lonely. On one of the runs to the lake, Vic and his crew were following Cooper in his borrowed Cadillac. Cooper took off and started running flat out, and when he topped a slight rise he became airborne. When the car hit the pavement, it ripped the exhaust pipe and muffler halfway off the car. By the time Edelbrock came sliding to a stop, Gordon was out of the car yanking the bent pieces off the car and tossing them into the weeds. Later, Vic remembered, he told us that with the muffler gone, "the car ran just a little quicker."

The race? In the end, the boat ran great and Cooper and Grissom drove like two old pros, but the stock pistons used in the engines just couldn't take the stress, and one of the engines blew.

So much work, so little time. Gus Grissom, left, and Gordon Cooper, right, were to drive the boat shown below. The Edelbrock crew scrambles to finish installation of a Chevy big-block engine. The space men drove the boat like they were old pros, but the stress was too much for the stock pistons and the engine blew before the end. Both Grissom and Cooper are gone, and those who knew them can only hope they are racing among the stars they loved so much.

In 1978, Camee Edelbrock retired from the horse show circuit and started water ski racing. She and her dad, who drove the boat, competed at places like Lake Havasu, top, in '79, Lake Mead, and Clear Lake in Northern California, above. Camee was part of the "Fun Team" when the term was first invented as a result of Vic's many wins as boat driver. During trophy presentations, every winning skier from the Edelbrock team was serenaded with a loud, repetitive phrase—Fun Team, Fun Team, Fun Team— a cheer that rattled the minds of the competition.

strong Danny Churchill to the team. At the time, he was a quarter-mile record holder on water skis, running over 110 mph. His first contest with Vic Edelbrock was the Catalina ski race, a round trip open ocean ski marathon between Long Beach, California, and Catalina Island.

"Heading out of the harbor at the start you hit very rough water," related Edelbrock of the fateful day. "Our boat began slamming hard and the compass was flying 180 degrees one way, then 360 degrees another, obviously not built to take a beating, and after a few minutes the instrument was junk. Because the boat had been converted from a family ski boat, the grips for the observer to hang onto were simple ropes and wooden handles and they tore out of their mountings at the start of the race. The observer was at the ocean's mercy and hung onto his seat.

"All I could do was take up a position behind several other boats, figuring that they had a compass that worked. Herbst had also told me to watch closely as we approached the island for a noticeable dip in the mountains on the left side of the island—that was the landmark for Avalon Harbor and we were to head directly for the dip. When the boats we had been following turned slightly right and I saw the dip, we turned slightly left and got to Avalon Harbor first— with a useless compass! We had cut a very quick time to the island.

"No one had yet completed the race in less than an hour, so if we kept our pace we could win and set a new record. We headed back to Long Beach by simply paralleling the late traffic coming to Catalina Island. Then we started tracking the seaplane used to transport passengers from Long Beach to the Island, but they only flew once every half hour.

"We were about to give up when a competitor running an Ocean Racer came flying up behind us and we started following his every move because I knew they carried inboard compasses. When the skyline of Long Beach appeared and we could find our way with landmarks, I pushed the throttle to pass, but power started falling off. Danny was going nuts and wanted to go faster. We thought a broken header had caused us to lose power. At the same time, a boat and skier, Chuck Sterns, was gaining on us, and there was nothing to do but watch. Chuck Sterns beat us by fifty feet. We later discovered the mag gear was worn out and caused the lost power. Not a happy ending! Danny, always a super competitor, stayed with me for one more race."

The following year, Edelbrock had a new skier named Jeff Wooten. Once again, the team had to be careful as they passed the breakwater where the water churned violently. Wooten went down a hundred yards off the start and Edelbrock retrieved him, but on the second start they hit fog that cut visibility down to about half a mile, and headed for the east end of Catalina Island to save time.

"The only thing to do was calculate our position by using a watch," confessed Edelbrock. "Most professional boat captains would be shaking their heads, but we ran flat-out through the fog hoping nothing got in our way. After forty-five minutes I began thinking we were lost when I spotted another boat with a skier directly in front of us. I knew it was one of the Australian skiers because of his skiing style—one hand behind his back.

"We started following these guys, but they were weaving all over the place and we realized they were as lost as we were. Totally bewildered, I stopped, pulled in Jeff, and tried to figure out our next move. Killing the engine created a new problem because there was no neutral gear in a direct drive system, so the engine had to be turned off when we pulled up. Restarting a hot engine equipped with a magneto and a very small battery is problematic. Suddenly, out of the fog like an apparition from an old sea story comes a thirty-foot schooner with people hanging onto the side railings, yelling and laughing. We lucked out, the engine started, and I steered over close by, asking, 'Where the hell is Catalina?' We heard remarks about our navigational skills and the wisdom of water skiing in the fog, but they pointed and shouted 'It's over there!' We followed the pointed fingers and, sure enough, the island appeared. We had missed by about two miles. It was not our best year."

"The ski races in the ocean were the most challenging, with water conditions ranging from glass smooth to white cap rough. I skied in the mixed doubles class with my friend Jim Cook. At Dana Point one year I crashed halfway through a 50-miler and broke my ankle, but still finished the race. We got 2nd in class. In '83, we skied the Catalina Race (52-miles across the shipping channel from Long Beach harbor to Catalina Island and back). It was super rough that year and many teams quit before they reached the breakwater. I fell so many times that my driver, Mike Toll, starting asking, 'Are you sure you want to keep going?' The answer was always 'YES' because I refused to quit. On the way back, Mike made a common mistake and didn't watch his compass. We ended up at the San Pedro harbor entrance instead of Long Beach, making the trip even longer. After a grueling 2 hours, 17 minutes, we crossed the finish line first in our class! The second place team wouldn't finish for another 43 minutes." —Camee Edelbrock

Fun on the Water

Vic continued water ski racing into the early 1980s. He pulled skiers using a wide variety of boats that included Rayson Craft, Kevlar Spectra Special, and even a borrowed Spectra from Herbst. Curt Hooker and Murray Jensen built the power plant for the race boats, equipped them with Edelbrock parts, and tested each one on the dyno. Vic's skiers covered many classes and varying age groups from nine years old and up. The skiers included Joe Brain, Clyde Horner, Buck Baker, Tim Herbst, Danny Mashburn, Melinda Bonderude, Dawna Brice and his own daughter, Camee. A number of successes racing at Clear Lake and other venues led to the christening of the Edelbrock crew as the Fun Team. Jerry Herbst and his sons got Vic started in the sport. They were serious racers who won many championships. Camee Edelbrock raced mostly in 50- and 75-mile marathons with partner Jim Cook in the Mixed Doubles Class.

Vic drove the boat in water ski races and his daughter Camee skied. She competed in the mixed doubles class, where two skiers of opposite genders were towed behind the same boat. Camee (left) and partner Jim Cook (right) won a high-point national championship in 1983. Later, Camee drove the Edelbrock 32-foot Spectra in several Catalina ski races, towing many fast women to top finishes.

A Great and Terrible Friendship

During his late teens and early twenties, Vic Jr. raced, and generally impressed the local boaters at Lake Arrowhead. Lifelong pal Jerry Herbst joined him ski racing and the pair soon gained a reputation as hard-core racers. The weekends of boat racing spawned a rivalry between them that got heated at times, but always in fun. Whether at USC as classmates, playing golf, or chasing girls at parties, Vic and Jerry shared a competitive spirit.

Herbst's father was a very successful service station owner who had been tagged "Terrible Herbst" by several of his competitors throughout the Midwest. When Herbst came west, he started a new service station called "Terrible Herbst." By the time Jerry had taken over his father's business, the franchise had grown to 120 stations in California, Nevada, Utah, Arizona, and Oregon. When Jerry's three sons joined the business, "Terrible Herbst" also included 30 giant truck stops and a partnership in a chain of resort/casino locations in Nevada.

"I met Vic Jr. during my freshman year at USC, about 1955," Jerry said. My wife Maryanna and Nancy Edelbrock also went to USC. Nancy was Maryana's big sister at the Theta Sorority house at USC. My parents and Vic's folks had a vacation home up at Lake Arrowhead. At the time, Lake Arrowhead was a little jewel, very pristine, out of the smog and hidden from the world. Nowadays, the boats are side-by-side nearly all the way around the lake, and you can't even smell the pine trees. Back then it was very different.

"I had a racing Chris Craft and Vic Jr. had a Higgins. We were both running around the lake, goofing off and entering the ski races held during the summer. We were both very competitive and we started getting after each other instantly. Vic was cocky; he thought his boat ran faster than my boat, plus he had backing from his dad's shop. A Hercules six-cylinder truck engine powered my boat—it had a Paxton blower and a pressurized carburetor.

"Vic Senior was still alive when I tore the engine down and took the rods, pistons, and crankshaft over to Edelbrock's shop on Jefferson. As soon as I walked into the shop, here comes Junior wanting to know

what I was doing at his dad's shop. I tell Senior, 'You guys are competitors, but I still respect your work. I want you to rework this engine with the same quality you use on your own stuff. I know you will do a super job, then I'll be able to beat you.' Vic Sr. tells me, 'no problem.' Junior got all uptight and believed that I was saying, 'your daddy is going to help me whip your ass.' I think he still believes that to be true."

Nevertheless, the two became very close friends. Both families, including Vic's girls and Herbst's three boys, spent many weekends and holidays together. When Herbst started ski racing on a serious level, Edelbrock's Fun Team joined him. Herbst had Team Terrible, and another good friend, John "Pete" Peters, ran Team Honcho. Edelbrock bought a boat and all the equipment needed to get serious about ski racing , and then proceeded to steal a couple of Herbst's best skiers.

"I think he was still mad about Arrowhead," Herbst said with a laugh. "Soon my sons were skiing at the 100 mph mark. At those speeds you have to be on top of your game every second, and since they were at the girl-chasing age and sneaking a beer or two, I started worrying—it was time to change to offshore racing"

The Herbst and Edelbrock families were always very close, and it was only natural that when Herbst went offshore racing, so did Vic. They bought a couple of hot Scarab boats and raced, all the while

having great fun with their sons and daughters. Herbst and Edelbrock also played golf, often partnering in tournaments.

"As our offshore racing got more serious and Vic got to be a better driver, we starting looking for the chance to race each other," noted Herbst. "The chance came at the 1985 National Championship event in Key West, Florida, but for some reason, Vic did not make the show. I wanted to win so I could brag about it, and rag on Vic for not showing up. My son Tim was driving, rigger Jerry Gilbert was the observer, and I was the throttle man. We hit an unexpected wind wave running about 90 mph, we flew into the air and slammed back down on the water. I was thrown from the boat—my left arm caught something and was literally torn to shreds. I lost the use of it, but was very lucky that it was not completely torn off. That ended not only my boat-racing career, but also put an end to playing competitive golf."

Soon after Herbst's crash, Edelbrock gave up boat racing, too. The idea of not being able to compete with his pal had taken much of the fun out of the racing and golfing.

Herbst's sons Ed, Tim, and Troy went off-road racing in Baja and won their share of races. Troy became the Class One Championship winner five times and was also the overall score Champion and Trophy Truck Champion.

As an only child, Vic Edelbrock Jr. never had a real brother, but his lifelong friend Jerry Herbst (left) came as close as possible to filling that void. Jerry and Vic raced boats, played golf, went to USC and enjoyed family outings together. When Jerry was critically injured in a boat crash, Vic gave up boat racing shortly after. The crash left Jerry unable to play golf, so Vic lost interest in the sport.

Jerry Herbst races across Lake Mead, left, in his offshore boat "Mr. Terrible." He once said that he enjoyed beating his friend Vic Edelbrock Jr. because he hates losing and it was fun watching him pout afterward. Herbst raced with his three sons, Ed, Tim and Troy and Vic raced with daughter Camee, while the rest of the Edelbrock clan was competing on horseback. Eventually the separation of family would help to end the offshore deal, but not before Vic and Camee raced under the Golden Gate Bridge in San Francisco, below left, finishing second overall behind the late Bob Nordskog.

Offshore Boat Racing

Jerry Herbst purchased a thirty-eight foot Scarab in 1984 to go offshore boat racing. He immediately challenged Edelbrock to follow. But Edelbrock was suddenly struck down by a heart attack, and everything stopped for a few weeks. While Vic recuperated at home, Herbst and fellow racer Pete Peters figured that the best medicine for the patient was to buy a new boat. The visitors came by with a model of a thirty-eight-foot Scarab, and told Edelbrock the real thing could be bought from land developer Tom Gentry in Hawaii. As soon as he was up and around, he bought the boat.

Offshore boat racing gave a whole new dimension to the Fun Team. This was the big leagues, high speeds, unlimited funds, and huge egos. Racing was dangerous, serious, and expensive. The Fun Team, Team Terrible, and Team Honcho were a trio of traveling offshore racers. Edelbrock set up a program at the shop to build engines specifically for his boat. Camee became the driver with Dad acting as throttle man and Curt Hooker as navigator. Just before Camee became pregnant with her daughter, Courtney, the team ran a marathon race in San Francisco Bay with the course passing under the Golden Gate Bridge. They lost an outdrive early in race and never made it to the bridge. After Courtney was born, the team ran one of its last marathon races—with Camee driving—so she could at last pass beneath the Golden Gate Bridge at the finish.

Edelbrock and the Liquid Thunder Phase

Like every other endeavor in his life, Vic Edelbrock Jr. attacked boat racing with an all-out effort. He raced offshore races and long distance ski events. He bought the best equipment, and when the Fun Team showed up at a race, all eyes turned in their direction. Clockwise, Vic Jr. and Wayne Murray talk race strategy after one of their offshore events. Murray, who is currently vice president of manufacturing, was part of the boat racing effort for 15 years. Vic, Camee and Curt Hooker in the number 37 offshore boat (a 38-foot Scarab) after a win at Lake Mead in Nevada. The winning Edelbrock team pulls into dock (left to right) Curt Hooker, Camee Edelbrock, and Vic Jr. Vic Jr. gives an interview to a TV crew after a race in the San Francisco Bay. *Opposite:* Top, Vic driving number 527 flat out as his observer hangs on for dear life during a ski race in the Colorado River. Below left, Vic raises his hand as he gets ready for a run in his first ski race boat, a Spectra.

"Our next racing venture was offshore boat racing with Bob Nordskog's association on the West Coast. We raced a 38-foot Scarab with two big-block Chevy engines. My dad worked the throttles, I was the driver and controlled the steering and Curt Hooker was the navigator. We raced all over the West Coast at speeds up to 100 mph. One of our most memorable races was in San Francisco in 1987. The race course included a long lap around the bay on smooth, fast water along with extremely rough water beyond the Golden Gate bridge. We were in second place overall, behind Bob Nordskog, when I noticed that Bob had negotiated the turn incorrectly. When this happens, you must turn back and re-negotiate the turn or be disqualified. I told my dad about this and he argued with me saying, "Bob never makes a mistake, follow him and do the turn the same way he did." I replied saying that I was sure he was wrong. Our navigator's radio was not working so we didn't get any help from him. We were going 95+ mph in San Francisco bay arguing about how to negotiate the next turn! Well, I was the one who had control of the steering so I went the way that I thought was correct. I was right! Bob had to re-negotiate the turn, putting us in first place overall. We got passed in the rough water and ended up back in 2nd place but this is one argument that I'll never forget! I tell our tour groups, "Thank goodness I was right, because if I'd been wrong, I probably wouldn't be working here today!" —**Camee Edelbrock**

Looking back, Curt Hooker recalled the grueling race schedule, but pointed out that as serious as the team was about winning, the crew was dedicated to having fun and that Edelbrock was the "CEO of the merriment."

"I was just a kid when we started ski racing," Hooker said. "Vic and the Fun Team were the hit of every event. It was crazy, and Vic would never let up. He became the leader—charging ahead, puffing on a big old cigar, seeing what trouble he could start. After a ski race and a couple of drinks in Northern California, a bunch of us headed for the local race track that was running an event featuring what they called 'Bomber Stockers', old junkers on their last legs. Vic and Southern California engine builder Paul Pfaff offered the locals a hundred bucks each to let them drive in a special race. A few others jumped in and the fans went nuts, they thought it's going to be a big fight. Pfaff sprinted into the lead and when Vic tried to pass, one of Pfaff's passengers (the Herbst boy), began pouring water out of holes in the floorboards, making the track slick. Pfaff won, and he kept buzzing around the track waving until the rest of the guys got him to stop. When he jumped out of the car, waving and cheering, you would have thought he won the Indy 500, winding up the wild ride by giving an interview to the local TV crew.

"Food fights were another premier event after every boat race, and Vic would start most of them, then pretend to stop things once they got out of hand. Once, at an upscale restaurant in an old mansion, we had a room of our own. Food fights usually started with butter pats, then bread, but on this occasion a fully-loaded baked potato—sour cream, butter, and all, went flying by my head and hit the wall. It got so bad that some guys grabbed their food and went out into the parking lot to eat. Vic would later compensate the place for the distasteful display of adolescence. Eventually we all grew out of the practice . . . sort of."

Nancy was spending most of her time at horse shows with Christi and Carey, while Vic went offshore racing with Camee. Nancy lost no opportunity to voice strong opinions about her fears of the dangers of racing. Expenses kept increasing, and by the late 1980s, offshore racing (which did not have much crowd appeal or media coverage) was costing Edelbrock Corporation more than it was worth in exposure. Because of the physical dangers involved, tension increased between Vic and Nancy. The Fun Team had some riotous good times, and won its share of races, including setting a speed record that stood for six years at the Catalina race, towing a champion racer Mason Thompson. Nevertheless, after Jerry Herbst's accident in Florida, Edelbrock lost interest in racing offshore. The thrill was gone.

"I have always considered Vic one of my closest friends. When it comes to private matters, I'm not a real expressive person, but one time Vic said to me, 'I never had a brother, so I have always thought of you as my brother.' We share the same business philosophy and we both spend as much time as possible with our children and grandchildren. The years would not have been as much fun if I hadn't been able to challenge Vic Edelbrock. I still like beating him. When Vic bought his 93-foot boat VictorE, we bought a 107-footer, just to aggravate him. It's great fun." —**Jerry Herbst**

Organic Horsepower

The Edelbrock Fun Team was more than fast boats and water skiers; it included a "natural horsepower" component as well. While Vic and daughter Camee were engaged in boat racing on the West Coast, the rest of the family went in for equine excitement. The family had owned horses since building a spacious ranch home in Rolling Hills in 1970. The Edelbrock girls—and even Dad—rode an old quarter horse named Dirty Mike.

Although Christi Edelbrock made the most of the family's involvement with horses by becoming a highly rated American competitor and later developing her own horse training business, Camee, Carey, mom Nancy, and even Vic Jr. did their share of riding. Camee, below left, competed in jumping competition as did her sister Carey. Nancy, below right, on her horse Hi Jack, rode and showed horses as well as acting as chaperone for Christi and Carey when they toured the East.

Carey Edelbrock Robb

Carey Edelbrock Robb, youngest of Vic and Nancy Edelbrock's daughters, thinks outside the box when it comes to living her life. She is an independent spirit, much the same as her mother and father. Although you will not see her suited up in a Nomex racing uniform, or dressed in jacket and hat bearing the Edelbrock logo, mingling with spectators at a major racing event, it does not mean that the desire to do so is not burning just below the exterior of her character.

Carey Edelbrock Robb admits that she loves racing, and although she is part of the most famous name in the performance industry, she has chosen to turn her attention to that of a higher calling. Her vocation requires many of the same attributes needed to succeed in business and in driving a race car; grit, determination, patience and a brave heart. Carey has given her life to being a wife and mother, raising her five children and devoting her energy to family. Her goals may differ from her siblings, yet they are similar in many ways. At one time, she equaled her sister, Christi, in equestrian competition. She could, at one time, water ski with the proficiency of her sister Camee.

"Being six years younger than Camee and five years younger than Christi, I was automatically the family baby and was pulled in whatever direction my sisters chose to go. When they started riding horses, I wanted to ride. When we all went water skiing with my parents, I wanted to ski with my sisters. Actually, being the baby, had its advantages, because I started doing all of the fun things much earlier than my sisters had, because my parents were not in a position to do all the fun stuff when Camee and Christi were babies. Another advantage I had was when Camee and Christi were seven or eight years old, they had each other to keep company, and sometimes my mom and dad would leave them with a relative when they would travel to a big event like the drag races. But when I came along, my sisters wanted to go to all of the exciting places, and my parents didn't want to leave me home alone, so I started having family fun early in my life.

"The first real separation for the family came

when I was about twelve. Christi was really making progress in her horse riding and programs, and I was following in her footsteps. I wanted to ride horses. So, when Camee entered USC and no longer rode horses, she and my dad went water ski racing while Christi and I went on the horse show circuit. At the time, I was totally dedicated to becoming a horse show winner and I didn't care much for boats or cars, so the family was divided into two camps. When Christi and I went back East to compete, things got even more tangled. Because I was too young to be on my own, my mom became bi-coastal. We bought a condo and my mother would stay with us, go to all of the events, and then fly home whenever possible to be with my dad and to help him with company events.

"On many occasions, my dad, who really enjoyed watching Christi and I compete, would fly back to our events, but it was extremely difficult for him, because of his schedule. He had to go to NHRA national events, big races like Indy and Daytona, plus he was very involved in boat racing. In reality, it was my mom who had the most difficult road when it came to keeping the family together. Our situation became more acceptable by the time I graduated from high school. Christi had begun training horses, and she had gotten married. She and her husband came back to California and opened a training center near our home. I gravitated toward Christi and her lifestyle, because I loved the horse business, but once back in California, there was the company and pressure to be part of that business. Camee was very involved with Edelbrock Corporation. She was working in the advertising department and still racing with my dad. I became a little confused, and had trouble sorting out my loyalties. So I took a year to work at the company between high school and beginning college at USC.

"I split my time between working at the company and training with Christi. Although I love my dad and my sister Camee, and I love the company, I was not comfortable. I wanted something different in my life. For many years I had harbored the desire to be a world-class chef. I told mom and dad I wanted to skip

USC and go to the Culinary Institute in New York City. My dad, who would be paying for much of my education, didn't think much of me becoming a chef, and suggested that I should first get my degree, then if I was still interested, go to New York. I agreed.

"During my first year at USC I met a young student named Bryan Robb, and that was that. We fell in love, I changed my major to teaching and Bryan and I were married. I became a teacher, never went to New York, and would only practice the art of gourmet cooking on my family. I found my calling. I loved teaching, especially small children; kindergarten and first grade. Soon however, we began raising a family and I discovered that my calling was not only teaching but being a mother and parent. I left the teaching profession and began nurturing my own children; the number grew to five (one set of twins). I believe that my time with my children is all-important, and I do not regret giving

Carey Edelbrock, youngest of the three Edelbrock daughters, below, (with her mom) is much like her grandfather, tough, reserved and competitive. Although Carey chose being a mom over a career, she was a fierce competitor in the horse jumping world. Carey won her share of events riding Man of Distinction, opposite.

"I regret the fact that I never got to know Vic Sr. I only heard stories from my grandma, Katie, my dad, Bobby Meeks, and Murray Jensen. When I hear all the stories, it makes me feel a little empty, and that I missed a lot by not knowing him." —**Carey Edelbrock**

up a professional career for that of being a full-on, 24-hour mom."

As for her relationship with the company, Carey feels strongly about the Edelbrock name, once telling her husband when they were first married, that she would always be an Edelbrock and that just

because she doesn't work at the company on a daily basis does not mean she has any less love for it than her dad, mom, or sisters.

"One thing that is very important to me is the fact that my mom and dad support my feelings and ideas dealing with my lifestyle, just as strongly as

they do Camee and Christi. They have always treated us equally. It just happens that I have gone in a slightly different direction. I love my kids, and raising them is what comes first in my life. My mom and dad understand my motives and that's what makes us a family."

At one point in her career as a champion Jumper and Hunter Class rider, Christi Edelbrock was on the short list to make the United States Olympic Team. She was considered one of the best riders in America.

Nancy had always been a horse lover. Her first horse was given to her by her dad who traded a used car for her horse at his car agency. Horse riding with Camee, Christi, and Carey started at the early ages of 9 and 10. Vic and Nancy went to most horse shows and Vic hauled the horses in a fifth-wheel trailer behind his pick-up. The rig held four horses and a small dressing room.

When Carey was born, Vic bought Nancy a horse to ride, which she did with Carey sleeping in her baby carriage, in the family station wagon. All three girls were riding, but Camee retired when she attended the University of Southern California. Christi and Carey continued riding up and down the West Coast entering more prestigious events, eventually ending up on the East Coast while Vic and Camee were water ski racing on the West Coast.

After Christi graduated from high school, she was invited east to show with a world-class trainer named George Morris. Hunterdon Farms is in New Jersey, and since Christi had only just turned 17, Nancy went with her so that she might make the most of the opportunity. Christi remembered the first show in 1979, the horse show in Devon Pennsylvania— the oldest outdoor horse show in the United States. "We shocked the establishment by bringing five horses. In those days it was unusual for contestants to come all the way from the West Coast—especially with five horses."

Christi's competitive nature emerged when she grew tired of simply showing her horses and began to participate in show jumping. She quickly moved to the difficult Jumper Division and traveled throughout the East entering both indoor and outdoor events. She was determined to take her shot at being a champion and she was soon placed on a long list of riders to be chosen for the American Olympic Team. She won the team gold medal and the individual silver medal for show jumping at the National Sports Festival before accepting an invitation to compete in Germany and Holland. She was the highest-placed American in one German event.

Christi had been accepted to USC, but she deferred enrollment twice to stay with her horse riding. But Christi's successes brought an invitation to the pinnacle of horse jumping elegance, the World Cup at New York's Madison Square Garden. Christi's biggest moment at the Garden came not in the World Cup events, but when she and her horse, Victor, entered the wall jumping (Puissance) event the night before the main contest. "I had entered several of the show and jumping events not really knowing how we would fare against the other riders. The night before the championship finals they held the Puissance Class. The crowd was so huge that the only way

Christi Edelbrock was a fearless rider, left and below, at Grand Prix events. During her career she competed in Europe, won gold and silver medals at the National Sports Festival and was the highest placed American in an event in Germany. But her greatest moment came in Madison Square Garden during the World Cup, when she jumped her horse over a 7-foot, 1½ inch solid wall. The crowd went wild.

The story of the 614 Corvette, center, goes back to 1962 and a race at Riverside Raceway called the "Times Three-Hour Invitational", when the father of the Corvette, Zora Duntov, right, with Vic Jr. at Laguna Seca in the late '80s, brought four Z06 Corvettes to run against the Cobra team. Vic restored the old 614 and still runs the car today. And, Zora and Vic, above, at the Car Craft Awards Banquet) stayed close friends until Duntov passed away.

to get space was to be a participant. I had very little experience in Puissance, but jumped cleanly (without mistake) in rounds one and two.

"George Morris, my trainer, saw that I was doing so well that he encouraged me to continue. As the third round approached, I wanted to see how high the wall had been raised, but the rules state a rider cannot pre-judge the jump, and I had to come out blind. My heart was pounding; I had a bad case of cottonmouth, but I figured since I had already done it twice I could do it again. It was too late to back out now, the crowd was cheering. The wall had been raised to 7-feet, 1½-inches and it looked insurmountable, but I didn't hesitate and took my shot. Victor gave a tremendous jolt of power launching us both into the air. We knocked off just a single block from the top of the wall. It was my moment. The next rider cleared and took the win, giving me a second-place finish. No other rider in the competition came close. When I called my mom and dad they couldn't believe that I had jumped such a height when I had only entered to gather a little experience. What a moment it was!"

Roaring into Vintage Fun

Horsepower seemed to permeate every aspect of an Edelbrock's life: in a boat hull, under a car hood, or attached to a saddle. Horses were the nucleus. So it shouldn't have been a surprise to Vic and Nancy when the next phase of their lives emerged at a horse show. Daughter Carey was riding at the Santa Barbara Show Grounds with Mom and Dad in her cheering section. Afterward, Nancy and Vic looked up an old friend, Joehnck, who ran an engine building shop in Santa Barbara since the fifties, and had been one of Senior's and Vic Jr.'s best friends.

During the visit and while in his shop, Joehnck pointed to an old hunk of a Corvette sitting under a canvas cover. When Edelbrock asked him about it, Joehnck replied, "That's the remains of one of the most famous Corvettes ever built, old number 614." Still puzzled, Edelbrock quizzed him further about what was so interesting about an old beat-up Corvette.

The car was one of the six original Zora Duntov factory racing Z-06 Corvettes. The 614 also ran in excess of 200 miles per hour on the Bonneville Salt Flats and then was sold several more times for drag racing and modified contests. Eventually it found its way back to Santa Barbara in the late 1980s, when a local guy came into Joehnck's shop asking about the old Corvette he

The 614 Corvette, driven by Vic, leading his daughter Camee at Laguna Seca, was the first Vintage race car restored by the Edelbrock Fun Team.

The Duntov Corvette

It is well known that Chevy exec Bunkie Knudsen wanted to improve the Corvette image, but Chevrolet could no longer sponsor racing teams. Although the new Corvette Sting Ray's styling is attributed to Bill Mitchell, the power train, suspension, and handling was the work of Zora Duntov. Chevrolet wanted the Corvette to look good at the Times Grand Prix in Riverside. Without GM's knowledge, Duntov went to the lower floor of the St. Louis plant and built six Z06 cars with better brakes, better engines, and 35-gallon gas tanks. He was unaware that Carroll Shelby was going to unleash the Cobra onto the sports car world, running a Ford small-block.

Shelley Washburn in Santa Barbara was one of four car owners who asked Joehnck to prepare the new Sting Ray. The problem was that the cars had to be picked up in St. Louis, and driven back to California. Although it was only the second annual race, the big push was to make the 1962 Times Three-Hour Invitational race at Riverside Raceway. The first contest had been held the previous year and was jointly organized by the California Sports Car Club and Sports Car Club of America. The Los Angeles Times returned as sponsor for the 1962 race, and this one would be an endurance sports car race contest on Saturday October 13, the day before the Times Grand Prix. As it worked out, the race would be a showdown between Cobra and Corvette.

"Bob Bondurant showed up with the car only a week and half before the race. There wasn't much we could do," lamented Bob Joehnck. "I put in a roll cage, seat belts, worked the engine, and made some decent headers. The brakes could have been better, but we had no time for testing. I got so pissed-off about the way we were preparing the car that I decided not to go."

That three-hour event with fifty-six entries became a cult classic in the chronicles of California sports-car racing. Started in Le Mans style where drivers run across the track to their cars, the race ended with a giant fireworks display. The 1962 version had an impressive lineup in the field: Dave MacDonald drove for Sting Ray dealer Don Steves, Jerry Grant was in another Z06 driving for SS Research & Development, the third Sting Ray saw Doug Hooper in Mickey Thompson's entry, and Bob Bondurant was in the Washburn number 614 car.

Although the Cobra team showed up with one Cobra driven by Ken Miles, it wasn't listed in the official program. World champion Sir Jack Brabham, Bruce McLaren, and Jerry Titus drove Sunbeam Alpines; Dick Guldstrand drove a Corvette; Jack Breskovich was in Los Angeles Chevrolet dealer Harry Mann's non-factory Sting Ray; future Can-Am and Trans-Am champion George Follmer entered with an Alfa-Romeo Super. Soon-to-be Cobra driver Lew Spencer was in a Morgan 4; Paul Reinhart, a 1960s superstar Corvette driver, drove a 1957 Corvette. Standing in the Formula Junior pit area waiting for his turn on the track was movie actor Steve McQueen, driving for John Cooper.

MacDonald and Miles waged a classic battle for a time until both cars broke. As for the 614 Corvette, Bob Bondurant said, "I had driven a '59 Corvette for Shelley Washburn and he wanted me to handle the new Z06. Joehnck worked his butt off trying to get the cars in shape but there was no time. When we got to Riverside I took one look at the Cobra and figured we were in deep trouble. During the race I could out-corner the Cobra, but it was lighter so Miles could get out of the corner quicker. The real problem was the brakes, and I ended up backing off for corners way early, but in the end for me it was an engine problem that put me out. Miles had the race in the bag, then something broke and Doug Hooper took over and won. It was a great win for Corvette, but the handwriting was on the wall—the Cobras were coming."

After the Riverside race, Bob Joehnck began working on the car, changing the chassis setup, reworking the brakes, and rebuilding the engine. Later on in the season he had a wild idea, one that would identify the car throughout history, and it started with the header flange hole saw that he used to cut holes in the chassis to reduce the weight by seventeen pounds. Club racer Tony Settember took over the driving chores when Bondurant left to drive Cobras, and the next installment of the 614 saga came when a local lawyer and racer Mark Dees bought the car to run 200 mph at the Bonneville Salt Flats and become a member of the 200 mph club.

Joehnck once again had set up the car and motor. "On our first attempt, we came close but no cigar," he recalled. "Mark called the factory engineers to see what they could tell him about improving the car's handling. When they found out how fast we were going, they about wet their pants. The engineers told Mark, no way should the car be going 200 mph, so he dropped them from the picture. We went back to the salt in 1968, after cutting off the top of the car and doing extensive streamlining. Mark got his wish and went 205.89 mph."

The Z06 Corvette, number 614—the pride of the Edelbrock Fun Team car collection.

To Vic — All the best — [signature]

The history of the 614 Corvette can be told with the two photos shown here. Back in the early 1960s, the 614 ran several races in California including the infamous Riverside three-Hour endurance event against the Cobras. It also ran various other events driven by Bob Bondurant, left, shown staying ahead of the Corvette roadster of Dick Guldstrand at the one and only event in the parking lot of Dodger Stadium.

The 614 was restored by Vic Edelbrock Jr., for vintage racing. Below, Vic runs hard at an event in Palm Springs, California.

Bob Joehnck, who set up the 614 for its original race at Riverside, knew the Corvette was too heavy, so he decided to lighten the chassis by boring holes in the main rails, above, with a header flange hole-saw. Today, the 614 has been restored, right, and has a solid chassis. According to Joehnck, the car is better today than it was back in 1962.

had bought. "When I saw the car, it was a hulk," Joehnck said. "But I could tell instantly that it was 614, it had holes in the frame, and there were certain brackets and modifications I had done, and they were recognizable. I bought the car on the spot, and took it back to my shop. I began rebuilding the car. The body was useless, so I found different nose and rear sections, and began putting things in place. I had no idea how long it would take or if I would ever get it back into running condition."

"What are you going to do with it?" asked Vic.

"Vintage race," came the reply.

Confused but still curious, Edelbrock asked, "What the hell is vintage car racing?"

Joehnck replied, "Oh, it's great, you build an old car and drive it around like a parade; no danger, no serious racing, just fun."

Nancy found the idea of historic car racing just marvelous, especially because the danger level was greatly reduced from that of offshore racing. She watched with amusement as Vic bought the car right on the spot, but only after promising Joehnck that he would finish the restoration. Racing vintage or historic cars had just begun to surface as a serious motor sport in the late 1980s.

"I bought the car, shipped it to the shop and knew exactly who I wanted to handle the restoration," Edelbrock recalled. "Mike Eddy, whose father had worked for Carroll Shelby, had just come to work full-time at the shop and was an excellent mechanic. I put him in charge of rebuilding the car to look original and make it safe, but thinking we were just going to drive around."

Mike Eddy is a big, tremendously skilled no-nonsense man, dedicated to the race car business. Possessed of a very dry sense of humor, he was always ready for a joke or prank. Race day was another matter. Eddy became a force to be avoided if you had frivolity on your mind. Get in his way when doing his job and you received a cutting stare—block his path further and he would

At one time, Mike Eddy drove the boat hauler, left. Today, he drives the company's transporter that carries four vintage race cars. Mike (right) has been crew chief, race car mechanic, and truck driver for the Fun Team for over two decades. He has overseen all of the Edelbrock vintage racecar restoration projects.

adjust your position. He was one of the very few who would argue with Edelbrock and convince him to see matters in a different perspective. Responsible for the Fun Team stable of cars, he worked on any restoration project that arrived into the shop; he also drove the Edelbrock 18-wheel hauler for the team when they went to races around the country.

"I had been with the Fun Team boat racing for several years when Vic asked me to work on the Corvette," said Eddy, "It was a piece of junk. We had a tough time just getting all the parts assembled so the thing would run. The first priority, as Meeks put it, 'was to make it safe, so the boss doesn't skin up his ass.' After months of labor the car was back in one piece, just barely drivable. We used the original chassis, with the holes drilled in the main rails, but I hated the first restoration."

After ordering a new slant-nose Porche 911 Turbo, Edelbrock went to a driving school at Hockingheim; he thought that would be enough. Besides, vintage racing would be easy, right? Edelbrock could handle boat racing, flying an airplane, running a business; having been engrossed in race cars all his life, what problem would there be in driving around with a bunch of other old cars?

"Mike Eddy worked nonstop for months on end," Edelbrock said, "He got the car sorted out and handling good enough that we took the car to the Monterey Historic Races in 1987, but I was not really ready for what was about to happen. Vintage car racing was not just a matter of parading in rank and file; the guys running vintage cars were serious runners. I quickly found out the way the car was set up that I was just a back marker."

It was nearly a year before Edelbrock ventured out again—this time better prepared for a Historic Motor Sports Association event at Sears Point International Raceway in the wine country near Sonoma, California. Excited to race, Edelbrock roared off and made it to turn eleven

The first driver and the current driver of the famed 614 Corvette stand together. Bob Bondurant (left) drove the Washburn Corvette in its first race in 1962 at Riverside Raceway. Vic Edelbrock Jr. (right) restored the car and now drives it in Vintage races.

before the clutch exploded. This little episode was the inspiration that led to number 614 becoming a more serious racer.

After their second historic race, the Fun Team stopped off at Bob Bondurant's Driving School, then at Sears Point, and Bob asked to drive the Corvette because he had driven it in the 1962 Riverside Race. Bondurant ran a couple of laps, came in and said, "On a scale of one to ten, ten being best, the car was a minus three." His comments sounded odd to Edelbrock, who thought the car handled pretty well.

Steve Earle

Steven J. Earle has taken Vintage Car racing to a higher level and has turned it into a major part of auto racing in the United States. Earle, a California native, loves the old cars, and is very close to the family of drivers who run his events. He does his best to preserve the heritage of the sport. Above, Carroll Shelby standing by one of his famed Cobra coupes, during an Earle event.

On the West Coast, historic automobile racing was a dream made manifest by one man: Steven J. Earle. Now considered the father of vintage automobile racing, he has made the Monterey race in August the most prestigious historic race in the United States. Earle was a California native raised in the hot rod culture, but unlike most kids of the late 1940s and early 1950s, he was always a sports car enthusiast. Fascinated by European cars from the age of ten, he picked his heroes from Phil Hill, Richie Ginther, and Dan Gurney. As an adult his interest never waned, and he went to Europe attending many sports car races, including the 1963 twenty-four-hours of Le Mans.

"I saw a Ferrari GTO running in that race, and eventually I bought that very car," said Earle. "Attending various Formula One races only fueled the fire and I continued to collect cars. I always thought these cars would some day race again, and people like me might enjoy seeing this type of historic machine. In the early 1970s there was a small club event put on by Classic Sports Racing Group in the little town of Cotati, California. Only about fifteen cars showed up, but I got the idea that a grander type of event was possible."

At the time, the family business was involved with General Racing, a sports marketing company with which Earle staged his first vintage-racing event. Nothing like an amateur club style program, Earle wanted a professional racing event complete with qualified corner workers, safety crews, and security to make the participants feel safe and not have to worry about anything but racing their cars.

"Without professional crews and wide safety margins," Earle added, "we could never convince the owners of rare and high-priced vintage cars to come out and run. It had to be professional from start to finish. I also knew there were many, many more people who were not in a position to own a vintage car, but they still loved them and would come out to watch. In 1974 my concept became reality when we held the first Monterey Historic Automobile Race at Laguna Seca Raceway in Monterey, California. We had about sixty cars, it was a huge success, and the word spread."

The rules for the event included a code of conduct. Although it was a race, the line was drawn at damaging another car, and drivers were expected to be gentlemen and ladies. With no prize money and no championship trophy, there would be nothing to win except pride. The cars were the important factor and they alone are on display. What Earle wanted to offer car owners was a chance to race their cars to the best of their ability and not worry about others who could drive faster or better. He enforced the rules just as hard with a famous ex-racer as with the newest novice.

Earle recognized that owners of vintage cars who had taken the time and money to restore a famous car once driven by a world-class driver wanted the chance to enjoy the driving experience in that car. The sport grew, and today hundreds of enthusiasts have taken the time and put up the money and effort to restore vintage race cars.

The next year after displaying the car at the SEMA show in Las Vegas, they entered it in a Palm Springs event that is run on public streets through downtown. Vic was driving, and remembered feeling very comfortable and he "began to stand on the gas harder. About the fourth lap, I was coming down the main street straightaway and just as I reached 120 mph, the ball joint pulled through the right lower A-arm and I turned right into a series of water barrels. When I hit, water went flying in the air like a mighty geyser. From the pit area, all Nancy and Camee could see was this explosion of water. The car did a few gyrations, shedding parts as it went. The roll cage and safety harness held

Vic Edelbrock Jr. got involved in vintage car racing in the late 1980s, after his efforts in offshore boat racing became too risky and expensive. His first car, right, was the famous 614 Corvette, once owned by a Santa Barbara car dealer named Shelly Washburn. The 614 was part of a four car Corvette Z06 team sent to Riverside in 1962 to race the Cobra Team of Carroll Shelby. Vic bought the car at the urging of his friend Bob Joehnck and it was restored by Mike Eddy and Bruce Kimmins. Shown here at Palm Springs, the Corvette continues to be Vic's favorite race car.

and I was only slightly shaken. When we got the car back to the shop, Mike Eddy put his large size foot down and told me, enough was enough, the Corvette was to be stripped down and the hole-drilled chassis was in the trash."

"Eddy had believed that the chassis was the problem since the beginning. It was a flexible-flyer and that's why the car won't handle. Close friend and restoration expert Bruce Kimmins said, 'Vic, you need a new chassis now!' We found a good front half and good rear section, welded the two together and then once again rebuilt the entire car. The "holey" chassis hangs on the wall of Vic's Garage. Today, the Washburn Corvette number 614 runs with the best of the bunch and is one of the best Corvette restorations of that period. The car has become simply a great car to drive, and it's fun to drive my products."

Finding and restoring the Washburn 614 Corvette was only the beginning of Edelbrock's interest in vintage car racing. Once in the driver's seat, his enthusiasm magnified, and if the Edelbrock name was to be involved with vintage racing, then he would do his best to garner respect for the company. When it was time to add a second car to the team, it had to be a classic that could be used to promote the equipment Edelbrock manufactured. All involved agreed the Fun Team should race what it made.

"Vic Edelbrock runs hard and offers up some tremendous cars for people to enjoy. Vintage racing is its own industry, and now retired crew chiefs, car builders, and fabricators who at one time would not be found dead around old race cars have started up business ventures that cater to vintage car restoration. The spectators at our events prove that we are on the right track. I am very proud that I have had a hand in bringing back to life many historic cars, and in turn brought those cars into the public eye to be enjoyed again. I always tell people that we took a hobby public. The spectators want to see great cars and could care less where the driver finishes in the race. The car is the star." —Steve Earle

If the 614 Corvette is considered a classic, then the Vic Edelbrock Jr. 1959 Lister-Corvette should be considered a jewel. Very rare, the Lister, left, was restored by Bruce and Colin Kimmins, Dave Dralle and Mike Eddy. Vic crashed the Lister in 2002, but it will be back in perfect condition very soon.

"After many telephone calls and networking within the vintage car world, I found a fellow who had the remains of a 1959 Lister that he had brought to the United States," explained Edelbrock, "At the time there were only about 25 Listers in circulation, so I bought what remained in England.

Brian Lister later told me that he built about fifty to sixty cars, but every time one crashed, a few clones would appear out of the wreckage with the same frame number. Road racing in England was very hot then. It seems that the English were not very interested in log books, frame numbers, or original pieces. The front end of a wrecked car would become part of one rebuilt car, the rear end part of another. The Lister arrived in California in boxes and crates. Eddy abducted Curt Hooker and the crew from the shop to get the Lister completed by late summer of 1991. When the parts got to the shop, Mike Eddy took one look at the remnants and gave me one of his famous looks, that says 'what the hell are you doing,' followed by a shake of his head."

The fun team was lucky—a good friend named Dave Dralle had found a Shelby, and passed the word on to Vic. So the team was now also involved with building a 1966 Shelby Mustang GT-350 (later signed by Carroll Shelby) that Camee Edelbrock would drive. The team was also actively racing the Corvette, but they dove in

"What we do here is fun. It's a social thing, and the racing is a release of our pent-up energy. There is no prize money, no million dollar deals, no championship to be won. Rusty Wallace or Roger Penske are not here looking for one of us to be picked up as their next prodigy. We race; we have lunch; we laugh and have a drink or two after the races, most of the time around Vic's trailer. In fact, Vic is part of the whole story, and we are part of his. He is perfect for this scene. He shares. He helps anyone who needs it. He is unaffected by the whole play. He does it for fun, not for ego." —Kenny Epsman

Laguna Seca

Racetracks come in the famous, infamous, and magical varieties. Indianapolis, Daytona, Le Mans, Monaco, Riverside, and Watkins Glen are the tracks considered legendary and famous. The deadly Puke Hollow corner at Langhorne and the high banks of Winchester, where many brave American dirt-track heroes met their end, qualify as infamous. Few possess the mystical hidden force of speed energy that invigorates speed gods like Laguna Seca does.

European-style sports car racing arrived here in the late forties, and was conducted on public roads surrounding Pebble Beach. Progress, land costs, spectator safety, and other considerations forced the racing enthusiasts, local businessmen, and civic leaders to form the Sports Car Racing Association of the Monterey Peninsula (SCRAMP). With the Sports Car Club of America (SCCA), SCRAMP approached the commander of Fort Ord in order to gain a lease of to build a racing facility. Negotiations included the Defense Department. A deal was struck. Within a couple of months, the track was born.

In November of 1957, the Pebble Beach National Championship Road Race gave up the public highways for the nine-turn, multi-elevation road course at Laguna Seca, and the site has been an active racing venue ever since. Its pavement has felt the awesome thunder of the Can-Am cars and the brutal speed of the open wheel racer. Even the first tentative turns of a novice are welcome at a school for speed.

Many of the racers who have contested Laguna Seca's corners and the famed corkscrew would be at home on the pages of a Steinbeck novel. They are among the best in the world and include Bruce McLaren, Phil Hill, Jim Hall, George Follmer, Peter Revson, John Surtees, Dan Gurney, Jackie Stewart, Mario Andretti, Mark Donohue, Parnelli Jones, A. J. Foyt, the Unsers, the Mears Gang, Roger Penske, Jo Siffert, and Swede Savage, among others.

Later, when historic racing became a popular way to exhibit racing machines without the cutting-edge competition, the legendary drivers returned to drive the cars again. Juan Manuel Fangio, Bill Stroppe, Sterling Moss, John Fitch, Hans Herrmann, and others returned to run the cars they once made famous: Ferrari, Mercedes Benz, Bentley, Bugatti, Aston Martin, Alfa Romeo, Porsche, Lancia, Auto Union, Cunningham, Talbot-Lago, Lotus, Maserati, Jaguar, Corvette, Cobra . . . the list goes on.

Former Trans-Am Champion George Follmer (left) talks to Vic Jr. about the number 16 Trans-Am Mustang, built by Bud Moore, driven by Follmer and now owned by Edelbrock. The car was part of the Ford factory team and partner to the Mustang driven by Parnelli Jones.

to the work on the Lister. Eddy wasted no time and called in Bruce Kimmins who had worked on the Corvette and was considered by Edelbrock to be the best in the business. The all-aluminum bodywork was hand-formed over a wooden shoe that was made from snapshots, and it proved to be an overwhelming job that took months of labor. When the restoration reached the chassis, Kimmins informed Edelbrock that the mild-steel chassis was cracking right in front his eyes as he tried to weld up the countless fractures. He suggested that they rebuild the chassis using chrome-moly seamless steel tube. Edelbrock agreed, and that decision would later prove to be a lifesaver.

A shakedown was conducted at Willow Springs Raceway in the Mojave Desert. After a full day of testing, Vic was satisfied that the Lister was ready to race and the champagne was poured in celebration of the new Fun Team car. The Lister ran beautifully until the 2000 vintage racing

season when the Fun Team arrived at Seattle International Raceway for a weekend of competition and a near-disaster.

Vic recalled the fateful day: "On the back side of the race course, coming out of turn three, the track is quite narrow with shallow ditches on both sides of the track. There are trees all around and it makes for a picturesque setting. From turn three, you hit a rise over a small hill. As my race started, I went into turn 3A, which is a hard right and then turn 3B, which is a hard left. Coming out of 3B I heard or felt a clunk. At first, I figured I had hit something thrown up by one of the other cars. So, I ignored it and kept running—the car was fine for the rest of the lap.

"Lap two, same noise, same corner. I spent the rest of that second lap trying to figure out what was going on. Lap three, a repeat of lap two, only this time as I crested the rise, the car turned left into the ditch, hit at about a forty-five-degree angle, nose-first, spun, and slid for another two hundred feet backwards in a ditch. A second shock hammered my body as the car hit a hole, flipped upside down onto the track and slid 20 to 30 feet on the roll bar. I'm alive only because I listened when

"I'll never forget how my father hired me. We were standing on the lawn at my USC graduation. It was a Thursday, and I was still in my cap and gown. He asked me what I was going to do for a career. I said, 'I'm not sure right now. I've been thinking about doing a little traveling before getting into the working world.' He replied, 'Well, if you want to work for me you better show up on Monday or don't show up at all!' Needless to say, I was at Edelbrock at 8 a.m. on Monday because I always knew I would work for my dad—it was in my blood!" —**Camee Edelbrock**

Vintage racing serves many purposes for Vic and his Fun Team. He is preserving several of the most famous cars in racing history for future generations. Vintage Racing permits Vic and the team to mingle with the greatest names in the history of U.S. racing, like Carroll Shelby, above, (talking with Vic) and allows the family tradition of racing to continue with participation of his daughter Camee, above right, in Vintage events.

Bruce Kimmins suggested that we rebuild the chassis using chrome-moly tubing and install a roll bar. My injuries were minor, two painfully bruised ribs and some sore muscles." The Lister sustained major damage, but could be saved and was sent back to Bruce for repair.

The Lister Corvette represents the grace and beauty of sports car racing, and the 614 Washburn Corvette offered a connection to the early days of Detroit's involvement in American road racing. Camee joined the team in 1991 at Willow Springs driving the 614 in the Novice Class. When she began racing her own car, the blue #27 Shelby Mustang GT-350, she was the only woman in the B-production class. Now the Fun Team had something for the Ford fans to appreciate.

Another member of the Fun Team stable, having joined in 1993, was one of the most talked-about cars to ever hit a racetrack: the Smokey Yunick Camaro. When the Edelbrock restoration began, it was a collaboration of Mike Eddy, Kimmins Coach Craft, DAH Exhaust Works, and John Briggs Painting. Edelbrock's Curt Hooker and Robert Jung tended to the 302 cubic-inch small block and built it to Trans-Am specifications. After a three-year refurbishment odyssey, Vic Edelbrock finally slid behind the wheel.

Originally the Ford factory's Trans-Am race car, the number 16 1969 Boss Mustang had quite a history. It was built by Ford's Kar Kraft skunk works. It had become part of the official Ford Factory Racing Team when Bud Moore ran the car only for the 1969 season. Powered by a Boss 302 built by the book it proved to be very competitive. Part of a two-car team with the number 15 driven by Parnelli Jones who won the series for Ford in 1970, the number 16 was driven by George Follmer who won a couple of races in the car. When a wheel broke coming out of turn nine at Riverside during the last race of the 1969 season and Follmer put the Mustang into the wall, Moore consigned it to the graveyard. It had been sitting behind Moore's building for twenty years among an ever-higher company of weeds and brush until a renowned car

restorer named Rick Rodeck spotted it, while looking for another car. He saw the number and George Follmer's name on the door and knew it was an important car, and bought it on the spot. Using all the archival photographs he could find, Rodeck meticulously restored the car, and Vic saw it at the Monterey historic car auction and bought it.

They took the car to the track on Sunday, and as it happened, George Follmer was there. Upon seeing the car in its restored condition, Follmer remarked with a tear in his eye, "As a kid I used to ride my bicycle down to Edelbrock's shop on Highland and stand behind the chain across the doors watching Vic Sr. work. We would also sneak into Gilmore Stadium on Thursday nights and root for Vic's V8-60 to whip up on the Offys. Seeing the Mustang in the Edelbrock Team is a real thrill for me."

With a five-star stable of vintage racing cars, Edelbrock's Fun Team has enjoyed the same popularity of vintage car racing as they had in boat racing. Historic automobile racing is the fastest growing motorsport today.

Second only to his 614 Corvette, Vic Jr. loves to drive the famed George Follmer Trans-Am Mustang, left, a true factory-built race car. Young female fans go wild when they cheer for Christi Edelbrock, above right, and her Shelby Mustang number 55. Christi loves racing and claims that car racing is less dangerous than jumping horses. Her Mustang was once owned by a friend named Brad, who died at a young age from a heart problem. Christi dedicates her racing to Brad's memory.

The Driving Family

In the early 1990s, Christi joined Dad and her sister Camee on the Fun Team and drove Camee's car for a couple of races at Willow Springs VARA events. Like her sister, Christi was to drive a 1966 Shelby. The car was bought from friends Tom and Susan Armstrong, whose son, Brad had owned the car. Only in his 30s, Brad had died of a heart attack while snow skiing. Vic and Nancy approached Tom and Susan later saying, "We'd be honored to own the car." Christi's Shelby was made race-ready by Mike Eddy with the original white-with-blue-stripes paint scheme. By 2002 Camee was driving two racecars—the Mustang and Smokey Yunick's Camaro. Camee was to drive the Camaro after they purchased the '69 Ford Boss 302 (Follmer Car). Vic said, "Camee, it's time you drive a Chevrolet and I'll drive a Ford.

Edelbrock's 1968 Trans Am Camaro

When Historic Trans-Am Registry president David Tom sold Edelbrock the legendary Camaro, it came with a controversial pedigree and undeniable Trans-Am notoriety. First constructed in 1967 to set speed records at the Bonneville Salt Flats, the Camaro quickly became part of the Smokey Yunick mystique. Some say he built the car just to torment the competition, but Vic Edelbrock says that the Camaro was a backhanded project from Chevrolet, who wanted to run the car in the FIA time trials at Bonneville to set records.

The Camaro was built in Yunick's Daytona shop with the chassis and roll cage constructed on a 360-degree rotational spit, similar to a rotisserie barbecue, to allow easy access from any angle. The innovations connected to the car are as plentiful as they are legendary. For instance, the front suspension points were relocated and the sub-frame was Z-cut and re-welded to allow a lower floor pan. The entire body was acid-dipped to reduce weight, the fenders and hood were reshaped to a wider and lower configuration, and every surface under the body was made smooth and shaped to reduce drag. The windshield was laid back and composed of thinner safety glass. The drip rails were pulled in flush with the body to reduce turbulence.

The engine was fitted with a pressurized quick connection that allowed the driver to quickly add oil from the interior during pit stops. A cable-ratchet mechanism from a military helicopter was used to release the shoulder harness so the driver could perform a variety of other tasks—a lot of trouble just to set a few speed records. Nevertheless, Smokey hooked the car to his shop pickup and towed it out west. He stopped at Riverside Raceway in California where Bud Moore's Cougar team was practicing for the Mission Bell 250. Yunick, who was always eager to annoy the Trans-Am competitors, phoned *Hot Rod* magazine's Jim McFarland and invited him to witness some fun. McFarland then called Bob Russo, the public relations man for the track, who was not aware of any planned events with Yunick, but drove out to the track anyway.

"Somehow Smokey bluffed his way into the track and unhitched the Camaro shod with a set of

sticker racing tires," recalled McFarland. "Lloyd Ruby jumped into the car and proceeded to break the Trans-Am qualifying record. The Ford guys protested vehemently and in the end Smokey had to pack up quickly and leave, but not before he had a great laugh. His next stop was Bonneville, where he broke a number of FIA records and headed back to Daytona."

When Smokey tried to run the Official Trans-Am series, the car was found to be in violation of rule book specs. It was a game for Smokey, who would change this or that and try again, always putting the fear of God in the starting field. The next owner was Chevrolet dealer and racer Don Yenko, who changed enough things to make the car legal, and ran it in several official Trans-Am races, winning some events. Many famous drivers drove the car, including Al and Bobby Unser, Mark Donohue, Dick Guldstrand, Jim Hall, Bruce McLaren, and Craig Fisher.

In 1966, Smokey Yunick showed up at the Indy 500 with his "Capsule Car," a race car with the engine mounted in a chassis and the driver located in a side pod next to the running gear. The establishment went bonkers. Smokey didn't care; the idea was his way of expressing his art form and that's all that mattered to him. The same held true for his 1968 Trans-Am Camaro, below. It bent the rules but the ideas were good and Smokey, above, just didn't give a damn what people thought.

It had taken a bit more effort for Christi to become acclimated to driving vintage race cars because she was used to the one-horsepower feel of horses. Camee made a similar transition, from horses to water ski racing, but both daughters survived the experience.

"My first race was at Willow Springs on a very cold morning in California's high desert," recalled Christi. "It took half an hour to defrost the car and warm it up enough to run. The novice driver's meeting followed with some chalkboard illustrations and instructions on the rules of driving. I panicked when I noticed ice patches on the track from the night before, as the crew started strapping me in the car. Worse, I had never been in the car before, but that didn't seem to matter because Camee and my dad both started giving me instructions. There was so much noise and confusion while backing the car out of our pit stall, I couldn't see out of the rear window, I was scared. As I rolled out past the pit wall, Bobby Meeks just stared at me shaking his head. The race starts, but I didn't have a clue as to what was going on and my dad, Camee, Bobby and Mike Eddy are all waving, trying to get me to go faster. I was going so slow that I was nearly black-flagged. After the race, my dad said, 'You're going back to Bob Bondurant's school.' From that point on, my fear evaporated and I improved each race."

Christi began to enjoy the art of pushing a car to its potential, being with her family, and adding her personality to the Fun Team. "After retiring from competitive jumping, I missed the excitement of competition, but even though I was interested in what Camee and Dad were doing, I didn't think I was capable of making the switch. I love cars, everyone encouraged me to try, and it only took a couple races to get me pumped after I discovered the best thing about the sport—family. I could race with my dad, and my sister Camee, who brings her daughter Courtney, Mom is in the pits cheering us on, my son Alex comes along—it is shared experience of teamwork and family. For me, the Fun Team is just that, fun."

To better understand the impact that the Edelbrock women have on race fans, you just need to wander by their Fun Team trailer after a race and stand around and watch as fans overrun the area looking for Camee, above left, and Christi, above center, to get an autograph. The women are close as sisters, but fierce as competitors. Fans, including Camee's daughter Courtney, right, (with mom) love to hang out with the Fun Team. Young girls really look up to the racing Edelbrock daughters.

Vintage Auto Racing, A Way to Preserve History

Vintage Auto Racing is far more than a whim for Vic Edelbrock Jr.; he is dedicated to the sport and to the preservation of rare and famous race cars. The banner under which the cars are raced is the "Fun Team" and it follows a family tradition dating back to the early days of the company and its founder Vic Sr.—when racing was a fun part of building the reputation of the Edelbrock name. Bruce Meyer, above, (right) is a fan of vintage racing and has his own collection of classic cars. Above right, Vic gets ready to drive Camee's Shelby at Willow Springs. Below right, Vic driving the Smokey Yunick Camaro at Limerock Park before it was turned over to Camee to race.

Continuing Past Glories

The Edelbrock Fun Team stable of Vintage Race cars is one of the finest in the sport. But unlike some collectors, Vic shares his cars with family and friends. Nancy, above, who keeps the family in line by recording their lap times at every race, shares a hug with Edelbrock's first employee, Bobby Meeks, who still goes to the races when he can. Vic Jr., top right, began racing his 614 Corvette in the late '80s, started a tradition of opening his pit area to the fans so they could enjoy the fun. The Edelbrock daughters, Camee and Christi, share the fun with their dad, driving a pair of 1966 Shelby Mustangs. Below left, Vic Jr. tries to make the fans part of his Fun Team program and one way he thrills fans around the country is by running his Ford Factory Trans-Am Mustang, below right, once driven by George Follmer. *Opposite:* Top, Camee in the Shelby Mustang leads her dad into turn eleven at Sears Point, locking up the period-correct drum brakes in an effort to keep her dad behind her. Below left, one of Vic's most coveted cars is the number 27 Lister Corvette. Both rare and beautiful, the Lister brings fans to thier feet whenever it runs. Below right, Camee buckles up and gets ready to do battle with her dad and sister.

Junior Johnson's Banana Car

Built by America's hero, Junior Johnson, this 1966 Ford Galaxy car, dubbed "Banana Car," occupies a controversial position in the chronicles of stock car history. Johnson was known for his own way of interpreting rules and regulations. The body shape was altered to transform the Galaxy into an aerodynamic projectile. The hood was reworked into a downward shape, the windshield laid back, the top was chopped ever so slightly and the rear deck lid was recontoured to produce a down-force effect.

How could a car like that be allowed to compete? NASCAR Grand National Racing officials knew the car took a liberal approach to car building, but turned a deaf ear, hoping to attract the attention of Ford Motor Company. At the time, Chrysler seemed unbeatable, and NASCAR needed to rekindle competition, so Junior Johnson's Banana Car was allowed to run in only one race. With Fred Lorenzen behind the wheel, Junior entered the Dixie 400 at the Atlanta Motor Speedway. Amid stares, howling accusations, and pointed fingers of the other teams, the car qualified, but a broken wheel made the car hit the wall while leading the race. The Galaxie never saw the spotlight again.

It was rebodied, run on dirt tracks in the southern short-track circuit, and fell into obscurity.

Years later, Kim Haynes, a NASCAR historian and restoration expert, brought the car to life, restoring its original shape. Edelbrock bought the car in 2001, and it became a member of the Fun Team's stable.

If the Banana Car illustrates the rebellious face of stock car racing's past, Vic's purchase in 2002 of the famed Kodak Chevrolet Lumina once driven by Ernie Irvan represents the new face of NASCAR Nextel Cup Racing and the rise in interest by corporate America. Vic may jump behind the wheel of the completely restored car and give fans a modern-day thrill.

If Smokey had a reputation for pushing the rule book, Junior Johnson wrote the book on avoiding the rules. When Junior, above, built the Banana Car, below, it was an example of rule bending to the highest degree. The car only ran once but the mystique still lingers.

That view remained strong despite the horrible news in 2001 when Christi was diagnosed with breast cancer that required immediate surgery to save her life. "The people we share the sport with are the best. We hang out, have a few laughs and reduce our stress level by a ton. After my surgery, the drivers and many fans urged me to come back and race." Christi returned to the driver's seat of her vintage Mustang with a transformed sense of welcome and belonging.

Camee has had her own share of battles, but in every case the worst part about it was not being able to race. Camee says, "I enjoyed water ski racing because it was the ultimate challenge, combining stamina and sheer determination to finish the long races in rough conditions. It truly was the Fun Team and it was great spending time with my dad and the Herbst family. The hiatus after we quite offshore boat racing was torture. When Vic asked if I wanted to go to Bondurant's, I jumped at the chance. As the saying goes, 'It's the most fun you can have with your clothes on!' After ten years of driving the Shelby, it feels like my best friend or an old shoe that fits perfectly, but reminds you when you've pushed too hard. But one of the best parts of vintage racing is the fans—they're awesome!"

What about Nancy Edelbrock—How did she feel about her husband and children climbing into racing machines? As "Mrs." and "Mom" she always supported her family in every endeavor. From the day when Vic took the reins of his father's company, she was as much a partner in business as she was in marriage. Working together at events, selling products, defending the company from any attack, Nancy and her husband developed such a close working relationship that the expression "joined at the hip" was often used to describe how they grew the Edelbrock name together.

"When Vic and Camee were offshore boat racing, that was my least favorite of all the things they ever did," confessed Nancy. "It was extremely dangerous and very difficult to ever watch because they were always far from shore. Crews and spectators could never get close to the action. The people involved in that level of boat racing are serious competitors made up of paid professional crews that are under a lot of pressure to do well, especially if sponsors were present.

Flying High

In March of 2000, Vic Edelbrock Jr. realized one of his most private lifelong goals. He had harbored a passion for flying since childhood, and as an adult, he took up flying first as a ROTC cadet and later as a private pilot. But one goal was to be reached, Vic had always wanted to fly a fighter jet. On March 6, 2000, he settled into the rear seat of a FA-18 fighter, about to take a ride with the most famous organization in aviation history, the Navy's Blue Angels.

The story actually begins with the aforementioned ROTC training and the fact that he gave up his career in military aviation to take his place in his father's business. The void between his days in a T-33 trainer and flying a fighter jet remained open for nearly 40 years. It closed on that day in March.

Jack Mayberry, a retired Navy captain, had come to work at Edelbrock Corporation as vice president of

After his ride with the Blue Angels, the crew placed an Edelbrock decal on the FA-18 used to give Vic his ride.

Research and Development. Through Mayberry's contacts, a special overnight junket was planned that would take Vic Edelbrock, Mayberry, chief operating officer Jeff Thompson and automotive journalist Jeff Smith, via fixed-wing aircraft to a landing on the aircraft carrier USS *Constellation*. As a goodwill gesture, the four would spend the night with the ship's crew, and Vic would sign autographs. In the morning, the group was shot off the carrier in a catapult take off. According to Vic, the experience was awesome. Next, during the annual Vintage Car Races in Corona Del Mar, California, Vic met Admiral Mike Bowman, who knew Jack Mayberry, and was aware that Vic had taken the carrier trip and wanted more. When Jack Mayberry contacted the admiral about a surprise flight for Vic with the Blue Angels, Bowman set it up.

When speaking about the experience, Vic gets as excited as he does when talking about racing. He uses hand gestures to describe the one-hour flight he took. He got the full treatment, including a straight up, afterburner takeoff, a diamond roll, a slip S roll, a complete loop, a gut-ripping 7.3G turn, and breaking the sound barrier. The pilot allowed Vic to actually fly the plane for about 40 minutes during the flight. After landing, the flight crew gathered around for some bench racing, and Vic got the honor of applying an Edelbrock decal to the FA-18 as a fitting conclusion to a once-in-a-lifetime experience.

For Vic Edelbrock Jr., half the fun of racing Vintage Race Cars is interacting with the fans. After the races, fans of all ages hang out at the Edelbrock trailer, above, and Vic, above right, never turns anyone away.

After Jerry Herbst was hurt I really didn't like boat racing. For a company making equipment for high-performance cars, we were not getting much in the way of exposure for the high costs required to participate.

"With Vintage Car Racing, winning isn't everything, and losing is just something to joke about, but many of the cars involved use our equipment, so the sport is a tremendous asset to our business. The fans come by the trailer for hats, T-shirts, and autographs. Vic and the girls love hanging out with the fans and other drivers. Fun is at the top of the list of reasons I love the sport, and also because I am part of the action. By timing laps for Camee, Christi, and Vic, I cannot only tell how each is doing, but when they come past the start/finish line, I know they are okay. If they turn up late, I start checking to see if anything happened. When Vic crashed the Lister, I was on the scene in minutes and I knew right off he was not seriously hurt.

"Vintage Racing is a family thing. Our grandchildren come to the races so we are watching them grow up. Often after the races other drivers and crews come by for a drink, a snack and the bench racing subjects range from cars to family life—local school systems, how the kids are doing, etc. We find that people all over the country have the same problems

"I have heard people say things about my dad; he is a tough boss, has an ego, and he is cold and distant. Wrong! The people who say those things, don't know him. Vic Edelbrock, my dad, considers family the best part of his life. He considers his close friends and employees part of his family. In fact, my dad can be considered a bit old-fashioned, he still believes in right and wrong, black and white, not grey and misunderstood. He was an only child, raised in a male-dominated world, and when he had three girls, he had to give in a lot; he had to adjust. It wasn't like having boys, doing macho things that men do—we played with dolls. He allowed us our freedom, and we in turn, took to water skiing, boat racing, horse riding, and things he could identify with. The bottom line was he raised us to be good people, and straight shooters." —Carey Edelbrock

Vintage racing for the Fun Team is truly about the fun! Camee (left), Nancy (center) and Vic, were presented the "Big Fun Award" at the Watkins Glen Vintage Race by Bob Fergus, who was the epitome of the vintage racing spirit. The Fun Team is one of the most popular and most accessible teams at any of the Vintage Car Races. Camee, Christi and Vic will spend an hour or more after an event just signing autographs, giving away caps and T-shirts or posing for photos.

Camee Edelbrock

The name "Camee" sounds like it was derived from "camshaft," but was actually created using the initials of her full name, Cathleen Ann Marie Edelbrock. She laughs every time she tells the story. As Edelbrock's vice president of Advertising, Camee strives for excellence with every project. Her passion for the industry, unrelenting enthusiasm, and competitive spirit is evident as she lives life at full throttle.

Camee first worked at Edelbrock as a teenager during her summer vacations. After graduating from the University of Southern California in 1982, she accepted a job in sales. When an advertising position was offered, Camee jumped at the chance. In the late '80s, the tools of the advertising trade did not include desktop publishing with computers, but it was creative, and that's what appealed to Camee. "We used a typesetter, stat machine and hot waxer to set up artwork. A simple flier took ten times longer than it does today. I enjoyed the creative process and seeing the results of my work: selling product. This remains true today."

Camee's daughter Courtney was born in 1987. After her maternity leave, making the decision about returning to work was difficult. "I called dad and told him I was going to be a full-time mom. His response was straightforward, 'I need you here.' That's all I really needed to hear."

In 1993, SEMA recognized Camee's efforts and named her "Young Executive of the Year." At the same time, Argus Publishers designated Camee a "Performance Pro." Today, her title at Edelbrock does not account for all of her duties. She represents the company through speaking engagements, radio interviews and appearances on television. On *Overhaulin'*, Camee has delivered crate engines and participated in several episodes. A Brizio-built '32 Roadster was built and delivered to Camee and Christi on the popular TV show *Rides*. Both shows air on TLC, a Discovery Network channel that reaches 90 million households

nationwide. Camee is also performance correspondent for Car and Driver Radio, which broadcasts live across the nation. She interviewed the women who designed the Volvo YCC concept car at the '04 Geneva Auto Show, which earned Camee a 2004 International Automotive Media Award in the radio news category. The IAMA program is designed to recognize excellence in all forms of automotive media. In fact, Camee received another award in '04, which she shares with her team, for the Edelbrock Performance catalog.

This Edelbrock daughter is truly an enthusiast, and she enjoys all forms of racing, from the Daytona 500 to Perris Speedway. Camee's own racing career started on water skis. When her nerves could no longer take the perils of speed skiing, she became the boat driver, towing several skiers to top ten finishes. Offshore boat racing came next. She says, "Racing under the Golden Gate Bridge in our 38-foot Scarab at 90+ miles per hour was unbelievable." After Bondurant's driving school, Camee started Vintage Car Racing. "At first, I was the only woman driver in the B-production class and the guys treated me like a little sister." Now, women racers are more common, but Camee still has fun challenging the men. She says, "My fans love to see me ahead of the guys! In fact, it's the fans that make this type of racing especially

rewarding. Kami from Seattle is one of my favorites. She not only has a great name, but unbelievable strength and courage. It's people like Kami that make this business so great!"

Both Camee and Christi Edelbrock have followed in their father and grandfather's footsteps becoming involved in the company. Camee, who graduated from USC, above, (with her dad and mom) in 1982, has been in the business the longest, over 20 years. Below, Camee, a true hot rod enthusiast and Edelbrock vice president of Advertising, shows off the company's products in a '32 roadster.

as we have at home. Local people bring their kids who look up to the vintage racers as role models. That is most important."

All in Fun

Mike Eddy is a trusted and valued Fun Team member who has a unique perspective of Edelbrock's zesty approach to competitive motorsports; he understands precisely why the Fun Team has become an intrinsic part of the Edelbrock Corporation and its promotion philosophy. Commenting on a parade run through the streets of Watson Glen—a reenactment of a 1940s event now run with the Vintage cars—Eddy shared how the Fun Team interacts with 20,000 spectators. "The town throws opens its collective doors, and after the cars run a few laps they are parked on the streets and the spectators allowed to mingle around. In 2002, fans swarmed Vic, Camee, and Christi. It was an unbelievable sight. People want Vic and the girls to autograph models of the Corvette and Mustangs, they bring pictures, and all sorts of memorabilia. They all know the Edelbrock name, and it is the fans who play a very important part in why the Fun Team exists: if people see the team at the track, they buy parts in the marketplace. It is good business."

On a typical day at the vintage races for the Edelbrock Fun Team, the big red eighteen-wheeler is in the vintage race pit area, "Edelbrock Race Team" emblazoned on the side. Parked alongside is a pair of Shelby Mustangs and a Z06 Corvette. A canopy covers the area where a portable staircase is positioned in the middle of the trailer.

"Someday, I am going to take my dad up on a promise. He told me he would send me to drag racing school so I can fulfill a lifelong dream of driving a dragster down the quarter-mile. Maybe I can get him to add a vintage dragster to the Fun Team stable." —**Carey Edelbrock**

The Edelbrock eighteen-wheeler at Limerock Park in Connecticut, below left, is the center of activity for the Fun Team. Below, Mike Eddy (right) is the glue that holds it all together, keeping Camee, (left), Christi and Vic race ready with cars in perfect tune.

Mike Eddy, left, talks to Vic Jr. about the setup for the day's events. Mike is crew chief for all of the cars. He is also one of the few people in the world that will argue with the Boss. When the day ends, the fuel burning, high horsepower feeling continues with the world's wildest Margarita maker, right, with Camee at the controls.

After a race, Edelbrock, with hair matted, face reddened, and eyes red with exertion, disappears into the confines of the trailer's living quarters to quickly change out of his sweat-soaked driving suit and into comfortable shorts, tennis shoes, T-shirt, and sunglasses. The next generation Edelbrock bench-racing ritual is about to begin, and he is the lynchpin for the impending fun. Held at the conclusion of every Vintage racing event, the Edelbrock Fun Team impromptu party is a "thank you" to course workers, emergency crews, volunteers, and fellow competitors whose hard work makes the event possible.

Christi and Camee stock a folding table with chips, spicy salsa, cold cuts, various snacks, and a selection of soda pop while crew chief Mike Eddy sets up a second table on which he places an odd-looking contraption with four legs, handlebars, a fuel tank, and a clear plastic container mounted on a flat surface platform. Underneath the legs rests a small weed-eater type engine, highly modified and sporting a custom-designed exhaust system. Your nose tells you the fuel mixture is methanol, tainted with a splash of nitromethane.

Camee Edelbrock confronts the machine like a high-priestess about to offer a sacrifice, yanks the starting cord, and the tiny engine barks to life filling the air with a high-pitch staccato that breaks the silence of the post-race calm. A cheer goes up. After twisting the throttle a few times, she kills the power, flips open the plastic container and fills it with the energy of a mad scientist. Splashes of citrus juice, ice, and tequila are blended together. Deftly, with the flick of a wrist, she brings the mighty-mite engine back to life pushing the rpms until the noise pains the ears. The ingredients are pulverized into a foaming broth. Suddenly, there is silence as the mixture settles. Camee Edelbrock has created the perfect margarita—now renamed the Camarita. A line forms and the contents of the machine are distributed to the waiting crowd. And the process begins anew. The Fun Team is in full swing.

In contrast to most CEO types, Vic Edelbrock Jr. is not a businessman who races, he is a real racer who runs a giant corporation. He carries on the traditions of the family and of the industry that made the name Edelbrock respected throughout the world. If the old man were still alive, he would point to all who would listen, that his son is a racer making products for racers. There is no compromise in what the Edelbrock Corporation stands for, Vic Sr. wouldn't tolerate compromise.

Vic Edelbrock Jr. is a hands-on person, and is as much of an enthusiast as his customers. Says Vic, "I use our products to be sure they work."

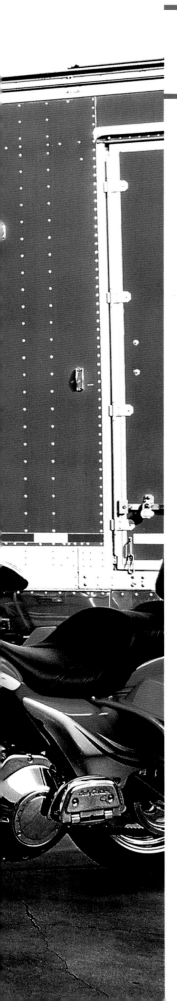

8 In Sight of the Goal

Vic Senior never wanted to be a rich man, but he did reach a point were he could look up from his labors and enjoy himself. He played golf, enjoyed taking Katie to dinner, and would take a few days off now and then. He once said to his daughter-in-law Nancy, "I like the company as it stands, everything is paid for, and I can take time off and enjoy things with Katie." Nancy remembers, "Vic Sr. told me that he didn't want to be a big company—he was a child of the Great Depression and always wanted to feel safe, and never get overextended."

The cover of the 1980 Edelbrock catalog depicted Vic Jr. posing with the company's new emissions control equipment. It didn't look like much to the untrained eye, but it was a window into how the company was changing. Much of the product information inside the catalog focused on emissions, and the fuel economy made possible with the new S.P.2-P. manifold designed for use on motor homes, campers, and large four wheel drive trucks. Set up for a narrow performance latitude operating from off-idle to a maximum 4500 rpm, the idea was to combine the best of both the single-plane and dual-plane manifold designs in one package.

The S.P.2-P. helped overcome the balkiness of stock anti-smog manifolds and became a popular choice to cure engine lag and improve off-road driveability for the four wheel drive enthusiast. Because California emissions laws disallowed changing from 2-bbl to 4-bbl carburetion, the company developed the S.P.2-P. 2-V that allowed the retention of the stock two-barrel carburetor without an adapter or linkage changes. These two models joined the Streetmaster single-plane as the fastest selling over-the-counter replacement parts used by the average street driver. Once again, Edelbrock Corporation proved its ability to find new customers in a challenging marketplace by overcoming emissions control problems and providing seat-of-the-pants performance at the best possible fuel economy. For the racer, a full line of manifold options remained, including the

> "It takes a lot to become a consumer-ready Edelbrock product. Our parts work or they get tossed."
> —**Vic Edelbrock Jr.**

Innovation

From a technical perspective, Edelbrock Equipment could always be counted upon to launch imaginative and controversial products. Some were far ahead of their time and some were less successful. Several of the most interesting ones came from the mind of Dawson Hadley, an old dry lakes racer. In the late 1970s, Hadley had developed a sequential electronic fuel injection system. The system was so far ahead of its time

that a great deal of effort was spent sorting out the timing sequence to aid in reliability. While dealing with the fuel injection system, Hadley released two other products, both promoted vigorously by Edelbrock. Thermalspark was designed to enhance ignition spark and work with his injection system. Another more controversial creation, labeled Vara-Jection—an electronic water injection—was, for its day, a very sophisticated piece of equipment. Gasoline prices had jumped from fifty cents a gallon to over a dollar, and everyone was trying to get better mileage. Newspapers and magazines suddenly featured "water injection" as a way to save gas. People actually thought that they could burn water. There were guys selling homemade water injection kits on the street corners. Most of the products were junk, but Hadley had an electronic system that really worked, and suppressed knocks and pings by controlling injection electronically. It was even certified legal for sale in California by the Air Resources Board. The system came with additional add-ons like "liquid power" mixed with water to prevent pre-ignition. Vara-Jection and Edelbrock's Vapormaster fuel atomization system served a purpose during the early days of emission controls and higher gas prices.

Victor Jr., Victor Ram, Tarantula, Scorpion, and Torker models. To adapt to the wishes of the environmentally sensitive customer, the performance industry needed new sales techniques.

Since the days when Vic Sr. spent evenings boxing shipments for customers, the Edelbrock Corporation had always packaged and shipped products in plain white or brown cardboard boxes, believing that the product was important, not the box. In 1981, Vic Jr. ordered all packaging to be redesigned and aimed directly at a point-of-purchase merchandising program. He deduced that the new breed of stores did not want to accept a product unless the packaging was four-color and had an easy-to-read content disclosure. The Edelbrock designs were bright and appealing, with the company logo displayed on all sides, and all product boxes were color-coordinated.

Answering New Challenges

It was obvious that the advent of smog laws in the 1980s would make things difficult for the performance aftermarket, so Jim McFarland expanded the catalog beyond a simple parts listing to a publication that included educational text on performance as the variety of products and services continued to

The early '70s were a tough period for the industry, requiring creative ideas to succeed. The engineers at Edelbrock, including Jim McFarland, above, had two goals, offer performance and save gas.

increase. Murray Jensen, an authority on carburetion, joined forces with his daughter and son-in-law, and began offering Calibrated Conversion gasoline and alcohol-fed carburetors for all types of racing and marine use in the Edelbrock catalog. As the decades passed, NASCAR racers looked to him as a fuel flow expert.

Using the catalog as an instructional tool, Edelbrock provided customers with guidance in choosing the correct application for their needs. The company's manifolds were divided into distinct categories for particular applications. Edelbrock added new manifolds for imports, bringing back a limited edition of the flathead for Fords, even producing high-tech toys like the DMI-7000 digital mileage instrument, which featured a flashing red warning light when the driver stepped too heavily on the gas pedal.

This significant marketing and merchandising upgrade was the result of customer feedback and the industry's difficulties in meeting emissions control restrictions in the mid-to late-1980s. Customers who bought the S.P.2-P. manifold for better mileage during the peak of the gas

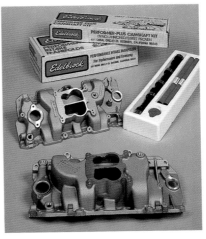

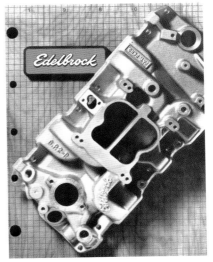

By 1972, the Edelbrock/Holley program was cooking, with Edelbrock introducing new manifolds like the Tarantula, left, being held by Frank Walter of Holley (left) and Murray Jensen (right), and the stock factory manifold (in the foreground). By 1975, all auto manufacturers would be using catalytic converter systems and unleaded gasoline. The first Power Package, top, matched camshaft and lifters to the proper manifold to ensure customer satisfaction. The gas crunch of 1974 forced Edelbrock to develop manifolds like the S.P.2-P., above.

crunch began making other changes to the engine that compromised the manifold's performance. Another problem cropped up when the government mandated drastically reduced gasoline octane ratings. Because of its small runner design and the high velocity of air the manifold moved, lower octane fuels caused pinging under heavy loads. The redesign was dubbed the Performer. The same thing happened with the S.P.2-P. manifold as it became popular with hot rodders. Designed for mild street performance and fuel efficiency, the addition of a performance carburetor and camshaft unbalanced the carefully engineered performance concept. Unhappy hot rodders often blamed the manifold. This created difficulties for the technical support team.

"My stepdad, Bob Joehnck, remarked that, years ago, you could do almost anything to a factory manifold and pick up horsepower. Nowadays it is extremely difficult. The end result is that nothing is old school, we have to think and plan way outside the box." —**Jack Mayberry**

Edelbrock and his staff realized that the growing epidemic of misplaced blame was going to hurt sales, so they went to work creating a solution. The result was the Power Package, a dyno-matched package of camshaft and lifters for a specific manifold to ensure the correct application. The camshaft coordination began when the customer purchased the Performer or Torker II camshafts for a domestic engine. Edelbrock's tech staff would then recommend the correct carburetor and exhaust header combination to complete the performance package. Gone was the guesswork regarding camshaft selection.

The package concept had first begun in 1946, when Vic Sr. conceived the idea of matching his manifolds with his own heads and a special "race" Winfield camshaft to complete a performance ensemble. All the parts were balanced, and he reworked carburetors that blended perfectly with the performance changes. With the renewed tradition, the package that was dyno-matched and tested put Edelbrock out front in the industry. In 1988 the concept changed from Power Package to Total Power Package when Edelbrock brand carburetors were added. And in 1992 Edelbrock-made overhead valve aluminum heads became part of the package. By 2002, the Power Package concept offered SBC combinations up to 400 horsepower .

A continuing leader in the performance industry.

In 1992 Edelbrock introduced its own brand of performance heads made from 356-T6 aluminum for the small-block Chevrolet engine. Customers could buy a pair of alloy heads machined and ready to run out of the box. Edelbrock did not carry a complete line of cylinder heads until the

Since the introduction of the very first catalog produced by Vic Edelbrock Sr., the concept of combining parts into complete packages was a primary goal. Vic Jr. continued the principal of packaging when he took over the company. The 1980s found the company matching camshafts and manifold combinations, below, to prevent the customer from making mistakes when combining manifold and camshaft on their own.

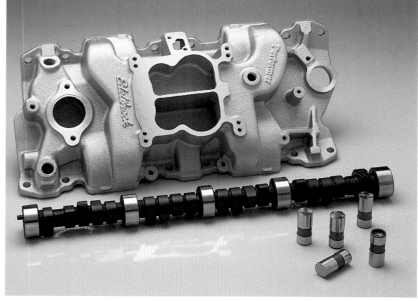

Vic Jr. believes that if a customer can buy a complete package, two purposes are served: if the parts are matched through a testing program, they will work as a complete unit. And, selling the package concept promotes overall sales. "The Total Package Concept" as Edelbrock advertises, allows the customer to put together the parts and pieces necessary to meet whatever horsepower goals they have before building the actual engine. Because of the Edelbrock research and testing programs, all of the parts, left, work as a single unit.

Edelbrock's packaging design was introduced in the early '80s. This design work, as well as other print ads and brochures, was done by their own advertising department. In fact, they received the SEMA New Packaging Award in 1982.

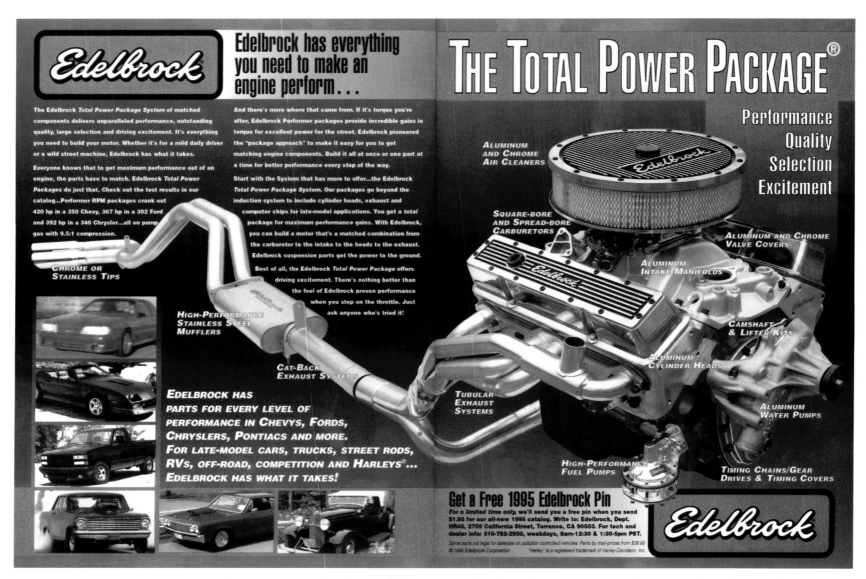
As the company grew in size and in the variation of its products, Vic Jr. realized that customers would have questions while making decisions on what products to choose in order to reach their goals. Therefore, Edelbrock decided to offer the novice as well as the expert a support platform to answer questions and provide assistance in making proper choices.

late 1990s. At the close of the 1980s, tubular exhaust systems, the Victor line of manifolds, and a long list of racing manifolds and cylinder heads for both drag racing and circle track competition were added to the product lineup. The Edelbrock name was acquiring a sizeable reputation in every form of motor sports.

The theme of Edelbrock's late 1980s catalog was Engineered Excitement, driving home the point that the development and testing of new products produced performance. Jim McFarland had organized a strong research operation for new products and the dyno room now featured two young lions—Curt Hooker and Robert Jung. The company's marketing tools were paying off in sales. The new packaging made sales easy for local speed shops and jobbers. The list of professional racers endorsing Edelbrock Products was long and illustrious, but the growth in sales was the result of satisfied hot rodders, street enthusiasts, and amateur track racers. The grassroots American car buffs loved Edelbrock and the company needed to nurture that relationship.

"We have not forgotten our racing heritage. Recently, we have placed new priorities on our products for racing. We have a full line of new cylinder heads and complete engine packages for the racer. And we have the only manifolds that are officially licensed by NASCAR. We love tough competition and the world of racing." —**Vic Edelbrock Jr.**

Since the birth of the company, the Edelbrock philosophy has remained constant. In order to build customer confidence, the company should provide as much information as possible to the public regarding their products. The methods have varied through the years, from a talking robot, left, to catalog information, to field work. Below left, key technicians like Curt Hooker (left) test products under real-world conditions and work with actual customers to solve problems or improve ideas.

Edelbrock Advertising: Three Generations, One Philosophy

It all started when Robert E. Petersen convinced Vic Edelbrock Sr. to place an ad in his national publication called *Hot Rod*. Throughout the years, one message has remained the same—Proven Performance. Vic Sr. sent this message through superior quality, record-setting speeds, and his first ad in *Hot Rod*. Vic Jr. continued this concept after his father passed away in 1962, and twenty years later, his daughter Camee joined the advertising team as a third generation Edelbrock.

Vic Jr. worked closely with his dad in the '50s and '60s, and now he works with his daughter in the same capacity. Heated discussions are the norm for the father/daughter duo, similar to the way Jr. and Sr. communicated. When Camee and her mother decided that Edelbrock needed a Web site, they approached Vic with lots of ideas. It took three years to get approval, but Edelbrock still beat the rest of the aftermarket industry to the internet.

Of course, the Web site was not the first business discussion to happen in the Edelbrock household. Slogans like "Engineered Excitement" and "The Total Power Package" were invented at the dinner table over classic meals like steak and salad. Camee says, "It was bench racing at its finest, we were just in the dining room instead of the dyno room." Catalog cover ideas, sportswear designs, ad concepts, and SEMA show outfits were just some of the topics reviewed in detail by the marketing team of Vic, Nancy and Camee Edelbrock. Camee's sisters were engaged in other activities during the mid- to late '80s. Christi ran a horse training facility at the Edelbrock ranch and Carey was attending the University of Southern California.

Part of Edelbrock's in-house strategy is keeping current with technology. Camee was director of advertising when the time came to consider going from traditional "paste-up and layout" to desktop publishing. She recalls, "The battle between IBM and Apple was crazy, with both sides claiming to be the best in every aspect. Apple was known for graphics, but I had strong opposition from the VPs. I finally convinced them to go with a Macintosh

computer. I think it had a hard drive that was only 256k and I can't believe we used that tiny screen to lay out type." Traditional ways were slowly replaced with computers as drafting tables went to storage. The digital age was here.

Advertising efforts have always been supported by event sponsorships and contingency programs. One of the biggest events that Edelbrock has supported consistently is the Hot Rod Power Tour. Since it's humble beginnings in 1995, Edelbrock has been a sponsor, and every year Vic insists on serving the best dinner available. In 2004, Edelbrock served 2,700 dinners in Davenport, IA and gave away 5,000 custom embroidered, limited edition hats. Camee and Dan Dragoo, a long-time employee, drove Edelbrock's new flamed '32 Roadster that was built by Brizio Street Rods for a show called "Rides." The show aired on TLC to about 90 million households and this roadster was recognized everywhere by young and old. Equipped with an Edelbrock Performer RPM crate engine, the roadster ran flawlessly, and cruised down the highway at speeds well over the speed limit! Of course, Camee says she'll never do that again. Proven performance is once again part of the Edelbrock campaign on the Hot Rod Power Tour. "When the tour goes anywhere close to Tennessee, we call Larry Price for his whole hog BBQ," says Camee. "It's awesome food and Larry is not only a great BBQ guy, but a huge supporter of children's charities."

In Edelbrock's history, the ad design has only been outsourced a few times. In the 1980s, a Torrance firm was hired and Camee was part of the advertising team. She remembers when Vic received a lunch invitation from Keith Harvey, long-time friend and distributor for Edelbrock. Vic and Camee met Keith at his facilities.

"Keith gave us the royal tour. Right from the start, he struck me as a straight shooting, no nonsense guy. I liked that part about him. Then at lunch he told us why we were there, 'Your ads are pretty, but they're not selling product." It was hard for me to hear a negative comment directed at Edelbrock. I was partly

responsible for a lousy ad campaign. We thanked Keith for lunch and the good advice. Back at the office, we divided the remaining budget into fractional ads to increase frequency and coverage. They were were definitely not pretty, but the minute these ads hit the newsstands, Keith Harvey made another phone call. This time he told Vic the news over the phone. Product was moving, the ads were a success. I remain grateful to this day and will never forget what I had learned. It doesn't have to be pretty to sell product."

Today, the Edelbrock Advertising Agency does more than print design and production. The list of projects includes video, DVD, web design, packaging, and much more. Basically, anything that requires design and implementation comes from this department. It's full service with in-house convenience. In fact, Edelbrock's in-house print shop is ready to go with one of three presses, bindery and complete finishing facilities.

When asked about her advertising team Camee says, "We do it all and we do it right."

Below, the cover of *Hot Bike* August '96 issue showing Vic and Camee with an Arlen Ness, Edelbrock special bike and a Harley Road King prepared by Bob Dron of Oakland, California.

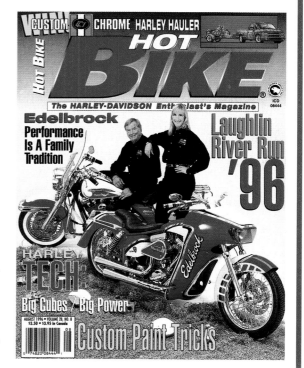

Moving Day

With growth came a greater responsibility to sustain robust development and testing programs to maintain the company's relationship with racers and generate new sales. Vic Sr. had moved six times from his first location on Venice and Hoover behind a Gilmore Service Station—each time because the workplace was nearly bursting at the seams. Vic Jr. had packed up after the first purpose-built facility at Jefferson Boulevard shop had become too small. As the El Segundo Coral Circle location fast approached maximum capacity and cramped conditions began to threaten productivity, something needed to be done.

By 1987, they had completely outgrown the Coral Circle facility. The problem was that the economy was flexing up and down along with the real estate market. Because Edelbrock was also in the construction business, developing a wide variety of commercial sites in California and Arizona, it should have been an easy fix. However, Vic did not have any available property that could accommodate a manufacturing plant, research center, dyno testing facility, and warehouse. He wanted to stay in the South Bay area, but nothing was available.

Tony Hollis got a tip from a real estate agent about a building for sale in Torrance, but Edelbrock, who was very familiar with the area, thought it was a joke when he first saw the address. Curiosity got the better of him, and he drove over to discover a well-used 1960s-style building he had never seen. As he walked around, he noticed that it was actually a complex of three buildings. Originally built in the early 1960s, it looked as if nothing had ever been done to maintain its integrity. It had been owned by Dow Chemical Company to manufacture foam cushion material, but its only inhabitants for some time had been pigeons while Dow had been trying to sell the place. The price was right and Vic bought the property. A brilliant architect named Tom Kowalski, who had designed many buildings for Edelbrock, began planning a structure to fit the company needs.

Edelbrock was struck with a nostalgic notion for the new facility and went to the city of Torrance to request a change of address to his lucky number—27. It was the same number his dad had used on the midget and Vic wanted the new place to be known as 2700 California Street. One of the old buildings was torn down and rebuilt as a 135,000-square-foot complex. Edelbrock was pleased with his new utopia, thinking it would take years to fill the entire building. They moved in on Halloween weekend in 1987, ten days after the stock market had plummeted 500 points. The new building would prove to be only a stopgap, and by 1994 Edelbrock purchased 4.6 acres to house the exhaust division in a 34,000 square foot building. The shock building of

Putting on the Brakes

Fame and fortune exact a toll on everyone, and in June 1984, Vic Edelbrock Jr. was presented his personal bill: a heart attack. Like many executives, he had been going a hundred miles an hour and thought he was indestructible. He had been taking medication to combat high blood pressure but his stress level was high, and even when he felt tired and overworked, Vic Jr. maintained the hard-charging pace. He had convinced himself everything was fine because he had passed his FAA pilot's medical check, but years of stress and long hours suddenly caught up with him.

One evening at home Vic just didn't feel up to par. "I started getting chest pains, began sweating, and felt really weird. Nancy knew the instant she saw my face what was wrong. I was hospitalized for a week and then recuperated at home for two more weeks. Everything was handled with medication. I did not have any surgery, and there was very little damage to my heart. It scared both of us, and we decided that I would turn my life around and stop trying to do everything."

The "new and improved" Edelbrock gave up boat racing, adjusted his diet, and began a regular exercise program. The staff was given more authority to handle day-to-day problems, and Steve Bell was hired as COO. Edelbrock marveled at how the old-time employees rallied around him—especially Bobby Meeks and Don Towle, whose stabilizing influence allowed Nancy and Vic to spend more time together.

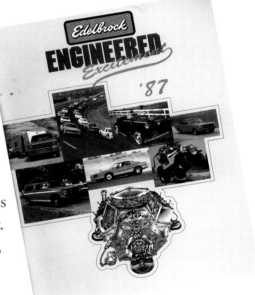

No single mind can grasp a subject in total. At Edelbrock Corporation, knowledge is a collective endeavor. Most of the engineers and technicians are hard-core racers who test the company's products under real-world conditions. For the customer, this experimentation is used as part of a support program that begins with their catalog, above.

A company photo taken at the headquarters in Torrance, California. Unlike most companies, the employees at Edelbrock Corporation are also customers for the products produced by the company. They are performance enthusiasts who actually use the company's products.

45,000 square feet was built in 1997. Then in 1998, 3.7 acres was purchased and a 65,000-square-foot building was built to house the Distribution Center and Vic's Garage.

The Performer Series

Other than the Murray Jensen line of racing products, the Edelbrock catalog displayed a marked absence of carburetors, despite the fact that the company had been instrumental in getting Holley into the performance business in the 1960s. Vic had always wanted to offer an Edelbrock brand carburetor that would be dyno-matched with its manifolds. When Carter Carburetor Company, owned by Federal-Mogul Performance, moved the carburetor production to Weber USA (whose parent company was Magneti-Marelli in Italy), the stage was set.

Red Line Products in Carson was owned by Peter Neuworth, a Vintage car racer like Edelbrock. Red Line Products had an exclusive distribution deal to sell Weber AFB carburetors in the eleven western states territory. Mike Rao of R&R Marketing had introduced Vic to Peter Neuworth, and was, by happy coincidence, also the Edelbrock sales representative. He was very aware of his client's desire to have a brand-name carburetor. Rao set up a meeting with both men, which began a process that saw the emergence of the Performer Carburetor Series. Mike Michalowski, president of Weber USA, got involved, and after a tour at Edelbrock he invited Vic to the plant in Sanford, North Carolina, where Magneti-Marelli would manufacture Carter AFB-style carburetors under the brand name Edelbrock Performer Series, totally recalibrated to match Edelbrock manifolds.

> "Believe it, when a new product is going through the stages of pre-production, Vic is there for every step. He checks every stage of progress, if his name is going on it, then it will be right." —**Jack Mayberry**

In an effort to control quality and prevent calibration and tuning problems with carburetors from vendors, Edelbrock introduced a complete line of carburetors of their own, to answer nearly every demand of the performance enthusiast. As part of their "Total Package Concept" the carburetors are manufactured by Magneti-Marelli Powertrain USA, and are engineered to match Edelbrock manifolds as well as their total package.

They announced Edelbrock Performer Series carburetors at the 1988 Performance Warehouse Association (PWA) meeting in Los Angeles. The carburetors were an instant hit. Made from aluminum, they did not have the heat distortion problems inherent in other brands made from zinc. The guesswork was gone, the carburetors worked right out of the box. Later, Magneti-Marelli began manufacturing Edelbrock's Q-Jet Performer series carburetors, and by 2000, the Edelbrock catalog offered applications for street and marine performance.

Quality Control

By the 1990s, technological advancements gave the manufacturing process not only speed, but reliable repeatability. No longer would the tedious labor be required as it was when Vic Edelbrock Sr.'s shop did 90 percent of the manufacturing process by hand, spending hours drilling and deburring rough castings. In 2004 the totally automated Edelbrock machine shop was populated with sophisticated machines able to select a block of aluminum and machine it into a precision part—hundreds of quality units per day. None of these machines have a handle.

California native Wayne Murray had worked at Edelbrock since his youth. Rugged, self-reliant, hard working, and outspoken, he started at the very bottom on a burr bench and progressed to running a drill press. Wayne and his dad and uncle had raced boats with Don Towle for many years. Towle put young Murray to work at Edelbrock the day after he graduated from high school. One enduring memory was Vic Jr.'s habit of working his way through the machine shop, checking over the day's labor, and conversing with each worker. "If you needed a haircut it was not unusual

One of the truly fascinating aspects of the Edelbrock product line is the fact that nearly every part, from concept to packaging, is handled in-house. Wayne Murray, left, vice president of Manufacturing says, "The company has the toughest in-house quality control in the industry." Steve Dorrell, right, conducts one of many product tests before a part is accepted.

for Vic to give long hair a tug. He would even go so far as providing the necessary cash and the time off to go to the barber," Murray fondly recalled.

Starting in the late 1970s, Wayne Murray saw the many castings moved in a pickup truck from Ed Barksdale's Buddy-Bar Castings foundry in South Gate and then helped deburr the castings, drill out the holes, and load the rough castings into crates. From there, they were hauled down to Sand Craft in Los Angeles, where the pieces were sand-blasted during the night so the crew could pick them up the following morning. This was long, labor-intensive and expensive. Sandblasting was soon replaced with the in-house, state-of-the-art Wheelabrator process to give manifolds a silvery sheen. While Murray learned more about the machine shop and the manufacturing process, he became friends with Larry Rusk and Chuck Davidson, who ran the manufacturing department at the time. Don Towle encouraged others to experiment with ways to improve the manufacturing process. Since there wasn't any custom equipment, they began building and modifying what was there. Up popped multi-spindle drilling machines and port mills to create all the different manifolds. In time, the entire machining cell program became more efficient and production increased.

A quality-control department was created where new tolerances were set and checked. Every product was subjected to exacting scrutiny. By the mid-1990s, a more sophisticated quality control room was planned that would rival those in the aerospace industry, complete with climate control, special air filters, and a Coordinated Measuring Machine (CMM). Today Edelbrock has six CMMs. Without such sophistication, manufacturers simply cannot compete in the performance industry. Currently there are in place over 40 CNC machines and cylinder heads with special lines for water pumps, camshafts, throttle bodies, gear drives, and other parts requiring machine work. In 2002 a new CNC center was installed that included an automated pallet loader and two Makino A88s, 4-axis machines capable of finishing a part from raw casting to a box-ready product at the touch of a "go" button.

"Senior would love the manifolds we produce today. His Slingshot was state-of-the-art then and it is the same today." —**Wayne Murray**

The Edelbrock manufacturing process is computer driven now. All the manifolds are designed and tested on a computer.

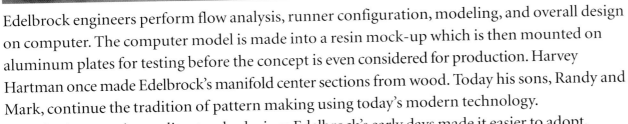

Vic Edelbrock Jr. has taken the company from a small business to a giant corporation. In the 1980s, above, Vic saw the need for more production and decided to expand his manufacturing facilty, above left, with the most modern machines available.

Edelbrock engineers perform flow analysis, runner configuration, modeling, and overall design on computer. The computer model is made into a resin mock-up which is then mounted on aluminum plates for testing before the concept is even considered for production. Harvey Hartman once made Edelbrock's manifold center sections from wood. Today his sons, Randy and Mark, continue the tradition of pattern making using today's modern technology.

Adhering to strict quality standards since Edelbrock's early days made it easier to adopt, implement, and become registered to Quality System Requirements QS-9000, an internationally recognized fundamental quality management system as demanded by the Big Three automakers: Ford, GM and Chrysler. In order to maintain Edelbrock's QS-9000 registration status, an external certification body audits Edelbrock's quality system at specific intervals, to ensure continued compliance to QS-9000. This status not only applies to product concept, design, quality, and manufacturing; it also applies to other areas of the company such as sales, marketing, advertising, and shipping. Edelbrock maintains its known high-quality reputation by requiring first production samples to be inspected for compliance to engineering blueprint specifications, which are defined and documented during the product development stage. Additionally, random samples from each production run are inspected at defined intervals and whenever a tool is changed, to ensure product quality is maintained. Although the production equipment used nowadays to produce high-quality parts is very different from that being used in Vic Sr.'s days, the result is the same: a sophisticated, quality-engineered product. Edelbrock became registered to QS-9000 in November of 1998. Future company quality system plans include the registration to Technical Specification TS-16949, an internationally accepted automotive industry-specific quality management system standard, which replaces QS-9000 in December of 2006.

Built by Enthusiasts

Vic Edelbrock Sr. had a brilliant mind for creating manifolds. When he began his business in 1938, the term for this type of development was "blacksmithing." It came from the days of horse and buggy—only a few years in the past—when nearly every product needed for transportation was made by hand. Many nights, Vic Sr. and his crew would cut manifolds apart and reshape them. If an idea had potential, Harvey Hartman turned the homespun effort into a carved wooden masterpiece. More cutting and milling and refining ensued until the finished lump of aluminum had become an Edelbrock manifold.

When Vic Jr. took over in 1962, new product development became a collective effort of the dyno room staff using a vast backlog of test results and several innovations. Bobby Meeks and Murray Jensen used a flow bench to work from the ports backward to the plenum chamber to create the correct length and shape runners. Then they made prototypes of plaster and fiberglass. When Jim McFarland came on board, he worked closely with race teams and engine builders coming to Edelbrock to use the dyno facility. In the late 1970s, Vic Jr. set up a separate engineering department. An engineer named Dennis Lowe was hired to help McFarland. A short time later, Brent McCarthy joined the team. In the early 1980s, Edelbrock installed a Super Flow engine dynamometer and began creating more sophisticated prototypes. In the 1980s the engineering department moved from the drafting board to a CAD-CAM computer design system.

Today products are no longer hacked up and welded together by a couple of the guys in the shop. The boss doesn't draw ideas on a note pad, and gone are the late-night sessions over cocktails. A staff of engineers led by the director of Engineering, Dr. Rick Roberts, creates and develops products to fill the catalog. Jack Mayberry, vice-president of Research and Development, administers the effort. He is the stepson of longtime Edelbrock family friend Bob Joehnck, so his relationship with the company reaches back to its founder.

Mayberry says, "The most significant transformation in our program has transpired within the last ten years. We moved from the CAD-CAM system to a Pro Engineering Program. With our old software, we created two-dimensional blueprints, which would go to the pattern shop. Now there is no blueprint or wooden pattern. The engineering department creates a three-dimensional computer drawing that is sent to a company to produce a prototype using a process called Stereolithography. The model, reinforced with fiberglass and using aluminum end plates, can be tested on an actual engine."

The process works equally well for all aluminum products. In the case of a cylinder head, a flow

It takes the blending of old school tradition and modern technology to produce a high-quality Edelbrock manifold. Engineers design a manifold on a computer, left, but the concept must be put into a tangible form. Mark Hartman, below, (left) and his brother Randy (right) are the sons of Harvey Hartman, pattern maker of the original Edelbrock manifold.

Today, Mark and Randy still produce the patterns for Edelbrock manifolds using methods their dad would have not believed possible in his day.

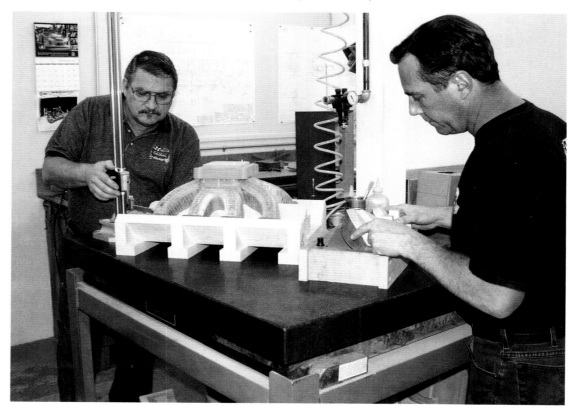

box—a mock-up of a single cylinder with intake and exhaust ports, and combustion chamber—is made. Engineers can then check how the ports flow without the expense of a complete head. This allows a more accurate prototype, and modifications can be made at low cost. With today's technology, Mayberry says, "a new product can be conceived, a prototype built, and the concept tested on a tight timeline. If it fails to meet our standards, it can be dismissed without a big loss."

Every step from concept to completion is handled in-house. Ideas approved at a "Futures" meeting are presented to Dr. Roberts, who assigns staff engineers to projects. Once given an idea, the engineer writes a new product proposal, including performance parameters, design goals, costs, and comparisons to competitive products. If approved, a final design is presented to the engineering staff. If accepted, the project engineer underwrites a

Stage A engineering release notice, which, with the approval the vice president of R&D, authorizes a prototype. A few handmade, machined samples are manufactured and tested. If all goes well, a Stage B production sample is produced. During this process, a pilot run of 20 units is produced and machined on production line equipment, with standards set at actual production levels.

Upon completion of the Stage B production pilot run testing, and approval by the engineering department, an engineering release notice sends the part into production and out to the consumer. Each part, from manifolds to shock absorbers to crate engines to water pumps, is done this way. Edelbrock has a 45,000-square-foot building specifically for their Performer Shocks, complete with custom-built, computerized testing equipment. Edelbrock is one of the few manufacturers with its own in-house State of California-certified

emissions lab, a definite advantage for the future.

With automakers offering advanced engine packages today, Edelbrock's focus is on developing power add-ons like nitrous systems, turbochargers, improved carburetor systems, exhaust headers, EFI systems, cylinder heads, and related parts. Import products like exhaust systems, suspension products, Russell fluid flow and plumbing products, and some space-age parts still on the drawing boards, are Edelbrock's future, according to Jack Mayberry. "The future will be equipment that is emissions-legal, with the emphasis on add-on products that improve performance without altering the factory engine configuration."

When a racer bought a part from the 1946 Edelbrock catalog, the company stood behind it. That tradition holds true in 2004. The years between have not diminished the quality of the product or the pride in the name.

Ulises Gonzalez, below left, works on our Super Flo SF1020 flow bench testing a prototype cylinder head stereo lithography flow box with combustion chamber intake and exhaust ports. This model is made from a Pro/E computer 3-dimensional model with a larger-syntering system. When proper flow numbers are achieved, Pro/E model and drawing files are changed. Actual patterns are made from these files at the correct size to assure proper performance. Below right,

Edelbrock's robotic welding machine making a first production sample of a new exhaust system. Once made, dyno tests are performed to assure performance gains.

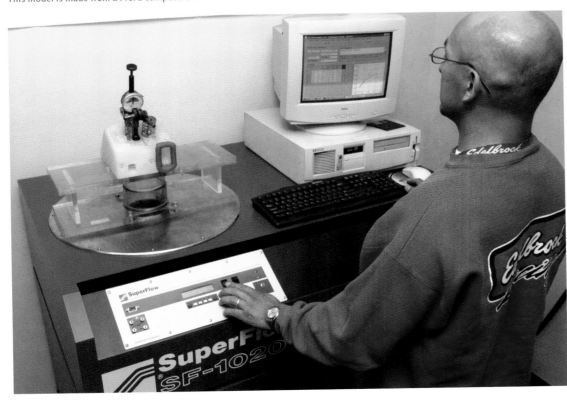

"At the time, computers had not taken over the design and development segment of manifold design, as they have today. In the late 1980s and even into the 1990s, there was still a lot of carry-over from the old days of hands-on, trial and error type design work. Jim McFarland and the rest of the crew were working hard to update everything, but like the days of Vic Sr., testing and running the dyno was a major part of every manifold. Vic Jr., was much like his dad, he wanted to be involved in every part of the process. He wanted to know every radius on every runner, the area cross-section in every manifold, the plenum dimensions, every detail. And, like his dad, Vic Jr. wanted to run every dyno test. Until the day I retired, one tradition was never altered—every manifold was tested until there was no doubt it worked. This was something that reverted back to the old man. Vic Jr. would always say, 'As long as it has my name on it, it won't go out until it works.' We eventually went to computers, and all the state of the art design stuff, but we never lost the tradition of the old days, and I always liked that." —**Don Waite**

Shortly after World War II, when Vic Sr. began production on his line of manifolds, the key issue to making quality merchandise lay in the aluminum casting process. He established a strong working relationship with Ed Barksdale, who owned Buddy Bar Casting. They continued to pour Edelbrock manifolds into the late 1980s. When the Barksdale family sold the company to Evans Industries, the relationship continued, because the castings remained under the supervision and control of Ron Webb, one of the most experienced foundry men in the country.

Because of the trust the company had in Webb, when he mentioned that he was leaving Buddy Bar foundry to strike out on his own, Edelbrock suggested that he and Ron could build a foundry together. The key to successful product design is a quality foundry, and Edelbrock had often thought of building his own to gain more control over the product manufacturing process. Webb agreed to run the operation, and the hunt for a suitable location began in 1988. A parcel of land was located near the city of San Jacinto, in Southern California, and by December 1989, the construction was completed, equipment installed, and employees hired.

The head man at the Edelbrock Foundry in San Jacinto, California, is Ron Webb (left) posing with Vic Jr. at the opening of the plant. At one time Webb worked for Buddy Bar—the foundry that poured castings for Edelbrock from the time of Vic Sr. until the late 1980s.

Within days of opening the doors, the first castings were poured in a modern foundry that was considered to be the most modern green sand foundry in the country. The key to this entire part of the process was having a real foundry man—Ron Webb—to run it.

Within the 73,000-square-foot facility were three automated molding lines—a green sand handling system capable of processing 100 tons of sand per hour and pouring a manifold every 45 seconds. Each mix, or batch, of aluminum alloy was analyzed for purity and consistency. Edelbrock uses two alloy mixtures: 808-alloy for manifolds because it was easy to machine and is not heat-treated; and a

There were several reasons for Vic Jr. to make the very difficult decision to build the company's own foundry. Reason One came when the company's original foundry, Buddy Bar, was sold. Secondly, Vic figured that with his own foundry, he could control the quality of his products, from pouring the casting to shipping the final package. And, it would all be made in America. The key to the program was the fact that Ron Webb agreed to run the operation.

stronger A-356 for heat-treated parts, to T6, like water pumps and cylinder heads. The foundry streamlined product creation, speeding the process from pattern to test samples. Testing new products proved quicker and less expensive. By pulling in the foundry, Edelbrock now completely controls its production, and its destiny.

An American Success Story

Edelbrock chief operating officer Jeff Thompson grew up in Southern California, and after he received an MBA he began working for Bank of America, where he tended to the needs of the Edelbrock Corporation. When Vic recognized Thompson's potential, he hired him to take part in the company's real estate holdings. "I was just 23 years old, recently married, and Vic was looking for someone with enthusiasm. It was a good match from the outset," commented the fellow who is unafraid to oppose Vic's opinions when it comes to what is best for the company.

"I believe in America and the idea of made in the good old USA. Obviously, not every single item in the catalog is made in our own shop. Cost, and other factors, make it impossible to manufacture some items in this country. So, we are forced to go offshore. But our primary products: manifolds, cylinder heads, water pumps, exhaust systems, suspension parts and shocks, are all made in-house." —**Vic Edelbrock Jr.**

"We have the latest and greatest in technology as it applies to software operating systems. We have a completely wireless shipping system at our distribution center. We are a state-of-the-art business. As big as we are, we all acknowledge each other's work, and everybody tries to make the process of earning a living more enjoyable. Vic treats the company and its employees the same way he treats his family, and in this day and age, it is something that is truly rare. The company philosophy is very unusual: "We are the Fun Team", and that motto really works. It is very easy to succeed at Edelbrock Corporation, but very difficult to fail, because we believe that we want everyone to make good, and we all go out of our way to help people overcome problems. You don't find that in many places." **—Arty Feles**

CFO Arty Feles began his working days in his father's San Bernardino garage business, which led to his interest in hot rodding and gave him a useful background, setting the stage for his Edelbrock position. However, his hiring in 1992 raised a few eyebrows when it became known he was a graduate of Notre Dame University. With Vic and Nancy Edelbrock active, devoted alumni of the University of Southern California, the act was something like Grant giving a job to Robert E. Lee. Despite the fierce football rivalry, Feles left a public accounting firm to accept a job after completing a public audit of Edelbrock. Feles explains that Edelbrock Corporation is "a Delaware Corporation, in which there are

A company that started out as a one-man operation, machining manifolds by hand, the Edelbrock Corporation has grown into a corporate giant that now includes hundreds of products, below, including a line of high-performance shock absorbers, and engine products from manifolds to crate motors. Edelbrock has now introduced a full line of Harley-Davidson motorcycle products.

two companies offering the stock; the greatest single most interesting difference between most companies our size and Edelbrock is vertical integration, meaning it controls its own destiny."

Starting with castings from its own foundry, parts are created and control is administered right through to final machining, to guarantee the quality of the product in every step. In 1995 Edelbrock began a new venture into manufacturing performance parts (heads, and manifolds) for Harley-Davidson motorcycles. The company also introduced an exhaust and suspension component division.Using the patented Ricor inertia active valve design, Edelbrock introduced

a complete line of shock absorbers for street,off-road, and sport utility vehicles. Adding to their full complement of aluminum heads, Edelbrock joined forces with Chapman Racing, to offer all-out racing heads. Other innovations include complete crate motors, nitrous systems, and Qwikdata data acquisition systems, and a complete line of sportswear. In 2001, Edelbrock bought Russell Performance Products. Edelbrock has become a one-stop performance mega-business.

With in-house marketing, advertising, and printing departments, the company controls almost every aspect of its products, from raw materials to on-shelf display. The Total Power Package gives the company a tremendous advantage over other manufacturers because it eliminates guesswork and offers packages in various degrees and costs. Customer service is provided at all levels, from big warehouse/distributors and mail order companies to the neighborhood parts store.

Edelbrock is very much an American company and plans to keep it that way, despite a great challenge from competitors that move offshore and make it difficult to match price points because they rely on a very inexpensive labor force. Also, there's the headache of dealing with knock-off copies of its products flowing into the United States.

Jeff Thompson believes that our government needs to do more to battle the situation. "Things cost more here because we have a better way of life. If everything is made offshore, then we are not feeding anything back into our economy in the form of wages. That means less and less money becomes available for research and development. At some point, there will be a deterio- ration of the American labor force and a lowering of our standard of living. We want to stay an American company, making American products. We like supporting the American economy and so do our customers." Producing

Modernization, Family Style

The growth of Edelbrock Corporation from 1938 through 2004 saw an evolution in technology as expansive as that of any Fortune 500 giant. From a core group of four, the company now employs nearly 700 workers who produce 7500 different products that generate annual sales of more than $124 million. The company went public in 1994 and is listed on NASDAQ Stock Exchange. In 2004 Vic Edelbrock took the company private again, acquiring all the outstanding stock Vic and the family didn't already own. Despite all of the modernization, the company has retained its founder's value that held family, tradition, and integrity as sacrosanct. When customers walked into the Highland Avenue location, owner Vic Edelbrock Sr. met them personally, sealed agreements with a handshake, always gave a little extra for the money spent, and all the while, he would rather work side by side with racers than mingle with strangers. Vic Jr. continued his father's traditions and work ethic.

The winner of a new Edelbrock manifold accepts his prize from Vic Jr. after a drawing at an Edelbrock/Holley seminar during the SEMA show in the late 1970s.

Vic personally bestows annual bonus checks to each employee—from executive level to floor-sweeper—complete with a handshake and "thank you." He signs every Christmas card himself. Whenever he is at the office, you will find him somewhere in the shop, perhaps in the dyno room checking out the tests and collecting the latest input. Every employee has an open-door policy to his office. Every product gets his approval before it is put into production. And like his father, he surrounds himself with the best and the brightest—including daughters Camee and Christi. Yes, he inherited a great name and market position in the business, but the truth is he made it happen by not squandering fatherly wisdom from lessons learned. All this and more is why executive vice president and chief operating officer of Edelbrock Corporation Jeff Thompson, who handles much of the day-to-day operation and makes major policy decisions, comfortably admits, "Make no mistake, Vic Edelbrock Jr., still runs the show."

"Vic Sr. believed in a debt-free business philosophy, and when Vic Jr. took over, he borrowed money to expand our move to the El Segundo facility, but the debt was always under control. Today, we still believe in the same rule. The basic function of the company has not changed." —**Arty Feles**

Vic's Partner, Nancy

"Believe it or not," Vic Jr. says, "When I was a young man, just out of college, I was shy and bashful around new people. Nancy, on the other hand, was very good with all things social, formal, and proper. When it came to dealing with people, presenting an appropriate image or being graceful under pressure, Nancy was in complete control. She made everything a game, and we had a great deal of fun together as she encouraged me to overcome my shortcomings. When my dad died I was really lost for a time, and Nancy was my backstop. She instituted a ritual we still follow to this day. When I would get home in the evening, we would sit down before dinner and discuss the day's events. She would tell me of her day and I would tell her about mine. I could open up and tell her the real story of my fears, doubts, worries, and the decisions I had to make.

"As the business grew, there were many tough times and Nancy never once backed off or complained, nor was there ever a time she didn't fully support me. Many times, Nancy set aside her problems and gave her time and efforts to solving mine. In the late 1960s we began marathon boat racing. Later on, in the mid-1980s, we raced offshore, and it was very difficult for Nancy to watch her husband and her daughter (Camee) race. When Jerry Herbst was hurt, it was Nancy who rose up and said, 'Offshore boat racing is too dangerous and it's time to do something different.' She was the driving force behind our decision to go Vintage Car racing. When Carey and Christi began showing horses and competing in jumping events, it was Nancy who went to the events, who took the girls back east, and worked day and night so they could fulfill their dreams.

"For a number of years, Nancy sacrificed her total life efforts to helping the girls on the East Coast, and commuting back to California whenever I needed her at an event or other company promotion. In the 1970s, we were involved in SEMA, NHRA drag racing, and other major events like the Daytona 500. Promotion was Nancy's calling, she was a magnet in drawing attention to our company. Everybody loved being around her. I would marvel at her ability to handle any situation. She could go from riding on the back of a scooter, carrying a satchel filled with tools and parts, racing around the pit area at a drag race, to running our display booth. She could be a strict disciplinarian, keeping racers in line as they waited for service at our booth, then turn around and play diplomat to the wives and girlfriends of VIPs that showed up at the races or trade shows. For more years than I want to remember, we were on the go, working trade shows, races, and visiting our distributors all over the country. It usually meant working from 9:00 a.m. to 6:00 p.m., then dinner to promote the company and on to a party for more of the same. Nancy never faded."

The loving bond between Vic and Nancy Edelbrock is the major reason why the company was able to grow and prosper. As a team they fought every battle the business world could throw at them.

high-performance automotive products of the utmost quality is the cornerstone of Edelbrock's business, and the company enjoys its leadership role in the performance industry by simply outperforming the competition.

Into the Future

Nearly every personal vehicle Vic Edelbrock Jr. drives is red, and the predominant color scheme throughout Edelbrock Corporation is red, because psychologists say it excites passion. As a USC graduate, Vic considers it an honor and an obligation to give back to the school that gave him the tools for building his success. Vic and Nancy give back much in the way of financial support as well as personal efforts. As an ex-football jock, Vic (and Nancy) are most proud of their endowment of the Trojans football team's quarterback. Vic attends games with lifelong buddy and fellow Trojan, Jerry Herbst, and hangs out with fellow alumni, fulfilling the high profile, excitement-driven side of his character.

"When I was going to Dorsey High School, I managed to make the football team. In my senior year, I received a letter from Jess Hill, head football coach at USC, about a scholarship for football. Use of this scholarship prompted me to go to USC. Getting that scholarship changed my life: I met Nancy, my best friend Jerry Herbst, and later, two of our three daughters went there. When I was able to return the favor, and when the endowment for the quarterback became available, we jumped at the chance to repay the school. Nancy and I have remained active in many programs at USC, and we travel to the football games whenever possible. For us, USC, is a tremendous part of our lives, and we both love the excitement of reliving our college days."

Giving back to his college is not the only payback Vic and Nancy offer, it is just their most exposed and public contribution. Vic also has a private side, and part of this inner self steers

From his childhood, Vic Edelbrock Jr. has loved cars. His collection of hot rods, above left, is filled with the coolest cars imaginable. Above, the Vic Sr. Scholarship is awarded each year to the most deserving automotive tech student at Northwest Kansas Technical College in Goodland, Kansas. Vic Jr. chose this school because his father was born nearby. Edelbrock also gives a yearly scholarship to Wyoming Technical Institute, known as Wyotech, in Laramie, Wyoming, a school very deserving of a Vic Edelbrock Sr. Scholarship.

him toward goals void of tribute or applause. Heading the list of very personal and unheralded humanitarian patronage is Vic's devotion to helping young people interested in the automotive industry. "For some time now, Nancy and I have been interested in the new wave of technical schools offering a student out of high school a chance to gain an education in a trade—if that student does not wish to, or cannot afford to attend a four year college. After all, not everyone can be a doctor or lawyer. There is a real need for professionally trained automotive technicians, simply because the automobile has become so sophisticated and high tech that the days of the self-taught mechanic are over. Just ask any auto dealer and they will tell you that it is very difficult to fill positions in dealership service departments.

"Actually, my interest in technical training schools goes back a few years. At one point, the SEMA organization put together a scholarship foundation to be implemented for students who wanted to go to technical schools, especially those schools dedicated to the automotive trade. I told them we would like to put money into a scholarship fund, if they would allow the scholarship to carry my father's name, and we wanted to choose the candidate. At the time, the powers in charge said no. We were very disappointed in SEMA, but we were still interested in promoting the scholarship idea.

"Vic is very open to new ideas; he is a team player and always allows his key people to make their own decisions. What I really like about the company is its traditions. Although we have nearly 700 employees, it is still a family, from Vic himself down to the youngest kid just starting. Vic takes very good care of his people, with free medical benefits, 401k plans, and even life insurance. So, being a family, we are all somewhat protected from the hazards of the outside world." —Jeff Thompson

Vic's Garage—Every Hot Rodder's Fantasy

Vic's garage is filled with his favorite cars, including the company's 1968 "test mule" Camaro, above, and cars his father made famous. There is even "Wa Wa II", a racing boat powered by one of the first small-block Chevy V-8 engines.

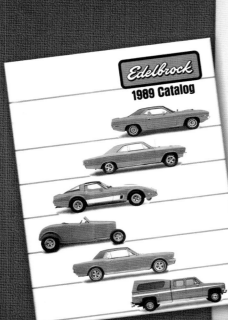

Edelbrock Cars Are Driven

The cars in the Edelbrock collection are symbols of the history of hot rodding and of the Edelbrock Corporation. Although the cars are on display in Vic's Garage, they are not untouchable. Vic shares his collection with the people who buy his products. For example, above, the *Hot Rod Magazine* Camaro is taken on the *Hot Rod* Power Tour through many towns in the Midwest. Camee and Christi, top right, take turns driving their super cool '32 roadster at Vintage races and hot rod meets around the nation. Below right, the famed number 27 midget, being hauled by a Nancy Edelbrock's 1946 Ford Woody Wagon, shown at Ascot Speedway only days before it was leveled, is taken to historic events throughout California. *Opposite:* Vic drives his cars whenever he can. Vic stands next to his 1957 Chevy shown on the cover *Hot Rod Magazine*, top left, considered by many as the most beauriful Chevys around. Photographers can take advantage of the collection, below left, to shoot photos for feature articles as shown here using four of the most famous cars to ever hit Ascot Speedway. At one of many Saturday company tours, below right, Camee talks to a crowd of enthusiasts before going on a complete tour of Edelbrock. Lunch and engine dyno runs are included at no charge.

The Edelbrock Credo

The Edelbrock Corporation maintains its independence from concept to finished product. Along with control comes the satisfaction that Edelbrock Products are made in the USA. Vic Jr. is very proud of his flag-waving, red, white, and blue stance concerning his products. He feels good knowning that he can look customers in the eye, and rest assured that they are going to be happy, and if not, he can fix the problem.

On the subject of offshore manufacturing, Vic has some strong opinions. Although forced to go offshore to compete with others in the business, he is critical of the practice and expresses his concern for the future. "I believe that this country has a very serious problem with its treatment of the hard-working, middle class, wage-earning, American family. Small manufacturing companies have now been put out of business by offshore manufacturing. I believe that if we continue to displace manufacturing and the jobs it creates, someday our country will lose the ability to manufacture its own needs, and other countries could have an advantage over us. We like to control every part of the creation of Edelbrock products. We are not dependent on a stranger, far away, manufacturing a product carrying our name. For example, I can follow a manifold from pouring the aluminum, to machining the raw casting, to putting the product in the box and loading it onto a truck. At any time, if I don't like what I see, I can yank it and toss it in the trash. Our government feels differently than I do, and many believe in advancing free trade and in American companies going offshore to manufacture products. I think it's unfair for a country to ship just about anything they manufacture into this country and then be very selective about what they allow America to ship into theirs. The result is a trade deficit. For me, it's black and white—you ship to us and we ship to you and all things are close to equal, end of story. I am committed to hang on as long as possible, and continue to manufacture in America using an American labor force. At present, we don't have to rely on others to make our products. I don't want products that may look good on the outside, but may be lesser quality on the inside. We know our products, and a huge amount of income from our products is returned in the form of research and development of new products. This is something offshore companies don't provide. I really don't care what other manufacturers in the performance business do; I am only concerned with the products carrying my name. I want our customers to be happy—if not, call and we'll make it right. We don't live on hype, we live on quality."

True to the tradition of the hot rod, Edelbrock products are made in America by American workers.

"In 1995, my public relations man, a fellow named Jim Losey, took a company project car back East to an event called the *Hot Rod Magazine* Power Tour, and on the way, Jim discovered a technical school called Northwest Kansas Tech School located in Goodland, Kansas. He suggested I take a look. When we went back for the Power Tour in 1996, we stopped, and I liked what we saw. They were taking young kids off of the farm and offering them a vocational choice in the automotive business. Farming is a very difficult business to succeed in, and this school offered a student a skill that can be taken anywhere in the country. It was perfect, my dad and his family had come to California from Kansas, so in effect, the Edelbrock Company history began in Kansas. The school agreed, so we introduced the annual Vic Edelbrock Sr. Scholarship Award for technical studies presented at the school each year by a member of our family. It has been such a success, that we are now looking at other programs, at many schools. We have now selected WYO Tech in the state of Wyoming to join our program. They do a great job, and offer many courses in the automotive trade, including those pertaining to racing. We have even ventured into programs with younger students. In 2003, our employees gave Nancy and I a fund for Christmas to do a local scholarship program, so we went to South High in Torrance and set one up. The school has a tremendous auto shop staffed by great teachers. Torrance has a strong legacy in auto racing, Parnelli Jones was raised in Torrance.

"I feel very strongly about bringing young people into our industry. I think all of the major organizations, SEMA, NASCAR, NHRA, should do as much as they can to promote interest in the automotive industry among young people. This country needs good people in the automotive trades. I never get tired of talking to kids about cars and racing. I can remember back to when I was eight or nine years old, and how I loved to be around the

"One of the beautiful things about giving is the act allows you to choose and support things that are meaningful to your life. For example, both Vic and I are active in our affiliation with the University of Southern California, and many of the things we do involve programs we both have interest in." —**Nancy Edelbrock**

cars in my dad's shop. Just let me drill a hole, in anything, as long as I was running a machine, or cleaning up the midget, sitting behind the wheel wiping off the gauges, and dreaming about flying around a dirt track with Rodger Ward chasing me. I tell young people that I meet, 'If you are not excited about getting up in the morning and going to work, you are in the wrong business.' I have never had a regret about the automotive business, and I would never trade my memories of my dad and the times in the shop when I was a kid. And, I cherish the fact that my wife and children have always loved the business as much as I have."

> "I have always felt, and I know Nancy has mentioned this, that if a young person, boy or girl, has a fascination toward the automobile, and comes home and works on a car in an evening, then that child will be less likely to get into trouble. One of the greatest underlying aspects of the performance industry is the family association—parents and children joined in a common endeavor. If proof is needed, just attend a street rod event or a drag race, and you will see the family unit working together." —Vic Edelbrock Jr.

An American Family

Back in Vic Sr.'s time, at the end of a bench racing session late into an evening's darkness, you stepped out into the cool night air with a clear reflection of the day's events. Perhaps there remained the aftertaste of one of Katie's dinners, and always, the scent of night-blooming jasmine coming from some unknown location. Heading home, there was always a sensation of contentment, a feeling of accomplishment that problems had been solved, and new ideas had been explored. Bench racing never ended without the sound of laughter, a racer's way of smoothing the edges off the day's vexations. Each ending was only a pause, the anticipation of the day ahead waiting, like tomorrow's promise. The story of the Edelbrock family and its sixty-seven-year history in business is not unlike the story of all American families, complex in many ways, while basic and simple in others.

Otis Victor Edelbrock Sr. was a racer, an innovator, and a genius. He was also a father, husband, and gentleman. Vic Sr., wife Katie, and son were a typical American family. They accepted those who came to work for them as additions to their family. Today, Vic Jr., his wife, Nancy, and their three daughters are a family who still believe that those who work with them are extended members of that family. And true to Edelbrock tradition, Vic Jr. is not a corporate mogul or a Fortune 500 celebrity. He is a car guy, a racer at heart. His biggest reward is in knowing that the products carrying his name are being enjoyed by everyone, from world-famous drivers to the unnamed, anonymous car enthusiasts. This is why the Edelbrock story is about life and family, and America's love for the automobile—nothing more, nothing less.

The Vic Edelbrock Jr. family in a rare moment—all three generations in one place, at the same time. There are a few missing on this Thanksgiving holiday, but not due to lack of interest. At the time this photograph was taken, Katie Edelbrock Higgins was 90 years old. And even though she was willing and able, the trip across country would have been as hard to endure. The phone was passed around, as always, so everyone could wish Katie and her husband Bob a "Happy Turkey Day". Shown from left to right top row are Brooke, Carey, Camee, Vic, Nancy and Christi. Lower row, Ashley, Kyle, Sean, Courtney, Alex, Grant, Bryan and Troy.

Many people helped with the research that went into this book. Many more would have, had I only the time or insight to ask them. There were so many early racers whose stories I never got to hear. One was Dean Batchelor, whom I had known for many years. We worked together at Argus Publishing Company in the late 1970s. I used his book, *The American Hot Rod,* as scripture for accuracy. Dean was always right with his facts. He passed on before this project began, so I never had the chance to hear him tell me how it was hanging out at the lakes, what was said over malts and burgers at the Triangle Drive In. If Dean could have told me the real story of his adventures with Wally and Alex, Bobby and Vic Sr., there would be more color to this story.

There is no way to fill the gap left by the absence of Don Towle as a firsthand witness to the Edelbrock story. A boat racer, lakes racer, and all-around hot rodder, Towle lived the Edelbrock story from two points of view. He was there when the

Two men author Tom Madigan expressed regret in not being able to interview for this book, noted Journalist and hot rod pioneer Dean Batchelor, above left, in his '32 roadster and Vic Edelbrock Sr., above right, talking to his driver Perry Grimm about their newest trophy.

company was fresh and struggling, working alongside the old man and Bobby Meeks. He continued on with the son. He saw the company evolve from one-man operation to corporate giant. He was trusted by both father and son, admired by real racers, and friendly to both Edelbrock loyalists and the competition. Towle was a calming voice when the fiery spirits of Bobby Meeks and Vic Sr. would clash, and when Jim McFarland, Murray Jensen, and Vic Jr. arrived at differing conclusions. This project is much less fulfilled than it would have been if Don Towle could have offered his input.

I also missed out on Fran Hernandez. I met Fran many years ago while covering a Ford project at the Bonneville salt flats, but except for an occasional phone call or meeting at a press function, I never really got to know Fran. When it came time for this project, Fran had taken ill and was unable to do an interview. Fran was very close to Vic Jr. when Junior was a youngster working in his dad's shop. As a long-time lakes racer and employee of Vic Sr., Fran could have provided more insight into the early growth of Edelbrock Equipment Company.

Early on in this project I called both Tom and Bill Spalding and suggested an interview. They both agreed. Time passed, however, and before I realized that I had neglected my obligation, Tom Spalding passed away. At the urging of Vic Hickey, a mutual friend, I contacted Bill and he invited me to his home hidden deep in a wooded patch of ground near the town of Pismo Beach, California. Considering his age, mid-80s, and the fact that he had lost his brother only weeks earlier, Bill was spry and cheerful. Bill talked at length about the old days, and when the subject came to Vic Sr. he laughed aloud as he told me how his mother was a great cook, and one of her specialties was

Bill Likes, above left, seated in his roadster and Fran Hernandez (not shown but who drove the roadster on many occasions) could have offered much in the way of detail on the early days of Edelbrock, but sadly, neither was available. Vic's mom Katie, above, did contribute her feelings to the story and helped connect the love between father and son.

baking pies—in particular, apple with a crust coated in cinnamon and butter. Vic Sr. was known to have driven from Hollywood to the Spalding ranch in Azusa just for a steaming wedge of Mom Spalding's apple pie.

I wish I could have spent more quality time with Katie Higgins, Vic Edelbrock Jr.'s mother. Katie, now in her late 80s, lives on the east coast, making personal interviews difficult. All of the conversations we had were over the phone. It would have been so much more natural to have been able to witness firsthand as she told stories of the early days. As it was, she filled in many gaps in the Edelbrock history, and she always ended a conversation by saying something about her son. She would say: "He was never spoiled. His dad made him start at the bottom, sweeping floors and cleaning toilets. And, no matter how rich and famous he had become, he never lost track of his roots."

Katie never accentuated her role in the Edelbrock story, yet she was always in the thick of the fight. She was a woman of great courage—as a child she flew in an open-cockpit biplane with a local barnstorming pilot. She drove Vic Sr.'s roadster like a true racer and endured the hazards of the dry lakes, once suffering sunstroke during a meet. True to family tradition, Katie was always cautious about divulging personal things about Vic Sr. and her son. It was not until the project was near completion and she felt more comfortable talking to a stranger that several unexpected revelations surfaced. According to Katie, after Vic Sr. passed away, Vic Jr. would talk to him during quiet times and ask his advice. (Vic admits he still does that today). When Vic Jr. visits his mom, she insists that he lead the prayer before the evening meal. And she admitted that, as a youngster, Vic Jr. got his share of spankings when he did things that really upset his father.

Bill Vukovich Sr., above, was a legend in the midget racing days of Vic Sr. and Wally Parks, above right, went from the dry lakes and being a member of the Road Runners, to establish the NHRA and help write drag racing history.

Back at the very first shop at Venice and Courtland, Bobby Meeks first became a part of the Edelbrock legend. Meeks had lived through the good times and bad, stood next to Vic Sr. at the dry lakes, and had bench raced with the likes of Perry Grimm, Walt Faulkner, Ward, Vukovich, and the rest of the legends. He knew the answers. Meeks labored through ten recording sessions, taping nearly twenty-eight hours of recollections. He supplied notes, books, magazine articles, and introductions to many other important players. He wanted the story to be right. This story could not have been told without Bobby Meeks.

Wally Parks went from a skinny kid running a hot rod at the dry lakes to the most famous figure in American drag racing. He built the NHRA into a world organization. Getting Wally to do an interview proved to be most difficult, as he was constantly traveling or attending an NHRA event. Finally, Wally suggested that I send him a list of questions and he would answer them. I sent a list of twenty or so questions. After a week went by I began to feel that maybe I wasn't going to get a reply. Then one morning the mailman brought a brown envelop with the answers from Parks. His skill as the one-time editor of *Hot Rod* magazine came through, and the answers provided much information, concluding with, "I'm out of gas, good luck with the project."

It took three weeks to finally get an answer from Bob Pierson, of the famed Pierson Brothers Coupe. It seems he was working day and night on a land speed record attempt at the Bonneville salt flats. Even in his late seventies Pierson is in demand. He agreed that the story of the coupe and his relationship with Vic Sr. and the early days of hot rodding was important. I didn't know it at the time, but Pierson lived in the mountains only sixteen miles from my home in northern

California. He showed up for his interview armed with scrapbooks, magazine articles, boxes of newspaper clippings, and a memory as sharp as any man half his age. He told stories at such a pace that the day flew by without lunch. The dry lakes, street racing in Los Angeles, the early days of drag racing, and running the salt flats all came back to life. He told me enough stories to fill a second book. Bob Pierson is still a madman.

If Pierson was wild and crazy, Bob Joehnck was the opposite. When I found him in the office of his shop in Santa Barbara, Joehnck was serious, shy, and reluctant to talk about any of his personal accomplishments. At our first meeting he declared, "I can be a grumpy old man at times, so don't get mad at me." Joehnck was key to much of the story of the early experimentation with the small-block Chevy. Joehnke was one of Vic Sr.'s first regular speed shop accounts, and he was the convincing voice behind Vic Jr. building a single four-barrel manifold for the small-block Chevy. He also convinced Vic Jr. to take up Vintage Car racing and to restore the number 614 Z06 Corvette. Having known Vic Jr. since he was born, Joehnck, like Meeks, was unafraid to spill the beans about the son of a famous hot rod pioneer. Unlike the others, Joehnck did not tell the whole story in one or two sessions. Rather, he would whisper a new story whenever our paths crossed.

I had met Alex Xydias in the early 1970s when I was editor of *Off-Road* and he produced the first SCORE show. We became close after our mutual friends, Mickey and Trudy Thompson (whom Alex worked for), were murdered. He provided me one of the most accurate accounts of the past. He filled in for his one-time partner, the late Dean Batchelor, with tales of their famed streamliner. Throughout the project Alex would call and ask if there was anything more he could do.

One of the most outrageous stories in the early history of Edelbrock Equipment was that of Bob Pierson and the record breaking string of cars built by him and his brother Dick (known simply as the Pierson Brothers). Above left, their chopped 1936 three-window coupe set records at the dry lakes and was the precursor to their famed Class D record 2D coupe. Bob Joehnck, above, (kneeling by his 1932 three-window coupe) was one of Vic Sr.'s first commercial accounts. He pushed Vic Jr. into creating the Edelbrock Chevy four-barrel manifold and he found the infamous 614 Corvette that Vic Jr. races today.

Applause for the most articulate interview turned in by one of the pioneers for this book went to Ray Brown, above, (second from right with white shop coat). This photo of Ray's 99C roadster is only one example of his long history in the performance industry. For his interview Ray actually wrote out a fifteen page script on his experiences with the Edelbrock family during the early years when he and Vic Sr. raced together.

Above right, three men who were part of the history of performance along with pioneers like Vic Sr., Robert E. Petersen, founder of Hot Rod magazine (left), Zora Arkus-Duntov, godfather of Chevy performance (center), and Wally Parks, founder of the NHRA (right).

One of the most surprising interviews came from Ray Brown. Although I had known Ray since his days as president of Superior Wheels and had heard stories about his exploits as a racer and engine builder, I didn't really know his history. In the summer of 2001, Ray was recovering from a serious health problem and was not at full strength, but when he found out that I needed help with the Edelbrock project, he brushed aside his problems and agreed to meet. Much to my surprise, Ray had created a handwritten script nearly twenty pages long recounting his relationship with the Edelbrock family, Vic Sr. and Vic Jr., as well as his racing experiences. To save time and effort, Ray simply read the script into the tape recorder and concluded the reading by asking me if there was anything more I needed. From that date to the completion of the project, Ray Brown faithfully called every month or so to offer encouragement.

It takes only a quick glance through the pages of *Hot Rod* magazine's first issues to understand how far back the relationship between the Edelbrock family and Robert E. (Pete) Petersen goes. Robert Petersen, founder of *Hot Rod*, developed Vic Sr.'s first magazine ad. The problem with a Robert Petersen interview was time. He has many business ventures, including a charter airline service, and his time is in demand. With help from Bruce Meyer (Petersen Automotive Museum) and Petersen's private secretary, Gigi Carleton, we set up a phone interview. Placed on a speakerphone, I asked questions and tried to record the answers on tape while taking notes on a yellow pad. The problem was, Mr. Petersen had a propensity for walking about the room while telling his stories. He would just get started telling a great tale, then begin walking away from the phone. I was getting a mixture of super stuff and muffled garble.

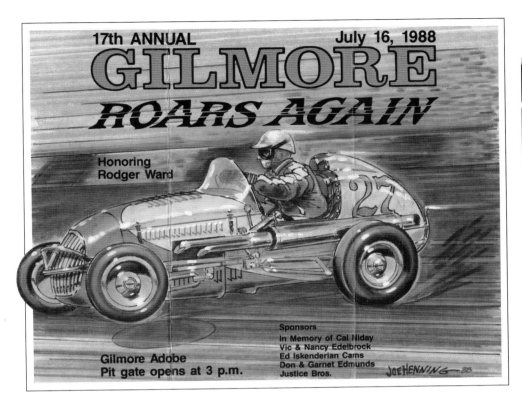

At one point he answered another phone in the middle of a story and, after conducting business, came back to finish. Over several months the phone stories continued until finally we sat down face to face at his museum and concluded his role in Edelbrock history. He never bragged about his success, claiming merely to have been at the right place and the right time. But in reality, without the foresight of Pete Petersen, the hot rod industry may not have turned out the way it did.

Among the things I never thought would happen was a spontaneous interview with America's first World Driving Champion, Phil Hill. Under a shade tree on the grounds of the Gilmore adobe at the "Gilmore Roars" party, Phil Hill sat at one of the picnic tables in the garden area and told stories of racing with Vic Edelbrock Sr. on the midget circuit and at the dry lakes. Urged on by hot rod legend Tom Sparks, Hill gave me several stories to add to the Edelbrock history. Hill is a man of action, and his stories were punctuated with waving arms, high-pitched laughter, and facial expressions worth a thousand words.

I have known Jim McFarland since his magazine days back in the 1960s. He helped me when I began racing and again when I started in the publishing trade. He went to work for Edelbrock in 1969 and stayed until 1988. During his tenure, all was not smooth sailing. Although responsible for many successes during the 1970s and '80s, McFarland left amid a somewhat strained relationship with Vic Jr. McFarland could have turned down my request for his remarks on the history of Edelbrock. In fact, he wasn't sure Vic would even want his comments in the book. To the contrary, Vic gave me specific orders to listen to what

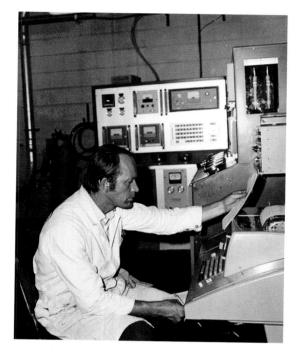

The history of the Edelbrock Corporation is a mix of old school and new ideas. When the performance world was hit by the 1970s gas crunch and government emissions regulations, Jim McFarland, above, helped the company work through the crisis. In the old days, Ed Iskenderian, above right, learned the camshaft grinding business, experimenting with designs used in engines built by Vic Edelbrock Sr.

McFarland had to say. In the end, McFarland offered up answers to many difficult questions concerning the development of several manifolds. He tackled issues like lawsuits, controversial dealings in emission controls, and product failures. He also provided some of the funniest stories about the inner circle of the company.

The worst thing for someone trying to record history is to hear that one of the key players in the story does not do interviews. This was what I'd heard about Bob Hedman. King of the racing exhaust header, Hedman had played a very significant role in the testing and development of many Edelbrock manifolds. I was told that he was retired, in poor health and did not want to be troubled by interviews. With some trepidation I remembered that I had worked with his son, Kenny, on several occasions, and although I had not spoken to him in many years, I called. Kenny laughed when I told him what I had heard, and while we spoke he called his dad on a cell phone. Bob had been troubled by health problems, but they were behind him, and when he heard that the interview was related to Edelbrock, he couldn't wait to have my wife and me at his home for a day of bench racing. So much for the rumor mill.

No hot rodder on the face of the planet can turn away once Ed Iskenderian begins telling stories. A rugged, tough-minded Armenian with a heart of gold and the comic timing of a burlesque comedian, "Isky" has seen it all and remembers most of it. At one time Ed had a shop directly across the street from Vic Sr. and the two men worked together developing combinations for the Ford flathead. When we sat down to talk about Edelbrock, Iskenderian was quick to credit Vic Sr. for helping him learn his trade. Isky could bring alive the feeling of the early days matter-of-factly,

as if the listener knew exactly what and who he was talking about. He said that he thought Vic Edelbrock Sr. was one of the smartest men he had ever met. Coming from Ed, that is a mouthful.

The saddest retrospection to come from this project was the loss of Murray Jensen and Ray Brock. Both men were good friends and both loved their relationship with the Edelbrock family. Ray Brock passed away only a month after we had sat down in his living room and spoke of his many experiences with the Edelbrock gang in the dyno room and how he had watched Vic Jr. take the company far beyond the original vision. Murray Jensen was the second person I interviewed at the start of this project. He spoke of how Vic Sr. had always taken care of him and his wife whenever they needed something. Murray spoke of how disappointed Vic Sr. was when he left to go around the world with Ford. And how Vic Jr. took him back years later with no hard feelings. Above all, Murray Jensen loved the boys Down South, the NASCAR racers—Junior Johnson, Dale Earnhardt, Benny Parsons, and the rest. During our interviews, he would often insist that I turn off the recorder and then he would tell an inside tale, followed by a caution not to say a word to anyone. Then he would laugh and continue his version for the public. I only wish that Murray and Ray could have seen the final result of their efforts.

There were several other players who dropped everything to help in this project. Among them, Ed Pink, master engine builder and long-time friend of the Edelbrock family. Also, taking time to record their experiences with the Edelbrock family were Tom Medley, Carl Olson (SEMA), Don Prieto, Steve Earle, Bob Bowen, Tony Nancy, Danny Eames, Mike Eddy, Mike Rao, Tom Sparks, Don Waite, Tom Shedden, Howard Gardner, Arty Feles, Jeff Thompson, Wayne Murray, Dennis

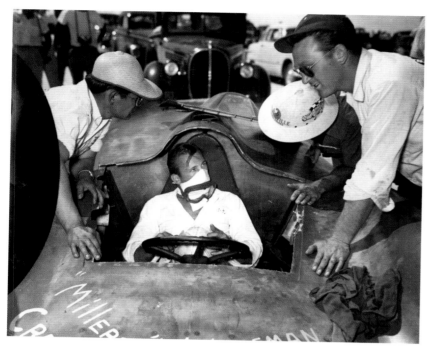

There could be no story told of hot rods and drag racing without the mention of the name Chrisman. Art Chrisman, above, along with his brother, Lloyd, built and raced countless history making cars. Uncle Jack Chrisman was a National Drag Racing champion and the legacy continues with Art's son Mike taking over the family business.

The late Rodger Ward, above right, once attributed his amazing career to his teaming with Vic Edelbrock Sr. during the wild years of Midget Racing in the '40s. Rodger was wild and needed a little guidance that was provided by Senior.

Edelbrock, Art Chrisman, Walt James, and Rodger Ward. I cannot forget the dyno room. Providing much of the laughter and many of the stories which made the Dyno Room infamous were Curt Hooker and Robert Jung.

This book is filled with photos that span the earliest days to present. Two people helped put the selection together and identify the subjects. First, Greg Sharp, California native son, hot rodder, ex-Los Angeles police officer, curator of the Wally Parks NHRA Motorsports Museum, and historian.

Longtime Edelbrock employee and golf instructor Ralph Guldahl Jr. not only provided his insights into the Edelbrock family, but logged, sorted, scrounged, and offered background to hundreds of photos and helped sort through the manuscript for factual accuracy.

As part of the family, I must list Jerry Herbst, simply because he is a lifelong friend of the Edelbrocks and offered insight into areas outside of the automotive business. Vic Jr. once commented that he had never had a brother, but Jerry was as close as the real thing. I owe Jerry Herbst a special thank you.

Vic and Nancy Edelbrock never once prevented me from interviewing anyone involved in this story. Never once did they impose their own will on the words I wrote. Vic and Nancy shared their life openly and without question, and they never once allowed their position to get in the way of being human. The entire Edelbrock family, including daughters Camee, Christi, and Carey, opened up and answered all of my questions without hesitation.

There were parts of the story I wish I could have told better. I was astonished by the camaraderie between all of the hot rodders when World War II turned American citizenry against one another.

Although I received part of the story from Thomas Shigekuni regarding his brother Tunney and Vic Edelbrock Sr., there was much left out. A friend of forty years, Kaz Watanabe, tried to gather information on some of the Los Angeles hot rodders who were sent to camp or who had records obliterated from the books because they were Japanese. Guys like Tom Ikanda, the Takashina brothers, Morimoto brothers, Gordon Ishimaru, Larry Shinoda, and Danny Sakai; many ran Edelbrock equipment. However, time and the fact that many Japanese families left Southern California after the war meant that many of the stories were lost to me.

African Americans, too, were very involved in the early days of California hot rodding. They had their own car clubs like the Mercuries and the Centuries. And, although accepted by the other racers, it was very difficult for an African American man to be accepted in Los Angeles during the 1930s, '40s, and '50s, let alone race around the streets in a hot rod. Only Mel Leighton, friend of Wally Parks and one-time treasurer of the SCTA, came to my attention as an African American hot rodder.

Mexican American culture has been an important part of the Los Angeles and Southern California heritage since the earliest historical records. Yet Mexican Americans suffered much the same from bigotry as other minorities. Despite their struggles, Mexican Americans played a part in the development of the performance industry. Where would the history of the dry lakes and early days of drag racing be without Joaquin Arnett and the Bean Bandits or the Marquez family? My rewards for telling the Edelbrock story would have been so much more had the stories of California's minorities been better told.

Tom Madigan, 2005

Two survivors of the World War II internment camps, Kaz Watanabe and Thomas Shigekuni told the stories of Japanese American racers, before and after the war. Vic Edelbrock Sr. befriended Tunney Shigekuni, Thomas' brother who used Edelbrock Equipment and was a member of the Road Runners Club. Vic Sr. supported many of the Japanese racers like Danny Sakai, above left.

Another famous racer who had to overcome a world of prejudice in the 1940s and '50s, San Diego-born Mexican American Joaquin Arnett, above with hat and trophy girl, and his club, the Bean Bandits.

Acknowledgments

This book could not have been written without the assistance of the following people. The author will be forever grateful.

Ed Almquist
"Ax" Axtell
Bill Bagnall
Jack Balch
Linda Barnikel
Jane Barrett
Bob Bondurant
Dana Bouey
Bob Bowen
Ray Brock
Ray Brown
Art Chrisman
Charlene Chronister
John Clinard (Ford Motor Company)
Tom Cobbs
Dave Cole
Mike Denney M.D./Ph.D
Jim Deist

Bob D'Olivo
Danny Eames
Steve Earle
Camee Edelbrock
Carey Edelbrock
Christi Edelbrock
Dennis Edelbrock
Nancy Edelbrock
Vic Edelbrock
Mike Eddy
Mary Faulkner
Arty Feles
George Follmer
Howard Gardner
Sheri Gray
Ralph Guldahl Jr.
Alice Hanks
Kai Hansen
Doug Harrison

C. J. Hart
Bob Hedman
Dave Henry
Jerry Herbst
Jim Herlinger
Vic Hickey
Katie Higgins (Edelbrock)
Phil Hill
Curt Hooker
Ed Iskenderian
Walt James
Murray Jensen
Bob Joehnck
Ralph Johnson
Judy Jones
Parnelli Jones
Robert Jung
Arlen Kurtis
Fern Long

Jim MacFarland
Darlene Madigan
Earl Mansell
Lorrie Marshall
Brent McCarthy
Tom Medley
Bobby Meeks
Jack Mendenhall
Bruce Meyer
Kathy Meyer
Ak Miller
Don Montgomery
Wayne Murray
Tony Nancy
Paul Nelson
Danny Oakes
Carl Olson
Kenny Parks
Wally Parks

Bob Pierson
Robert E. Petersen
Ed Pink
Dr. Robert Post
Don Prieto
Mike Rao
Paul Reinhart
Donna Reusck
Eric Rickman
Jan Schield
Carmen Schroeder
Lou Senter
Greg Sharp
Tom Shedden
Nancy Sherbert
Thomas Shigekuni
Bill Spalding
Tom Spalding
Tom Sparks

Jim Spoonhower
Robert Stack
Richard Stocker
Jeffrey Thompson
Don Waite
Dick Wallen
Rodger Ward
Kaz Watanabe
Ron Webb
Joan Weiand
Dick Wells
Deborah Westler
John Wolf
Alex Xydias
Smokey Yunick

Sources

Books

Almquist, Ed. *Hot Rod Pioneers: The Creators of the Fastest Sport on Wheels.* Warrendale, PA: The Society of Automotive Engineers, 2000.

Batchelor, Dean. *The American Hot Rod.* Osceola, WI: Motorbooks International, 1995.

Post, Robert C. *High Performance: The Culture and Technology of Drag Racing 1950 – 2000.* Baltimore, MD: John Hopkins University Press, 2001 (revised edition).

Drake, Albert. *Flat Out: California Dry Lake Time Trials 1930 – 1950.* Portland, OR: Flat Out Press, 1994.

Montgomery, Don. *Hot Rods in the Forties.* Fallbrook, CA: Don Montgomery, 1987.

Editors of Hot Rod Magazine. *Hot Rod Magazine: The First 12 Issues.* Osceola, WI: Motorbooks International, 1995.

Mansell, Earl A. *My Life Story* (unpublished memoir).

Yunick, Henry "Smokey." *Best Damn Garage in Town: The World According to Smokey.* Daytona Beach, FL: Carbon Press, LC, 2002 (second edition).

Ludvigsen, Karl. *Corvette: America's Star-Spangled Sports Car: The Complete History.* New Albany, IN: Automobile Quarterly, 1989 (third edition).

Stolley, Richard B. *Life: Our Century in Pictures.* Boston, MA: Bulfinch, 1999.

Jennings, Peter, and Todd Brewster. *The Century.* New York, NY: Doubleday, 1998.

Popely, Rick. *Indianapolis 500 Chronicle.* Lincolnwood, IL: Publications International, 1998.

Wallen, Dick. *Roar From the Sixties: American Championship Racing.* Phoenix, AZ: Ben Franklin Publishing, 1997.

Riverside Raceway Palace of Speed. Phoenix, Arizona: Ben Franklin Publishing.

Fabulous Fifties: American Championship Racing. Phoenix, AZ: Ben Franklin Publishing.

Distant Thunder: When Midgets were Mighty. Phoenix, AZ: Ben Franklin Publishing.

Lyons, Pete. *Can-Am: Photo History.* Osceola, WI: Motorbooks International, 1999.

Neely, Bill. *Daytona U.S.A.: The Official History of Daytona and Ormand Beach Racing from 1902 to Today's NASCAR Super Speedways.* Tucson, AZ: Aztex Corporation, 1979.

Osmer, Harold L. *Where They Raced.* Harold L. Osmer Publishing, 1996.

Sims, Carol Anderson. *Troy: The Story of Indy's Youngest Winner.* TIS, Incorporated, 1999.

Time Life Books. *Our American Century: Turbulent Years: The 60s.* Richmond, VA: Time-Life, 1998.

Time Life Books. *Our American Century: The American Dream: The 50s.* Richmond, VA: Time-Life, 1998.

Time Life Books. *The Home Front: U.S.A.* Richmond, VA: Time-Life, 1978.

White, Gordon Eliot. *Offenhauser: The Legendary Racing Engine and the Men Who Built It.* Osceola, WI: Motorbooks International, 1996.

Bochroch, Albert R. *Trans-Am Racing 1966–85.* Osceola, WI: Motorbooks International, 1987.

Orr, Veda. *Lakes Pictorial 1946.*

Redd, T.C. *When the Coliseum Roared.* Croyden, Surrey, UK: D.T.S. Publishing Company, 1983.

Fetherston, David A. *Heroes of Hot Rodding.* Osceola, WI: Motorbooks International, 1992.

Smith, Tex. *Tex Smith's Hot Rod History: Tom Medley.*

Fox, Jack C. *The Mighty Midgets: The Illustrated History of Midget Auto Racing.* Speedway, IN: Carl Hungness Publishing, 1985.

Kaplan, Sam Hall. *L.A. Lost and Found: An Architectural History of Los Angeles.* Santa Monica, CA: Hennessey & Ingalls, 2000.

Magazine Articles

Brown, Racer. "229 Horsepower Chevy V-8." *Hot Rod,* January 1956.

Brown, Racer. "Head Hunting." *Hot Rod,* February 1955.

Brown, Racer. "Six In a Row: How to Make Them Go!" *Hot Rod,* April 1954.

Catlin, Russ. "Midgets Tried Again . . . and won!" *Speed Age,* 1951.

Author unknown. "Smooth, Fast and Single." *Hot Rod,* December 1952.

Cumberford, Robert. "Go Fast, Last Long." Pilgrimages/Ford Motor Co.

Hop Up, August 1953.

Hot Rod Magazine Yearbook 1961

Hot Rod Staff "Coupes in Competition." *Hot Rod,* March 1954.

Hot Rod Staff. "Running with Russetta." *Hot Rod,* July 1951.

Hot Rod Staff. "Touring The Hot Rod Shops: Edelbrock." *Hot Rod,* October 1951.

Jacobs, Ken, and John Christy. "Gas Class Go-Buggy." *Hot Rod,* January 1953.

Likes, Bill. "Engineering vs. Chemistry" *Hot Rod,* December 1952.

Madigan, Tom. "Reviving the Past." *Circle Track,* December 1989.

Madigan, Tom. "V8-60 Revisited." *Circle Track,* December 1989.

O'Reilly, Don. "Speed Duel in the Sun." *Speed Age,* December 1953.

Osborn, Harold. "Seven Records Fall at Russetta Meet." *Hot Rod,* July 1950.

Prieto, Don. "Clean Air Engine." *Hot Rod Industry News,* December 1971.

Rickman, Eric. "Flathead One More Time." *Hot Rod,* December 1957.

Rickman, Eric, and Pete Petersen. "Bonneville '52." *Auto Speed and Sport,* November 1952.

Rickman, Eric, Parks, Wally, Petersen, Pete, and Brown, W.G.. "1952 Bonneville Nationals." *Hot Rod,* November 1952.

Rudow, Pete. "Edelbrock Z06." *Sports Car International,* May 1991, May 1991.

Speed Age August 1951.

Speed Age, February 1953.

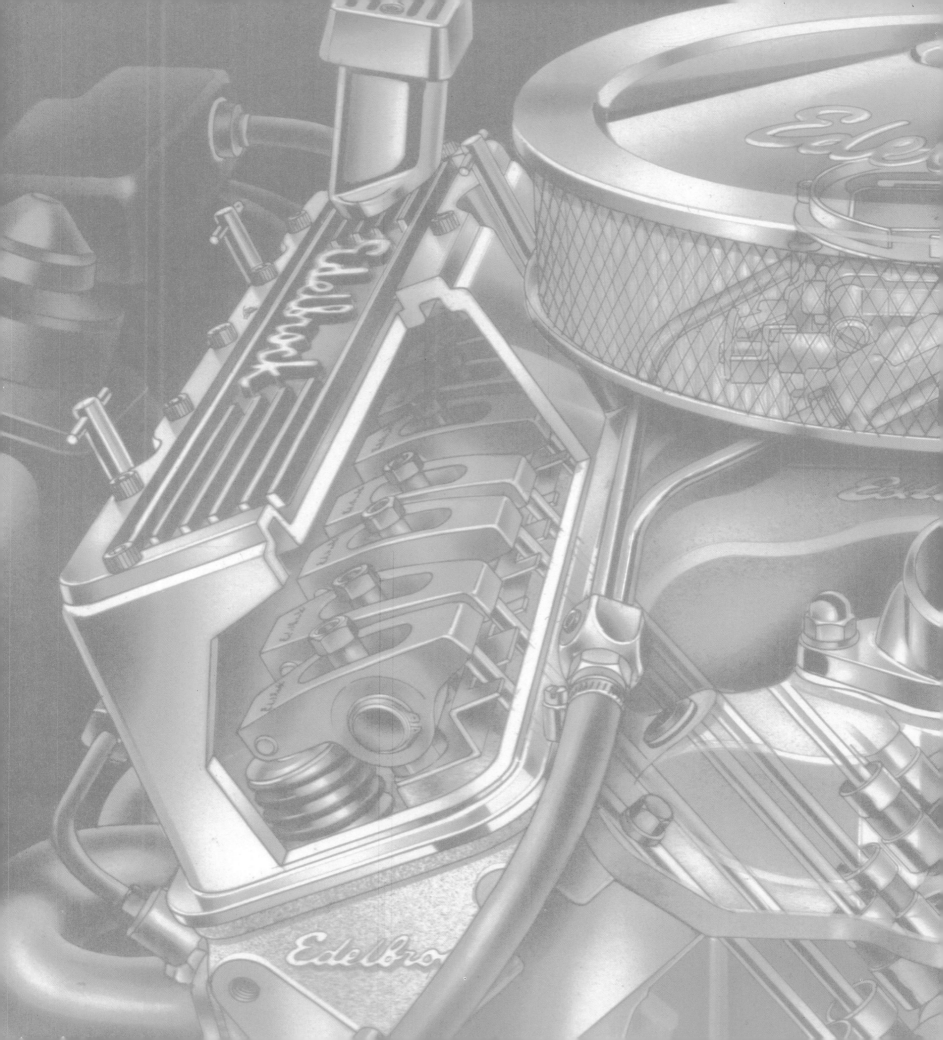